Children's Writer ®
Guide to 2008

Writer's Institute
Publications ™

Editor: Susan M. Tierney

Contributing Writers:

Pegi Deitz Shea
Jan Fields

Judy Bradbury
Virginia Castleman
Chris Eboch
Sue Bradford Edwards
Christina Hamlett
Mindy Hardwick
Lisa Harkrader

Mark Haverstock
Veda Boyd Jones
Suzanne Lieurance
Joanne Mattern
Sharelle Byars Moranville
Paula Morrow
Darcy Pattison
Katherine Swarts
Leslie J. Wyatt

Contributing Editor: Marni McNiff

Copy Editors: Meredith DeSousa, Sandra Horning

Production: Joanna Horvath

Cover Art: Melanie Williamson

Publisher: Prescott V. Kelly

International Standard Book Number 978-1-889715-38-4

1-800-443-6078. www.writersbookstore.com
e-mail: services@writersbookstore.com

Printed and bound in Canada.

Table of Contents

Markets

Book Publishing Overview, R.E.S.P.E.C.T.: Find Out
    What It Means to You   7
    Pegi Deitz Shea

Magazine Publishing Overview, The Big World of
    Small Magazine Communities   25
    Jan Fields

Creative Nonfiction for Today's Eager Reader   49
    Sue Bradford Edwards

Winner or Wannabe? Topics for a Preschool Audience   57
    Paula Morrow

Specialize or Diversify? Build on What You Know   65
    Sue Bradford Edwards

Bring Legends to Life with Historical Fantasy   73
    Chris Eboch

The Thrill of Horror and Things that Go Bump in the Night   85
    Chris Eboch

Breaking into Educational Publishing Today   95
    Joanne Mattern

A Matter of Conscience: Writing on Social Responsibility   105
    Pegi Deitz Shea

Busy Hands, Happy Hands: Crafts, Games, Activities   115
    Paula Morrow

News of the Year   125
    Marni McNiff

Style

When More Than One Voice Tells the Story 143
Mindy Hardwick

Life as Story, Story as Life: Short Stories for Ages 6 to 12 149
Paula Morrow

Spice Up Your Writing with Vivid Images 159
Darcy Pattison

No Cheap Theatrics, Please! Avoid Cliché and Melodrama 167
Katherine Swarts

In Transition 177
Leslie J. Wyatt

Cooking Up a Theme 187
Virginia Castleman

The Light Dawned: Improve Your Character Epiphanies 195
Darcy Pattison

Who Said That? Using Dialogue and Idiom to Define Character 203
Sue Bradford Edwards

Coming of Age—Again! 213
Sharelle Byars Moranville

The (New and Improved) Truth About Autobiography 221
Christina Hamlett

Business

Taking Care of Business: Magazine Contracts and Payments 231
Mark Haverstock

The Questions, Quandary, and Quest for an Agent 243
Judy Bradbury

The Gamut of Professional Organizations 255
Veda Boyd Jones

Into the Readers' Hands: How the
    Book Distribution Process Works   263
    Christina Hamlett

Making a Career Splash   271
    Chris Eboch

Software to Simplify the Writer's Life   281
    Christina Hamlett

Create an Author Website   289
    Mark Haverstock

Ideas

Prime the Pumps and Start the Ideas Flowing   301
    Sue Bradford Edwards

Backstory: Life's Breath of Frontstory   309
    Sharelle Byars Moranville

The Fine Art of Brainstorming   321
    Katherine Swarts

Writing Coaches: Help Getting to the Top of Your Game   331
    Suzanne Lieurance

Research

Oh, the Places You Can't Go! Researching Place   337
    Lisa Harkrader

Worth a Thousand Words: Photos for Nonfiction   347
    Lisa Harkrader

Add to the Writing Fun with Hands-on Research   357
    Mark Haverstock

Becoming Expert at Finding Experts   367
    Christina Hamlett

Contests and Conferences

Details Make the Difference at the Annual SCBWI Conference   373
     Judy Bradbury

Writers' Conferences
   Conferences Devoted to Writing for Children
       General Conferences   383
       Society of Children's Book Writers & Illustrators   385
   Conferences with Sessions on Writing for Children
       University or Regional Conferences   391
       Religious Writing Conferences   398

Writers' Contests & Awards   401

Index   439

R.E.S.P. E.C.T.: Find Out What It Means to You

By Pegi Deitz Shea

Respect: Ever hear comedian Rodney Dangerfield's shtick about not getting any? In the "danger" field of publishing, children's books are finally getting some. While teachers, librarians, and independent booksellers have always recognized the value and quality of juvenile literature, the mainstream press and the general populace are now according increasing respect to those who create books for young people.

Several factors have contributed to this new approbation, and the success of J. K. Rowling is indisputably among them. Rowling put a non-celebrity face on children's books, got kids hooked on novels of more than 100 pages, inspired many parents and others to read children's books both for themselves and to children, generated massive media coverage for children's publishing, and made money for herself (and others) to rival the contracts of professional athletes—and no one questions that it's deserved.

The media is itself another factor in the increased attention paid, particularly the Internet. Word of mouth and hand-selling used to mean distribution by one person to another. Now with blogs, IMs, and websites —Word of Web—more voices distribute more writing to immeasurably more potential buyers, making children's publishing an increasingly powerful industry. Search engines can help those buyers find what they want, and make their purchases with a couple clicks of the mouse. Readers even create online communities that "live" beyond a book's last page. A downside of the new media is that bookstores, especially the independents, have suffered from slowing traffic as more sales occur online.

The publishing developments that come with the increased value placed on children's books seem two-sided: Licensing is expanding and boosting revenues, but some see it as allowing less room for new voices. Successful adult authors are steadily moving into books for young readers, contributing to a renaissance of young adult fiction that, fortunately, is also allowing room for talented new children's writers to succeed. But picture book authors struggling in a weak market cringe with each celebrity who suddenly believes they can write for kids. Series seem to be slowing, at the same time that new visual and textual formats are pushing boundaries across children's publishing.

Victorious Circle

Licensing has also contributed to increased respect for children's books. Children's writers can be snobbish about licensed books, but like it or not, lifting characters off the pages and pasting them on backpacks and games increases the visibility of a book or series. It is an ever-growing segment of children's publishing and one to be aware of, and accord some respect.

Instead of a vicious circle, call it a victorious circle: Mom learns of Lisi Harrison's Clique book series on *Oprah* and orders one from Amazon. Daughter likes it and asks for the Clique Steamer Trunk boxed set. Daughter becomes a walking/IMing advertisement for everything Clique, including the books and the new DVD. The whole time, daughter is flaunting her Clique-ness on her My-Space, and checking out the quizzes and games on Little, Brown's Clique website. (Little, Brown's new imprint, Poppy, is a chick-lit imprint, now handling the Gossip Girls books and its new TV show as well.)

Some authors and illustrators shiver at this process of branding—it feels and smells like cashing in. Maybe so, but Rowling is shivering her way to the bank and her publishers are too. Licensing increases the

number of revenue streams to a company. With today's major children's book publishers owned by international corporations, their executives' most required reading is the bottom line.

Licensing can be sparked by a single title, even in picture books. Recently, Eric Rohmann's Caldecott winner *My Friend Rabbit* (Roaring Brook) debuted in animated form on NBC and Telemundo. Nelvana, Ltd., a "multi-platform children's content provider," has also worked with other children's book creators, including the Berenstains, William Joyce, and Maurice Sendak. Who knows what merchandise this adorable friendly rabbit will inspire? Wouldn't you rather the merchants push items inspired by books, rather than by TV shows?

Licensing is like a stuffed Paddington bear—nothing new, but it has long proven valuable. Today, however, the items and images that can be licensed are new and expanding every year.

It's not vital that an editor have licensing deals in the pocket when presenting a new project, says Douglas Whiteman, President of Penguin Group USA. "We realize that [licensing deals] are few and far between. And, in fact, a number of things have been launched with the intention of being spun off into merchandise but simply never got off the ground. We look at the book project itself on its own merits, and if anything happens in TV, film, or merchandise down the line, that's gravy."

The gravy at Penguin comes in the flavors of *The Little Engine that Could*, its top-selling title of all time, *Corduroy, Madeline,* and *The Very Hungry Caterpillar*.

A Golden Age of YA

Respect for children's literature, especially YA fiction, is also being bestowed by the likes of adult mega-authors James Patterson and Joyce Carol Oates, and poets Marilyn Nelson and Nikki Giovanni.

Admit it, authors, your hackles stand up when seeing children's books by Madonna, Billy Crystal, and the *celeb du jour* in the front windows of Borders. They're not the ones who need the placement and the promotion dollars. When renowned writers of books for adults turn their talents to teen or tween fiction, however, it's like a pat on the back to those of us who have been toiling lovingly and painfully at this work. Of course, these authors want a piece of the growing juvenile pie; but they're willing to put in the hours of rolling the dough and baking.

They're saying that children's literature is valuable, as valuable as that written for older readers. After all, some of the best fiction written for adult readers featured child or young adult protagonists. Where would John Irving and J. D. Salinger be without them?

Publishers are looking more at fiction that can succeed in both adult and teen or even tween markets. Young readers are responding to the books being published for them with real purchasing power and literary appreciation. The YA market comprises more than 30 million teens, who are buying books like never before. In the *Seattle Post Intelligencer*, reporter Cecelia Goodnow quotes Holly Koelling, a librarian and the editor of the most recent American Library Association (ALA) *Best Books for Young Adults:* "There has been an increase in the age of the protagonist, the complexity of the plotting, and the gravity of the content . . . I think it may be a reflection of a more sophisticated teenage population." ("Teens Buying Books at Fastest Rate in Decades, New 'Golden Age of Young Adult Literature' Declared," March 7, 2007.)

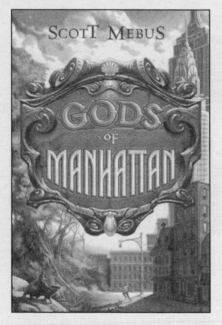

The article indicates just how much more respect publishers are giving teen readers. It also quotes Judy Nelson, President of the ALA's Young Adult Library Services Association (YALSA), as saying, "Teens have a lot of disposable income, and they're willing to spend it. They buy books. They (especially) buy paperbacks." It isn't just about that favorite teen activity, shopping, though. Young adult literature is also rivaling adult fiction in library circulation.

Recent examples of crossover YA/adult titles include *The Book Thief* (Knopf), by Markus Zusak; *My Sister's Keeper* (Atria/Simon & Schuster) and other books by Jodi Picoult; *Twilight* (Little, Brown) and its sequels, by Stephenie Meyer; and *Running with Scissors* (Picador), by Augusten Burroughs.

While some authors of books for adults may just be dipping into the juvenile pool and children's editors may be cautious, Dutton President and Publisher Stephanie Owens Lurie was thrilled to sign Scott Mebus and his book, *Gods of Manhattan*. "This, his first novel for children, is a

The veritable golden age of teen literature is enabling new authors to emerge.

dream come true," Lurie declares. Mebus's work for adults has consisted of humorous bachelor books, but Lurie calls his children's fantasy "ingenious." The book reveals a world full of warrior cockroaches, kung fu rodents, and hungry gargoyles ruled by New York notables such as Babe Ruth, Boss Tweed, and Peter Stuyvesant. The hero, 12-year-old Rory, must free American Indians who have been trapped in Central Park for 150 years.

At Atheneum Books, Haven Kimmel has a new entry in the juvenile market. Her adult books include the best-selling childhood-based novel *A Girl Named Zippy* and its sequel *She Got Up Off the Couch*. Editorial Director Caitlyn Dlouhy comments on Kimmel's middle-grade debut *Kaline Klattermaster's Tree House:* "You'll not only fall in love with Kaline, you'll want to bring him home and feed him a big slab of chocolate cake."

A New Author Welcome Mat

This veritable golden age of teen literature is particularly welcome because it is enabling new authors to emerge and YA imprints to expand.

Publishers Weekly has cited three "fresh voices" in particular. Irish author Siobhan Dowd, had two novels in 2007, and 2008's *Bog Child* (all published with Random House/David Finkling Books). Lizabeth Zindel, daughter of Pulitzer Prize-winning author Paul Zindel, debuted with *Girl of the Moment*, which she followed up with *The Secret Rites of Social Butterflies* (both from Viking). Melissa Marr's *Wicked Lovely,* described as a twenty-first-century fairy tale, was published by HarperCollins last summer, and Marr has contracted for three new books related to *Wicked Lovely*, though not technically sequels.

The list at Wendy Lamb Books, an imprint of Random House, also has room for new novelists. *The Opposite of Invisible,* by Liz Gallagher, is set in artsy Seattle and explores the lines between friendship, crushes, and love. If new novelists are silver at Wendy Lamb, then established ones like Patricia Reilly Giff are gold. Giff's latest is the middle-grade novel, *Eleven*. It depicts an unlikely friendship between a girl who can't stop reading and a boy who can't begin.

Writers are stretching between YA genres, too. Flux, the still new teen imprint of Llewellyn Worldwide, is coming out with a first novel by the nonfiction author Stacy DeKeyser. *Jump the Cracks* follows a girl who rescues an abused child on the train, only to be hunted down as a kidnapper.

Flux Publicist Marissa Pederson cites other titles the growing imprint is proud to publish: *The Shape of Water,* by Anne Spollen, is "wonderful for readers aged 12 and older who are interested in dark, surreal stories with characters who must learn to deal with real and troubling issues." The follow-up to Carrie Jones's *Tips on Having a Gay (ex)Boyfriend* is edgy in a different way. *Love (and Other Uses for Duct Tape)* explores Belle's changing relationships as high school ends, with her best girlfriend, her ex, her mother, and especially with a new, straight guy with whom "nothing is happening."

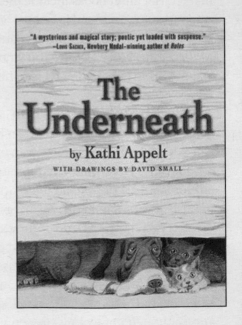

"A mysterious and magical story; poetic yet loaded with suspense."
—Louis Sachar, Newbery Medal-winning author of *Holes*

The Underneath
by Kathi Appelt
WITH DRAWINGS BY DAVID SMALL

New YA Titles from Award Winners

Kathi Appelt has more than 20 award-winning children's books under her belt. Even so, her young adult debut novel, *The Underneath* (Atheneum) succeeds with sheer storytelling. Editorial Director Caitlyn Dlouhy has only superlatives about the title: "The adventures are monumental, mythic, multi-dimensional, and thrilling. As I was reading the manuscript for the first time, I was terrified, not only for the kittens and dog in the story, but because I was scared that the author wouldn't be able to sustain the exquisite level of story and storytelling that she'd started with. But she did!"

Clarion Books, an imprint of Houghton Mifflin, is bringing out the big guns of storytelling this year. In *Keeping Score,* Newbery winner Linda Sue Park weaves major league baseball and the Korean War into a thought-provoking novel. In *Trouble*, Newbery Honor and Printz Honor winner Gary D. Schmidt tells the tale of a teenage boy who climbs the highest mountain in Maine while trying to deal with the loss of a brother.

Under the Penguin Group umbrella, many best-selling authors and award winners turned out new works for 2008. Titles include *Peeled*, by Newbery Honor author Joan Bauer (Putnam); *The Fold,* by Printz winner An Na (Putnam); *The Big Field,* by best-selling author Mike Lupica (Philomel); *Lock and Key,* by Sarah Dessen (Viking); and *Paper Towns* (Dutton), by Printz winner John Green (Dutton).

While the novel market has been booming over the past few years, Chronicle Books and Charlesbridge Publishing did not stand idly by. Both long known for their strong nonfiction lines, their recent moves to publishing novels has already paid off. "The reception to our older books has been quite wonderful," says Yolanda LeRoy, Editorial Director of Charlesbridge. "People seem very supportive of the new direction and happy to have a fresh face in the crowd." When asked about increased respect for children's publishing, LeRoy responds, "I don't know that I'd say there's more or less respect. Respect comes from publishing consistently good books, no matter what the genre or target age group. Perhaps there's been more respect from other publishers, though. I think the new line of books has made our colleagues see us more as a full-service children's publisher."

Among the recent fiction titles at Charlesbridge, *Secrets of the Cirque Medrano* is getting much buzz. The middle-grade novel by Elaine Scott tells the story of an orphaned Polish girl living in Paris with her aunt and uncle, who run a café frequented by bohemian writers and artists.

Chronicle has seen its fiction segment grow so much that Bill Boedeker, Children's Publishing Director, announced, "We are acquiring more middle-grade and YA projects and are currently searching for a senior editor to lead our growth in these two areas."

Series Slowing?

Young adult fiction has had substantial success in the form of series over the last score of years, as has middle-grade fiction, but fiction and nonfiction series publishing may be riding the brakes for now.

At Penguin, Whiteman estimates that series account for less than 10 percent of the company's new titles. Whereas some publishers see a decline in fiction and nonfiction series, Chronicle's Boedeker sees them as a huge revenue generator. "Approximately 30 percent of our 2008 titles are part of series."

"Series are actually becoming harder to launch and maintain," says Whiteman. "This tends to be a cyclical issue, as bookstores tire of series every few years if no new series has emerged in a big way. Undeniably some teen/YA series are working right now, but middle-grade series are tough these days."

It might not sound like it, but Penguin is publishing fewer series than in the last two years. New series and sequel titles at Penguin Group include *Return to Fairyopolis,* by Cicely Mary Barker (Warne); *Ranger's Apprentice Book Five, The Sorceror in the North,* by John Flanagan (Philomel); *Monster Blood Tattoo,* book two of the Lamplighter series, by D. M. Cornish (Putnam); *Talent,* by Zoey Dean (Razorbill);

and *Hank Zipzer #14 Super Special: The Life of Me (Enter at Your Own Risk),* by Henry Winkler and Lin Oliver (Grosset & Dunlap).

Walker Books, part of Bloomsbury USA and distributed by Macmillan U.S., is going serial with a new YA paranormal suspense series penned by national best-selling author, Wendy Corsi Staub. Publisher Emily Easton is excited about the second volume in the series. *Lily Dale: Believing,* set in the real town of Lily Dale, is "about a girl who is being tracked by a serial killer after her newfound psychic abilities emerge." Walker also has the nonfiction 101 Things series, by Tracey Turner and illustrated by Richard Horne, which debuted with *101 Things to Do Before You're Old and Boring.* The success of this book in the teen and adult

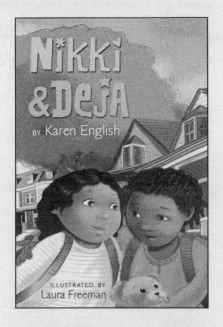

crossover market led to a second book, *101 Things You Need to Know . . . And Some You Don't!* which is also selling strongly. These titles are to be followed by *101 Things You Wish You'd Invented and Some You Wish No One Had.*

Clarion is publishing the second of what may become an illustrated chapter book series for younger readers, *Nikki and Deja: Birthday Blues.* Written by Karen English and illustrated by Laura Freeman, the books capture "the small betrayals and triumphs" of two African American third-grade girls. The first book is told from Nikki's point of view, and the second, from Deja's. "Once again," says Editor Lynne Polvino, English delivers "a delightful multicultural story that doesn't make an issue out of race, and features characters with both traditional and nontraditional families."

Charlesbridge does not publish series in the traditional sense, but it does have books that are tied, explains Charlesbridge Publishing Associate Editor Randi Rivers. "Two of our 2008 picture book titles are part of a series: *Come Look with Me: Asian Art,* by Kimberly Lane, one of a multi-authored series, and *Ralph Masiello's Ancient Egypt Drawing Book,*" which follows the same author's books on drawing dragons, bugs, dinosaurs, and oceanic creatures. "Generally, if the first in the series is successful, then, yes, it can be easier to acquire the next. However, the next book in the series still needs to be well developed and organized. If an idea doesn't work, it's back to the drawing board."

Boedeker agrees, and adds that a series is not guaranteed a long run. "Nothing gets a free ride. Each title must qualify before staff time, money, and resources can be devoted to acquiring, printing, and promoting."

Innovation and Artistry

Innovative production and artistry continue to strengthen in children's and YA publishing, with continuing appreciation given to the graphic novel and comic art forms. These genres have inspired new formats, hybrids, and mixes of children's books. In fact, corporations like Hachette Book Group, which includes Little, Brown Books for

Young Readers, are making deals with giants such as DC Comics. There are bound to be more innovative collaborations in the near future.

The success of Brian Selznick's *The Invention of Hugo Cabret* (Scholastic) shows publishers that there are worlds of creativity to be rediscovered on another side of the literary tracks. After all, illustrated books for adults are ancient. Think of medieval illuminated manuscripts, the woodcuts of Dürer and Holbein in early printed books, William Blake's art illustrating his books of poetry, and in nineteenth-century novels, Charles Dickens's collaboration with Phiz and Lewis Carroll's *Alice in Wonderland* and *Through the Looking Glass,* illustrated by John Tenniel, a political newspaper cartoonist.

Think of what the Dickens-Phiz or Carroll-Tenniel collaboration could imagine and accomplish with today's technology and color palettes. Perhaps the format might be familiar but striking, as in Mary Cuffe-Perez's *Skylar*, which is illustrated by Renata Liwska in "the tradition of *Charlotte's Web*," according to Philomel Books Editorial Assistant Katie Carella. Or some readers may prefer the more truly graphic images in *Yummy: The Last Days of a Southside Shorty*, by G. Neri, illustrated by Randy DuBurke and published by Lee & Low Books.

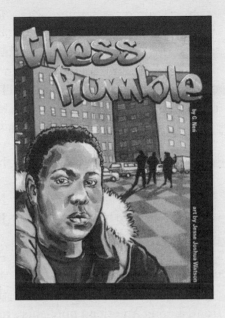

According to Editor Jennifer Fox, this graphic novel is based on real events in the life of Robert "Yummy" Sandifer, an 11-year-old gang member from Chicago's Southside who shot a girl and was later murdered by his own gang. Neri's first book was the middle-grade *Chess Rumble*, also graphically illustrated, by Jesse Joshua Watson.

While developing *The Underneath*, Atheneum's Dlouhy was thinking of making Kathi Appelt's book even more special, through illustrations. "It wasn't a definite at that time, but I let the author know that it could be a possibility from the get-go." Dlouhy turned to David Small (who also has a picture book, *That Bookwoman*, coming out with Atheneum). There are 15 pencil and watercolor wash illustrations "sprinkled through the manuscript." In the Texan bayou, a kitten must avoid becoming alligator bait. Dlouhy dares to say the middle-grade novel "is destined to be a classic."

Front Street, an imprint of Boyds Mills Press, is offering several groundbreaking books. *Run Far, Run Fast*, by Timothy Decker, looks like a picture book and smells like a picture book, but tastes like a graphic novel. The book takes place in fourteenth-century Europe, where the pestilence is ravaging whole cities. A girl, who had been told to run far and fast from an ever-sickening village, witnesses the ignorant ways

people try to prevent and cure the illness. Each two-page spread in the book has a different composition of variously sized frames. The black pen-and-ink illustrations evoke the time when few people could read. The look is ancient, but each frame expands the narrative and fills in historical detail.

New Directions in Picture Books

Another strong volume from Front Street exemplifies the risk literary texts take, and the excitement they can generate. It also points to a trend among American publishers toward buying more international projects, some via the Bologna and Frankfurt Book Fairs.

The Australian team of Margaret Wild and Anne Spudvilas have created a startling picture book for older readers, *Woolvs in the Sitee*, about a homeless boy named Ben and his elderly friend, who goes missing from the abandoned buildings that are their home. Violently colored, stark illustrations suggest a post-apocalyptic city devoid of most humanity and basic resources like clean water and education. The type and misspellings reveal semi-literate characters.

At the other end of the mood spectrum is the Philomel picture book, *The Lord Is My Shepherd*, a depiction of Psalm 23 released in time to aim at the Easter market. Artist Gennady Spirin created a work in "the classic style of illustration—painted in rich and painstaking detail," says Carella. How the narrative was painted is innovative. Spirin created a large painting, then took sections of it to illustrate each spread. "The book's end is a foldout spread that shows the entire painting," Carella explains.

Are psalms and poetry in picture book form fiction or nonfiction? Just as visual artistry is expanding the forms of novels and picture books, the verbal structure is also crossing boundaries. Think of the heartrending, history-based, poetic narrative in the Newbery winner, *Out of the Dust* (Scholastic), by Karen Hesse. Who, in children's literature, had ever delivered the Dust Bowl before with such beautiful language? Wordsong, the poetry imprint of Boyds Mills Press, has taken on that mantle with three new books revealing periods of African American life. *Birmingham, 1963* is written by award-winning poet Carole Boston Weatherford. A fictitious girl narrator, an admirer of the four girls who died in the Sixteenth Street Baptist Church bombing, is turning ten in 1963 but wishes she were still nine. Her powerful witness to her own idealistic passion and efforts for civil rights couples with a naivete as she speaks four poetic eulogies for each of the four girls.

Birmingham, 1963
CAROLE BOSTON WEATHERFORD

Award-winning poet Marilyn Nelson, author of *Carver: A Life in Poems* (Hand Print) has teamed up with poet Elizabeth Alexander to produce an evocative history for older readers, *Miss Crandall's School for Young Ladies & Little Misses of Color*. A call-and-response format structures this collection of sonnets that chronicle Prudence Crandall's school's existence amid protest from the white townsfolk of Canterbury, Connecticut. Well before slavery ended for the whole country, Crandall flouted segregation. The school was closed after only two years, in 1832, but in 1984, designated a National Historic Landmark, it opened as a museum. The volume is illustrated by Floyd Cooper, who also created the pictures for Wordsong's poetry collection *Tough Boy Sonatas*, written by Curtis L. Crisler. Cooper uses a unique technique called a *subtraction process*. After he paints a canvas, he strategically draws with an eraser to make the images impressionistic. Poems and pictures combine in a soft realism.

Poetry isn't the only format that straddles fiction and nonfiction. Historical picture book stories can add beauty and pathos to a topic. This is the case in a Clarion picture book for older readers that is in the works, with the tentative title *A Story of the Young Jimi Hendrix*. Written by Gary Golio and illustrated by Javaka Steptoe, the book focuses on the poor boyhood of the legendary rock musician who played air guitar on his broomstick. "It's also a book about the process of creation: inspiration, hard work, determination, and vision," Polvino explains.

Nonfiction Shines

Biographies have always been a staple of publishers, no matter their size or independent corporate status. In addition to the Hendrix biography, Clarion's list includes *She Touched the World: Laura Bridgman, Deaf-Blind Pioneer*, by Sally Hobart Alexander and Robert Alexander. Bridgman, who lived 50 years before Helen Keller, learned to read, write, and perform on stage, despite her disabilities. She became famous in her time, but few people today have heard of her. Polvino calls it "fascinating and moving," and long overdue.

Also fascinating is the Susanna Reich biography *Painting the Wild Frontier: The Art and Adventures of George Catlin*. Polvino says Catlin was "the Indiana Jones of the nineteenth-century art world because of his adventures in the wilds of North and South America." He was most famous for his portraits of Americans, and graced the palaces of Europe with his art.

Charlesbridge biographies include a picture book about the first woman to run for U.S. president on a major-party ticket. *Margaret Chase Smith: A Woman for President* is written by Lynn Plourde and illustrated by David McPhail. Smith served as a U.S. representative from Maine from 1940 to 1949, senator from 1949 to 1973, and ran for president in 1964. "What makes this book stand out for me," says LeRoy, "is the innovative use of timelines running throughout the book. These timelines are on such historical subjects as women in politics or the Cold War, and create a sense of context and relevance for the main biography."

The workings of art in picture books is the subject of a nonfiction Chronicle book, *Show and Tell,* by Dilys Evans. Founder of the Original Art Exhibition (sponsored by the Society of Illustrators in New York), Evans is regularly called upon by Caldecott committees to talk about how to look at picture book art. In this book, she highlights the work of twelve seminal picture book artists, including David Weisner, Trina Schart Hyman, Lane Smith, Brian Selznick, and David Shannon.

A talented writing choir speaks in Atheneum's *Voices in First Person: Reflections on Latino Identity*. Compiled by Lori Carlson and edited by Dlouhy, this collection features monologues written by the most influential, esteemed Latino writers today, including Oscar Hijuelos, Sandra Cisneros, Gary Soto, and Ana Castillo. Dlouhy says, "Each writes about what it's like to be a Latino youth in America. Each has something different to say, and they hold no punches. The monologues are raw, gritty, yearning, hopeful, desperate, heartbreaking, joyous." The audience for this volume is not only Latinos, but all young readers. The essays "capture the myriad of emotions all teens go through," Dlouhy says. "There's nothing like this out there, and it's impossible to read without feeling, somehow, changed. Black-and-white photographs heavy with symbolism and graffiti art accompany the text, so it's also a very visual package that doesn't need to be read in a linear fashion."

Shared human experiences are what make history come alive. Publishers are eager to offer true stories that may not appear in any social studies textbook.

An example is *The Mayflower and the Pilgrims' New World*, Nathaniel

Philbrick's middle-grade book, adapted from his National Book Award-winning book for adults, *Mayflower: A Story of Courage, Community, and War.* Putnam Senior Editor Timothy Travaglini says that Philbrick shines the spotlight on little-known events in the colonists' first years. Particularly chilling is the account of King Philip's War in 1675, which pitted the English against an alliance of Native American tribes. "Over 14 horrifying months, the war claimed more than 5,000 lives, and irreversibly decimated the Native American population in southern New England," Travaglini explains.

Walker Books plumbs the eighteenth century to find the measure of a tragic circumstance with *Duel: Burr and Hamilton's Deadly War of Words,* by Dennis Brindell Fradin and illustrated by Larry Day. Most schoolchildren have heard of the duel but don't know the specifics. Easton says Fradin's book explains "how the lifelong rivalry escalated into a deadly duel involving a U.S. vice president and a founding father." These very personal stories of the past and their impact on a larger society echo in current times.

Easton speaks of what she seeks in the coming year: "As books have to compete more and more with other media for kids' time and attention, we are looking for fresh formats to bring information to readers, stories—both factual and fictional—that inspire and intrigue, and illustrations that make you take a second look. Writers are tired of this familiar answer, but the truth is, editors are always looking for a compelling author's voice and a fresh angle on important perennial topics. There's less patience for a quiet book that takes time to build. You have to grab a reader's attention right away in order for them to take that journey with you, no matter what kind of story you're trying to tell."

Impact, information about issues, activism, and interactivity with text are qualities some publishers are taking to an international level. Small but mighty Tilbury House isn't afraid to publish picture books on difficult subjects, or to use extensive backmatter to turn readers into activists (usually with the help of their teachers). According to Editor Karen Fisk, *Give a Goat* is such a book. The author is Jan West Schrock, whose father founded Heifer International, a nonprofit organization that battles poverty and hunger. In this true story, a school class works together to buy a needy family a goat, which can provide milk for dairy products. Humorous illustrations by Aileen Darragh show the process of identifying a charity and doing fundraising. "*Give a Goat* is the perfect template both for those who work with children and want them to experience the satisfaction of giving to others, and for kids who are looking for ways to make a difference," says Fisk.

Tilbury House, whose books are largely multicultural, is also publishing *Amadi's Snowman,* by Katia Novet Saint-Lot and illustrated by Dimitrea Tokunbo. Set in Nigeria, Amadi resists his mother's encouragement to read, and would rather play at "business" at the market. Soon he finds an older boy reading about a snowman, and curiosity changes Amadi's mind about reading.

The current and upcoming children's literature lineups are not all issues and important language. There is still plenty of room for silly books, holiday books, and bright concept books. Editor Kristin Daly at HarperCollins can't wait for December, hoping that many copies of *When Santa Lost His Ho! Ho! Ho!* will be under Christmas trees. Written and illustrated by Laura Rader, this is the third book in the Santa trilogy. "Laura has such a great picture book voice—her text is simple and snappy, and both text and art are full of little laugh-out-loud details."

From Simon & Schuster Books for Young Readers, *Fartiste,* by Kathleen Krull and Paul Brewer, illustrated by Boris Kulikov, is based on a true story. There was once a Moulin Rouge "who could make his pants dance." No kidding—this comes from David Gale, Vice President and Editorial Director.

As usual, there is something new for every reader. Silly or serious, series or single title, children's books and their authors are respectfully yours.

The Big World of Small Magazine Communities

By Jan Fields

In the sometimes glamorous and high-powered world of publishing, the annual number of magazine launches is closely observed for vacillating trends. What is the pulse of the market? Are e-zines undermining print circulations? Will advertising revenues drop? But in any given year, trade periodicals and magazine associations broadcast different numbers and vary in their predictions about the health of magazines. Consider the recent data below. What's a writer to think?

➤ *Media Life* reports that a recent rise in new general interest magazines reversed markedly last year, though— relying on the research of journalist professor Samir Husni— it also says that debuts are succeeding at a higher rate. Husni determined that the survival rate for new magazines a decade ago was about 18 percent, while today it is closer to 40 percent.

➤ The Magazine Publishers of America (MPA) found a 7 percent increase in projected launches over the first half of the preceding year. Even better news may be that the MPA found that magazine readership increased by about 7 percent over the last decade, with particularly strong growth in the last five years.

➤ A survey by the media marketing company McPheters & Company found that younger readers read more magazines than adults, as reported by Marketingcharts.com.

Magazine writers should feel heartened: an increasing readership, highest interest among teens and tweens, and staying power by new publications. These positives are joined by other encouraging factors in the magazine marketplace at the end of the first decade of the twenty-first century. Digital media publishing ventures are widening, and a steady stream of new niche magazines are entering the arena.

The magazine industry remains fretful as postal rates continue to rise, distribution grows more competitive, and technology encroaches and beckons. One way to deal with these changes is for publishers, small and large, to be solidly realistic about making magazines work. For writers, that's good news, but they have to do their part in being grounded in reality. More than ever, magazine writers must know the market and produce quality work. An important key is to pay attention to those small magazines that more and more are slipping into the cracks of underserved markets and meeting readers' needs so well that even the big players are taking note.

Sources

➢ Nelson, Katy: "Abrupt Slowing in Magazine Launches." *Media Life Magazine,* 23 July 2007. www.medialifemagazine.com

➢ "Hispanic/Latino Market Profile." Magazine Publishers of America. www.magazine.org/Advertising_and_PIB/MPAHispMktPro.pdf

➢ "Younger Readers Read More Magazines than Older Peers." www.marketingcharts.com/print/younger-adults-read-more-magazines-than-older-peers-423/

➢ Samir Husni, Chair of the Journalism Department, University of Mississippi. www.mrmagazine.com

Meet Me in the Niches

A readership group piquing the interest of publishers from major media giants to small entrepreneurs is the Hispanic community, and for good reason. The Latino population in the United States grew 58 percent from 1990 to 2000, and that growth has come with purchasing power—an estimated $798 billion in the last year surveyed.

When *Quince Girl* launched a little over two years ago to meet the needs of Hispanic teens, it was the first national magazine to focus on the *quinceañera,* the cultural and religious coming-of-age celebration for Latino girls turning fifteen. A year after its launch, *Quince Girl* was generating revenue in the high six figures and had a circulation around 300,000.

With those earnings, and 400,000 Hispanic girls turning fifteen each year, even a media giant can become interested. Hearst followed by producing *Mis Quince* as a promotional insert in the October issues of *CosmoGIRL!, Seventeen,* and *Teen* magazines. The next step was for Hearst Digital Media, in September 2007, to launch *Misquincemag.com,* an online magazine for girls approaching their quinceañera.

Not every audience is as large as the American Hispanic community, and certainly market segments—readership communities—are divided by interests, age, and geography, as well as ethnicity. One of the paradoxes of widening global communication over the Internet is that those readership communities—smaller segments or niches—seem to be the wave of the print future.

With the growing number of such targeted magazines and the clear signs that today's niche can become tomorrow's major market, writers benefit from stretching into these new arenas. Magazines can match nearly every writer's interests. In every case, successful niche magazines began by someone recognizing an underserved population.

"We've had a general sense of an absence of materials for our community for a long time," says Ausma Khan, Editor in Chief of *Muslim Girl.* "But things became more urgent when members of our publishing team attended the Islamic Society of North America conference. There they heard from many young people and women about feelings of isolation and alienation from the larger culture. There was a real sense of being marginalized and excluded. We did some research and determined that the market for the magazine was large and viable and we knew there was a huge need for it, so we started planning."

Publisher Ayal Korczak launched *LàTeen* in October 2007 because he sensed some of the same absence of material to meet the needs of young Latinos. "Not many other entities are vying for the attention of Latino teens," says Korczak. A teacher, he saw major magazines, like *Sports Illustrated,* produce Spanish versions but he found it difficult to locate entertaining and informative materials for his Hispanic students' specific needs. The publication describes its purpose on its website: "*LàTeen Magazine* provides the Latino teen community with positive reading material that is relevant to the Hispanic experience. We strive to empower and educate the next generation of Hispanics through articles that highlight Hispanic success. We believe in education, equality, and pride in being brown."

For *LàTeen*, the plan to reach the readership includes essential newsstand placement, connecting with educators, and extending the scope of the magazine's content. "We plan to go on the newsstands across the nation; we have gone to a quarterly model with a higher page count," Korczak says. "We hope to include supplements for teachers to guide class discussions on some of the topics in the magazine. We are adding more Spanish content to increase the variety of readers. We are spotlighting where the different Hispanic groups hail from in America. We are also placing a strong emphasis on college."

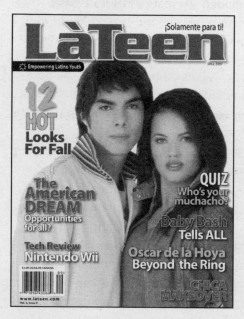

Making sales to community-focused niche markets depends on understanding the community being served. "*Muslim Girl* is open to freelancers," says Khan, but because of the very specific needs of Muslim readers, the editorial staff recognizes that not every freelance writer is able to produce what they need. "Every subject we address is measured against core Islamic values practiced by our community, which means that we don't talk about boys, dating, and fashion in the same way that other teen magazines do. We talk about these issues from a values-based and girl-empowerment perspective."

Community style is as essential as community topics. Korczak says, "Writers need to keep in mind that *LàTeen* readers need simple sentence structure and fun, interesting topics appealing to Latino teens ages 13 to 17. Some of our readers are [English as a] second language learners and therefore the writers need to cater to their reading abilities."

Filling a niche can also go beyond ethnicity to meeting special needs. *Logan Magazine* launched in 2007, targeting young adults with disabilities. At 16, Logan Olsen sustained a brain injury. When she came home from rehabilitation, she and her mother Laurie looked for a magazine that would meet her needs and interests. It was a search that led to frustration and eventually to creative solutions. "When we didn't find what Logan was looking for, we decided to create a cut-and-paste dream magazine," says Laurie Olsen. "Logan's brother and friend took pictures of Logan in downtown Spokane and we used Photoshop to create a mock-up magazine. The more people we shared our homemade magazine with, the more help and advice we received to really get this going."

That humble beginning launched a project that surprised everyone. "The response has been overwhelming," says Joy Carlsen, a feature writer and Editor of *Logan*. "Typically, a publication our size ends up with about 50 new subscribers for every issue they release. We had more than 500 new subscribers after the launch issue debuted. We are hearing from people all over the U.S. and now, Canada. We are hearing from people living with disabilities, but lots of people without as well. We have subscribers who just liked the look and content of the first issue so much they subscribed. We are being asked to expand the features, add new ones, and grow into a national publication."

Carlsen adds that *Logan* is open to freelancers who can focus on the young women rather than on the disability they may have. "We are always interested in hearing ideas for new features, as well as entertaining options for single-run articles. The mission of *Logan* is to inspire, encourage, and inform young women with disabilities about how to lead a lifestyle that is productive, purposeful, and pleasurable. Our goal is to motivate young women to live, work, play, dream big, and look great experiencing all life has to offer."

Fun and Games

Although many teen and tween girl magazines are thriving, new publications continue to launch with the purpose of focusing on the interests of specific groups. Some of these concentrate on activities, such as *Kiki Magazine* for girls interested in the fashion industry, and *Golfer Girl* for readers involved in competitive junior golf.

The impetus for starting *Golfer Girl* is familiar—but with a sporting twist. Publisher Claude Hooton identified an underserved community, the approximately two million girls who golf—180,000 of whom play eight or more regulation rounds each year. "My three daughters are all competitive junior golfers," Hooton says. "We often heard from the players that, although there were many golf magazines, there wasn't a magazine specifically for them. Golf is a wonderful sport but there is still a perception that it is a sport for males."

To be certain of creating a magazine that directly addressed the interests of the young female golfer, Hooton turned to his daughters for ideas and staff. His approach is not unlike that of *New Moon*, the successful, award-winning magazine for girls that integrates the girls themselves in the editorial staff. Hooton says, "My oldest daughter, Libby, loves to write, so we have given her the position of Editor in Chief. She likes having the responsibility and opportunity. She is still learning how to do the tasks of the position."

Having a young staff doesn't mean Hooton has approached the magazine haphazardly. "When we decided to take the big step of starting this magazine, there were three primary goals: to provide a mechanism for our daughters to learn the fundamentals of running a business while focusing on their passion, which is golf (and fashion, also covered in the magazine); to help develop and coordinate the community of junior girl golfers; and to develop the business so that it is financially viable. We are well on our way to accomplishing those goals." The current circulation is about 10,000.

Kiki Magazine was launched in fall 2007 with similar girl-oriented ideas: to serve the interests of fashion-minded girls, ages 9 to 14, while focusing on age-appropriate material only. *Kiki* founder Jamie Gleich

Bryant says too many teen and tween magazines present sexualized images of girls and women. She wanted to see a magazine that would meet a young girl's interest in fashion without the sexual overtones. "In *Kiki*, there's no gossip, no boyfriends, no sensuality, no instructions on how to kiss, no tips on getting sexy abs."

Instead, Bryant says, fashion and creativity are front and center. "Our goal is not to push fashion on girls but to let fashion be a lens through

The goal is to be a lens through which girls explore creativity and develop self-expression.

which girls can explore their own creativity and develop their sense of self-expression. Because fashion is multifaceted (art, craft, expression, industry, etc.), it provides a rich entry point for personal expression and development. We want to give our readers a place to encounter fashion as a design student would and to explore how fashion relates to their lives—how they use it, how they make it, how they change it, how they feel about it, and so on. Being able to interact with fashion is elemental to the whole concept of *Kiki*."

Part of the interactivity is encouraging readers to write and draw directly on the magazine pages, transforming it into a kind of creative journal. Among its departments are From the Studio, on design, textiles, shoes, fixing clothes; World Beat, profiling cities with design traditions and cultural trends; Biz Buzz, on managing money; and Your Style, on readers' everyday life.

Audience Recalibration

Large magazine companies smartly react to market vacillations with shifts in focus, moving to identify and serve their audience better, and of course stay appealing to advertisers and keep revenue flowing at a goodly pace. When *Nick Jr. Family Magazine* experienced a newsstand sales plunge of almost 150 percent, parent company MTV Network decided to stop publication of the magazine with the April 2007 issue. The plummet, however, was matched by an increased interest in magazines for very young children, so *Nick Jr.* experienced an inversion, and

Sports Markets

➤ *American Cheerleader:* 110 William Street, New York, NY 10038.

➤ *American Girl:* 8400 Fairway Place, Middleton, WI 53562.

➤ *Baseball Youth:* P.O. Box 983, Morehead, KY 40351.

➤ *Boys' Life:* 1325 West Walnut Lane, P.O. Box 152079, Irving, TX 75015.

➤ *Boys' Quest* and *Hopscotch:* P.O. Box 227, Bluffton, OH 45817.

➤ *Canoe & Kayak:* 10526 NE 68th Street, Kirkland, WA 98033.

➤ *Golfer Girl:* P.O. Box 804, Del Mar, CA 92014.

➤ *International Gymnast:* P.O. Box 721020, Norman, OK 73070.

➤ *JAKES:* P.O. Box 530, Edgefield, SC 29824.

➤ *Junior Baseball:* P.O. Box 9099, Canoga Park, CA 91309.

➤ *Skating:* 20 First Street, Colorado Springs, CO 80906.

➤ *Slap:* 1303 Underwood Avenue, San Francisco, CA 94124.

➤ *Softball Youth GA:* P.O. Box 1137, Watkinsville, GA 30677.

➤ *SportingKid:* 3650 Brookside Parkway, Alpharetta, GA 30022.

➤ *Sports Illustrated for Kids:* 1271 Avenue of the Americas, New York, NY 10020.

➤ *Thrasher:* 1303 Underwood Avenue, San Francisco, CA 94124.

➤ *USA Gymnastics:* 201 S. Capitol Avenue, Indianapolis, IN 46225.

many writers may not have noticed the change. *Nick Jr.* is on the newsstands with a nearly identical look. The new magazine has far fewer pages and concentrates on content for kids rather than parents. The magazine may seem to have only gotten slimmer, but its content is radically different.

Another magazine to undergo a refocusing was Bauer Publishing's tween girl celebrity magazine *Twist*. Again, the magazine looks much the same on the newsstand. It's still pink. It's still covered with young celebrity faces. But now *Twist* offers practical content, with celebrity examples. A double issue last year added departments on self-image issues, such as Is This Normal? and Body Insecurities. Bauer's media kit touts the new editorial focus as 51 percent celebrity/entertainment, 14 percent relationship, and 21 percent fashion and beauty, with health, self-improvement, and general interest in the mix.

For most magazines, change is constant and carefully planned. As a classic example, in 1945 Youth for Christ launched a magazine by the same name, a name held until 1965 when it was changed to *Campus Life*. In 1985, *Campus Life* was purchased by Christianity Today International and kept the same title until 2006, when it became *Ignite Your Faith*. The magazine's title changed because many readers interpreted *campus* as meaning the magazine targeted college students instead of high school students.

With the most recent name change came a major re-visioning. *Ignite Your Faith* now has a focus that Editor Christopher Lutes says grew out of his realization of teens' interest in deepening their faith and spiritual walk. "With this emphasis on committed Christian teens who are seeking to live their faith, we still realize that kids are in the process of growing," says Lutes, and, thus, experiencing some difficult and troubling physical, spiritual, emotional, and mental growing pains. So, we continue to deal empathetically and sensitively with huge issues like anorexia, depression, homosexuality, parental be-

trayal, and sexual promiscuity." Among them is a first-person story of a Christian girl who struggled with oral sex, "Everything but All the Way" (June/July 2008).

One change that *Ignite Your Faith* readers will see is an increase in using popular culture and technology to explore spiritual truths. "Along with encouraging discernment of questionable content in today's entertainment, we have also been taking a more positive approach to media," Lutes explains, "through lively, youth-talk styled Bible studies that use movies and movie characters to convey biblical principle, values, and truth. He cites "More Than a Game," by Tom WP Kapr [as the author chooses to spell his name] (September/October 2007), which looks at Christian principles found in popular sports movies.

Lutes is aware of how much time teens spend online. "To stay in tune with the current generation, we are always seeking new ways to connect on the Web and with an Internet-savvy generation. We

What a Girl Wants

Anastasia Goodstein, Editor of the online journal *Ypulse: Media for the Next Generation,* spends considerable time thinking about teen media. With stiff competition for teen money and time, especially from new technology and the Internet, she sees teen magazines needing to face certain realities to survive. "Print is definitely competing with online for teens' time and for advertiser dollars," she says. "Yes, you can't take MySpace to the beach with you, but that doesn't mean teens will ask their parents to subscribe to a magazine for them versus just picking up single copies at the drug store for that purpose." She sees other shifts that magazines and their writers will have to face:

➤ "Teens, and especially teen girls, are growing up faster. They're exposed to more media and marketing at earlier ages and their tastes are more sophisticated. They may want to read teen titles when they're 11, but when they hit 13, most of them grab the adult fashion or celebrity magazine. I think that's why the tween titles like *Tiger Beat* and *J14* continue to do well, especially on the newsstand. Tween girls love their idols and still want to tear out their pictures."

➤ "Teens can now create their own content. The role of the teen magazine was always this big sister persona, with editors in the know helping teens with beauty, boys, and fashion. The power has shifted and now teens are creating their own zines online, or blogs, or videos, or MySpace layouts. They will not accept being a passive reader or audience any longer. I posted the other day about a teen who created a magazine that

have recently increased our exclusive online content, created a MySpace page, and we are getting ready to release an online video cartoon."

A Teeny Tiny Boom

The transformation of *Nick Jr.* isn't the only sign that tots are hot in the magazine market. Research continues to show that parents who read to infants and toddlers build their language skills and vocabulary. A 2006 study in the professional journal *Child Development* indicated that the tie between reading to children and their development in language and cognition begins even earlier than had been thought:

What a Girl Wants

was made using Condé Nast's new Flipbook application Flip.com."

➤ "Magazines can't keep up with the Internet when it comes to celebrity news and gossip. Blogs like Perez Hilton's and Pink is the New Blog, and websites like TMZ, are going to break news before any print magazine can, which kind of makes that news feel like yesterday's news. Teen magazines have to run exclusive celebrity content like specially produced fashion spreads or interviews versus just running the same paparazzi photos you can get online or in the celebrity weeklies."

"I think the real challenge is that even if magazines can marry top-notch editorial with applications that encourage user-generated content, feedback, and community (like Flip.com), they still have to compete with sites like MySpace, Facebook, and other social networks that already have millions of teens spending lots of time there. And teens don't have that much free time. I think that's why Hearst bought eCrush and eSpin. I think you'll see more magazine companies buying or partnering with popular teen websites/communities, especially if building their own just isn't attracting the numbers these sites already have."

So what does that mean for writers? It means getting to know the teens of today, not the teens of yesterday. It means becoming familiar with the changing face of technology because that technology is going to continue to change teen magazines. It means writing from the viewpoint that isn't parental, but much more peer to peer. To write for teens, you need to know them and respect them, not aim to fix them.

Better vocabulary and language comprehension were clear by age two. (Raikes, H. *Child Development,* July/August 2006; vol 7. Society for Research in Child Development.)

Parents and publishers responded. Toddler magazines comprise a growing market, with *National Geographic Little Kids* and *The Little Lutheran* joining the still fairly new *Highlights High Five* and the now venerable *Babybug.* Launched in July, *The Little Lutheran* is a 24-page, art-based magazine for children ages six and younger, and is published ten times a year. Editor Elizabeth Hunter envisioned the publication as "one that parents, godparents, grandparents, teachers, and friends could use to help nurture the faith of young children."

National Geographic Little Kids debuted last spring, and targets children ages three to six. Its stated mission is to give preschoolers "a head start into reading, logical reasoning, counting, and cultural awareness" through content about animals, nature, and science.

Writers should be aware that the high standards of these early magazines can make them tough markets for freelancers. Part of the problem is the difficulty in writing very short material that is also unique. *Highlights High Five* rarely uses material over 150 words. At *The Little Lutheran*, all pieces range from 25 to 200 words. The word count for nonfiction maxes out at ten words at *Babybug*.

Bonus Pull-out Pages: Make Your Own Sewing Cards

Unsolicited submissions are less likely to make headway than approaching publications with a writing résumé, with the hope of assignments, or entering side-doors. Editor Kathleen Hayes, of *Highlights High Five*, explains, "At this time we are commissioning most of the stories and poems that appear in the magazine and most of the features are being written in-house." Some very short material for the youngest reader that is submitted to *Highlights for Children* eventually ends up in *Highlights High Five*, giving writers another possible entrance into writing for the very youngest readers.

Babybug is accepting manuscripts and Editor Alice Letvin says she could use more material for the youngest of Carus Publishing's *bug* magazines. She warns that writing for such young readers is difficult, and most submissions she receives are better suited for older children.

The news is similar at *The Little Lutheran*: "Submissions from outside writers are reviewed, but rarely accepted," says Hunter. "For our readers, we require writers to be knowledgeable about ELCA (Evangelical Lutheran Church in America) theology and practice, as well as skilled at writing for very young children. So many people want to write

Cobblestone:
History Comes Alive

American history is a subject that makes some adults cringe with memories of dry and seemingly endless lists of facts and figures. *Cobblestone*, published by a division of Carus Publishing, is a terrific cure for an irrational fear of history. The magazine proves that history can excite the reader's imagination if you see it as a journey to the past instead of a collection of dull facts. Cobblestone Publishing's Editorial Director Lou Waryncia is excited about creating a magazine that makes that journey again and again.

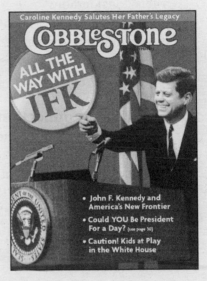

"We publish *Cobblestone* with the belief that American history is about our shared American experience," he explains. "History is about our lives. It's filled with heroes, exciting events, and amazing inventions, as well as everyday stories of real people, some notable, some not. Each person's contribution made us the people and country we are today. Best of all, these stories are real."

Aware of the place *Cobblestone* has in classrooms, the editors also always look for ways to expand beyond the basics of what children need to learn in school. Choosing themes for each issue is a complex process. Waryncia says, "We have a running list of theme ideas. It probably has more than 100 items on it. Each year we get to choose nine. We talk to our advisory board and get each member's opinion on themes. We look to see what our readers want. Editorial staff members add their own ideas. We look at upcoming events and commemorations. Sometimes we work with museums, historians, and filmmakers in collaboration with projects they are doing."

In everything, though, *Cobblestone* keeps the reader in mind. "We take a lively, kid-friendly approach to our material that's well written, highly descriptive, age-appropriate, and understandable. I like to say 'I want to know how dirty a person's fingernails are.' I think our material has a sense of fun, too. Of course, we try to present the text with the best photos and illustrations to make each page interesting to read."

for young children because they believe it's easier than writing for adults. But, really, it's exactly the opposite. It's difficult to find writers who can write material for very young children that is both developmentally appropriate and, from an ELCA perspective, theologically solid. The best writers express theologically complex teachings in a way that honors the God-given worth and curiosity of young children, while managing to communicate something of value to children at varying developmental levels and abilities. This narrows the field of writers considerably."

For writers who have spent time studying these magazines and understand the developmental needs of the young audience, opportunities are likely to continue to increase as parents look for readalouds for their little ones.

Educational Connections

Teachers have always valued the use of magazines for older children in the classroom. According to a Rutgers University study, cited by Scholastic, Inc., 92 percent of the teachers surveyed believe magazines increase interest in reading. (See http://teacher.scholastic.com/products/classmags/files/RESEARCH.pdf.) The two "big dogs" in classroom magazines are Scholastic and Weekly Reader Corporation—and both have been working to increase their publications' usefulness to teachers and students.

According to Bryon Cahill, Editor of Weekly Reader's teen classroom magazine *READ*, the magazine's 56-year history of success doesn't mean the editorial staff can afford to let *READ* stagnate. "Last year we increased the physical size of *READ*. It had always been digest-sized and we decided that, by blowing it up a little, we had more room to breathe." Cahill says this change translates into more opportunities to make literature come alive for students. "Sometimes when kids read, they tend to forget that someone (maybe someone just like them) was behind the words on the page. We try to bring that out in the open with everything we do. We would have found considerable difficulty doing this type of thing in the original, digest size."

Weekly Reader has also been aware of the value of technology in reaching its audience. "*READ* has gone electronic over the past couple of years," Cahill explains. "Together with *Writing*, we launched

WORD, Weekly Reader's literary blog (www.readandwriting.com). At WORD, we are able to deliver book news, author interviews, writing tips, and pretty much anything even remotely related to the literary world in an immediate fashion. We want students to know that we are actual people sitting on the other end of the magazines they hold in their hands. WORD allows us to connect with them on a level that print publications cannot."

Cahill says WORD has also allowed more publication of student writing. "We have many writing prompts in our magazines that direct students to our blog (or *bloggy* as I lovingly like to call it). We ask them to share what they are writing with us and we get a lot of great writing from all ages. We try to post student writing on WORD as much as we can. It's important, not only for the student who wrote a piece to see his or her work published, but also to other student readers. When a student sees that someone his or her own age can do it, then they may become more courageous in their writing. It's win-win."

Encouraging student writing is an important feature of Scholastic's online magazine *Write It*, which is designed to help student writers in grades 7 to 12 and give them a place to publish.

The classroom magazines rarely accept unsolicited submissions—but that doesn't mean they're uninterested in those freelance writers who can provide strong, timely information. According to Cody Crane, Associate Editor of Scholastic's *Science World*, the best way for experienced writers to connect with Scholastic classroom magazines is through a solid package of résumé, clips, and a strong query.

Teachers often go beyond traditional classroom magazines when integrating content into the classroom. Magazines can help round out the curriculum in new and exciting ways. For example, many teachers

Classroom and Teacher Magazines

➤ **Scholastic Magazines:** 557 Broadway, New York, NY 10012. *Action, ART, Choices, DynaMath, Instructor, Junior Scholastic, MATH, Scholastic News, Science World, Scope, Storyworks, SuperScience, Upfront.*

➤ **Weekly Reader Magazines:** 1 Reader's Digest Road, Pleasantville, NY 10570. *Career World, Current Events, Current Health 1 & 2, Know Your World, READ, Weekly Reader, Weekly Reader Science, Writing.*

Other Titles

➤ *Art Education:* Virginia Commonwealth University, P.O. Box 843084, Richmond, VA 23284.

➤ *Arts & Activities:* 12345 World Trade Drive, San Diego, CA 92128.

➤ *Childhood Education:* 17904 Georgia Avenue, Olney, MA 20832.

➤ *Education Week:* 6935 Arlington Road, Bethesda, MD 20814.

➤ *Gifted Education Press Quarterly:* 10201 Yuma Court, P.O. Box 1586, Manassas, VA 20109.

➤ *Language Arts:* National Council of Teachers of English, Ohio State University, 333 Arps Hall, 1945 North High Street, Columbus, OH 43210.

➤ *Learning and Leading with Technology:* 175 West Broadway, Eugene, OR 97401.

➤ *The Reading Teacher* and *Reading Today:* International Reading Association, 800 Barksdale Road, P.O. Box 8139, Newark, DE 19714.

➤ *SchoolArts:* 2223 Parkside Drive, Denton, TX 76201.

➤ *Science Activities:* 1319 18th Street NW, Washington, DC 20036.

➤ *The Science Teacher:* National Science Teachers Association, 1840 Wilson Boulevard, Arlington, VA 22201.

➤ *Science Weekly:* 2141 Industrial Parkway, Silver Spring, MD 20904.

➤ *Social Studies and the Young Learner:* University of Missouri-Columbia, 303 Townsend Hall, Columbia, MO 65211.

➤ *Teaching Music:* National Association for Music Education, 1806 Robert Fulton Drive, Reston, VA 20191.

➤ *Teaching PreK-8:* 40 Richards Avenue, Norwalk, CT 06854.

➤ *Technology & Learning:* 1111 Bayhill Drive, San Bruno, CA 94066.

and homeschool families love *Cobblestone* for the adventure it brings to American history. Lou Waryncia is Editorial Director of Cobblestone Publishing and Editor of the flagship publication. Waryncia explains that the Cobblestone publications approach history as important literature. "These are real stories. They can be written about and presented in a manner that's not boring, not just a list of dates and facts. I think our material has a sense of fun, too." Cobblestone Publishing also offers *Calliope*, about world history; *AppleSeeds*, which explores topics based on people of the past and present; and *Faces*, on cultures around the world.

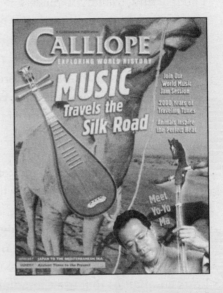

Moo-Cow Fan Club went from a print publication to an online magazine last year, and also has its share of fans among teachers. Editor Becky Ances says switching to an online format also allows *Moo-Cow Fan Club* to go beyond the capabilities of a print magazine. "The educational articles are now blog entries by the characters. They still do the same things that they did in the magazine, but more often and with timely information. For instance, we had a phoebe bird build a nest on the front door of *Moo-Cow Fan Club* headquarters. Right away Kiweenie, a bird himself, began blogging about the birds. Readers could follow along in almost real time and watch the birth of the baby birds!"

Like the classroom magazines, going online has opened up Ances's ability to share more reader writing. "Readers can write to the characters themselves and ask questions, and become part of the dialogue. That was something we were never able to do in the magazine outside of the Letters to the Editor section. We are also going to add videos and podcasts—such as videos explaining how to do crafts (like a mini *Martha Stewart* episode), and just some fun stuff."

Online opportunities have opened the door for educational niche magazines as well. Michele Regenold, Editor of *Go! Exploring the World of Transportation*, a teen magazine focused on careers in the transportation industry, says the decision to launch online was purely financial. "Our original plan was for a print magazine, but it was cost prohibitive. Printing and distribution costs would make our total costs soar by about ten times. It was much easier to find sponsors/donors for $30,000 than for $300,000 (and that wasn't easy)."

Although less expensive to produce, e-zines offer other challenges—like reaching the target audience. "Marketing to teens directly online can be tricky," Regenold says. "We continue to try new strategies. In terms of e-mail marketing directly to teens, we've gone through Iowa State University (which publishes *Go!*). We've e-mailed current freshmen through juniors in about 20 different majors. We've also e-mailed prospective Iowa State students. We'll contact new freshmen the same way again when our first issue of the fall comes out."

Beyond Borders

The Canadian magazine market for young readers seems to be in the middle of a new market boom, with print magazines like *Crow Toes Quarterly, Girls Can Do Anything, Six78th,* and *Zamoof!* popping up.

Writers in the U.S. should recognize that Canadian publishers may favor Canadian authors, not just out of national allegiance, but because arts and regional councils often earmark funding to magazines and book companies that use Canadian writers and target content to Canadian interests and audiences. Some magazines accept submissions only from Canadian writers, but many want to keep the door open for the really good piece, no matter where the writer is from.

Zamoof! is available across the U.S. and Canada, and targets ages 6 to 12 with fun and educational materials that prepare them for their adolescent years. Founder and Editor TeLeni Koochin has in-house writers but definitely leaves space for freelance submissions. She wants the magazine to have a variety of voices, and to give writers the opportunity to work with other writers. "Due to our desire to qualify for future Canadian grants, we do lean toward Canadian writers at this time. *Zamoof!* has also been designed to give youth the chance to be published so we work closely with many classroom settings for our writing needs. As far as freelance goes, we generally are only seeking short stories."

Publication Websites

➤ *Be Well:* www.bewellmagazine.com
➤ *Boys' Life:* www.boyslife.org
➤ **Carus Publishing:** Cobblestone Publishing and Cricket Publishing, www.cobblestonepub.com
➤ *Crow Toes Quarterly:* www.crowtoesquarterly.com
➤ *Go! Exploring the World of Transportation:* www.go-explore-trans.org
➤ *Golfer Girl:* www.golfergirlmagazine.com
➤ **Hearst Magazines:** www.hearstcorp.com
➤ *Highlights for Children, Highlights High Five:* www.highlights.com
➤ *Ignite Your Faith:* www.christianitytoday.com/teens
➤ *Kiki:* www.kikimag.com
➤ *LàTeen:* www.lateen.com
➤ *The Little Lutheran:* www.thelittlelutheran.org/little
➤ *Logan:* www.loganmagazine.com
➤ *Mis Quince:* www.misquincemag.com
➤ **MOM:** www.mommagazine.ca
➤ *Moo-Cow Fan Club:* www.moocowfanclub.com
➤ *Motherwords:* www.motherwords.org
➤ *Muslim Girl:* www.muslimgirlmagazine.com
➤ *National Geographic Little Kids:* http://littlekids.nationalgeographic.com/littlekids
➤ *Nick Jr. Family:* www.nick.com/all_nick/everything_nick/enter_mag.jhtml
➤ *Quince Girl:* www.quincegirl.com
➤ **Scholastic, Inc.:** www.scholastic.com
➤ *Six78th:* www.six78th.com
➤ *SM, The Magazine for Single Mothers:* www.singlemothermag.com
➤ **Weekly Reader Corporation:** www.weeklyreader.com
➤ *Zamoof!:* www.zamoofmag.com

The vision of *Zamoof!* is educational, but with plenty of kid appeal. "Apart from all the fun that kids commonly seek in a publication, we aim for creativity and new slants," says Koochin. "The magazine was mainly developed to educate youth in social issues to prepare them for the teen years ahead. We hope it becomes a real teaching tool for parents and educators alike, along with inspiring youth to seek out the creativity within themselves."

Another Canadian magazine open to freelancers is *Crow Toes Quarterly*, which publishes funny, frightening, wondrous stories for ages 8 to 13. Managing Editor Christopher Millin says, "Though we limit the amount of international content we publish, we would definitely never want to pass up a great story." The publication has no particular interest in educating the reader, but rather in entertaining with stories that are "playfully dark." Millin describes the origin of the magazine, giving insight to the stories it wants: "*Crow Toes Quarterly* was born out of my love for dark, quirky children's literature. I grew up on the stories of Roald Dahl, Lewis Carroll, Ray Bradbury, and the Brothers Grimm, and more recently I have become a huge Lemony Snicket fan."

Like other magazines for younger readers up through tweens, Canadian magazines work at formulating voices and audiences that are unique. As *Six78th*, a girls' "junior high lifestyle magazine," Publisher Angie Rangel says, "It's been a struggle getting most to understand that we have created a magazine for girls that aren't quite ready for teen magazines just yet." Unlike many tween magazines that try for the voice of a cool big sister or cool aunt, *Six78th* recognizes the importance of parents in the lives of tween girls. "Although we definitely have an enormous amount of respect for the existing and emerging tween magazines, we are attempting an entirely new approach and feel that we have something special to offer."

Being a new magazine comes with a host of challenges that must be met early if it is to thrive, and the biggest is getting into the hands of readers. "Definitely I'd have to say breaking into the market with *Zamoof!* has been slower than expected," Koochin says. "That is the reality of the industry. As confident as we are, it is all about having the tools and finances to see it through long-term, to where we ultimately want to be, versus depending on any quick leaps."

Staying the Course

For longtime magazines, some of the planning for the future involves ignoring so-called conventional wisdom, and staying the course. Certain truisms are proven false every day by the success of magazines as diverse as *Boys' Life* and *Seventeen.*

Flying in the face of the bromide that "boys don't read, and certainly don't read fiction," *Boys' Life* continues to thrive. Managing Editor Michael Goldman says the reason is respect. "We treat our audience as

> Sensory material brings stories to life. Leg muscles burn at altitude. Mountain air smells sweet. Sweat tastes salty. Nerves tense at the sight of bears.

interested, and interesting, readers, not children. How do we do that? By listening to our readers and giving them what they want to read about. We must always keep in mind that *Boys' Life* is for the boys, not their parents or the editorial staff."

Goldman explains that the magazine's stories for ages 6 to 18 are full of concrete details. "Our fiction pieces have action, with the young protagonists actually doing what's being said. We give readers a taste of the trip or of the game or of the meeting in the schoolyard. Sensory material—smell, touch, taste—brings stories to life, draws readers in, and keeps readers until the end. Leg muscles and lungs burn at altitude. Mountain air smells sweet. Sweat tastes salty. Nerves tense at the sight of bears. *Boys' Life* fiction brings the action to the reader, and puts the reader into the action."

Another discordant truism that has become popular in the last few years is that young readers aren't interested in print, and that magazine websites actually meet the reader's need for information, making the magazine obsolete. This is simply not true, says Chuck Cordray, Vice President and General Manager at Hearst Magazines Digital Media, the parent company of *Seventeen* and *CosmoGirl!*, in a Q&A with media journalist Mark Glaser for *MediaShift*, a PBS weblog. Cordray says

Hearst's expansion into different media has been good for the magazines because the chance that a Web surfer to their sites would subscribe to the print publication had as much as doubled. He attributed that increase to "brand experience. If you have a good experience online, you might subscribe to the print publication." (Glaser, Mark. "Hearst Uses Startup Mentality in Revamp of Magazine Sites." *MediaShift*, 15 Aug. 2007. http://www.pbs.org/mediashift/2007/08.)

Goldman agrees with the value of online connections. "Our website is a critical component in reaching our readership and our goals. Online content provides multimedia and sensory experiences that are just not available via the printed page. The magazine and website complement each other, drawing readers seamlessly from one to the other, without cannibalizing content." Websites also offer quick reader response, Goldman says, "We have always been very receptive to reader feedback and get a great deal of it each month. Certainly, more is received electronically these days, and with the increase in quantity comes a general increase in quality, too."

Online may also be one option for Carus Publishing's teen magazine, *Cicada*. Editor Deborah Vetter explains, "We know that teenagers' interests and tastes constantly evolve, and we want *Cicada* to evolve with them. Therefore, we have been examining the scope, focus, and format of *Cicada*. We've launched an exciting new redesign in January/February 2008 and will be exploring ideas for an enhanced Web presence to augment The Slam, our popular online poetry and microfiction forum."

Parents Are People Too

The growth of practical parenting content online has been explosive. As a result, print parenting magazines for the general interest market are struggling. The twist here is that families appear to be more interested in magazines that look at being a parent as part of a broader lifestyle category, as last year's success stories with *Cookie* and *Wondertime* show.

More recent launches that take a parenting lifestyle approach are *SM, The Magazine for Single Mothers*; *Be Well*; and *MOM Magazine*. Each has a slightly different approach to addressing the needs of parents and families.

Publisher Crystal H. Jennings is a single mother and professional who was frustrated by the difficulty in finding legal, financial, and emotional information specific to single mothers. Her publication's mission statement says, *SM* is "not just another parenting magazine. [*SM*] is a fierce supporter of the needs and rights of the reader as a woman first—in fact, a woman with many roles in her life that must comfortably coexist with being a single parent. Thus, rather than addressing her narrowly as a single mother, *SM* will speak to her as the multidimensional woman that she is."

Editorial content provides women with practical tools to manage life, help with multitasking, make informed decisions, be proactive, and find ways to live optimally for herself and her family. *SM* is open to contributions from freelance writers on subjects such as family law, health, relationships, spirituality, money, co-parenting, and lifestyle issues.

Another family lifestyle magazine open to freelancers is *Be Well*, a magazine with a unique focus. "To literally *be well* is to nurture the physical, mental, emotional, and spiritual self," says Editor Suzanne Manning. "True wellness can only come from the care, feeding and exercise of all." Total wellness, she continues, comes from dealing with all of the most common life stresses, including money. "The magazine incorporates a money/finance section geared toward general financial interest, which helps keep readers financially fit and well." With this in mind, Manning says, "Writers can wow our editors by sending submissions that pertain specifically to everyday wellness, but staying clear of product pitches and self-endorsements."

The creation of *Be Well* arose from one magazine pointing the way to another. Manning explains that she was working in the area of healthy lifestyles with a magazine called *Q*, about quitting smoking. She found that there was a gap in publications that address everyday wellness. "Everyone talks about being well and living healthy. We wanted to create a publication that addressed this directly to interested readers," she says. "*Be Well* doesn't exclude one gender or another, as universally we all tie together and the whole human being revolves around the relationships we form."

Launched last September, Canadian newcomer *MOM* is based on the premise that all moms are goddesses. Publisher Tamara Plant says one way its vision plays out is in appreciating actual mothers. "Our cover moms are real women. They are not posed with kids that aren't even their own. They have curves in all the right places. They are local faces. We want women to celebrate every part of themselves—every curve, every stretch mark, every wrinkle, *everything*. We believe moms of all stages are beautiful, inside and out."

Appreciating the beauty in ordinary women is part of what makes *MOM* stand out. "We have had so many women thank us for putting out this magazine," Plant says. "We are connecting with moms on a totally different level than they are used to. Instead of being advised on how to raise their kids or what to cook for dinner, they are being shown how to reconnect with their inner goddess in spite of the fact that they have kids. Being a mom doesn't mean your life as a woman is over. We have sent that message to 20,000 moms locally, plus the crazy number of Web hits we get each week—an average of 12,000." Plant seeks content from all kinds of mothers. "Our website features content from moms everywhere. We offer a voice to moms and we want them to use it!"

As always, the number of parenting titles in regional markets also continues to climb, offering content to fit the needs of very specific regions. One of the very newest of these titles is *Motherwords*, targeting the northern Boston area, with a January 2008 launch. *Motherwords*'s slant is an irreverent but realistic look at motherhood, with editorial that encourages, celebrates, and allows mothers to share. The guidelines say, "We welcome submissions from women and men from all over the world. After all, we are all in this together. What could be more universal than child rearing?"

Writing for children and families is similarly universal, whatever the trends that surge through the magazine industry. But for now, niche magazines will continue to launch and thrive, technology will continue to spread through the industry keeping it vital and offering challenges. One factor that never changes: The content that sells best speaks to young people where they are today. Stay informed, stay current, and to echo a coined phrase, think global and act local, writing well for a receptive community of readers.

Creative Nonfiction for Today's Eager Reader

By Sue Bradford Edwards

Are creativity and nonfiction basically at odds? Journalism and other arenas of writing have debated the question for almost half a century, back to *In Cold Blood*, by Truman Capote, who is often credited with inventing the genre. Today, creative nonfiction is valued, widespread, and yet still sometimes controversial—and it is more dynamic than ever.

In creative nonfiction, also called narrative or literary journalism, authors use fictional techniques to tell a completely factual story. The genre gives writers drawn to nonfiction a wider array of tools to make their work appealing and artful. It gives writers drawn to fiction another avenue for their work—and from a practical standpoint, magazines, trade books, and educational markets all want and need much more nonfiction than fiction. Creative nonfiction gives those children's writers who love nonfiction more opportunity to flex our imaginative muscles.

BY KELLY MILNER HALLS

Defining Terms

"The purpose of all nonfiction is to relate fact-based information," says author Carla McClafferty. "That information

49

can be written in a dry, boring, encyclopedic way or it can be written in an exciting, interesting way that is a pleasure to read. In creative nonfiction, readers are caught up so much in the story that they forget they are learning something."

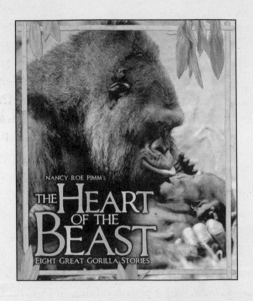

Whether creative nonfiction is journalism is one of the points of debate. "It differs in that straight reporting is required to be neutral," says author Kelly Milner Halls. "Creative nonfiction is factual, but can be crafted without regard for that kind of journalistic balance."

Creative nonfiction often delivers a clear message from the author. Halls's *Mysteries of the Mummy Kids* (Darby Creek) relates a wealth of information on mummies, but the fact that these mummies were clearly people who were loved and cherished and must now be treated with respect grabs at the mind and heart. In *The Heart of the Beast: Eight Great Gorilla Stories* (Darby Creek), author Nancy Roe Pimm makes it clear that she believes that gorillas think and feel. Unlike a journalistic piece, the book gives no space to those who disagree with Pimm's theory, because that is not the story she is telling.

While all nonfiction relays information, creative nonfiction borrows from fiction techniques—not creating fiction, but using its methods—to tell a story. "Creative nonfiction uses literary elements, or fictional techniques, in order to tell a true story," says Charlesbridge Publishing Associate Editor Randi Rivers. Just as they help to tell the story in fiction, scene, setting, and character build the story in creative nonfiction.

Scene and Setting

Perhaps the most important of these fictional elements is scene. Used properly, the description of a place and the people in it may be entirely factual and pull the reader into a real event. See how it works in the opening paragraph of *The Heart of the Beast:*

One hot August afternoon in Chicago in 1996, a young
mother sat holding her baby. Suddenly she heard a loud thud
and turned to look when another mother started screaming.
Nearby a small boy had just fallen from a height of almost
twenty feet—and tumbled into the bottom of a ravine. The
first mother, still holding her seventeen-month-old baby,
headed toward the motionless child.

Everything in this paragraph is fact. On August 16, 1996, a three-year-
old boy climbed the wall surrounding the gorilla enclosure at the
Brookfield Zoo in Illinois. He slipped and fell. His mother screamed. In
the enclosure was a young female gorilla, Binti Jua, carrying her baby.
The gorilla heard the fall and the scream. She knuckle-walked to the
boy. These are the facts. But how much more compelling is the scene
created by Pimm? It allows the reader to be there when it happens.

For the same power, create scenes rich in detail. "Your setting needs
to be so vivid in your reader's mind that they can visualize it," says Mc-
Clafferty. Use all five senses to provide vivid specifics. Choose information that creates suspense or sets up the human drama behind the
story.

"Creative nonfiction writers pay a little more attention to setting the
stage, painting a broader picture, than straight nonfiction writers
might," says Halls. In setting the scene in *Mysteries of the Mummy Kids,*
she describes the cold and wind researchers face in the Andes, as well
as the altitude sickness that hampers their work. She describes land-
slides and lightning strikes. All of this creates immediacy that pulls the
reader into the setting and the emotion of the story, and therefore into
the facts laid out by Halls.

Character

Perhaps you already use setting and scene in your nonfiction. The
best writers of creative nonfiction also use them to establish character.
The actual people who talk and walk across the page, acting out scenes
in real life settings, are characters. How you portray them and the traits
you highlight depend on the story to be told.

"Even though your character is a real person, you pick and choose
how you characterize them," says McClafferty. The scenes you shape

depict a person as careful or careless, secretive or open. Scene allows you to craft an artful piece that shows relevant character traits, without direct statements—"she worked hard" or "he looked after his neighbors"—that can simply fall flat.

Some character traits are fairly easy to depict. A person's innermost feelings are not, and yet it is possible to convey them creatively in nonfiction. Author Ginger Wadsworth discovered this researching *Rachel Carson, Voice for the Earth* (Lerner Publishing). "After Rachel Carson completed *Silent Spring,* she sat down and listened to Beethoven. And then she wept. Her book represented four hard years of research and work, and she knew that *Silent Spring* would create a national controversy. This was a very private, introspective moment in Rachel Carson's life, at a time when she was slowly dying of cancer," says Wadsworth. "How do I know this? From various sources, starting with the letters she wrote to her dear friend, Dorothy Freeman. I read a National Council of Women lecture Rachel gave and fan mail as well." Wadsworth visited Yale University's Beinecke Library and read everything she could find related to Carson. "Each piece," Wadsworth says, "added to a very personal, poignant moment in her life."

Letters written to a person, articles and books about them, the writing they do themselves: All offer different types of information from which to draw in revealing a real character in nonfiction. "You have to know as much as you can from as many sources as you can to know what the person was like," says author Nancy Warren Ferrell, whose titles include *Alaska's Heroes: A Call to Courage* (Alaska Northwest Books). "If he wrote something that was short and angry, you could draw some inference from that. You want to do as much reading and as much research as you can." No matter what form your nonfiction takes, Ferrell says, "your bibliography is still very important."

Scene, setting, and character combine with other fictional qualities to make for a compelling creative nonfiction read. "Virtually all elements of good fiction can be found in good nonfiction, including plot, dialogue, active language, character development, descriptive language, rhythm, voice, and so forth," says Sneed B. Collard III, author of such books as *Shep: Our Most Loyal Dog* (Sleeping Bear Press) and *The Prairie Builders: Reconstructing America's Lost Grasslands* (Houghton Mifflin). "Or put more simply, good nonfiction is literature, just as good

fiction is." It is up to you to find the supporting facts and bring them out in your carefully crafted story.

Working with Nonfiction

Perhaps it is because good creative nonfiction reads like a well-crafted story that it confuses some who have yet to master it. The most important point to remember? The writing remains nonfiction. "If you want to put a tang of the type of person this was or the culture," says Ferrell, "you have to have it real and correct even as you bring out the

> # In creative nonfiction, each and every fact can be documented— including dialogue.

flavor." Writers bring out a particular tone, not by fudging fact but by selecting which facts to include.

"That's True with a capital T," Rivers says of adhering to the facts. "Authors who write in this genre do not make up dialogue or create scenes or events that never occurred. The idea is to do your research and craft a dramatic, compelling story around the facts."

The proper selection of information after extensive research is core. For example, McClafferty says, "In a biography, you cannot write about every detail of your subject's life, so in a way your plot develops from the events from their life you choose to highlight. You also need good pacing to pull the reader through the story."

The Bumblebee Queen
April Pulley Sayre • Illustrated by Patricia J. Wynne

In *The Bumblebee Queen* (Charlesbridge), tension comes through the bee's search for a nesting site and food and from the drive to build a colony. Every possible danger is not included nor is every ho-hum day. The facts are selected and arranged to create a compelling

Weeding Out Fictionalized Sources

Just because you follow exacting standards in writing nonfiction doesn't mean other writers have done so. "A couple of years ago, I began researching *Shep: Our Most Loyal Dog,* a true story of a Montana dog that lived back in the 1930s and 40s," says Sneed B. Collard III. "Hundreds of articles and stories had been written about Shep, but I found that in many of them, the writer created outright fiction in trying to create a better story. To me, this is unconscionable. If you're embellishing, or making things up, you are no longer writing nonfiction and you should be forthright and label your work as fiction."

Whenever a source fictionalized part of the information, Collard looked for corroboration. If he couldn't find it, he didn't use it. The adherence to factual sources, and the integrity of the sources, allowed Collard and Sleeping Bear Press to publish *Shep* as nonfiction.

story arc. Author April Pulley Sayre never followed a bumblebee queen through a season as depicted in the book, but the book does relate typical bumblebee events and behavior. Nothing vital has been eliminated, nothing fictional added.

In creative nonfiction, each and every fact can be documented. "When I look back at nonfiction books from the days when I was a child, I see fictional dialogue in them," says McClafferty. This is not the case today. "For example, in my book *Something Out of Nothing: Marie Curie and Radium* (Farrar, Straus and Giroux), if I quote Marie Curie," says McClafferty, "I have a documented source to prove it. For each and every quote, I provided my editor with a hard copy."

What if your research fails to find quotable dialogue? Even short phrases can give a feel for a person's speech. "President Theodore Roosevelt often expressed certain words or phrases, like 'bully' or 'this is bully,' so it would be appropriate to have him say these words when he was enthusiastic about something," says Wadsworth. Be careful: Simulating dialogue that uses such phrases can push a work into historical fiction. Saying something along the lines of, "Roosevelt's typical response would have been to say with great enthusiasm, 'Bully!'" allows the writing to remain pure creative nonfiction.

The same standards of research hold in creating vivid scenes. "Through details you find in research, you create the setting for your scene, but even then you can't make anything up. For example, you can't say the drapes were blue unless you have a source that says the drapes were blue," says McClafferty. "To write some scenes in my books, I've combined research from many different sources, like books, magazines, journals, and newspapers, to get enough information to re-create the scene. I've used the subject's own writings. I also use the writings of others who were there who also wrote about the same thing from a different viewpoint, using different details. When the time comes to write the scene, I know the facts of the scene including the dialogue, so then I try to find a way to make that scene come to life on the page."

Other sources might be museums, historical homes, and so on. In the case of Teddy Roosevelt, for instance, a visit to his Sagamore Hill home and discussion with the experts there might reveal the color of those drapes in the bedroom the year he became president.

Diverging from accuracy remains unacceptable. "It's a very thin line, a tough tightrope to traverse. Step too far from the facts as the rest of the world knows them, and you risk serious public scorn and the loss of credibility. And that's as it should be," says Halls. "If the living players can discount your work, you've gone way too far. The best way to guard against it is to work closely with the people involved in the actual events, or with their surviving relatives or intimates. It's not easy. It requires partnership and repeated revisions. But it's probably the only way to be sure you don't step over the line. That's what I would do."

If you're writing biography or history, talk to those who were there. For science, turn to the experts to make sure your facts remain accurate. It's worth the time and effort to have someone point out where you have made an assumption that goes a bit too far.

If you are already writing nonfiction, you are probably using some of these creative narrative techniques. Is it worth your while to perfect the delicate balance between creative approach and fact? Will it really have a discernable impact on your writing? Read the following from Russell Freedman's *The Voice that Challenged a Nation: Marian Anderson and the Struggle for Equal Rights* (Clarion Books) before you decide:

> The massive figure of Abraham Lincoln gazed down at her as she looked out at the expectant throng. Silencing the ovation with a slight wave of her hand, she paused. A profound hush settled over the crowd. For that moment, Marian Anderson seemed vulnerable and alone. Then she closed her eyes, lifted her head, clasped her hands before her, and began to sing.

Says Wadsworth, "Read this paragraph to get a sense of how Freedman steps in, but oh so quietly, to set a scene, introduce a character, hook the reader, and more." All of this with one carefully crafted scene.

How the facts are expressed varies from author to author and project to project. "Many authors write creative nonfiction in the form of a narrative. I've also seen people use poetry," Rivers says. "To my mind, though, creative nonfiction is constantly evolving. Authors keep finding ways to push the genre in new directions." Learn to be truly creative with your nonfiction, and you will find editors at a variety of houses hungry for work sure to satisfy adventurous young minds.

Winner or Wannabe? Topics for a Preschool Audience

By Paula Morrow

"**A**gain!"

If you ever read to preschoolers, you've heard this demand countless times. No sooner do you pronounce the last word of the story than chubby hands reach out to push the pages back to the beginning. That's how you know a picture book or a magazine story is a success.

But if your moppet wiggles off the sofa or burrows under the bedspread, that's a clue that the story you are reading doesn't make the cut.

The preschool writer has to please three audiences, all with different agendas. The wide-eyed toddler or energetic preschooler is your intended audience, of course, but first you must get past the editor who has one eye on possible awards and one eye on the publishing company's bottom line. Then you have to please the parent, grandparent, or gift-giver who will buy the book or pay for the magazine subscription and who will have to read your story out loud hundreds of times.

Kevin Lewis, Executive Editor of Simon & Schuster Books for Young Readers, lists three touchstones he considers essential for the success of a preschool book, but they all apply equally to picture books or magazine stories.

"First and foremost," he says, "it has to be a joy for parents to read over and over again. Second, rhythm and rhyme (or rhythm in structure) are key. Rhyming texts, when done right, are a gas to read. They invite the reader to lose themselves in energy of the verse. Basically, you get carried away. Third is relevance to the child's world. Texts that feature things familiar to a child have a much easier time attracting the child. The theme can be whatever the writer chooses, but the elements have to be of interest to the child."

Topic and Treatment

Relevance relates to topic and treatment. Whether two feet tall or six foot two, a reader first notices the topic. An acquiring editor scanning a cover letter knows (or should know) right away what the manuscript is about: Trains. Goldfish. Bedtime. In a library or bookstore, the picture on a book's cover announces what the story is about before the customer picks it up. Some subjects have automatic appeal to kids at certain stages, and let's face it, there's a built-in gender bias even in the most liberated families. Little girls do love purses, as witness Kevin Henkes's popular Lilly. It would be hard to find a four-year-old boy who doesn't pore over pictures of diggers and dozers and other heavy machines. Kittens and puppies and dinosaurs all have their faithful followings.

A good author can still come up with new treatments for the tried and true, and the world is filled with other areas just waiting to be explored. Whether the topic is familiar or unique, the trick is to present the material in a way that speaks to a young child—and for that, it's important to be familiar with developmental stages preschoolers go through and developmental tasks they are mastering.

Sally Nurss, author of *The Well-Centered Child*, a newsletter for parents of preschoolers, and a child development specialist, suggests that before writing for children of a particular age, an author should find opportunities to watch them being read to. "Observing a group of children who are close in age can be a particularly helpful way of discovering the range of their needs and interests," she says. "Try to visit a library story hour or a child-care setting. Watch the children's eyes as they listen to stories. What do they respond to? Watch their physical reactions. What kinds of stories make them inch forward with interest? Which stories do they ask to hear again?"

Nurss also offers some basic developmental guidelines with which aspiring writers should become familiar. She notes important characteristics of toddlers from one to three years old:

➤ They are interested in relationships with family, care-givers, other toddlers, and pets.

➤ They are concerned about separation because their sense of time is still developing.

➤ They are able to realize that an illustration on the page may represent something real in their world.

➤ Toddlers want to feel in control and to be able to partic-ipate in parents' routines of caring for the house or yard.

➤ They are beginning to understand reciprocity (taking turns).

➤ Pretend play is limited to their own actions and experi-ences, such as pretending to be asleep or feeding a doll.

Your successful toddler book or magazine story will appeal to one or more of these developmental areas. Keep the cast of characters small and focus on the toddler and on people who are familiar. If a parent goes away, be sure that parent comes back—as in the charming picture book *Mama Always Comes Home* (HarperTrophy), by Karma Wilson and illustrated by Brooke Dyer.

Write about simple, recognizable events. Julie Peterson, Assistant Editor of *Babybug* magazine for ages six months to two years, suggests "topics that are familiar to a young child's life, such as eating, sleeping, playing." Stories about teddy bears and toys and common backyard creatures work well. So do stories about helping Daddy do laundry or helping Mama in the garden or chasing butterflies.

In the classic *The Bundle Book*, by Ruth Krauss (written in 1951 and unfortunately out of print, but ask at your library), a child hides under the covers and the mother "guesses" what that bed lump might be—an early bit of pretend play that's just right for a toddler. Avoid didacticism ("Nice little boys and girls share their toys"), but a story in which first Katy hops, then Chip hops, or Joey and Megan roll a ball back and forth can show, not tell, how to take turns.

Young children are learning new words and developing an ear for the rhythms and inflections of language. Writers for this age should treat their topics simply yet with sensitivity to the sounds of the text. Peterson notes that the successful author appeals to a child's five senses and uses "memorable words, rhythms, and rhymes that make stories and poems outstanding, interesting, and fun to hear over and over again."

Next Stages

Toddlers grow up all too quickly, and soon some topics may seem too limited for the wider interests of a preschooler. Characteristics of the three- to six-year-old child, says Nurss, include:

➤ They continue to be interested in relationships, especially friendships with other children.

➤ Pretend play is of major importance; it becomes in-

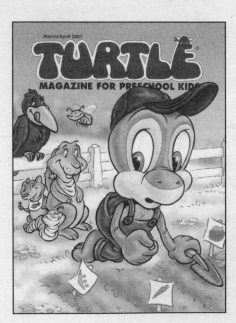

creasingly elaborate and reaches a peak around age six. Preschoolers use pretend play to deal with stress, to understand what it's like to be another person, especially powerful people (teachers, firefighters, superheroes), and to pretend to do things they aren't allowed to do in real life.

➤ They spend a lot of time negotiating play situations with friends: problem-solving and arguing about who will have which role, and about sharing.

Terry Harshman, Editor of *Turtle* magazine for ages two to five years, advises that what works best for this age is "a simple story with identifiable characters and lots of humor. Rhyme and wordplay work well for this age group, too. I think little children love a sense of adventure as long as they feel secure and protected."

The treatment of topics for these older preschool children can be tricky. Parents who aren't familiar with developmental theory may object to a book that shows children doing something that their own child is not allowed to do, not realizing that pretend play is a child's way of learning.

Therefore, many editors are reluctant to accept a story in which a four-year-old crosses the street alone or a six-year-old washes the new car with doggie shampoo—unless the behavior is clearly hyperbole (jumping on the bed in *Ten Naughty Little Monkeys* (HarperCollins), by Suzanne Williams and illustrated by Suzanne Watts) or obviously pretend play (going into the ocean alone in John Burningham's delightfully absurd *Come Away from the Water, Shirley* (Random House/Red Fox)).

For this age, stories that show friends playing together are popular. Again, there's a fine line to walk between fun and didactic. Children do disagree while they're playing and need opportunities to practice working out their disagreements. In *Yes We Can!* (HarperCollins), by Sam McBratney and illustrated by Charles Fuge, a helpful mother intervenes and solves a dispute for the children. In contrast, *Help! A Story of Friendship* (Greenwillow), by Holly Keller, shows the participants dealing with their problem themselves.

In addition to a child's natural interests, any number of important developmental tasks may be worked into a storyline—never in a schoolish way, but as underlying structure. That is, don't necessarily show characters actually doing the tasks, which can get too preachy or didactic, but build the task into the concepts behind the story so that readers are vicariously experiencing them. Some of these big-picture tasks include:

> ➤ recognizing same and different
> ➤ building
> ➤ collecting and sorting
> ➤ patterns and relationships
> ➤ shadows

Many traditional tales include these elements. Goldilocks sees items that are the same (three bowls, three chairs, three beds) yet different (large, medium, and small). She also discovers that the large-medium-small pattern repeats itself in each room she enters. The three little pigs build houses and discover something about materials. The gingerbread man illustrates building of a different sort, as each person or animal joins the chase, building a chain of participants in a cumulative story. Yet these developmental concepts are not stressed or superimposed; they are an intrinsic part of the plots. Story comes first! Children focus on the bears, the pigs, the wolf, absorbing the concepts in the process.

Preparation

A good writer can stack the deck, so to speak, so that a story or poem helps a child prepare for future tasks such as learning to read. Kathleen Hayes, Editor of *Highlights High Five*, points out that for her magazine, "the poems must be short—and it is helpful if most of them have some rhyming element—to support phonological awareness. We are stressing with teachers and parents that talking together about what you see on the page is one of the best ways to prepare young children for the task of learning to read. We take the notion of visual literacy—learning how to read a picture—very seriously. We want to make sure that all our features and stories and poems can be clearly illustrated, to support young children's ability to make sense of the magazine." The writer who thinks in varied visual images while writing will have a clear edge in appealing to editors, and illustrators, of preschool literature.

The wise writer never sets out specifically to teach children something, but rather to tell a good story. The learning will happen through the story.

Barbara Seuling, former editor and now the author of more than 60 children's books, says, "I found, as an editor, that it was always story that appealed most to children, and this seems only right to me, as it is what appeals to me as an adult reader as well. We all want stories. Stories tell us how other people live, how they behave, how we ourselves might fit in, or make changes. They are models for us to follow or to ponder, learning all the while about ourselves and our own choices.

The lasting gift that a child receives from reading can be found in the stories he keeps in his head.

Certainly, the wide variety of books available to children is one of the joys of contemporary life, and each has its place: action books for the energetic child who wants to see everything go fast, and with lots of color and noise; concept books that help shape a child's ideas of how the world works; books that have wheels or handles or pockets attached so they can function as toys when they are not being read. But the lasting gift that a child receives from reading can be found in the stories he keeps in his head."

Wistful writers looking for story ideas sometimes lament, "That's been done before. What else is there to say about it?" And nearly every author who submits often enough will sooner or later receive a form rejection on which some kindly first reader has noted, "We've already done this." Even the Old Testament author of *Ecclesiastes* acknowledged this dilemma, writing, "That which has been is what will be, that which is done is what will be done, and there is nothing new under the sun. Is there anything of which it may be said, 'See, this is new'?"

There is, according to Sandy Asher, noted author and playwright, who draws upon the Bard himself. Yes, Shakespeare, master of the English language, wrote in Sonnet 76, "So all my best is dressing old words new." Asher says, "No matter what genre you name, there are plenty of those kinds of stories already. And yet, there's always room for another good story. As editors and readers, we can't get enough of the thrill that comes with hearing a truly unique voice. Sure, it's telling an old truth, but in a bright new way. I encourage my students to delve into their own personalities and experiences to find the stories that only they can tell."

As writers, we often spend hours, even days, struggling, pacing, erasing, searching for a new way to say what's been said before. The answer is elusive, because we usually search for it outside ourselves when it really lies within. No two of us have experienced the world in the same way. We are each the sum total of where we've been, whom we know, and what we've done.

"Think of any good story with a happy ending," Seuling advises. "Keep to these basic tenets. Give it a contemporary spin—think of the world we live in now, not the one in which you grew up—and you will find your way."

Specialize or Diversify? Build on What You Know

By Sue Bradford Edwards

In writers' magazines and e-zines, in college courses and writers' conferences, in books on writing, you see the same advice again and again: Develop a specialty to build a career. This would seem to go hand in hand with an even more common truism, to write what you know. But is it good advice?

Some people start out writing a wide variety of material and, despite no single focus, develop tidy careers and even win awards in the process. Other writers create a specialty for themselves and thus build their careers. Whether successful writers are known in many genres or in only one, they delve into subjects about which they are passionate —as those interviewed here illustrate. That said, some start out someplace slightly different from where they end up.

Building a Specialty

Known today for her historical nonfiction picture books, Cheryl Harness turned to history only after writing fairy tales, *The Windchild* and *The Queen with Bees in Her Hair*, which were essentially ignored by book buyers. Getting those contracts and seeing the

Rip Tide Warning:
Violating the Write-What-You-Know Rule

Although 'write what you know' is a principle that may be violated with great success in fiction, it's more difficult to do in complicated nonfiction topics such as science. "When I wrote *1,000 Years Ago on Planet Earth,* I knew absolutely nothing about ancient civilizations," says Sneed B. Collard III. "The book, in fact, turned out to be one of the hardest to research."

Natural science topics often cross beyond what Collard knows, but his general familiarity in this area has translated into expanded interests. "Even within my natural science books, I also often tackle subjects I know very little about," says Collard. "In fact, it's through my books that I've learned about and developed real interest in birds and butterflies."

But working in a totally unfamiliar area brought greater unease. "The difficulty of that book makes me think twice about subjects totally outside my expertise. I really would caution writers with no experience in topics such as science to think carefully before venturing into those areas."

Unfortunately, some authors are tempted by a paycheck and travel too far into unfamiliar territory. "Not long ago, I read a science book written by a well-known fiction writer," says Collard. "The topic was great, but it was clear that she was out of her depth. She misinterpreted many of the concepts she had learned about and generally made a muddle of the subject. I also find many, many errors in science books written by writer generalists who are taking on science topics just to get book contracts."

Write what you know. Perhaps better advice would be "write what you are willing to learn about." Even when the going gets really tough.

books in print was good, but Harness wanted to be read. So, she turned to a longstanding personal favorite, history, and there she struck gold.

"My penchant for adding in extra hoohah worked well with my first historical picture book, *Three Young Pilgrims*," she says. She is an artist as well as a writer, and her representational style of illustration meshed well with her chosen historic topics. Book followed book. Among the most recent is *The Trailblazing Life of Daniel Boone: How Early Americans Took to the Road* (National Geographic Children's Books).

Sneed B. Collard III started out writing fiction. "The first four children's pieces I ever sold were fiction," he says. "Eventually, though, my passion for nature and the environment led me to begin trying science articles for *Highlights for Children* and *Cricket*." He paired a background in science with another trait that made his work stand out. "I assumed in my writing that children could understand and would be interested in virtually any topic that interested scientists. It set my work apart from other submissions."

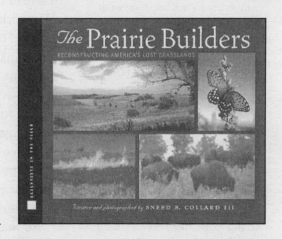

Combining respect for the reader with a strong background and a clear voice, Collard quickly developed a specialty in unique picture books and picture storybooks featuring the natural world. "I've been able to present science in creative ways that people hadn't thought of before. *Animal Dads* (Houghton Mifflin) and *Beaks!* (Charlesbridge), for instance, both look at science in very whimsical, poetic ways. *The Prairie Builders: Reconstructing America's Lost Grasslands* (Houghton Mifflin) presents science in a purely storytelling mode, sharing how scientists became impassioned with creating a new tallgrass prairie from scratch," he says. "These approaches, together with a strong writer's voice, have definitely helped make people think of me when they think of children's science books."

As librarians and teachers discovered that Harness and Collard's work was accurate, lively, and fun, these writers' titles found places on shelves nationwide and they built solid careers. Unfortunately, even solid careers come with a few minuses.

Dealing with Drawbacks

Especially with school-oriented nonfiction, these authors often find their work missing from or hidden away in bookstores. "In big bookstores, if they're there at all," says Harness, "my books are stuck in the

Learn What's Best for You

Deciding whether to specialize or diversify means knowing what works for you. While author Elaine Marie Alphin moves well from one project to another, she has her limits. "I don't think I could shift gears easily from one novel to another," says Alphin, who thinks that voice might be a problem.

Other authors find it difficult to transition from fiction to nonfiction. "It's hard sometimes to shift gears from nonfiction to fiction and vice versa. After I've done one type of writing for six months or a year, it can take me several weeks to get comfortable with a different type," says Gary Blackwood, "kind of like breaking in a new pair of shoes."

Authors must also be comfortable when writing something not meant for another part of their audience. "No child who has read one of my younger books has picked up *Counterfeit Son*," published by Puffin, says Alphin. The only one of her YA books she discusses with younger audiences is *The Perfect Shot* (Carolrhoda).

Some authors solve this problem by using pen names. "One essential aspect of my diversity as a writer was the decision to use a pen name to separate different types of books," says author Susan Vaught. "My romances are under a name and persona completely separate from my children's writing."

history ghetto. I'm condemned to the margins. Fortunately, one can live pretty well there, sort of like a character actor who'll never get the lead but nonetheless gets regular work."

Wait! Don't skim ahead because you think diversity will solve this problem. It simply creates another issue, says a children's author known for the breadth of materials she writes. "The bad news is that no one can ever shelve me in the same place," says Jane Yolen. "I am scattered throughout bookstores and libraries."

No matter how successful within a specialty, most writers eventually get hit with an idea that takes them into another arena. Breaking out can be tough. "I think there's always a tendency for editors to pigeonhole writers," says Collard. "I have fought this somewhat by writing many different types and styles of science books from the beginning, but I think it's made some editors take my fiction less seriously." This is ironic since Collard first sold fiction.

Perseverance pays off both for beginners and for career writers trying to break into new areas. Quality of writing and sales potential are very translatable. The proof is in Collard's nonfiction book *Shep: Our Most Loyal Dog*

(Sleeping Bear Press) and Harness's *Just for You to Know* (Harper-Collins). "Certainly, all of that nonfiction heavy lifting built up my writing muscles," says Harness, "and whether the subject is real or imagined, you want the writing to be lively."

Whether it's by desire to reach into other kinds of work or by the strong need for a larger paycheck, does the fact that authors like Collard and Harness had to work hard to succeed beyond a specialty make diversification a bad idea? Not necessarily. Having a specialty helps an author develop name recognition and repeat sales. This can help authors become known factors sought out by editors for their writing and by teachers for the possibilities that come alive in their school visits.

If you have a passion or interest that will sell, this may be the path for you to take. Even if your interests are diverse, this may be a way for you to work up a number of sales and develop a writer's résumé.

Still, not all authors specialize and some of them never have.

Variety, the Spice of Life

Some writers are generalists simply because their interests vary greatly and so does what they know. "When I was in high school, I was going to be a doctor, so I started college in premed and took lots of science," says author Elaine Marie Alphin, whose broad interests still have not narrowed. "I have a lot of things I love and that I'm fascinated by. I discovered this was a really good thing in my writing. The magazine market is the perfect place to write about a wide range of topics."

Getting a wide variety of magazine work out there paid off for Alphin, who had published several works of fiction before she was approached by an editor and asked to write a nonfiction book. "My first nonfiction book was *Vacuum Cleaners*, from Carolrhoda," she says. "The editor contacted me because she saw my piece on the history of vacuums in *Cricket*."

For Alphin and many other authors, diversity reflects something other than write what you know. Yolen says, "It reflects 'Write what you want to learn about!'"

But isn't it easier to research within a single specialty? Doesn't it waste time to research a range of topics, one after another? As writers research what they are curious about, the information they locate sometimes fuels multiple projects. This is the case with Gary Blackwood, novelist, nonfiction author, and playwright.

"All those different types of writing really aren't so different," Blackwood says. "The research I do for a nonfiction book often gets used for a novel or a play as well. When I was taking notes for the *Paranormal Powers* volume of the Secrets of the Unexplained series (Benchmark/Marshall Cavendish), I came upon a detailed description of a mind reading act that was performed in music halls in the early 1900s. A couple of years later, that became the basis of my historical novel, *Second Sight* (Dutton)." Whether a writer specializes or not, research that fuels project after project pays off.

For other writers, being diverse reflects not only broad interests but a wide range of stories they simply must tell. After all, each story dictates its own best form—one might be a novel while the next is a short story. Some writers, like Linda Sue Park, don't consciously determine a genre until a story is written. "I just sit down and start writing a story. I don't know what it's going to be until I'm finished. I started out *Seesaw Girl* and thought it would probably be a picture book, but my first draft was 3,000 words long. When I rewrote it, it was 5,000 words and I thought, 'It isn't getting shorter.' When I finished it was middle-grade."

Park correlates her diversity in writing—middle-grade, picture books, historic, contemporary, fantasy—with the diversity in her reading. "More than anything, it reflects that I'm a reader. What I read is a great inspiration. The only thing I have not tried, and I probably won't try, are easy readers because I think they're the most difficult genre to write well."

Doesn't this generalist approach make it more difficult to shape your writing career? Not necessarily.

Fueling Growth

For many writers, one plus of working in a variety of categories is the likelihood of continued sales despite market changes. "I have weathered both death by fire and death by ice, when several of the things I had loved to write—concept picture books, art fairy tales, retold folktales, historical novels—became extinct," says Yolen. "Publishing is like that."

When one type of writing no longer sells, authors with diverse skills can concentrate more heavily on what is still selling. They are more likely to be ready to take advantage of market changes when something begins to sell again.

Although writers often avoid discussing it, and will always say to write what you love, many decisions are necessarily based on the need to pay bills. "My choice to write in a variety of genres is more economic than anything," says author Susan Vaught, whose titles include *Trigger* and *Stormwitch*. "I learned years ago that in business, it's best to have several streams of income, and since I have a family to support, I'm still following that maxim."

In addition to her young adult novels, Vaught is working on a picture book, has chapters in nonfiction books, and also writes self-described "spicy" romances under another name. "Writing romance has allowed me to reduce the hours I work at my day job, and focus more fully on my craft and books," says Vaught.

Money isn't the only benefit of writing diversely. Artistic growth is another. "I believe that at base, the diversity has allowed me to learn and grow enough to write better, stronger stories," Vaught says.

Jeanie Ransom agrees. "Most of my sales have been a result of ignoring this *rule*" of specializing, she says. "I mean, how can you keep learning and growing, both as an author and as a human being, if you don't?"

Still not sure if you would benefit from writing diversely? If you are a writer who sometimes has problems with writer's block, this may be one way to work around it. "I'm working on two short chapter books, one fiction and one historical fiction using made-up dialogue; a beginning reader; a young adult nonfiction book about a historical event; and a young adult novel," says Alphin, who admits that she sometimes runs dry on working projects. When this happens, she simply sets that one aside and turns to another. "I can make progress on another book," she says.

Build On It

For some writers, developing a specialty works well, but others form equally strong careers as generalists. They take the basic advice of write what you know seriously, but then use it to delve into the unfamiliar.

"*Stormwitch* had four primary elements: Southern history with respect to racial conflict (specifically, Mississippi history), Hurricane Camille, Haitian history, and the history of Dahomey, Africa's War Women—the real Amazons," says Vaught. "Now, the first two elements, I knew intimately, from my childhood experiences. The second two elements I had to immerse myself in and research extensively."

While Vaught didn't know Haitian history or the history of Dahomey, she had other expertise that served her well. "My experiences in graduate school, earning my doctorate, did teach me much about how to do research thoroughly and well, so I had the tools I needed to tackle something I didn't know." By the time she was ready to write, Vaught knew the topics in question. Like Harness and Collard, she had made them her own.

Write what you know.

It's not bad advice. In fact, it can help you build a specialty and name recognition. But diversity can fuel growth and can also build a career.

Knowledge fueled by curiosity.

Perhaps that is truly the best way to go, whether you write about one thing or many.

Bring Legends to Life with Historical Fantasy

By Chris Eboch

At a glance, historical fiction and fantasy appear to be opposing genres. Historical fiction requires intensive research to portray a specific era with accuracy. In fantasy, the author may create the setting from pure imagination. Yet some writers combine the two into historical fantasy.

Historical precision does vary in this mixed genre, but without some adherence to the facts, history is taken out of the dynamic. *How to Train Your Dragon* (Little, Brown), by Cressida Cowell, claims an old Norse setting but is only loosely based on historical Vikings. Megan Whalen

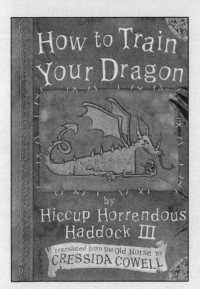

Turner's Attolia series (Eos/HarperTeen) reminds the reader of ancient Greece, but includes anachronisms such as guns. Catherine Fisher's Oracle Prophecies trilogy (Eos/HarperTeen) combines ancient Greece and ancient Egypt. These books are more inspired by history than based in historical fact.

Other books are purposely set in a clear historical time and place. Donna Jo Napoli's *Beast* (Atheneum/Simon Pulse) sets the story of Beauty and the Beast in ancient Persia. Walter Mosley's *47* (Little, Brown) is set on an American slave plantation, but includes a character from a distant world.

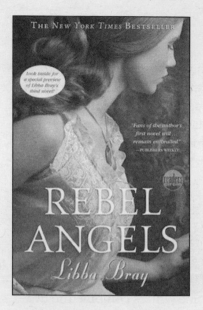

Many traditional fantasy books draw upon medieval England for setting and mythology. This era is popular for many reasons, including appealing legends used in the works of great writers of the past, such as the medievalist J. R. R. Tolkien. While Tolkien used medieval history and legend as an inspiration to create fantasy, some authors take extra care to portray the past with specific historical accuracy. Janet Lee Carey says of her novel, "*Dragon's Keep* (Harcourt) started out as a novelized fairy tale about a princess with a dragon's claw. The story begins in 1145 and takes place on a fictitious island that was once an English prison colony." Her story is solidly grounded in English history.

Other arenas of British history also fuel historical fantasy. Clare B. Dunkle set *By These Ten Bones* (Henry Holt) in the Scottish Highlands of the late Middle Ages and used fantasy elements derived from the beliefs of medieval Highlanders. She says, "Folklore-based fantasy has always been a favorite of mine. I made a study of the folklore of Britain when I was in school, so it was a natural choice when I decided to write."

More recent historical Britain is another popular fantasy setting. Dunkle's Hollow Kingdom trilogy (Henry Holt) is staged in England from 1815 to 1854, and characters include magical beings common to European folklore. Libba Bray's *A Great and Terrible Beauty* (Delacorte) and its sequels, such as *Rebel Angels*, are also set in Victorian England. The books have an accurate setting, but a few characters access the fantasy world. In contrast, fantasy elements are an accepted part of everyday life in the Sorcery and Cecilia series (Harcourt), by Patricia Wrede and Caroline Stevermer. Reka Simonsen, Senior Editor at Henry Holt and Company, says, "I'm not sure if the English setting fascinates so much because the current generation of YA readers has grown up with Harry Potter, or because Victorian London is the birthplace of the most famous classic horror and ghost stories, or if there's some other reason entirely."

Other books push the boundaries into ancient times and places. Tracy Barrett is working on a novel tentatively titled *King of Ithaka*, based on Odysseus's son Telemachus. "I'm trying to keep all the day-to-day details of late Bronze Age Greece accurate. The centaurs, nymphs, sea creatures, and other imaginary creatures that are in the story are interwoven with these realistic details," she says. "A professor of Greek history has read it and fact-checked the realistic sections."

American history has many fans, too, in historical fantasy. Carla Jablonski's *Silent Echoes* (Razorbill/Penguin) involves characters in New York City in 1882 and the present. Jablonski was inspired by research about a historical figure for another project. Jablonski says of the protagonist in *Silent Echoes*, "If she claimed these things today, they'd assume she was crazy. That got me thinking about context; about how values, attitudes, even sanity and reality are determined by the historical time period. The fantasy element allowed me to contrast how the same behavior would be perceived and experienced differently in different times."

Tiffany Trent's Hallowmere series title *In the Serpent's Coils* involves a magic school in post-Civil War Virginia. The historical reality spurs the fantasy almost beyond the possibilities for any imagined war; history also helps set up a realistic internal character conflict. "Often, fantasy books feature some sort of conflict that culminates in an epic battle," says Trent. "But what if the epic battle has already happened? I wanted to give the sense that my character Corrine, at 15, had lived through a tremendous amount before she even got involved with dark and mysterious Fey."

The Painful Truth

Many fantasy authors appreciate the gritty realistic details that come from history. Carey says, "The fantastical elements require solid ground. The reader needs to feel grounded in a real place. The filth and stench of the middle ages helped me ground the story of *Dragon's Keep* in reality. Medieval times offered so many strange and often gory details simply as it was. I found the time fascinating from fleas and famine to bizarre medicinal cures. Did you know that goose droppings liberally applied

A Fictional History

Historical fantasy has a sister genre in *speculative fiction,* which uses an alternate history. Louise Spiegler's *The Amethyst Road* (Clarion Books) has a setting much like the Pacific Northwest, but it is a world where gypsies are common and persecuted. "This is an archetypical story—the story of the heroine's journey through trials," says Spiegler. "One reason I didn't tell this as a straight contemporary story was to tap into these archetypes, and to create a world that is rich with allusion and poetry."

Once you accept the basic premise of Spiegler's world, it still follows all the rules of ours. No one uses magic; there are no dragons or fairies. Yet the Science Fiction and Fantasy Writers of America considered the book a strong enough fantasy to name it a finalist for the Andre Norton Award.

Spiegler says, "The research made my created group feel much more real to me, and certainly made the experience of racism come across more powerfully, and yet the speculative fiction form allowed me to integrate these invented people into this more archetypical story I was telling."

were believed to cure baldness?"

Dunkle comments, "Anchoring *By These Ten Bones* within a historical setting gave the book its strength. The Highlanders had a fascinating superstitious lore. They wouldn't have been surprised to find a werewolf in their midst, and they would have known exactly which brutal course of action to employ."

Editors also see advantages to the mixture of fantasy and history. Susan Van Metre, Executive Editor of Abrams Books for Young Readers and Amulet Books, says, "The history helps ground the fantasy and the fantasy enlivens the history."

Kathy Dawson, Associate Editorial Director at Harcourt Children's Books, says, "Historical fantasy offers that one foot set in reality that I need to get absorbed in fantasy. There's such a beautiful tension where magic meets the mundane, and historical fantasy offers that in a great way."

Agent Marcia Wernick of the Sheldon Fogelman Agency posits, "History is fantastical to contemporary readers. It's different. Fact sometimes speaks louder than speculation." Barrett agrees. "To most people, the Bronze Age is as fantastical a setting as Venus!"

An unusual historical setting may also help a book stand out from the crowd. "I suppose the combination of history and fantasy can help a book feel more original in the current, very flooded fantasy market," says Simonsen.

A Crossover Market

Historical fiction and fantasy independently have avid readers. Drawing fans from both genres can boost sales. "Many readers have confided that they don't usually like reading fantasy, yet they enjoyed *Dragon's Keep*," says Carey. "My guess is that a rich historical setting will definitely bring in more readers."

Dunkle thinks, "The fantasy elements sold the Hollow Kingdom books. They certainly made me want to write them." Yet she also points out that "a number of reviewers mentioned the setting [of *By These Ten Bones*] favorably. I was surprised when an amateur reviewer on the Web called the book historical fiction rather than fantasy. The review said, 'This is how it would have been if the legends of werewolves were true.'"

The combination of history and fantasy also gives publishers promotional options. Simonsen says, "If a book seems like it has potential in the school and library market because the historical setting is part of school curriculum, then we might play up the historical aspect—make it a feature book at library conferences, etc. But generally, fantasy is the bigger selling point these days, so the book would most likely be marketed as a fresh new fantasy novel that just happens to be set in some other time."

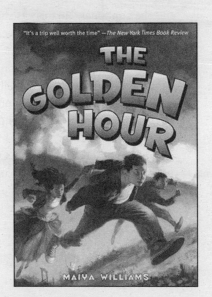

Van Metre says that Abrams would "probably play up the fantasy, but it depends. Certainly Libba Bray's books look more historical than fantastical. For *The Golden Hour*, by Maiya Williams, the hardcover played up fantasy, but we decided to emphasize historical adventure on the paperback edition."

At G. P. Putnam's Sons, Senior Editor Timothy Travaglini says, "It depends on the project, but I would certainly

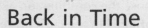

Back in Time

Time travel books have long been popular in children's literature. Often, time travel is the only fantasy element, while both the present world and the past are strictly realistic. In Susan Cooper's *King of Shadows* (Margaret K. McElderry), a young actor winds up in Shakespeare's time. In Kimberly Little's *The Last Snake Runner* (Knopf), a Native American boy travels back to the Acoma Pueblo of 1598. These books take place mainly in the past, as seen through the eyes of a contemporary character.

A few books weave contemporary and past stories together with multiple trips through time. In *On Etruscan Time* (Henry Holt), by Tracy Barrett, a boy on an archaeology dig visits an Etruscan village of 2000 years ago. He and his friend from the past move between each other's worlds several times.

Louise Spiegler, author of *The Amethyst Road* (Clarion Books), is working on a novel where the main character travels back and forth between the early days of the American invasion of Iraq and World War I. Of *The Jewel and the Key*, Spiegler says, "My subject demanded time travel. I felt a strong resonance between the two time periods, between the two wars—the questionable reasons for our involvement, the strong voices raised against it, the antagonism toward dissent, the curtailment of civil liberties."

She continues, "In this case, the advantage over straight historical fiction is the introduction of a perspective that characters who are embedded in their own time period can't have. My World War I characters can't know—as my twenty-first century characters do, for example—that World War I won't be the war to end all wars."

In the Golden Hour series (Amulet), Maiya Williams's characters travel to periods ranging from the French Revolution to Cleopatra's Egypt to the California Gold Rush. "I'd rather write about contemporary people experiencing the past than write about people who were actually from that time," says Williams. "There are more opportunities for humor that way, and the narrative is more engaging to the young reader, with relatable characters to guide them through the history."

play up the fantasy. If, for example, we were publishing a novel about Abraham Lincoln but in the story he can do magic, then you want to make that ability readily apparent. There is no purpose in trying to disguise the fact that it is about Abraham Lincoln, though."

Editors, like readers, have their personal tastes and often want to explore new directions. Travaglini says, "So much of our English literature, naturally enough, has been grounded in European traditions. I love seeing settings and stories influenced by other parts of the world."

"There are just naturally settings that I'm drawn to or dislike," acknowledges Simonsen. "But the decision is also influenced by lots of other factors, including what else is out there. If a lot of books are set in one place, for example, an editor might feel that there isn't really room for another—unless the writing is truly breathtaking, of course."

Any era can work, says Wernick. "It's how it merges with the character. I don't think any particular time periods are precluded." She makes the point that for young, contemporary readers, even the history is "otherworldly."

Authentic History, Fresh Fantasy

Merging genres has its advantages, but also its challenges. Historical fantasy must meet the standards of both historical fiction and fantasy. "The world in which a story is set has to be as authentic and real feeling as possible," Simonsen says, "whether it's a completely invented world or one that is based on well-documented history. So, my standards for historical fantasy aren't much different than for regular historical or even contemporary fiction; it's just that a writer has to do twice as much work to create both a believable new fantasy world and get all the historical aspects right as well."

Though some writers use history only as inspiration, many are committed to historical accuracy. Jablonski says, "The research helped inspire events that took place in *Silent Echoes*. I think the more realistic the setting, the more absolutely rooted in the truth, the more your reader will go with you in the fantasy."

"I also write nonfiction," Trent says, "so I'm a stickler for being as accurate as I can, no matter what I'm writing. In the Hallowmere books, I used as much factual detail as I could, even down to finding out the days of the week corresponding to the 1865 calendar, so I knew whether

79

I was scheduling events at the proper time. I do admit to a few liberties when absolutely necessary, but on the whole, I don't feel excused from historical fact just because I'm writing fantasy."

Dunkle comments, "Because the Hollow Kingdom trilogy takes place mostly within the confines of the fantasy part of that world, I didn't have to do too much research. For *By These Ten Bones*, however, I probably did more research than I would have done for straight historical fiction because I needed to know not just the historical details of life in a Highland township, but superstitions, pagan practices, and religious beliefs as well."

As an editor, Simonsen appreciates authors' research. "There has to be some rationale, some real reason that the fantasy element is set in that exact time and place, rather than just a sense that the author thought 'wouldn't it be fun if . . . ?' Good research is a must—an author needs to know all the details of the world she's writing about before she starts to play with the reality, or something is going to ring false. For me, a seamless blending of the real and invented aspects of that world is crucial. I have to believe in both absolutely, so that I can get swept up in the tale the author is telling, rather than tripped up on some anomaly that takes me right out of the story."

On the other hand, historical research shouldn't take over. "A darned good story arc is needed," Simonsen insists. "I've seen many manuscripts where the author got so caught up in the fascinating historical details that the story didn't actually go anywhere."

Travaglini says, "Whether the world is wholly original—where every facet is built up from scratch—or wholly modern and contemporary, it must always be utterly authentic, utterly. Great writing makes historical fantasy believable. Nothing can trump a compelling voice, immediacy, narrative tension, and great storytelling. No matter what the genre is, these factors contribute the most to making books popular."

The Messy Details

Historical accuracy can help create a realistic world, but it can also be a burden for the writer. Trent notes, "You may want to get your character somewhere quicker than is really possible in the time period you're using. You may not want to deal with all the messy details of life in a certain historical period—eating, washing up, and the like. There's always the problem of accurately representing the way people thought or spoke. My biggest challenge has to do with diction, especially with as many nationalities, classes, and eras as I worked with" in the Hallow-mere series.

For Dunkle, "The historical setting of *By These Ten Bones* began to feel constricting after a time because I couldn't just go with any flight of fancy. I felt compelled to get it right. This led me to obsess over crazy details, such as how the medieval Scottish chickens looked. I also had to piece together the mental and spiritual perspective of the medieval Highlander, which meant that I was working with characters who didn't think the way I do. This can be uncomfortable for an author, but I dislike books that dress modern characters up in medieval costumes and call them historical."

Of *Dragon's Keep*, Carey says, "It's all made up, of course, but tying into the Arthurian legend in the prologue and setting, the story a little more than six hundred years later had its responsibilities." She cites "the frustration of making the dates in the story fit snugly into English history. I had to do extensive research into England's civil war between Empress Matilda and King Stephen, but it was worth it."

Jablonski explains what she found challenging: "Making sure the fantasy element is believable, making the transitions between worlds seamless and grounded in credible reasoning—I paid a lot of attention to that."

A realistic setting grounds the fantasy, while fantasy elements breathe fresh life into old times. Simonsen says, "I think history is fascinating to most people, really; it's just the dry, textbook approach that turns so many of us away from it. But when a talented author revisits a long-ago time or place and brings the people there to life, the results can be captivating."

Selected Historical Fantasy Titles

➤ Alexander, Lloyd. *The Golden Dream of Carlo Chuchio* (Henry Holt). Based on the Middle East and Mediterranean in the fifteenth century.

➤ Bray, Libba. *A Great and Terrible Beauty*; *Rebel Angels*; *The Sweet Far Thing* (Delacorte). Victorian England.

➤ Carey, Janet Lee. *Dragon's Keep* (Harcourt). Twelfth-century England.

➤ Cowell, Cressida. *How to Train Your Dragon* (Little, Brown). Old Norse.

➤ Dunkle, Clare B. *By These Ten Bones* (Henry Holt). Sixteenth-century Scottish Highlands; the Hollow Kingdom trilogy: *The Hollow Kingdom*; *Close Kin*; *In the Coils of the Snake* (Henry Holt). Nineteenth-century England.

➤ Fagan, Deva. *Fortune's Folly* (Henry Holt). Based on Renaissance Venice.

➤ Fisher, Catherine. Oracle Prophecies trilogy: *The Oracle Betrayed*; *The Sphere of Secrets*; *Day of the Scarab* (Greenwillow). Combination of ancient Greece and ancient Egypt.

➤ Jablonski, Carla. *Silent Echoes* (Razorbill). America, 1882 and contemporary times.

➤ Kolosov, Jacqueline. *The Red Queen's Daughter* (Hyperion). 1557 at the court of Queen Elizabeth I.

➤ Michaelis, Antonia. *Tiger Moon* (Amulet). Colonial India.

➤ Mosley, Walter. *47* (Little, Brown). American slave plantation, 1832.

➤ Napoli, Donna Jo. *Beast* (Atheneum). Ancient Persia; *The Wager* (Henry Holt, 2009). Twelfth-century Sicily.

➤ Sensel, Joni. *The Humming of Numbers* (Henry Holt). Tenth-century Ireland.

➤ Tomlinson, Heather. *The Swan Maiden* (Henry Holt). Medieval Provence.

➤ Trent, Tiffany. Hallowmere series: *In the Serpent's Coils*, Virginia during Reconstruction; *By Venom's Sweet Sting*, Victorian Scotland; *Between Golden Jaws*, Victorian London (Mirrorstone). Future books will be set everywhere from pre-Civil War South Carolina to ancient Greece.

➤ Turner, Megan Whalen. *The Thief*; *The Queen of Attolia*; *The King of Attolia* (Greenwillow). Similar to ancient Greece.

➤ Wrede, Patricia and Stevermer, Caroline. Sorcery and Cecilia series: *Sorcery and Cecilia or the Enchanted Chocolate Pot*; *The Grand Tour*; *Magicians of Quality*; *The Mislaid Magician* (Harcourt). Regency England.

Selected Historical Fantasy Titles

Time Travel History

➤ Barrett, Tracy. *On Etruscan Time* (Henry Holt). Etruscan village, two thousand years ago.

➤ Cooper, Susan. *King of Shadows* (Margaret K. McElderry). Shakespearean England.

➤ Little, Kimberly. *The Last Snake Runner* (Knopf). Acoma Pueblo, New Mexico, 1598.

➤ Williams, Maiya. Golden Hour series: *The Golden Hour*, French Revolution; *Hour of the Cobra*, Cleopatra's Egypt; *Hour of the Outlaw*, California Gold Rush (Abrams).

Alternate History

➤ Aiken, Joan. Wolves Chronicles, 13 titles (Delacorte). Alternate eighteenth-century England.

➤ Jones, Diana Wynne. Chronicles of Chrestomanci series, (Greenwillow). Series set in parallel England and Italy.

➤ Spiegler, Louise. *The Amethyst Road* (Clarion). Alternate contemporary America.

➤ Stroud, Jonathan. Bartimaeus trilogy: *The Amulet of Samarkand*; *The Golem's Eye*; *Ptolemy's Gate*, (Miramax/Hyperion). Alternate modern London.

The Thrill of Horror and Things that Go Bump in the Night

By Chris Eboch

From ghost stories around the campfire to summer slasher flicks, many children and teenagers enjoy the thrills of being scared.

"Growing up is intrinsically horrific," author Cynthia Leitich Smith says. "You're a shape-shifter in your changing body. You're a vampire in your thirst for life. Your emotions can turn you from Dr. Jekyll to Mr. Hyde. Essentially, gothic fantasy is all about reflecting this reality through metaphor that asks the hard questions and tackles the classic themes, but in a fresh—sometimes bloody fresh—and sometimes funny way."

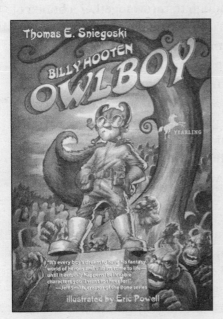

Many authors are drawn to this genre because of their own childhood love of the macabre. "As a kid, I adored anything scary: ghosts, monsters, mummies, you name it," says Laura Ruby, author of *The Chaos King* (Eos) and *Lily's Ghosts* (HarperTrophy). "So, when I sat down to write my own books, I wrote the ones I would have liked to read when I was a kid."

85

"Maybe it's the adrenaline rush that we get from being frightened," muses Tom Sniegoski, whose titles include *Billy Hooten: Owlboy* (Yearling) and *Sleeper Code* (Razorbill). "There's also something about the effect an author can have over his reader with this material. There isn't anything cooler than to find out from a reader that you scared or disturbed them in some way."

Plus, for people who enjoy the spooky, the research and brainstorming is fun. Lois Szymanski writes the Gettysburg Ghost Gang series (White Mane) with Shelley Sykes. "We love the research that goes into writing about Civil War-era ghosts," Szymanski says. "We really go out on ghost hunts with ghost researchers who use all the modern gadgets—from tape recorders and cameras to electromagnetic field detectors, radiation meters, and infrared cameras, thermometers, and motion detectors."

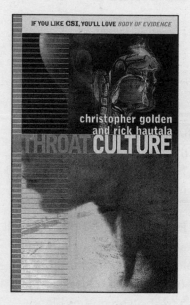

Who could resist the chance to tell scary stories for enthusiastic fans? But it's not enough to throw together a bunch of ghosts or monsters. Horror stories have been around since prehistoric people tried to explain the things that go bump in the night. Authors who want to catch a reader's attention today have to do something different. "Often I attempt to take the conventions of the genre and subvert them," says Christopher Golden, who is author of the Outcast series (Aladdin/ Simon & Schuster), with Sniegoski; the Body of Evidence series (Simon Pulse), with Rick Hautala; and the new *Poison Ink* (Delacorte/Random House). "I try to find my own explanations for why we've come to believe certain legends over the ages."

"Horror has its quintessential themes," Smith says. "The key is in your twist or twisted retelling. In crafting *Tantalize* (Candlewick), I drew my initial inspiration from Bram Stoker's *Dracula*. Stoker's classic includes a Texan, Quincy P. Morris, among its original vampire hunters. I brought the mythology home to Texas, offering my new protagonist,

Quincie P. Morris—an updated and gender-flipped nod to Stoker's old school."

Ideas can come from everywhere, including real life facts or mysteries. Ruby wrote *Lily's Ghosts* based on stories a friend told her about her family's haunted house. Linda Joy Singleton says, "Sometimes I'll hear something on a news report that will trigger an idea. Or sometimes a character just comes to me out of dreams, like Sabine in the Seer series." A recent title in that series is *Fatal Charm* (Llewellyn).

Q. L. Pearce, author of three scary story collections for Price Stern Sloan, says, "I look at average people in supermarkets, shopping malls, etc., and ask myself, 'What are they hiding?' Then I let my imagination run wild. I also love antique stores and swap meets. There are objects in such places that just scream a story."

Gettysburg Ghost Gang fuses a contemporary setting with its nineteenth-century ghosts. "Our ideas come from our history research and our experiences on actual ghost investigations," Szymanski says. "For instance, in our history research we found that hundreds of women fought in the Civil War dressed as men." This inspired *A Whisper of War*.

Sniegoski says, "Just flip on the evening news, or open a newspaper. There's plenty of stuff to be afraid of. In *Sleeper Code*, I have these untrustworthy government agencies set up for the good of the people, but their true purpose is anything but."

The Monsters Among Us

With so many human monsters in the real world (not to mention dangerous beasts, scary diseases, and the basic fear of death), readers may find it easy to believe in fictional monsters. Still, horror stories need a grounding in reality. Human characters should be realistically human, points out literary agent Ashley Grayson. "No juvenile novel

The Ghosts of Magazines

In magazines, true horror stories are generally reserved for publications with a young adult audience that may cross over to adults. Magazines for younger children may publish some scary stories, but usually keep them light.

According to Judy Burke, Managing Editor of *Highlights for Children,* "Because our audience includes 6-year-olds as well as 12-year-olds, we publish only moderately scary stories that often have a logical explanation at the end. For example, in our October 2006 issue, we published "The Basement Ghost," by Barbara Kanninen, in which two girls hear a noise coming from the basement and one girl becomes convinced that it's a ghost. After they gather their courage to check it out, they discover that the noise is their sneakers thumping around in the dryer." Burke continues, "Many of our successful ghost stories are really mystery stories, in which a child figures out what the supposed ghost really is. We find that incorporating humor can work well, too, since humor can give a reader temporary relief from the tension of a scary story."

Consider the magazine's mission before submitting a ghost story. For example, religious magazines are unlikely to use a story that portrays ghosts as real. Even at *Highlights*, Burke says, "It's tough to do a real ghost story in a way that works for us and our audience. In the one story that I can recall, a boy who gets lost in a snowstorm feels guided to do what he needs to do to survive by the ghost of his father, but in the end, the reader isn't really sure if it was truly the ghost of his dad or if it was just the boy's own recall of what to do in such an emergency, enhanced by how the extreme cold and conditions were affecting him. We probably wouldn't publish a realistic story in which a ghost is confirmed as existing."

today can omit cell phones, the Internet, and the new relationships kids have. As one teen told us: 'No girl I know would go anywhere without her friends and certainly not into the woods. If she did have to go alone, she'd IM or SMS her friends the whole time.' Ask yourself, would this story be scary if the protagonist could make a cell call to his or her best friends within moments?"

"Any good story is about the character dynamics first, and how the plot events act as a catalyst on those dynamics," Golden says. "It isn't just about the reader being able to identify with the characters. The author needs to identify with them, to believe in them, to see through their eyes."

Fantastical elements should ring true as well. "Monsters, ghosts, supernatural creatures of any kind should be described in the same sort of physical detail that any human would," Ruby says. "They should also have distinct personalities, personal tics, etc., to round them out."

Andrew Karre, Acquisitions Editor at Llewellyn Worldwide and its YA fiction imprint Flux, says, "The impact of good horror or suspense writing is directly proportional to the author's ability to describe scenes, situations, and characters in surprising yet evocative ways. How can you translate whatever gruesome thing you've conjured up in your imagination into words that seem simultaneously surprising and true?"

Some authors don't worry quite so much about believability. For Singleton, "Since I write about psychics, I figure those people who believe in psychics will believe my books. Skeptics will consider it fantasy. As long as they enjoy my books, I'm content." Her new Dead Girl series from Flux debuts with *Dead Girl Walking,* in a genre Singleton calls paranormal romantic dramedy.

Susan Van Metre, Executive Editor at Abrams Books for Young Readers, concedes, "Perhaps there's more of an emphasis on fun and a little less concern about logic [in horror] than for other sorts of books." However, believability benefits "when the fear or concept has some basis in reality. Peni R. Griffin wrote *The Ghost Sitter* about a girl killed in a fireworks accident (Didn't we all worry about that growing up, after all our parents' dire warnings?) who haunts her suburban home until a family with a girl her age moves in, and the girl helps free her. So it became a wonderful novel about the power of friendship to reach across a seemingly impossible divide."

Delacorte Press Editor Krista Marino says, "By nature, these are plot-driven stories." The characters have to behave in a believable way, however. "I look for fear in the character. I'd be terrified by a ghost. If the protagonist isn't, there's something wrong. Not only that: It's no longer a horror story."

I want to go where angels fear to tread, but you have to coax me there.

There's no point in writing horror if you're not going to make it spooky. "Mood and atmosphere appeal to me as a reader," Candlewick Executive Editor Deborah Noyes Wayshak says. "I want to go where angels fear to tread, but you have to coax me there."

Pearce suggests, "What frightens most people is a loss of control. That's why the midnight ramble through a haunted house can be so eerie. Even if you don't believe in ghosts, you don't know what might be hidden in the shadows. In general, characters in a scary story have to be helpless to some degree, though they can ultimately triumph."

The best horror also goes beyond the merely spooky or grotesque and touches some deep truth. "The most engaging horror or ghost stories are psychologically complex," Wayshak says. "The horror or haunting reflects the protagonist's psyche in some way, what she or he is hiding or suffering or grieving on the mundane plane."

To find these deeper truths, authors must be emotionally honest and willing to take risks. "The main challenge is writing into the heart of the horror—what's on the page, what's inside oneself—without protecting or skirting or

The Ghastly Truth

Jeff Belanger is the Ghost Guy. He runs Ghostvillage.com and writes nonfiction about ghosts. "I'm looking for real haunts, true eyewitness accounts, and sometimes gruesome history that can support the evidence of hauntings. You can't study ghosts without also looking into history. If a ghost is really still hanging around, why is it still here? What happened in this location? I began to see ghosts as an innovative way to teach history to children." This led to his first children's book, *Who Is Haunting the White House?* (Sterling).

"One of my greatest challenges in writing for children is to balance the history lesson with the ghost accounts," Belanger says. "I try to bring in an element of mystery as well so my readers can be hooked by the sensational (the ghost), delve a bit into the history (backstory), and reach some conclusions as to why a ghost may still be around (solve the mystery). I also get to empower kids by turning them into ghost and history hunters. You can't be afraid of something you hunt. And I get to help foster a way of thinking that leads to lots of big questions that each reader will have to answer for themselves."

With ghosts popular in books, on TV, and on the Web, the nonfiction horror market has room to grow, Belanger believes. "On bookstore shelves, nonfiction for children has limited space. Perhaps if we can dress up the package with a ghost or two, we'll be able to push the boundaries of the nonfiction section and bring in more readers to those often neglected shelves."

offering apologies," Smith says. "The challenge is in unleashing your own monster within."

Joshua Glazer, Editor at Scholastic, is the author of *Encyclopedia Horrifica: The Terrifying Truth about Vampires, Ghosts, Monsters, and More*, under the pseudonym Joshua Gee. "I ask myself what it means to bleed or to scream or to feel preyed upon," he says. "I try to give those abstractions a name or a face or, when applicable, lots of slimy tentacles. Sometimes these effigies already exist in the form of, say, vampires or werewolves. Other times, these real world emotions and instincts lead to something new." With his editor hat on, Glazer adds, "Even if a horror submission is judged to be a good story well told, does that automatically

More Horrifying Tales

> Brooks, Max. *World War Z: An Oral History of the Zombie War* (Crown).
> Keene, Brian. *Ghoul* and *Dead Sea* (Dorchester).
> Meyer, Stephenie. Twilight series: *Twilight, New Moon, Eclipse* (Little, Brown).
> Noyes, Deborah. *Gothic: Ten Original Dark Tales* (Candlewick).
> Pearce, Q. L. *Super Scary Stories for Sleep-Overs, More Super Scary Stories for Sleep-Overs, Scary Stories for Stormy Nights, No. 5* (Lowell House).
> Ruby, Laura. *Lily's Ghosts, The Wall and the Wing, The Chaos King* (HarperCollins).
> Shan, Darren. *Cirque du Freak* (Little, Brown).
> Sleator, William. *The Boy Who Couldn't Die* (Graphia).
> Smith, Cynthia Leitich. *Eternal* (to be published by Candlewick).
> Sniegoski, Tom. *Sleeper Code, Sleeper Agenda,* Fallen Series (Razorbill).
> Szymanski, Lois and Sykes, Shelley. *The Soldier in the Cellar,* Gettysburg Ghost Gang series (White Mane).
> Whitcomb, Laura. *A Certain Slant of Light* (Graphia).

mean it's a good horror story horrifically told?" The protagonist's fears must speak to the reader in a realistic way.

Growing Up Scared

The interest in horror seems to be growing, especially for teenagers. "There's definitely been a rise in the popularity of thrillers, ghost stories, and stories based on the paranormal," Marino says. "The most popular books are the ones that set the ghost story in the contemporary world. There's something about believing those things are out there right now that is thrilling for young readers."

"Pure horror will probably never explode the way fantasy or sci-fi have exploded at different times," Glazer says, "but the wave of terror ebbs and flows. During any given year, some subgenre or another seems to take off. For the past couple years, apocalyptic zombie stories have been big, thanks to Max Brooks, Brian Keene, and others."

At Llewellyn, says Karre, "We see good, steady demand for well-done paranormal thrillers, books that might even be called dark fantasy or urban fantasy, especially for girls. Witty, graphic horror, such as the books by Darren Shan, seems to work well for boys."

In Wayshak's opinion, "I think we'll see more graphic fare in all of these areas as the graphic novel continues to gain popularity. It's a natural fit." In contrast, "Alice Seybold's crossover novel *The Lovely Bones* (Little, Brown) opened a whole new audience for teen fare about ghosts and the afterlife, and some interesting literary YA sprang from that soil: *A Certain Slant of Light* (Graphia), by Laura Whitcomb, *Elsewhere* (Farrar, Straus and Giroux), by Gabrielle Zevin, and *Lessons from a Dead Girl* (Candlewick), by Jo Knowles. For middle-grade readers and younger, the emphasis seems to be on series publishing and story collections, while YA readers range more between genre/series fare and lush, literary novels like *Twilight* (Little, Brown)."

"I think it's part of our process in accepting death to think about all the terrible ways one can die from the relative safety of youth," Van Metre says. "Perhaps we've seen a soft decline in such series as Goosebumps and Fear Street, but this is more than made up for by the rise of short series like Cirque du Freak and one offs like William Sleator's *The Boy Who Couldn't Die* (Graphia)."

Children of all ages might enjoy horror, but they don't enjoy the same kinds of horror. Stories for younger children tend to balance fear with humor. Plots are spooky but not terrifying. Teen novels, on the other hand, can include more gore and death. Writers have to find the right balance for their books.

"We write for grade school children, so we add lighter scenes to balance darker moments," Szymanski says. "Having the kids befriend a ghost corporal who stays with them throughout the Gettysburg Ghost Gang series also helps us in a big way. The corporal offers a safe place to run and to find advice and answers."

Younger kids need to return to that safe place. "The youngest readers are more likely to enjoy what you might call the *gotcha!* scares," Glazer says. "Middle-graders want to be surprised on every page, but not necessarily terrified. Finally, younger kids usually prefer a little humor with their horror. Goosebumps is a great example."

Grayson points out that different age groups have different fears.

"The scariest thing for a 12-year-old is the idea their parents might die. Typical YAs almost hope they would, so most YAs are fearful of loss of social capital or that their boy/girlfriend is a psycho or vampire."

Pearce says, "I am writing an early reader ghost story and a YA horror. In the early reader story, the ghost is discovered early on and is actually a sympathetic character, so the protagonists are never in any real danger. The setting is the scary part. The YA is very dark and the horror arises from the characters themselves. The main characters are always in danger, in some ways from people they trust."

"There's material in my YA stuff that I'd never think of including in my middle-grade books," Sniegoski comments. "It's not that I don't think younger readers can handle the dark stuff, it's just how that dark stuff is portrayed in the particular book. The delivery of the material is very important."

According to Van Metre, "YA novels are pretty limitless in the amount of gore; one would try to soften this or have it happen off-stage for middle-grade readers. Also, the occasional bleak ending is okay for teens; not so much for middle-graders."

"The younger the age level, the more debates we have about content issues," Glazer notes. "However, when it comes to horror, less is often more. Content limitations can lead to creative solutions that require the author to suggest something horrific without explicitly showing it. Ironically, when something is left to the reader's imagination, the scene might become ten times spookier!"

Does the world really need more monsters? Maybe so, if scary books can help young people deal with real life. "One of my all-time favorite books is *Where the Wild Things Are,* by Maurice Sendak," Glazer says. "It introduced me to my first monsters—and taught me how to make friends with them. I think that's the role of scary literature in a kid's life. It provides a safe and neutral realm where kids may engage their fears without becoming consumed by them. From an early age, Mr. Sendak's words and pictures taught me that, yes, the world is a scary place, but it's also a magical, surprising place. It can't be one without being the other."

Breaking into Educational Publishing Today

By Joanne Mattern

Classroom readers, textbooks, encyclopedias and other references, workbooks, biographies, teacher resources, hi-lo readers, activity books, classroom magazines: All are products of educational publishers. All require writers. The educational market is a promising and productive arena for new or established writers, but just as in school, educational publishing has its own rules and lessons to be learned.

The common denominator for the many kinds of educational materials is that they are sold primarily to schools and libraries, with a small but growing market among homeschoolers. As Barbara Mitchell, Publisher of Mitchell Lane Publishers, explains, "In educational publishing, we are trying to fill the needs of classroom teachers and school children. Most of our books will be used for research, reports, or to strengthen reading skills when reading for pleasure."

Editors at educational publishers take their responsibilities to children and educators very seriously. When asked about the challenges and rewards of educational publishing, Sue Thies, Editorial Director of Perfection Learning, replies, "Creating a product that works for our diverse population of students. It becomes increasingly difficult to do so, but rewarding when we make teachers' lives easier and students successful."

Morgan Reynolds Acquisitions Editor Sharon Doorasamy agrees: "Our reward is knowing that we've produced a title that is compelling, informative, well written, and well received by students, librarians, and reviewers." Writers are an important part of that production formula.

Formats and Categories

Publishers create a wide variety of educational materials, as do book producers, who are hired by publishers to create books and other products. In the words of Molly Smith, Executive Editor of the book producer Jump Start Press, "We are hired by the school publishers to assist in conceptualizing, writing, and editing basal textbooks, readers, and other supplemental materials."

For those interested in, but new to the educational market, the best advice is to learn more about these kinds of materials, their function, and who produces them. Also consider some of the genres very specific to educational publishing, such as hi-lo books and classroom readers.

➤ **Basal readers** are very structured readers for beginners that include basic vocabulary, with words regularly repeated to help children become familiar with them. Basal readers are often phonics-based, teaching letter sounds and spelling patterns to young readers. They are a vital part of the elementary educational market.

➤ **Classroom readers** are usually short—anywhere from 8 to 32 pages— and used to enhance curriculum topics in a classroom. For example, a lesson on fractions might incorporate a reader about cooking; a geology lesson might include a reader about volcanoes. Classroom readers generally include specific vocabulary targeted to the grade level and also include a glossary, index, and a list of other books or websites on the topic.

➤ **Hi-lo readers** are books of high interest for children who function at a low reading level for their ages. These books feature topics that will appeal strongly to young people, such as sports subjects, disasters, or adventure stories. The audience for these books is reluctant or struggling readers, and the goal is to hook their interest without scaring them away with difficult vocabulary or syntax. Do not mistake these for being simplified in concept, however. Children having difficulty with reading do not necessarily have difficulty with understanding concepts appropriate for their age.

➤ **Reference books** are another important category in educational publishing. These books include encyclopedias, almanacs, dictionaries, and other forms of nonfiction. Reference books tend to be about broader topics

Formats and Categories

than a trade nonfiction book and often include many short entries about a variety of topics. James Chambers, Editor in Chief of Facts on File and its Ferguson imprint, points out another difference between reference books and other educational titles: "In general, reference books can have a much longer lifespan. Strong reference books are prone to becoming good backlist titles with a steady demand and the possibility of new editions over the years."

➤ **Test materials.** Many writers have found a niche creating test items and test passages. The increasing use of standardized tests all over the United States has led to a thriving market in this area. Usually, test passages are short—200 to 600 words is the average—and must be written for a specific grade level. They must also be written to reinforce specific strategies, such as fact versus opinion or finding supporting ideas. Passages can be in any format, including fiction, poetry, nonfiction, instructional, or drama. Questions, or test items, are then written to quiz students on the material they just read. Writing for standardized tests can feel restrictive to some authors because topics are assigned and the material must be clear enough for students to comprehend without any background and under the pressure of taking a test. Test passages also must be very noncontroversial, with strict rules dictating acceptable plots and language. Still, the wide range of projects and the good pay in this market makes it attractive to many writers.

➤ **Magazines.** Last but not least are classroom magazines. There are two types of classroom magazines: those geared to educators and those geared to students. Both welcome authors who have a teaching background and a familiarity with curriculum standards. Teachers are always looking for new approaches to lessons and exciting ways to bring material to life for their students.

What to Write About

Educational publishing covers all genres—science, history, math, the arts, biography, languages—and all ages and skill levels. It embraces special needs children and gifted children. With such a spectrum, how do editors and writers decide what is worth writing about?

Doorasamy explains the methods of many publishers. "We rely on school librarians, comments from reviewers, and our own good scholarly sense when deciding which titles to publish or what kind of series to develop. We also try to keep abreast of market trends by reading industry publications, attending conferences, and talking to others in the industry."

Beth Townsend, Editor of Enslow Publishers, also stresses the importance of researching the market. She provides a glimpse into the process by explaining that Enslow's editors "ask librarians what types of books are being asked for by teachers and students. If we see trends forming regarding certain topics, we research those trends. Then we have meetings to decide what topics are worth publishing. The meetings consist of our editor in chief, managing editor, the vice president, and president of the company. Together we discuss the marketability of a topic. If we all agree, then we do it. If not, we choose a different topic or a different approach."

School requirements obviously contribute to publishers' determinations of what to publish. Gillia Olson, Associate Managing Editor of Capstone Press, says, "We focus on curriculum needs. We are focused either on delivering books that help children learn with curriculum content, or simply delivering high-interest topics to get children to read." Needs are joined by student wants. "We really try to look at what kids are interested in right now." Interest in a topic is a key ingredient to getting a child to pick up a book.

Most publishers develop their own ideas for books or series, rather than rely on queries from freelancers. Writers can also suggest ideas, however, provided they have done their research as well—into what curriculum and current interests call for, and also into the needs of the particular publisher and the makeup of its list.

JoAnn Early Macken is the author of more than 100 books for children. She has also worked as a managing editor for a major educational publisher, which gives her a unique viewpoint from both sides of the desk. Macken explains, "As a writer, I try to suggest topics I find interesting that I think kids would enjoy learning about. As an editor, I also had to consider other factors, such as how well a book would sell, how well the topic was already covered by competitors, whether we could offer an original approach, and whether a topic fit into the school curriculum."

Writers can discover subjects that will sell by talking to teachers and librarians to find out more about the topics covered in curriculums, and where they see gaps that could benefit from original ideas. Look up curriculum guides and standards at each state's Department of Education website. If possible, review the textbooks used in local schools. Browse the shelves of your library's nonfiction section to get an idea of who publishes in this market and what types of books they do. Volunteering in the classroom is another way a writer can get his or her finger on the pulse of the education community.

The State of the Market

Among the challenges to writers today's educational market presents, unsurprisingly, is money. In the past, libraries and schools received sizable amounts from state and federal governments and could afford to buy a large number of different books. Those days are long gone. "Libraries and schools do not have the funds to purchase all the new, worthwhile books being published today," says Mitchell.

Tamara L. Britton is the Editorial Director of ABDO Publishing, whose imprints include SandCastle, Buddy Books, Checkerboard Library, and ABDO & Daughters. Britton's take is that "educational publishing is a highly competitive market. Educational publishers are producing thousands of titles each year that are all based on the same national curriculum standards. This is good for librarians, educators, parents, and students in that it provides a wide array of book choices with which to educate kids. But it makes for a tight market in which a publisher's books must be top-notch or their products will not be purchased."

Olson agrees that today's market has its hurdles. "The last few years have been a bit tough for school library publishing," she says. "Customers, both librarians and kids, expect more than ever before out of a book. It's not enough to have a book about the moon. You must have value-added features to make that book really stand out from all the other moon books. In that respect, I see trade and library publishing coming a little closer together."

Advice from the Experts

We asked editors and writers for advice on how an author can build a successful career in educational publishing. Here's what they had to say:

➤ **Tamara Britton, ABDO Publishing:** "It is important to know your audience to serve it well. An author interested in working in educational publishing must familiarize him or herself with the audience and the market. Read book reviews, study vocabulary lists, and talk to teachers and librarians. Talk to kids and ask them about what they like to read and why."

➤ **James Chambers, Facts on File:** "It can help to concentrate on a couple of key topic areas to establish some credentials writing on those subjects. That's something we look for in new authors: an understanding and working knowledge of the topic at hand."

➤ **Lorin Driggs, *Time for Kids:*** "Understand what goes on in schools, know how standards and standardized testing affect content, and know how to write to grade level."

➤ **Sharon Doorasamy, Morgan Reynolds:** "Writers should learn to work with and not against editors. Writer and folklorist Zora Neale Hurston once told an editor, 'Please remember that I am neither Moses nor any of the writing apostles. Nothing that I set down is sacred. Any word or sentence can be changed or even cut out. What we want is success, not my deification.' Writers who follow her example will do well."

➤ **JoAnn Early Macken, author:** "Network! I've found other writers to be generous with information about editors who need writers, projects being assigned, and tips for working successfully."

➤ **Barbara Mitchell, Mitchell Lane Publishers:** "If you want to be the one to get lots of assignments each year, be sure to meet all deadlines and be cooperative with your editor and project manager. If you are easy to work with, you are more likely to get additional assignments."

➤ **Gillia Olson, Capstone Press:** "If you want to be a writer, always research companies you want to write for and make sure your writing goals or ideas fit in with their market."

➤ **Sue Thies, Perfection Learning:** "Don't pretend to be something you aren't. Be honest about your strengths and make inquiries. It's often a case of being in the right place at the right time."

➤ **Beth Townsend, Enslow Publishers:** "Keep writing, keep trying. Do research on the company for which you would like to write. Don't send your pet project of fiction short stories to a publisher that only deals with nonfiction. You may be the best writer in the world, but they're not going to publish your work."

Indeed, library books, classroom readers, and textbooks look more like trade books every day. No one is interested in books filled with huge blocks of stylistically bare text and maybe a few black-and-white photos to break up the monotony. Educational books now feature short, lively text, with sidebars and other informational boxes to make pages more appealing to readers, not to mention lots of colorful photos, illustrations, and other design elements. For young readers used to playing colorful, action-packed video games, and watching high-definition television, these features are a must for drawing them in and holding their attention. Still, as Olson points out, the basics never change. "We will always need to cover curriculum content that remains similar over the years. The approach is what changes."

Technology's core place in children's lives also requires that books add references or interactive elements. For some, these are as basic as a list of websites, but some texts extend their contents through online activities. Other companies have made the Internet an even more integral part of their publications.

Julie Carnagie Pitlock is a Senior Content Project Editor in Global Production Media Services for Thomson Gale, which is made up of many educational and reference imprints for adults and children, including U·X·L, Greenhaven Press, Lucent Books, KidHaven Press, Blackbirch Press, and Sleeping Bear Press. Many of Pitlock's projects include online elements. "It is a bit of a struggle for the market today, but Gale is finding creative ways to deal with it," she says. "Instead of just continuing to market to libraries, Gale has begun to offer some of its content over the Internet. That content includes biographical and informational databases that students can access for research. A product can be print, online, e-book, or Web-based."

How to Break In

Most educational publishers work differently than trade publishers when it comes to submissions. Since educational publishers work so closely with school curriculums, they usually assign topics rather than accept submissions from authors, and they operate on a work-for-hire basis. The process of becoming a writer for an educational company generally involves sending a résumé, writing samples, and miscellaneous other materials.

Educational Submissions

> **ABDO Publishing:** 8000 West 78th Street, Suite 310, Edina, MN 55439. ABDO does not accept unsolicited manuscripts or proposals. Writers who wish to be considered for assignments may submit résumés at the company's website, www.abdopublishing.com.

> **Capstone Press:** Editorial Department, 151 Good Counsel Drive, Mankato, MN 56002. Capstone does not accept unsolicited manuscripts but does accept queries. Writers who wish to be added to Capstone's database should send writing samples (published or unpublished) and a list of topics that interest them.

> **Enslow Publishers:** Box 398, 40 Industrial Road, Berkeley Heights, NJ 07922. Enslow does not accept unsolicited manuscripts. Instead, send a résumé, query letter, or book idea to Dorothy Goeller, Editor in Chief.

> **Facts on File:** 132 West 31st Street, New York, NY 10001. Facts on File accepts unsolicited manuscripts. Writers should read the submission guidelines on the company's website, www.factsonfile.com.

> **Jump Start Press:** 144 West 27th Street, #7R, New York, NY 10001. Jump Start only accepts résumés from writers with experience in the school market. The company does not accept manuscripts or queries.

> **Mitchell Lane Publishers:** P.O. Box 196, Hockessin, DE 19707. Mitchell Lane does not accept manuscripts but will accept a cover letter,

"ABDO publishes books for a specific audience based on school curriculum standards. Because of our curriculum-driven list and specialized market, we do not accept unsolicited manuscripts or proposals," says Britton. Capstone Press has a similar policy. Olson explains, "We don't accept unsolicited manuscripts. The topics we publish come from our planning department and are assigned through our editorial department."

Book producers also do not accept unsolicited manuscripts. At Jump Start, says Smith, "Everything we do is work-for-hire, so we are never in a position to publish a manuscript" that comes over the transom. Lorin Driggs is a Senior Editor with Time Learning Ventures, the licensing arm of *Time for Kids*. She works to provide content to various publishers of textbooks and supplementary materials for the educational market.

Educational Submissions

along with a résumé listing education, publishing background, and a list of previously published works.

➤ **Morgan Reynolds:** 620 South Elm Street, Suite 223, Greensboro, NC 27406. Morgan Reynolds accepts unsolicited manuscripts and also assigns topics. Writers should review the publisher's catalogue and several of its books, and study the company's guidelines at www.morganreynolds.com.

➤ **Perfection Learning:** 1000 North Second Avenue, P.O. Box 500, Logan, IA 51546. Perfection accepts unsolicited manuscripts and also assigns topics.

➤ **Thomson Gale:** 27500 Drake Road, Farmington Hills, MI 48331. Thomson Gale's editors only work with authors listed in the company's Contractor Database. Writers can contact the company with their information and will then receive a form to fill out to be added to the database. The company does not accept unsolicited manuscripts or queries.

➤ *Time for Kids:* 1271 Avenue of the Americas, 22-415A, New York, NY 10020. *Time for Kids* does not accept unsolicited manuscripts but will file résumés for possible future assignment. The company prefers to work with experienced writers.

➤ JoAnn Early Macken's website, www.joannmacken.com, includes an extensive list of additional educational publishers' websites.

"We must assign topics, since we are not a publisher," she says. "We do not accept or have use for unsolicited manuscripts."

Most producers and packagers accept writing samples, queries, and résumés. Driggs says, "We look at and file résumés and review them when starting new projects." Olson encourages writers to contact Capstone, saying, "Many of our new writers come from those who write to us expressing an interest in receiving work-for-hire projects. We have a database of writers, both potential and current authors. We accept queries to be added to that pool."

Macken knows that keeping your name in the front of an editor's mind is a great way to get an assignment. She recommends, "Send résumés and writing samples, and then follow up from time to time with updates."

Some educational publishers accept queries, however. Townsend explains Enslow's policy: "A potential author can send a résumé, a query letter, or their great nonfiction idea. If an author fits a topic we're looking for, we may give them a shot. Potential authors should also be open to writing about topics other than the ones they may have presented." It is very common for a writer to submit a book idea that might not be accepted, only to be contacted later and offered another project to write.

Educational publishing can be a particularly rewarding part of the business. James Chambers, Editor in Chief of Ferguson Publishing and Arts and Humanities for Facts on File, appreciates that the books he works on allow readers "to find information that can have a direct impact on their lives." Olson says, "Ultimately, we are helping kids learn to read and love to learn. Most people would rank the education of our children among the most important of society's goals. It's great to be a part of that." Britton agrees, saying simply, "I know that my work serves a higher purpose."

Writers also get a special sense of enjoyment out of this genre. For Macken, "The variety of work is nearly unlimited. I am never bored because there are so many interesting topics to explore and research." Perhaps Pitlock sums up the rewards of educational publishing best when she says, "Trade publishing may be considered more fun, but I think educational publishing is more fulfilling."

A Matter of Conscience: Writing on Social Responsibility

By Pegi Deitz Shea

The Oprahs, Phils, and Maurys give so much air time to issues affecting children, whether it's poor health, dysfunctional relationships, or poverty, that it's tempting to ask why is there still a market for books on topics like these. Aren't young readers saturated and satisfied with content from their iPod, Internet, and TV?

Apparently, and thankfully, not. While publishers are most attuned to the bottom line, they also listen for cries of help. Publishers—especially corporate ones—have a fiscal responsibility to shareholders, but they also take on a social responsibility to create books that advocate a better world, or at least, offer better responses to kids' problems.

War and Peace

Lee & Low was founded in 1991 with the mission to meet the need for stories that children of color can identify with and that all children can enjoy. Senior Editor Jennifer Fox explains, "As a socially aware company specializing in books that represent the experiences of people of color for children, many if not most of our books fit into the category of social responsibility in one way or another."

One of the company's first books was *Baseball Saved Us,* by Ken Mochizuki and illustrated by Dom Lee. It is about a Japanese American child living in a World War II internment camp. "This continues to be one of our best-known, best-selling titles, and really serves as a touchstone for our continued social responsibility in publishing," says Fox.

Several titles this year that aim to open readers' minds include *Buffalo Song,* by Joseph Bruchac and illustrated by Bill Farnsworth. This nonfiction title chronicles the Native American efforts to bring bison back from the brink of extinction. *Yummy: The Last Days of a Southside Shorty*, a graphic novel by G. Neri and illustrated by Randy DuBurke, is based on real events of an 11-year-old gang member from Chicago's Southside who shot a girl and was later murdered.

Lee & Low, whose policy is to publish ethnic authors and illustrators, often focuses on global issues. Nonviolence and understanding are the messages in *Sharing Our Homeland,* by Trish Marx and photographed by Cindy Karp. An Israeli boy and a Palestinian girl attend Peace Camp, where they develop understanding and friendship, despite their countries' warring past and present.

As difficult as it is, the exposure of past horrors even in the form of picture books is intended to inspire young readers to act upon their consciences. *Song for Cambodia*, written by Michelle Lord and illustrated by Shino Arihara, documents the childhood of Arn Chorn-Pond, an activist and musician who survived the Killing Fields in 1970s Cambodia.

Fox says, "Children should be exposed to stories that show them people from all backgrounds and walks of life—people like themselves and people who are different; people they can relate to and people they can learn from. Reading these types of stories as children can help them grow into socially aware and responsible adults."

The Marginalized

The Northland imprints, Rising Moon and Luna Rising (all recently acquired by Cooper Square), also make a point of publishing socially responsible books. Managing Editor Theresa Howell explains, "We've been doing it for years and feel strongly that children's books are a beautiful way to bring the world to children and show them all sorts of new things and experiences. It's also important to remember that not all children have the same experiences in life, and we make an effort to publish books that children who are marginalized by the general market will be able to relate to." One example is a picture book that shows the journey of a Cuban refugee, *My Name is Celia: The Life of Celia Cruz,* by Monica Brown and illustrated by Rafael Lopez.

"Books about bullying, abuse, and other social issues have been part of our list for decades, part of our Concept Books line, which covers a whole range of topics," said Wendy McClure, Senior Editor of Albert Whitman and Company. "We usually publish at least two Concept Books each season; this is one of the things librarians and booksellers expect from Albert Whitman." One of the 2008 standouts is *The Truth About Truman School*, by Dori Hillestad Butler, about cyber-bullying at a middle school.

In an increasingly global market, teachers and librarians work hard to expose kids to other cultures' traditions and attitudes. One recent book tackles a religious standard for modesty, which makes many American children suspicious or derisive. Scholastic Senior Editor Lisa Sandell talks about a YA novel titled *Does My Head Look Big in This?* by Randa Abdel-Fattah. "It's about a Muslim Australian girl who decides to wear the *hijab* full-time and has to deal with the fallout at her uppity prep school."

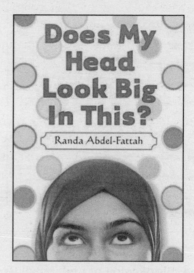

According to Susan Kochan, Associate Editorial Director at Putnam, one of their new novels also examines attitudes about appearance, and the lengths to which people will go to change theirs, for better or worse. An Na, who won the Michael Printz Award for *A Step from Heaven*, takes on the issue of plastic surgery in *The Fold*. The Asian protagonist Joyce is tempted by a rich aunt to "fix" her eyes so that she appears more "American." The book makes readers wonder about the validity of beauty standards.

The beauty standard of an ideal weight makes many businesses into billion-dollar companies—doctors, drug companies, food producers, fashion designers, retail stores, exercise equipment manufacturers, gyms, publishers of DVDs, books, infomercials. The health benefits of maintaining an ideal weight prevent this issue from being simply good versus bad, right versus wrong.

Forthcoming Putnam picture book, *I Get So Hungry*, by Bebe Moore

Campbell, illustrated by Amy Bates, focuses on health and weight, says Kochan. Moore Campbell, who passed away in late 2006, wrote this book because she felt strongly about the worth and necessity of the story's message. In the book, a plump girl's teacher is taken to the hospital because of a weight-related illness. Nikki, her mother, and her teacher plan a healthier lifestyle for all of them.

A different, dangerous lifestyle is temporarily glamorized in Jacqueline Woodson's new novel, *After Tupac and D Foster* (Putnam). Neeka and her friends get a taste of "real ghetto" when D Foster moves into their safe Queens neighborhood. But Tupac Shakur's lyrics become too personal when the rapper is fatally shot, and D is suddenly reclaimed and removed by her mother. Neeka realizes that even all too brief connections can touch deeply.

Quality Comes First

Putnam is a large company, part of an enormous conglomerate, and has no specific mission such as Lee & Low's purpose of publishing about people of color, or making all its books lift readers' consciousness. But Kochan says, "We publish books we think kids will enjoy and relate to, and if they offer insight into brave ways to stand up for what's right, all the better."

Chronicle Children's Group takes the same approach. "We don't go out of our way to publish books that explore social issues," says Melissa Manlove, Assistant Editor. "But we're not avoiding it by any means. We're very enthusiastic about social responsibility when it is done in an accessible, appealing, and non-preachy way."

After Tupac and D Foster is a good example of showing through good storytelling, not telling readers a message. Kochan explains how writers can avoid a teachy tone. "Be true to the characters. Show what they're going through in an accessible way without adding judgments or pointed interpretations of what things mean."

Writers need to focus on the craft of storytelling," McClure advises. "It's not enough to say, 'This is a very important topic'; there needs to be a purpose beyond that. Characters need to do things, they need to act and react, not just serve as mouthpieces."

Lee Wade, Vice President and Co-director of the Random House imprint Schwartz & Wade, is in accord. "Don't spell anything out," she advises. "Readers need to get to the message on their own, so there needs to be subtlety in the writing."

Characters need to act and react, not just serve as mouthpieces.

In *Does My Head Look Big in This?* Abdel-Fattah deals with a rather serious topic—Islamic practices in a secular world—says Sandell, but "she uses a light hand and wonderful humor."

Fox expounds, "An open, honest, age-appropriate telling is extremely important when handling strong themes for children. The information should be clear and concise, not overly emotional nor dumbed down." She cites the fictional *Brothers in Hope: The Story of the Lost Boys of Sudan,* by Mary Williams and illustrated by R. Gregory Christie. The book is based on the true stories of 8- to 15-year-old boys who were forced to be soldiers, became refugees, and struggled to survive. The author had worked in Africa with UNESCO and the International Rescue Committee. Because of that experience, "she was able to give the story a genuine and straightforward voice," Fox believes.

"Raising social awareness of an important issue, group of people, or part of history is a good reason to tell a story," Fox says, but "authors also have to make sure the quality of writing backs up the good intentions."

One great example from Albert Whitman is *Not in Room 204,* by Shannon Riggs. McClure explains, "We've seen many manuscripts that attempt to address the subject of sexual abuse, but this is one of the most thoughtful stories we've ever read. Sometimes a topic like this is so overwhelming, there's so much to say, especially when you want the book to be helpful. But here the author chose to focus on one crucial

step—how to tell someone about the abuse—and relates it as a story. It's so important for a book like this to be reassuring rather than cause further anxiety, and Riggs accomplishes this beautifully by keeping the story simple."

Although Schwartz & Wade publishes mostly picture books for very young children, Wade says, "We try not to shy away from touchy issues in general. Last summer, we published a book for critically ill children, *The Purple Balloon*, by Chris Raschka." Children's Hospice International (CHI) realized the need for a book for dying children. CHI approached Raschka and he approached the publisher. Wade explains, "Chris created balloon characters out of potato prints to tell a story of a sick child. He used disarmingly simple and direct language to make a gentle and reassuring book for seriously ill children and the people who love them."

Working on the book, Wade says, "reminded us of why we get up and come to work everyday. It is gratifying to think that we are publishing a book that could help a child or a family in a significant way."

Inherent Responsibility?

Suggestions of social responsibility are bound to emerge in almost any children's book. Examine the mass market end of the spectrum—say, one of the Clifford the Big Red Dog books (Scholastic). Clifford is always helping someone, even if he squashes that someone's car in the meantime. At the literary end of the spectrum, consider *The Invention of Hugo Cabret*, by Brian Selznick (Scholastic), which shows resourcefulness and artistic creation in the midst of extreme poverty. The general nature of the content in children's books depicts good over evil, triumph over challenge. In nonfiction, biographies tend to be written about good people who succeed despite the odds and people who apply their energy and talent to a worthy cause.

"When I examined our 2008 list for the interview [for this article]," Northland's Howell recalls, "I had to think about which of our books would apply because none of them purport to be anything other than good stories for kids that by chance have a larger message. *Going and Going*, for instance, never once comes out and says that despite this girl's poor living conditions she is able to find beauty. Instead it's written from her per-

spective so we see what she sees: 'the lovely details of a child's life,' regardless of her whereabouts—not what someone else thinks we should be seeing given the settings."

The picture book, by Juan Felipe Herrera and illustrated by Rafael Lopez, is about a young migrant worker whose family is always moving. Howell quotes:

> "Pretty soon we'll have to leave," Mama says. "Pretty soon, we'll have to go and gather otra cosecha, a new harvest."
> "Going! And going! And going!" [Juanita] says.
> "We must be like the sun, Juanita," she says. "Fill yourself up with the friendship of the sky, and then carry it wherever you go."

Howell notes that another book, Amy Costales's *This House Is Ours*, does carry a more obvious message. "But we consciously decided to tell a story that needs to be heard. People can take all sorts of things from it." The book is about one family's journey from Mexico and the pride they feel at owning their own house. "The story juxtaposes a little girl's memories of the hard times and hard work her family has experienced and her appreciation for what they have now."

Nonfiction from histories to how-to's can convey overt messages with the actual words and images of the book's subject or voice of an expert. Readers expect to learn when they pick up nonfiction. This takes some of the onus off the author and lets the subjects speak for themselves on an issue. Wade cites *Muhammad Ali, Champion of the World*, written by Jonah Winter and illustrated by Francois Roca. "In this book, it is mentioned that Ali protested the Vietnam War and that he was sentenced to jail. The text reads: 'Muhammad Ali said NO. Boxing was one thing, but killing people was wrong.'"

Then there is *Some Helpful Tips for a Better World and a Happier Life*. Rebecca Doughty's picture book "is a sort of *Life's Little Instruction Book* for kids," Wade explains. "The book presents 20 straightforward and kid-friendly suggestions for enriching life." The tips range from the silly ("Begin each day making funny faces in the mirror") to the more serious ("Help someone in need").

Also offering tips is Scholastic's nonfiction ecological release, *The Down-to-Earth Guide to Global Warming*, by Laurie David and Cambria Gordon. "It is a large format book loaded with information, photographs, and illustrations, and should be *the* global warming book for kids," says Sandell.

Marketing Responsibility

The creators of books with themes of social responsibility and justice have an important power. The decision to write, illustrate, and publish such fiction or nonfiction is a political stand in and of itself. Who would write a children's book that says global warming is a good thing or that child soldiering is a healthy preteen experience? What editors would contribute?

The creators of these books extend their power throughout all stages of publication. They decide which illustrator and style to use; which photos and quotes to use; how they'll be arranged on the pages; how many pages; when to release it, how to promote it, if it will be nominated for an award, whether to do a paperback edition, and how long the book stays on the backlist.

When asked if they market socially responsible books in different ways than other titles, McClure explains, "If there are specific organizations dedicated to an issue that we cover in one of our books, we certainly try to market our book to these groups." Wade gives the example of working with CHI "to approach the various hospice and health care organizations that might be interested in *The Purple Balloon*."

Other groups involved in targeted marketing include the National Council of Social Studies, National Health Institutes, International Reading Association, and international aid and other organizations addressing more specific problems such as discrimination, religious tolerance, abuse, housing, disease, etc. Some of these organizations generate notable book lists, which are used by teachers and librarians.

Chronicle's Manlove mentions a few awards given to books with social responsibility themes: the Jane Addams Children's Book Award for the best book promoting peace, social justice, and world community; the Christopher Awards, for the "highest values of the human spirit"; and the Carter G. Woodson Award, which honors books that accurately portray cultural and ethnic diversity. Manlove enthuses, "These are just some of the wonderful programs that support and help get the word out about books with a message. Books with a social responsibility theme often have more of a hook for publicity and for promotion; they get nominated for special citations, reviews, etc., much more than other books that are mainly for enjoyment."

Such acclamations could mean that the particular books remain on a publisher's backlist for a longer time. Some companies, such as Albert Whitman, categorize and market titles to niches. "Sometimes a book will stay in print longer if it's listed in a specialty catalogue, where there's a steady stream of orders year after year," McClure explains. "That's also true of lots of books in our other subject categories—multicultural, holiday, etc."

These types of books may not get much exposure on the shelves of chain bookstores and retail stores, but the school and library markets love them. "Teachers and librarians make special efforts to expose children to diverse, socially aware materials that expand young minds and reflect a wide variety of life experiences," Fox says. Because of Lee & Low's reputation for these materials, she adds that the company has had very few books go out of print.

Rising Moon also enjoys healthy sales of its backlist books. "We've been publishing bilingual books for over 12 years. Many subtly deal with topics such as immigration, discrimination, etc. We always publish with the backlist in mind. Some of our socially responsible books are timely and may coincide with what's going on in the world. These books are largely marketed by word of mouth and their sales gain momentum with time," says Howell.

Putnam's Kochan concludes that socially responsible books "stand on the quality of their writing. Books that handle issues in intelligent, sensitive ways that resonate with kids have the best chance of lasting a long time. We always aspire to that, but kids, parents, teachers, and librarians decide which books have achieved it."

Quality will come when writers "don't think of telling a story with a message," McClure says. "Instead, try to find the story *in* the message."

Busy Hands, Happy Hands: Crafts, Games, Activities

By Paula Morrow

Busy hands are happy hands. Many a grandmother has spoken that adage, and she wasn't referring to a joystick or a remote control. Traditionally, children have entertained themselves with a wide variety of lively and challenging games, handicrafts, and other creative activities, usually using simple, inexpensive materials or no materials at all.

Children's book and magazine publishers are an eager market for crafts and games that lure children away from video screens and engage their minds, hands, and bodies in fun, fascinating activities. A glance at writers' guidelines or market guides reveals that most want ideas that are out of the ordinary, "something we haven't seen a dozen times already." That doesn't mean complicated. "Sometimes even the simplest crafts with a creative spin are just what we are looking for," says Tiffany Hoffman, Editorial Assistant at *Highlights for Children.* She mentions "a bird toy made with popsicle sticks, beads, and string. It's not complicated, but it's unique and interesting."

Where Do You Get Your Ideas?

Fresh is important, but many good ideas are waiting to be recycled in a more contemporary form. Children are pretty much the same the world over—born with an innate curiosity and energy. Yet every generation enters a new world, with different styles, attitudes, concerns, and inventions. A 1950s birthday party usually included a game of pin the tail on the donkey. For today's children, the game might become tape the tiara on the princess or Velcro the NASCAR driver on the finish line.

The key is to give your idea a contemporary spin while making sure that the project or game really works, is fun, and is age-appropriate. Meg Chorlian, Editor at *Cobblestone*, has praise for an author who sent her a how-to article on a myriopticon (a form of moving diorama), with "the simple steps to make this nineteenth-century toy out of twenty-first-century materials."

Hoffman, who is in charge of crafts at *Highlights*, says, "All of the materials must be easily accessible to our readers." She offers several examples. "Recently, I've received some really great crafts including a tambourine made with an oatmeal container and lid, a basketball hoop and backboard made from a two-liter bottle and cardboard, and a *scytale* [rhymes with Italy], made from strips of paper and a paper towel tube. Up until recently, I thought *Highlights* had exhausted crafts made from paper towel tubes, but this particular contributor researched an ancient Greek communication method for sending secret messages, and she found a way to make it accessible to kids."

Note the mention of research. Some ideas spring ready-made from your imagination, but many more will be unearthed, or enhanced, by some digging. Author Amy Houts was assigned to write a book entitled *Clap Clap: Clapping Games* for Pearson to be published in the next year. "In my research I learned that clapping games are typically for girls and a sign of friendship," she explains. "All my research had to be documented, which was hard because clapping games are part of folklore, part of an oral tradition. While I could easily find the words to clapping games, the hand movements were difficult to find. I searched the Internet, books, and magazines. What worked best was finding and talking to people of different countries. It was a time-consuming process, but I am proud of this book and hope that children enjoy reading it, as well as trying the games."

Magazine editors are most enthusiastic when an activity ties in with an issue theme or an individual article or story. Chorlian says, "One person in particular always gives me great hands-on activities to include in *Cobblestone*. His name is Nick D'Alto, and his ideas are not only creative, but they fit the themes so perfectly, which is important to us." She gives two examples from a recent *Cobblestone* issue on steamboats. "Nick even provided two articles to work with the activities. One was on how steamboats used whistles to communicate with one another. With the article, he included a simple way to make a steamboat whistle out of toilet paper rolls. The second article was on how steamboats measure the depth of water to know if it was safe for travel. Nick included an activity that showed our readers how to make a lead line using string, paper clips, and construction paper."

Patricia Pingry, Project Editor for Williamson Books's craft titles, gives an example from the Williamson list. "*China,* by Debbi Michiko Florence, fits into the Kaleidoscope Kids line, in which each book aims to introduce children to how kids live in another country." Pingry says telegraphically, "China. Here is history: the Great Wall and the terracotta army of warriors, horses, and chariots of the first emperor. Culture: jade bracelets, New

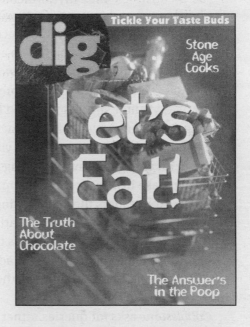

Year's celebrations, religions of Tao and Buddhist, the philosophies of Confucius and feng-shui, as well as Dragon Races and Moon Goddess Day." The book, targeted to ages 7 to 13, contains more than 40 activities, all related to specific facts in the text.

Almost any nonfiction topic can lend itself to an associated activity, craft, or game, and almost any activity can include a tidbit of nonfiction to enhance its attractiveness to an editor.

Planning

If the activity writer begins with a nonfiction topic, the first decision is what type of craft or game to consider. Rosalie Baker, Editor of *Calliope* and *Dig,* explains, "Some topics lend themselves to hands-on projects, so it seems a given that I should include a couple." She describes a craft from *Calliope* that was included in their issue on Galileo. "One really neat activity was how to build a Galileo telescope using simple stock items: lenses (magnifying glasses, plastic magnifiers, or reading glasses), cardboard tubes, aluminum foil, and tape or glue." Baker continues, "Other topics, like the Mythical Monsters issue (February 2008), seem to want wordplay and the like." Word games can be an excellent way to reinforce a topic's vocabulary, and a bit of humor is always a plus.

Chorlian warns, however, "Crossword puzzles are always fun, but I find they are easy to do in-house since I know exactly what vocabulary words will appear in an issue. There are programs now that will create a puzzle once you have chosen your words and clues."

Style and tone are important in presenting an activity to children. Nearly every editor stresses the need for the idea to sound fun and appealing. At *Highlights*, says Hoffman, the article should be "kid-friendly, fun." Chorlian explains yet another virtue of D'Alto's work, "Nick always writes in an engaging way. The thing I like best about his activities is that they make history active and fun." She cites the example of a craft that walks the readers through making an engraving using a piece of styrofoam. "This activity is particularly great because readers have to travel back in time and see the steps that it took to create a picture for publication before electricity, fax machines, printers, etc. Nick's activities always seem to do that—make the readers feel like time-traveling inventors and creators."

Cobblestone asks for queries rather than complete manuscripts, and Baker is aware of tone even before requesting a manuscript. She says she's not sure how to describe exactly what catches her eye, but at least one important element is "the tone of the query—enthusiastic, knowledgeable, and keenly interested in creating an activity that young people will love to do."

Some projects and games seem to appeal to children of one gender or the other, which is useful for magazines such as *American Girl, Hopscotch, Boys' Quest,* or *Boys' Life.* There's always a need, however, for more universal activities. According to Hoffman, a craft for making a simple basketball backboard "was exciting because we know that it will appeal to both boys and girls. We always try to balance our crafts so that they appeal to both genders, but sometimes it's difficult. This activity (and another craft submission called 'Bocce in a Box') gives our readers something that they can make and then play with. We always try to publish at least one craft game in each issue of the magazine."

Another vital consideration is difficulty, which relates to age level. It's wise to test a craft, game, or project with children of the target age, to be sure it's within their abilities and appropriate to their interests. For her clapping games book, Houts knew, "The games couldn't be too easy or babyish for second graders (no patty cake, patty cake), but not so challenging that they wouldn't want to try them. The four games I included had slightly differing levels of difficulty. Another issue related to age-appropriateness is vocabulary and sentence structure. The sentences followed a simple structure with few hard words."

It's tempting to indicate a broad age range on a submission, in hopes of attracting a wider audience, but this almost never works. Sheila Barry, Editor in Chief at Kids Can Press, is clear about this: "The manuscript should be designed for children within a specific and appropriate age range. So, I am not interested in a craft book that claims to be 'for kids of all ages.'" Recent craft books from the publisher include *123 I Can Paint* and *123 I Can Sculpt*, by Irene Luxbacher.

Sometimes a craft that's too difficult can be simplified (but not dumbed down!) for a younger audience. A puppet that would be sewn together by an older child might be completed with fabric glue, instead of needle and thread, for a younger child; or, the face could be added with fabric markers rather than embroidered features. A solid knowledge of children's skill levels is a valuable asset to the project writer.

Safety considerations are paramount too. Hoffman points out, "we do not publish crafts that use a glue gun, knives, etc." Using adult assistance is appropriate at times, but should not be overdone. A recipe that calls for baking may say, "Ask an adult to set the oven at 350 degrees" or "ask an adult to hold the heavy bowl while you scrape out the batter."

A skillful writer does have some wiggle room concerning difficulty. "While degree of difficulty matters," says Baker, "we have had some

Crafts and Activities Markets

Magazines

➤ **American Girl:** 8400 Fairway Place, Middleton, WI 53562. www.americangirl.com

➤ **Boys' Quest, Hopscotch, Fun for Kidz:** P.O. Box 227, Bluffton, OH 45817. www.funforkidz.com

➤ **Carus Publishing:** 70 East Lake Street, Chicago, IL 60601. www.cobblestonepub.com

➤ **FamilyFun:** 47 Pleasant Street, Northampton, MA 01060. www.familyfun.com

➤ **Highlights for Children:** 803 Church Street, Honesdale, PA 18431. www.highlights.com

➤ **Kid Zone:** 801 W. Norton Avenue, Muskegon, MI 49411. www.scottpublications.com

➤ **Pack-o-Fun:** 2400 Devon, Des Plaines, IL 60018. www.pack-o-fun.com

Books

➤ **Humanics Learning:** 12 South Dixie Highway, Lake Worth, FL 33460. www.humanicspub.com

➤ **Kids Can Press:** 29 Birch Avenue, Toronto, Ontario M4V 1E2 Canada. www.kidscanpress.com

➤ **Lark Books:** 67 Broadway, Asheville, NC 28801. www.larkbooks.com

➤ **Meadowbrook Press:** 5451 Smetana Drive, Minnetonka, MN 55343. www.meadowbrookpress.com

➤ **Millbrook Press:** 241 First Avenue N., Minneapolis, MN 55401. www.lernerbooks.com. A division of Lerner Publishing.

➤ **Penguin Book Group:** 375 Hudson Street, New York, NY 10014. www.penguin.com. Check individual Penguin divisions.

➤ **Rainbow Publishers:** P.O. Box 261129, San Diego, CA 92196. www.rainbowpublishers.com

➤ **Sterling Publishing:** 387 Park Avenue South, New York, NY 10016. www.sterlingpublishing.com.

➤ **Wiley Children's Books:** 111 River Street, Hoboken, NJ 07030. www.wiley.com/children

➤ **Williamson Books:** 535 Metroplex Drive, Nashville, TN 37211. www.williamsonbooks.com. A division of Ideals Books.

➤ **Workman Publishing:** 225 Varick Street, New York, NY 10014. www.workman.com

activities that were quite difficult to do and involved complicated principles, but the author translated the difficulty into simple, logical steps that led you from gathering the necessary items to putting them together in the correct sequence to making the craft do what it was supposed to do."

Once the topic and target have been selected, the research done, it's time to concentrate on presentation.

Treatment and Presentation

Be sure that the materials needed are not only inexpensive but easy to obtain. Double-check on any commercial products recommended. The Internet contains hundreds of craft recipes that call for Ivory Flakes, for example, even though the detergent was discontinued by the manufacturer in 1978. Games often need materials, too; don't forget to mention up front that children will need a handkerchief or spoons or a piece of chalk or whatever is necessary.

Something mentioned by virtually every editor is that the instructions for playing the game, completing the craft, or doing the activity must be clear. Barry looks for "authors who can write concise step-by-step instructions, which is a harder thing to do than you might think." For *Clap Clap: Clapping Games,* Houts specifies, "I used clapping games that could be explained in numbered steps within a two-page spread."

Don't send artwork unless you're an artist, of course, but simple diagrams can be very helpful to an editor or an art director in understanding the project. Chorlian is pleased when an author "provides sketches of the steps, so when we need to illustrate his activities, we can pass along the visuals for guidance."

Always test the project by asking children to make the craft, play the game, or try the activity. It's helpful to take pictures of this testing stage, not for publication but as reference. For a craft, samples are a plus. "The best are those that the authors make and then send me," says Baker.

When compiling a book of crafts or games, the collection should have a central focus. At Kids Can Press, Barry says, "When I evaluate craft book proposals, I look for manuscripts that are organized either thematically (for example, Halloween crafts) or by skill (for example, a book of knitting projects)." The Kids Can list includes books that are not just sewing projects but have specific focus: *Beanbag Buddies and Other Stuffed Toys* and *All-American Quilts*.

Angela Wiechmann, Senior Editor at Meadowbrook Press, says, "We see many submissions that are little more than parents' collections of the homespun activities they enjoy with their own children. Due to the nature of the genre, many parents (or childcare providers) consider themselves children's activity experts. Yes, there are a lot of great ideas floating out there, but most submissions go straight into the reject pile because the authors show no publishing and marketing savvy." For an example of an excellent submission that Meadowbrook did accept, see the sidebar on page 123.

Lasting Value

A Chinese proverb says, "Tell me and I'll forget; show me and I may remember; involve me, and I'll understand."

In the introduction to Steven Caney's *Kids' America* (Workman), possibly the best activity book ever published and now unfortunately out of print, the author states, "By sampling the hundreds of games, recipes, crafts, toys, and ideas in *Kids' America*, you may gradually begin to understand just why America is so special." The book's theme, obviously, is the New World, and it includes crafts, hobbies, tales, legends, games, projects, and other adventures to keep children busy and happy for a long, long time. Learning history and sociology and geography and horticulture and physics and all the rest a child will absorb is not a stated goal, nor will the child be aware of (or care about) the broader implications of the activities. Everything in the book is fascinating fun, and that's enough.

Notice how many times the word *fun* appears in the editors' quotes in this article and make that a first priority. To compete with television and computer games and handheld devices, an activity must be even more appealing than electronics.

At the same time, activities and games can include deeper value. "Anything that gives kids a taste of other cultures is a great idea to submit to *Highlights*," says Hoffman. "Right now, our greatest need is probably for multicultural and holiday crafts. We often receive Christmas crafts, but we rarely get anything for Hanukkah, Kwanzaa, Purim,

Case Study of an Activities Book

Angela Wiechmann, Senior Editor at Meadowbrook Press, describes the process of a new book Meadowbrook had taken on. The contract had been signed a year before, and the final manuscript was just arriving for review.

"As you'll see, I discuss a book we haven't even edited yet, but we already know it's a great addition to our activity line. The book is tentatively titled *The Siblings Busy Book*, by Lisa Hanson and Heather Kempskie. It's a collection of activities designed for siblings to enjoy as a group—from baby to toddler to preschooler to school-age child. They submitted their proposal in October 2006, and as soon as we saw it, we knew it was heads and shoulders above anything else in our submission pile. We ended up working with them to refocus their original idea into something that could fit into our popular Busy Book series, and the book was scheduled to be published in August 2008.

"The proposal stood out in many ways. First, the proposal itself was professional, thorough, and engaging. It immediately communicated a great deal about their project and themselves. They clearly explained their idea, which was fresh and well executed. They knew their subject matter and the general market well enough to convince us quickly that parents would want to buy this book. We agreed, and to make it even more marketable, we worked with Lisa and Heather to fashion it into our bestselling Busy Book line.

"More important, their proposal indicated that Lisa and Heather would not only write a terrific manuscript, but also effectively promote it once it was published. They smartly emphasized their backgrounds and connections in child development (which highlighted their expertise with the subject matter) and in parenting media circles (which highlighted their marketing potential). They also emphasized the fact that they're identical twins, which is a fun and unique publicity hook."

Divali, etc. Crafts for nonreligious holidays are also great. Any crafts from other cultures that are kid-friendly are fantastic. For example, the March 2008 issue of *Highlights* includes a friendship card with the Claddagh on the front. With that craft, we are printing a few lines that talk about the significance of the Claddagh ring in Ireland." Hoffman concludes, "We strive to help kids learn more about the world around them, not only in the stories, but in our crafts, activities, and in every-thing we do."

Houts expresses a similar goal for *Clap Clap: Clapping Games.* "By teaching clapping games from different countries—India, Ghana, the United States, and the United Kingdom—I felt I was teaching tolerance and bringing the world closer together. After all, the games children play are similar no matter where they live and the experience of fun and friendship is similar, too. The more we learn about each other, the more we can accept one another."

Busy hands, happy hands . . . the writer of children's activities, games, and crafts provides fun for today and may be making a very real contribution to the future.

News of the Year

Anniversaries

➤ The beloved *The Cat in the Hat,* by Theodor Seuss Geisel, aka Dr. Seuss, turned 50. With more than 10.5 million copies sold, this classic is credited with encouraging children to enjoy a lifetime of reading. Random House marked the anniversary with *The Cat in the Hat Party Edition* and *The Annotated Cat in the Hat: Under the Hats of Seuss and His Cats.*

➤ Tundra Books, the oldest children's book publisher in Canada, celebrated its fortieth anniversary. The publisher was founded by May Cutler.

➤ S. E. Hinton's bestselling novel *The Outsiders* turned 40. Finishing the novel at 16, Hinton went on to win the first Margaret A. Edwards Award for a distinguished contribution to young adult literature.

➤ Forty years after the publication of *Brown Bear, Brown Bear What Do You See?* Henry Holt has released *Baby Bear, Baby Bear What Do You See?* It is the final collaboration of the best-selling author-illustrator team Bill Martin Jr. and Eric Carle.

Awards

➤ The American Library Association (ALA) presented the John Newbery Medal to Susan Patron for *The Higher Power of Lucky* (Simon & Schuster/Richard Jackson Books). Honor Books were *Penny from Heaven,* by Jennifer L. Holm (Random House); *Hattie Big Sky,* by Kirby Larson (Delacorte); and *Rules,* by Cynthia Lord (Scholastic).

➤ The ALA Randolph Caldecott Medal for picture book illustration was awarded to David Wiesner for *Flotsam* (Clarion). Wiesner had won the medal previously for *The Three Pigs* and *Tuesday.* Honor Books were

Gone Wild: An Endangered Animal Alphabet, by David McLimans (Walker); and *Moses: When Harriet Tubman Led Her People to Freedom*, illustrated by Kadir Nelson, written by Carole Boston Weatherford (Hyperion/Jump at the Sun).

➤ The ALA Michael L. Printz Award for excellence in YA literature was presented to Gene Luen Yang for *American Born Chinese* (Roaring Brook/First Second). Four Honor Books were also named: *The Astonishing Life of Octavian Nothing*, by M. T. Anderson (Candlewick); *An Abundance of Katherines*, by John Green (Dutton); *Surrender*, by Sonya Hartnett (Candlewick); and *The Book Thief*, by Markus Zusak (Knopf).

➤ The ALA's Coretta Scott King Author and Illustrator Awards, given to inspiring African American authors, were presented to Sharon Draper for the writing of *Copper Sun* (Atheneum) and Kadir Nelson for illustrating *Moses*. The author Honor Book was *The Road to Paris*, by Nikki Grimes (Putnam). Illustrator honors went to Christopher Myers for *Jazz*, written by Walter Dean Myers (Holiday House); and Benny Andrews, for *Poetry for Young People: Langston Hughes* (Sterling).

The King awards also recognize new talent in the form of the John Steptoe Award, given to Traci L. Jones for *Standing Against the Wind* (Farrar, Straus and Giroux).

➤ The Young Adult Library Services Association (YALSA), a division of the ALA, announced a new award for the coming year, to honor longtime Vice President and Director of Library Promotion at HarperCollins Children's Books, Bill Morris. The William C. Morris Award will be presented annually to a first novelist "who has made a strong literary debut in writing for young adult readers."

➤ The ALA also created the Odyssey Award for Audiobook Excellence to recognize the best in audiobooks for children.

➤ National Book Award finalists for young people's literature were *The Absolutely True Diary of a Part-Time Indian*, by Sherman Alexie (Little, Brown); *Skin Hunger: A Resurrection of Magic*, by Kathleen Duey (Atheneum); *Touching Snow*, by M. Sindy Felin (Atheneum); *The Invention of Hugo Cabret*, by Brian Selznick (Atheneum); and *Story of a Girl*, by Sara Zarr (Little, Brown).

➤ The Boston Globe-Horn Book Awards went to *The Astonishing Life of Octavian Nothing*, by M. T. Anderson, for fiction/poetry; *Dog and*

Bear: Two Friends, Three Stories, by Laura Vaccaro Seeger (Roaring Brook/ Neal Porter Books), for picture book; and *The Strongest Man in the World: Louis Cyr,* by Nicolas Debon (Groundwood), for nonfiction.

➤ The Society of Children's Book Writers and Illustrators (SCBWI) presented the Golden Kite Awards to *Fireflies,* by Tony Abbott (Little, Brown), for fiction; *The Adventures of Marco Polo,* by Russell Freedman (Arthur A. Levine/Scholastic), for nonfiction; *Jazz,* by Walter Dean Myers, for picture book text; and picture book illustrator Larry Day for *Afraid of Dogs* (Walker), written by Susanna Pitzer.

➤ The Quill Award for YA fiction went to *Sold,* by Patricia McCormick (Hyperion). *Flotsam,* by David Wiesner, took the picture book prize. The chapter book/middle-grade winner was *The Invention of Hugo Cabret,* by Brian Selznick. Scott McCloud's *Making Comics: Storytelling Secrets of Comics, Manga and Graphic Novels* (Harper) won for graphic novels.

➤ The Mystery Writers of America presented its Edgar Awards to *Room One: A Mystery or Two,* by Andrew Clements (Simon & Schuster), for best juvenile novel; and *Buried,* by Robin Merroe MacCready (Dutton), for best YA novel.

➤ The Ezra Jack Keats Book Award recognizes authors and illustrators new to children's books. Kelly Cunane won for *For You Are a Kenyan Child* (Atheneum), and Kristen Balouch won for her illustration of *Mystery Bottle* (Hyperion).

➤ The Margaret A. Edwards Award, created to honor popular YA authors and their bodies of work, was presented to Lois Lowry.

➤ *Moon Plane,* by Peter McCarthy (Henry Holt), won the Charlotte Zolotow Award for outstanding picture book, from the Cooperative Children's Book Center (CCBC) of the University of Wisconsin-Madison.

➤ Matteo Pericoli won the Gryphon Award for *The True Story of Stellina* (Knopf), sponsored by the Center for Children's Books, Graduate School of Library and Information Science at the University of Illinois in Urbana-Champaign.

➤ The fifth annual James Madison Book Award was presented to *A Dangerous Engine: Benjamin Franklin, from Scientist to Diplomat,* by Joan Dash (Farrar, Straus/Frances Foster Books).

➤ The Jane Addams Award honors books that promote peace, justice, world community, and equality. The winner in the category of younger children was *A Place Where Sunflowers Grow,* by Amy Lee-Tai (Children's

Book Press). Cynthia Kadohata's *Weedflower* (Atheneum) won for books for older children.

➤ The Association of Jewish Libraries named the winners of the Sydney Taylor Book Awards. *Hanukkah at Valley Forge,* by Stephen Krensky and Greg Harlin (Dutton), won in the younger readers category (grades one to five). *Julia's Kitchen,* by Brenda Ferber (Farrar, Straus), won for older readers (grades four to eight); and a teen award was given for the first time, to *The Book Thief,* by Markus Zusak (Knopf).

➤ The Andre Norton Award for Young Adult Science Fiction and Fantasy, among the Science Fiction Writers of America's Nebula Awards, went to Justine Larbalestier for *Magic or Madness* (Razorbill).

➤ Formerly the Whitbread Award, the Costa Book Award was given to *Set in Stone,* by Linda Newbery (Random House/David Fickling Books).

➤ Meg Rosoff won the Carnegie Medal for *Just in Case* (Puffin), which deals with anxiety, depression, and coming of age.

➤ Mini Grey won the Kate Greenaway Medal for *The Adventures of the Dish and the Spoon* (Jonathan Cape).

➤ Michael Rosen became the first poet to become Britain's children's laureate. He will hold the title for two years.

Mergers, Acquisitions, & Reorganizations

➤ The Ripplewood-Led Group, owner of Weekly Reader Corporation, purchased Reader's Digest Association for about $1.6 billion. The deal moves Reader's Digest from a publicly traded to a privately held company.

➤ Reference publisher Facts on File is reacquiring the Facts on File News Services from Reader's Digest Association.

➤ The publishing assets of T&N Children's Publishing, including its Two-Can and NorthWord Books imprints, were acquired by Cooper Square Publishing, a joint venture of Rowman & Littlefield Publishing Group and a private equity firm.

➤ Cooper Square also acquired the assets of Northland Publishing, with its Rising Moon and Luna Rising imprints. Distribution of Northland's titles was taken over by the National Book Network. Although Cooper Square owns the company's backlist, Northland may broker a deal that allows it to continue publishing new frontlist titles.

➤ AuthorHouse acquired one of its largest competitors, iUniverse. In a *Publishers Weekly* interview, iUniverse President Susan Driscoll and

AuthorHouse President Bryan Smith noted that the companies target different segments of the self-publishing market. iUniverse provides a wider array of publishing services, while AuthorHouse gives authors more control over their work.

➤ Meredith Books left the children's market and reduced the number of titles produced by its New York office. Its book program will focus on its core areas of home and garden. Trade publishing Editorial Director Linda Cunningham left the company. Executive Editor Lisa Berkowitz is managing New York operations.

➤ Holtzbrinck's Pan Macmillan division acquired British children's publisher Kingfisher from Houghton Mifflin. Simon Boughton, Publisher of Holtzbrinck's Roaring Press imprint, is in charge of operations for Kingfisher, which publishes about 100 titles a year and will be a Macmillan Children's Books imprint.

➤ Simon & Schuster is moving the Simon Spotlight Entertainment imprint from the children's division to the adult division's Pocket Books. The editorial focus of the fast-growing imprint will remain the same.

➤ Simon & Schuster's Children's Division is encouraging the publication of comics and graphic novels. Although it will not launch a separate graphic novel imprint, Simon & Schuster plans to produce and market more graphic novels in each of its existing imprints.

➤ Running Press acquired the primary Peanuts children's publishing license from United Media and is creating a novelty line from the Charles Schulz comic strip and television specials. *The Great Pumpkin, Charlie Brown* was the first title.

➤ Lerner Publishing added a trade line specializing in educational hardcover and paperback comics to its Graphic Universe imprint. Shannon Barefield is Editorial Director.

➤ With the acquisition of Avalon Books by Perseus Book Group, Perseus imprint Da Capo Press absorbed the Avalon imprint Marlowe & Company into Da Capo's Lifelong Books.

➤ Hoping to ignite a wider acceptance of graphic novels, DC Comics switched its book trade distribution from Warner Books/Hachette to Random House Publisher Services, the book industry's largest distributor. DC is also investing in Flex Comics, a Japanese production company creating original manga for Web and audio distribution.

➤ A top digital photo company, Shutterfly, has acquired Make It About

Me, which produces customized children's books that allow parents to place their child's picture into a story's illustrations.

➢ Chelsea Green acquired the environmentally conscious children's series Gaia Girls. Author Lee Welles originally self-published the books through her Daisyworld Press. Chelsea Green hopes to attract younger readers through this acquisition. *Enter the Earth* is the first title.

➢ Naughty Ma Xiaotao, a Chinese series for ages seven to nine, written by Yang Hongying, was acquired by HarperCollins UK. The series chronicles the adventures of a young boy and his father and has sold more than 12 million copies in China.

➢ A preliminary agreement was reached for Taylor & Francis to acquire Haworth Press, publisher of academic books and journals. Haworth's fiction imprint, Harrington Park Press, is being sold separately.

Launches & Ventures
Books

➢ Kids Play is the new preschool novelty market imprint from DK Publishing. Its focus is books and novelty material that reinforce early learning concepts through play.

➢ Zest Books is a new line of teen self-help, how-to, and craft books from book packager Orange Avenue. The company plans to publish about five books each season.

➢ Answering the call of tweens everywhere, Simon & Schuster Children's Publishing created its first tween imprint, Aladdin MIX. Vice President and Associate Publisher Ellen Krieger heads up the imprint. Debut titles include *There's a Girl in My Hammerlock,* by Jerry Spinelli, and *The Melting of Maggie Bean,* by Tricia Rayburn.

➢ Smith & Sons, the new middle-grade fiction imprint from Smith & Kraus, was created after Publisher Marisa Kraus's son Peter read the manuscript for *Middleworld,* by Pamela and John Voelkel. The 14-year-old could not tear himself away and had to read the next two novels in the series. His excitement led to this new venture for Smith & Kraus, which is best known for its theater books. Smith & Sons will publish adventure fiction and books of interest to middle-grade readers.

➢ Brenda Bowen is set to launch a yet unnamed imprint at HarperCollins Children's Books that will offer graphic novels and books on cultural trends for readers of all ages.

➤ Poppy is the new Little, Brown imprint under the direction of Cindy Eagan. Its list will include series that Eagan has edited since their inception, including Gossip Girl and a new series, Poseur, by Rachel Maude.

➤ The ABDO Publishing Group launched a new publishing company called Magic Wagon, which will focus on picture and graphic books for the preK through eighth-grade market. Magic Wagon debuted with two imprints, Graphic Planet and Looking Glass Library. Plans for a third imprint are also in the works.

➤ Learning Books is the new imprint stemming from the partnership of Random House Information Group and Sylvan Learning. It will publish trade educational paperbacks for preK to grade 12 students.

➤ Marimba Books is a joint venture of Kensington Publishing and Hudson Publishing, a new company from Wade and Cheryl Hudson, the founders of Just Us Books. The imprint will target the African American and multicultural children's market.

➤ Boxing Day Books is the new publishing house of Paula Morrow, former Executive Editor at Cricket Magazine Group, and Ron McCutchan, former Senior Art Director at Cricket. The first release is Barbara Seuling's *Say It with Music,* a biography of singer Jane Froman. Boxing Day Books will publish titles for children and adults.

➤ Random House's Robin Corey Books launched its debut list, a mix of pop-up and other novelty titles.

➤ Little Scholastic is a developmental book program for birth to age three offering board books from across Scholastic's imprints. The books feature interactive components, bright colors, and rhyming, repetitive text to promote language comprehension and listening skills, as well as suggestions for using the books with children.

➤ Supermarket continuity-program developer Advance Publishers debuted its first mystery book series, based on Scooby Doo.

Magazines

➤ Targeting children ages three to six and their parents, *National Geographic Little Kids* premiered under the direction of Editor in Chief Melinda Bellows. The magazine covers animals, science, and people around the world. A new classroom magazine for grades two to six, *National Geographic Explorer* provides science and social studies articles with vibrant photographs to engage readers.

➤ *Hieroglyphics Magazine* debuts in print and online. The monthly magazine is a cross-cultural African history magazine that features history and science articles, and futuristic fiction for children ages 2 to 12.

➤ *Plushie Pals* is a new publication from Beckett Media about collecting the popular Webkinz stuffed animals, and offers games and new product information. The bimonthly caters to girls ages 6 to 14.

➤ Subtitled "a quarterly magazine for girls with style *and* substance," *Kiki Magazine* debuted in September. It offers age-appropriate style advice and confidence-building material for girls ages 9 to 14.

➤ Targeting the three million female student athletes in the U.S., *Girl* focuses on sports coverage, lifestyle articles, and articles on social issues in each quarterly issue.

➤ Young female golfers ages 8 to 17 are the target audience of *Golfer Girl.* Publisher Claude Hooton says the magazine "is interested in topics of general interest to teenage girls, but we prefer stories that are relevant to the health, fitness, and strategy of young females on the golf circuit."

➤ Debuting in August, the quarterly *Junior Shooters* targets young people, ages 8 to 21, who are interested in the sport of shooting. Andy Fink is Editor in Chief.

➤ *Young Urban Viewz* aims at African American teens. Editor in Chief Trina Graves describes the quarterly as "different from other YA publications in that our focus is mainly about providing thought-provoking, forward-thinking articles. We are mostly interested in articles that bring awareness to things that are going on in different communities."

➤ Publisher Ayal Korczak's mission for *LàTeen* is to encourage Latin American teens to read for enjoyment. The magazine features positive material relevant to Hispanic life.

➤ New YA magazine *PresenTense* covers Jewish life, news, and views. Editor Ariel Beery says, "*PresenTense* seeks to invigorate Hebrew culture by providing a nuturing environment where Jewish youth will be able to explore and enrich their Jewish identity within a civilizational framework."

➤ Helping children to age six learn about God's love for them and the world in which they live is the mission of newcomer *The Little Lutheran,* published 10 times a year by the Evangelical Lutheran Church in America.

➤ *Muslim Girl* targets girls ages 12 to 19. Editor in Chief Ausma Khan is "interested in stories about issues that matter to teen girls and that focus on girls' self-esteem, education, and empowerment."

➤ Muslim youth in Canada are the target audience of *Aver Magazine*. It covers topics including sports, fashion, and profiles of unique and inspiring Muslims.

➤ *Logan* serves young women ages 14 to 25 who are living with disabilities. Logan Olson, who is disabled, and her mother Laurie founded the magazine, which offers professional success stories, tools to make everyday tasks easier, and fashion ideas.

➤ Parents sharing ideas with each other is the premise of *Parents for Parents*. Editor Linda Deane looks for practical solutions to everyday parenting struggles.

➤ Suburban parents in the greater New Jersey area are the primary audience of *The Family Groove*. Offering general parenting information, current trends, and ideas, the magazine plans to expland into Massachusetts, California, Maryland, Florida, and Arizona.

➤ Women ages 22 to 42 turn to *Baby Couture* for fashion advice for infants and toddlers, celebrity baby news, and parenting information.

➤ *Family Circle* expanded its target audience to include mothers of tweens and teens by offering new product information and general parenting information for mothers of older children.

➤ Written by and for 15- to 29-year-old women in the Sault Ste. Marie area of Ontario, Canada, *Fresh.Magazine* offers articles on politics, education, careers, technology, and health.

➤ *Secular Homeschooling* debuted in October and provides quarterly coverage of teaching methods and styles for homeschooling parents.

➤ According to Editor Heather Janssen, the goal of *Get Born* is to nurture mothers. "We offer realistic material that helps mothers to know that they don't have to have it all together." The quarterly features personal essays on spiritual growth and inspirational fiction.

➤ *Acadiana Moms* targets mothers in the Lafayette, Louisiana, region with advice on organizing, crafts for kids, and general parenting articles.

Multimedia

➤ *The Dangerous Book for Boys* is coming to the big screen thanks to Disney. The best-selling book by Conn and Hal Iggulden covers topics such as tying knots, hunting, science experiments, and carpentry.

➤ Harcourt Children's Books became the distributor for Full Cast Audio's children's audiobooks. Full Cast had handled its own distribution to schools and libraries. This venture now expands Full Cast's marketing of family listening titles, such as *Fairest,* by Gail Carson Levine.

➤ HarperCollins teamed with LibreDigital, a division of NewsStand Inc., to offer digital services to other publishers, including typesetting, production, digital warehousing, Internet distribution, and marketing.

➤ Holtzbrinck established an online network of audio bytes in an effort to enter podcasting. QuickandDirtyTips.com began as the brainchild of Mignon Fogarty, best known as Grammar Girl.

➤ Zudacomics.com is the new Webcomics imprint of DC Comics. The online imprint solicits original material from fans for publication.

➤ Simon & Schuster and Turn-Here, Inc. launched Booksvideo.tv, described as a "book-centric video channel" that will promote Simon & Schuster authors and their books.

➤ Lisi Harrison's best-selling series Clique (Little, Brown) was optioned by Warner Premiere, a division of Warner Bros., for a series of direct-to-consumer DVDs.

Book Deals

➤ R. L. Stine, author of the Goosebumps series, and Scholastic are publishing a 12-book series titled Goosebumps Horrorland. The series will feature some familiar villains, along with several new characters.

➤ Scholastic is publishing three new series by Meg Cabot. Allie Finkle's Rules for Girls targets girls ages 8 to 12. Two trilogies for teens titled Airhead and Abandon are scheduled for release in the next year.

➤ Wendy Loggia at Delacorte secured a deal to publish *Parties & Potions,* the next title in Sarah Mlynowski's Magic in Manhattan series. The three previous books in the series have sold a combined 250,000 copies. Delacorte will also publish Mlynowski's standalone title, *Gimme a Call.*

➤ Barry Cunningham, Publisher and Managing Editor of the U.K. publisher Chicken House and the editor who discovered J. K. Rowling when he was at Bloomsbury, acquired a new fantasy series. Written by Roderick Gordon and Brian Williams, the first book is *Tunnels.*

➤ Michael P. Spradin's trilogy the Youngest Templar was acquired by Timothy Travaglini at Putnam. The first book to be published is *The Keeper of the Grail.*

➤ Penguin Group's Young Readers Division made a deal with writer/ illustrator Salina Yoon for an eponymous line of novelty books. The first titles were *Just for Daddy!* and *Just for Mommy!*

➤ Jean Feiwel's Square Fish imprint at Holtzbrinck became the new paperback publisher of Madeleine L'Engle's *A Wrinkle in Time*. The book was released in May along with four other titles by L'Engle. Dubbed the Time Quintet, the books were treated as new releases complete with new cover art and a movie-style trailer.

➤ Renowned physicist Steven Hawking signed with Simon & Schuster to write a children's book, *George's Secret Key to the Universe*. The middle-grade novel follows a boy who goes on myriad adventures across the universe.

➤ HarperCollins acquired world rights to a children's book by First Lady Laura Bush and her daughter Jenna. The yet untitled book is the story of a young boy who doesn't like to read.

➤ Former New York Yankees third baseman Alex Rodriguez penned a picture book, *Out of the Ball Park* (HarperCollins).

➤ Simon & Schuster bought world rights for an inspirational picture book by former NFL player and coach Tony Dungy. *You Can Do It* will be published by the Howard Kids/Little Simon Inspirations imprint.

➤ *A Box Full of Kittens* (Atheneum) is the new picture book from Sonia Manzano, who plays Maria on *Sesame Street*.

Other News

➤ New language in Simon & Schuster's author contracts was challenged by the Authors Guild, which felt that the altered clause was an unreasonable attempt to retain copyright beyond standard industry practice. The Guild argues that the language could be used by publishers to claim that a book has never gone out of print. In response, Simon & Schuster agreed that in-print status could be negotiated on a case-by-case basis. The Guild remains cautious.

➤ The Ambassador for Children's Literature is the new government-recognized post instituted by the Children's Book Council and the Library of Congress to support children's literature and highlight the importance of reading. The position will be given to renowned children's authors and illustrators of both fiction and nonfiction.

➤ 2008 sees the final conversion from 10-digit to 13-digit ISBN numbers. Although most of the industry has already switched to 13 digits, 10-digit ISBNs were still being accepted.

➤ Penguin U.K. launched a book website run by a teen editorial board, www.pinebreakers.co.uk, in an effort to reach teens through Internet marketing.

➤ Little, Brown Books for Young Readers released the controversial *Tintin in the Congo* for the first time in the U.S. since it was written in 1930. The book caused an uproar over racial content in the U.K. A note on the parent company's website (Hachette Book Group) says that the book "may be considered somewhat controversial, as it reflects the colonial attitudes of the time it was created. . . . but in this edition it will be contextualized for the reader in an explanatory preface."

➤ Litigation over the unauthorized importation and sale of U.S. textbooks intended for sale in foreign markets was resolved in separate settlements with Pearson Education, John Wiley, Thomson Learning, and McGraw-Hill Education. The publishers will receive "significant" damages from the two defendants, who operated out of Texas, Michigan, and Singapore under various names.

➤ The Associated Press discontinued its book-review package, although books will be covered periodically as arts and entertainment features or reviews.

People

Books

➤ President of Simon & Schuster Jack Romanos stepped down and was succeeded by Carolyn Reidy.

➤ Elizabeth Law, Vice President and Associate Publisher of Simon & Schuster Books for Young Readers, left the company.

➤ Mark McVeigh joined Simon & Schuster's Aladdin Books as Editorial Director. McVeigh, who had been Senior Editor at Dutton, reports to Ellen Krieger.

➤ Carl Raymond was named Associate Publisher for Simon Spotlight Entertainment. He was most recently Publishing Director for adult lifestyle titles at DK Publishing.

➤ Dial Books for Young Readers, part of Penguin, hired Alisha Niehaus as an Editor. She had been Associate Editor at DK Publishing.

➤ Eamon Dolan succeeded Scott Moyers at Penguin Press as Editor in Chief. Dolan left his similar position at Houghton Mifflin.

➤ Marian Lizzi stepped into the newly created position of Editor in

Chief at Penguin's Perigee Books.

➤ Candlewick's first Editor, Amy Ehrlich, retired from the company.

➤ Liz Van Doren, Editorial Director of Harcourt's Children's Division, left the company after a reorganization. She had been with the company since 1988. Children's editorial was integrated under Editor in Chief Allyn Johnston, who reports to Children's Publisher Lori Benton.

➤ Weeks after leaving Disney, Brenda Bowen moved to HarperCollins Children's Books to start her own imprint.

➤ Steve Ross was named President and Publisher of HarperCollins U.S. division, a role previously held by Joe Tessitore. Ross had been Senior Vice President and Publisher at Random House's Crown Books.

➤ Tina Constable took over Ross's position at Crown Books. Philip Patrick, Vice President and Director of Marketing at Crown, added President and Publisher of Three Rivers Press and Publisher of e-books and digital content to his titles.

➤ Tim Ditlow, longtime Publisher of Random House's children's audiobook imprint Listening Library, is now Vice President and Publisher at Large for Random House Audio. Ditlow's parents, Anthony and Helen Ditlow, co-founded Listening Library in 1955. Amy Metsch took on the newly created position of Editorial Director at Random House Audio. Her position includes overseeing editorial acquisitions for Listening Library, Books on Tape, and Random House Audio and Large Print.

➤ Daniel Menaker left his position of Vice President and Executive Editor at Random House Publishing Group.

➤ Gary Krebs made the move to a newly created position of Group Publisher at Globe Pequot Press. Krebs had been Publisher at Adams Media where he had worked with Scott Watrous, who is now President of Globe Pequot.

➤ Sarah Davies left her position as Publishing Director at the U.K.'s Macmillan Children's Books to start up a literary agency in the U.S. for the British book producer Working Partners.

➤ Doug Lockhart, CEO at Zondervan, stepped down from his post in June. Former President and CEO Bruce Ryskamp, who retired from the company a few years ago, is serving as interim president and CEO.

➤ Annette Bourland was named Vice President and Publisher at Zonderkidz Children's Group. She was previously Managing Editor at *Clubhouse Jr.*

➤ Lauren Wohl was named Associate Publisher at Roaring Brook Press. She served as Marketing Director since Roaring Brook's acquisition by Holtzbrinck four years ago. Deirdre Langeland joined as Senior Editor, and will develop titles for a new nonfiction program.

➤ Lexa Hillyer was hired as Editor at Razorbill.

➤ Carlo DeVito has taken over responsibilities for Sterling Publishing's Hearst imprint and all puzzle and games titles, as Vice President and Editorial Director. Philip Turner, Vice President of Editorial, has assumed responsibility for Sterling's non-illustrated titles and continues to oversee the Union Square imprint. Michael Fragnito has responsibility for illustrated categories, also with the title of Vice President, Editorial Director.

➤ Former Senior Director of Acquisitions and Development at Tyndale House Ken Peterson was named to the new position of Vice President and Publishing Director at Multnomah Books. He reports to Steve Cobb, President of the WaterBrook Multnomah Publishing Group.

➤ Beth Ford was named COO and Executive Vice President at Hachette Book Group USA. She reports to Chairman and CEO David Young.

➤ Page Edmunds assumed the role of Associate Publisher at Workman Publishing after Katie Workman left the company.

➤ Will Balliett left Da Capo Press to take the position of Editoral Director at Hyperion.

➤ Lisa Lyons was named President of Kids Can Press. She had previously been interim president.

➤ Vice President and Editor in Chief at Holiday House Regina Griffin stepped down. Mary Cash was named as her replacement.

➤ Cal Morgan, former Editorial Director of Regan Books, was appointed Vice President and Editorial Director at Harper Perennial. Morgan succeeds David Roth-Ey.

➤ Richard Charkin resigned as CEO of Macmillan UK to become Executive Director at Bloomsbury.

Magazines

➤ Jenny Gillespie signed on as Submissions Editor at *Babybug* and *Ladybug*.

➤ Ann Shoket is the new Editor in Chief at *Seventeen*.

➤ Romana Profopin took over as Submissions Editor at *ASK*.

➤ Martha Krienke took over as the Associate Editor of *Brio*. She replaces Susie Shellenberger.

➤ Meredith Matthews is the new editor of Weekly Reader Corporation's *Current Health 2*. She replaces Anne Flounders.

➤ *Ranger Rick* hired Mary Dalheim as Editor. She replaces Gerald Bishop.

➤ Lisa Singer Moran has stepped down as Executive Editor of *Baby Talk* and *Baby Talk First Months* and moved to *Time Out New York Kids* with a similar title.

➤ Entertainment digest *The Magazine* hired Karen Wong as Editor.

Closings
Books

➤ New Age Dimensions

Magazines

➤ *Above and Beyond*
➤ *Amazing Journeys Magazine*
➤ *American Cheerleader Junior*
➤ *Anime*
➤ *The Blue Review*
➤ *Child*
➤ *Club Connection*
➤ *CollegeBound Teen*
➤ *Dane County Kids*
➤ *Disney Adventures*
➤ *Dragon*
➤ *Family Energy*
➤ *Guideposts Sweet 16*
➤ *Kids' Rooms, Etc.*
➤ *Leading Student Ministry*
➤ *Magic: The Gathering*
➤ *My Friend*
➤ *National PAL CopsNKids Chronicles*
➤ *Natural Jewish Parenting*
➤ *Nick Jr. Family Magazine*

➢ *North Texas Teens*
➢ *Positive Teens*
➢ *Puget Sound Parent*
➢ *Real Sports*
➢ *Resource*
➢ *Teacher Magazine*
➢ *Teaching Elementary Physical Education*
➢ *Teen Light*
➢ *Teen People*
➢ *Think & Discover*
➢ *Three Leaping Frogs*
➢ *Tiny Tummies*
➢ *U*S*Kids*
➢ *What's Hers*
➢ *World Pulse*
➢ *Yu-Gi-Oh*

Deaths

➢ *A Wrinkle in Time* author Madeleine L'Engle passed away at age 89. The Newbery Medal winner wrote more than 60 books including fantasies, poetry, and memoirs, often highlighting spiritual themes and her Christian faith. *A Wrinkle in Time* was one of the most banned books in the U.S. after accusations that it offered an "inaccurate protrayal of God" and nurtured the beliefs of myth and fantasy.

➢ Mary Stolz, author of more than 60 children's books, including *To Tell Your Love* and Newbery Honor Book *Belling the Tiger*, passed away at 86.

➢ Carol Otis Hurst died at 76. The former teacher and librarian penned the novels *Terrible Storm, You Come to Yokum,* and *Torchlight*.

➢ Book agent Dorothy Markinko passed away at age 80. She is credited with establishing the children's department at McIntosh & Otis, where she worked until her retirement in 2001. Authors she represented included Scott O'Dell and Virginia Hamilton.

➢ Joe Ann Daly passed away at 82. A longtime book editor, Daly began her own imprint, Cobblehill Books, at Dutton.

➢ Clyde Robert Bulla died at 93. He wrote more than 60 titles, including *The Donkey Cart* and *The Chalk Box Kid*.

➢ Children's fantasy author and Newbery Medalist Lloyd Alexander died at 83 after a long illness. *The High King, The Black Cauldron,* and *The Marvelous Misadventures of Sebastian* were among his children's titles. His final novel, *The Golden Dreams of Carlo Chuchio* (Henry Holt), was published last year.

➤ Illustrator Bruce Wood died at age 34. Wood collaborated with his mother Audrey Wood on several titles, including *The Christmas Adventure of Space Elf Sam* (Scholastic), the first picture book to use 3-D computer art.

➤ Scholastic Vice President and Senior Editorial Director Craig Walker died at 63. Walker joined Scholastic in 1983 as an assistant editor of the See Saw Book Club. He left the company for a period and returned in 1994 as Editorial Director of trade paperbacks.

➤ Jan Nathan, Executive Director of PMA, the Independent Book Publishers Association, died at age 68.

➤ Howie Schneider, a cartoonist and picture book author best known for his Eek and Meek comic strip, died at 77. He authored the children's books *Chewy Louie; Wilky, the White House Cockroach;* and *No Dogs Allowed!*

When More Than One Voice Tells the Story

By Mindy Hardwick

Writing my current novel, a romance, I first assumed it would have a single-voice narrative. The boy would tell the story and the girl would be a strong secondary character. But when my character sketches came together, both characters had a strong arc and each was trying to tell their side of the story. Did I have two books on my hands, one for her and one for him? Whose story was I writing? Liza Ketchum, author of the two-voice historical novel *Where the Great Hawk Flies* (Clarion Books), read the sketches. Her advice was to try writing my novel using multiple voices.

Intersections and Arcs

In a multiple-voice novel, more than one character tells the story. The characters intersect with each other, but each has an arc that drives the storytelling of the whole. Separate voices allow the story to be seen from two sides, and give a novel complexity and depth distinct from that of a single-voice narrative.

In Wendelin Van Draanen's young adult novel *Flipped* (Knopf), the voices belong to seventh-grader Bryce and next door neighbor Juli. At the beginning of the book, Juli absolutely adores Bryce but he wants nothing to do with her and thinks she is a pest. As the novel progresses, the characters learn more about themselves and more about the other person, shaping and reshaping how they see each other. At the end, Bryce adores Juli and says, "If I've learned one thing from Juli Baker, it's that I've got to put my whole heart and soul into it and try." Meanwhile, Juli's feelings about Bryce have changed and she tells her Mom, "All those years that I liked him, I never really knew him. All I knew was that he had the most beautiful eyes I'd ever seen and that his smile melted my heart like the sun melts butter. But now I know that inside he's a coward and a snake, so I've got to get over what he's like on the outside."

A multiple-voice novel may have two or three, and sometimes considerably more narrators. In *Seedfolks* (Joanna Cotler/HarperTeen), by Paul Fleischman, 13 voices take turns telling how a vacant lot was transformed into a neighborhood garden. Ron Koertge's *Brimstone Journals* (Candlewick) has 15 voices. The story is about the fictional class of 2001 at Branston High school; each character is a different type of high school student. Koertge says, "It was fun for me to work out what the high school types sounded like—jock, punk, etc.—and to be consistent without falling completely into caricature." *Brimstone Journals* is written in verse, with the poems strung together to make up the story. "The first poems came at me in a pretty fragmented way, so I never really entertained the idea of a regular narrative," Koertge says.

Alternative Perspectives

Multiple-voice narratives offer advantages of perspective. In *Where the Great Hawk Flies,* the characters present the viewpoints and experiences of two cultures living in 1780s Vermont. Daniel is a 13-year-old

half-Pequot and half-English boy. Hiram's family has lost nearly everything in the Vermont Indian raid of 1780. "Writing in two voices gave me the chance to see the conflict from both sides, and this is an asset since any conflict is often more complex than just a black or white, right or wrong, good versus evil situation," says Ketchum.

Character complexities draw some writers to multiple voices. "I wanted to show that Daniel wasn't a perfect character," says Ketchum. "He's as flawed in his own way as Hiram is, and we see that more clearly through Hiram's eyes."

The same is true in Annette Curtis Klause's *The Silver Kiss* (Delacorte), in which the vampire Simon and 16-year-old Zoe take turns telling the story. The form allows readers to feel compassion for Simon, who is lonely and doomed to eternal life, and also to understand Zoe's attraction to him while she struggles through fears about her mother's illness and death.

Time can take on fascinating dimensions in multiple-voice novels, which often remove stories from a traditional linear structure. Brent Hartinger's *Grand & Humble* (HarperTeen) plays with the question of whether the circumstances of our lives would change because of a single action. Would we be different people? What would our lives look like? In the novel, 17-year-old Harlan is popular, wealthy, and has what appears to be an ideal life. He's having panic attacks, however, that he can't quite make go away. Seventeen-year-old Manny lives with his single dad, is a theater geek, and although happy with his life, is having nightmares that he doesn't understand. The characters lead parallel lives until the end of the novel, when they come together at Grand and Humble streets for one moment in time. By telling the novel in dual voices, Hartinger allows us to see the separate and then merging paths of each character.

Adele Griffin's two-voice novel *Where I Want to Be* (Putnam) explores the concept of alternate realities. The story is told through the eyes of two sisters: Jane, who has died, and Lily, who is still very much alive and trying to come to terms with her sister's death. By giving Jane a voice in the novel, Griffin reveals the complexities of the sisters' relationship and how each comes to terms with that relationship after death.

Essentials

As creative and satisfying as multiple voices can be in a novel, and as much as some stories simply cry out for them, they present problems

that writers must overcome. Plotting and characterization are much more complex in a multiple-voice novel. If you are up to the challenge, consider these techniques:

➤ *Create distinctive character voices.* Voice is exponentially more important in stories told by several people. Each point-of-view character should have a distinctive personality and way of speaking.

For historical fiction writers such as Ketchum, finding the right character qualities can be especially problematic. Ketchum says, "The most difficult challenge I faced in writing *Where the Great Hawk Flies* was to capture Hiram and Daniel's speech. The story takes place long before recorded speech, and my editor insisted that I cast both voices in the first person—which made the challenge of capturing their syntax, rhythm, and vocabulary even more difficult. In addition, the British had made it a crime for the Pequots to speak their own language, so it is almost extinct. I only had access to a short list of Pequot words given to me by the staff at the Mashantucket Research Library." Ketchum solved the problem when she visited the Massachusetts Historical Society in Boston and found diaries written by young people from the time period. She says, "As I read these diaries, I jotted down the contemporary phrases, idioms, unusual vocabulary, and syntax. Later, I typed them up in a large font and tacked them up above my desk so that each time I looked up, those eighteenth-century phrases were in front of me. I repeated them inside my head until they became like a familiar melody."

Ketchum also spent time reading *A Treasury of New England Folklore.* "Much to my surprise, I realized that some common eighteenth-century phrases are ones I heard when I was a child in Dorset, Vermont. Some survive today. One of our Vermont neighbors still says he's going 'up to the meader,' or that he's going to 'fix his chimbley.'"

In *Boy Girl Boy* (Harcourt), says Koertge, the challenge was "making sure X sounded like X and not like Y or Z. It was a bit like making the great Japanese film *Rashomon*, since the three kids often reported the same thing from three different points of view. Characters had better *sound* different and not just be different reporters."

➤ *Find suitable viewpoints.* Experiment with the point of view when writing a multiple-voice novel. Koertge explains that when writing *Boy Girl Boy*, "I tried conventional ways: omniscient first, then first person using the girl only. Nothing really satisfied me and my enthusiasm would trickle away after 40 pages or so. Then I saw a movie using multiple points of view and I wondered what that would be like if I tried different points of view for each narrator."

One structural possibility for a multiple-voice novel is to shift point of view by chapter, each with a different character speaking. Joyce Carol Oates did this in *Big Mouth & Ugly Girl* (HarperTeen). In the novel, Matt Donaghy has been accused of threatening to blow up the school. Ursula Riggs knows he is not guilty and stands up for him. The voices alternate, with Ursula's story told in the third person and Matt's in the first. Each voice remains distinctive and supports the character's perspective.

➤ *Create strong character arcs.* A novel with several voices is never about simply retelling the same story in different words. Story is about change; each of your point-of-view characters should grow and change. Each chapter should move your story forward. The voice characters must each have their own arc. Ask yourself:

> What does each character want?
> What or who stands in their way?
> What's at stake?
> What happens if they don't get what they want?
> How will each character change in the story?
> How will each scene move the story forward?

If you find that one of your characters is flat and static while another is dynamic, ask yourself if your book is truly a multiple-voice novel.

➤ *Know the purpose of multiple voices.* Multiple-voice novels are not a trend or a fad to follow simply because it might sell in the current market. Quality sells, and comes from a book that is well structured, a story that is well told, and characters whom readers find worth hearing. There should be a strong reason to tell the story with several voices rather than just one. As Koertge says in the opening chapter of *Boy Girl Boy*, "Everything looks different told from different ways."

Novels with several voices often revolve around an issue or an event. Each character needs to tell one part of the story or offer a unique perspective so that the sum of the parts adds up to greater than the whole. The novel should be better for all those voices, as in Joyce McDonald's *Swallowing Stones* (Delacorte). Michael receives a new rifle on his seventeenth birthday. He shoots the gun into the air, but the bullet travels for a mile and kills Jenna's father, who is on his roof repairing shingles. The novel tells the story of Jenna and Michael as each come to terms with the devastating consequences of Michael's actions.

Be clear in your multiple-voice novel that an issue or event is best addressed when seen from more than one side, that it will further the characters and the story. How will each character show a different side of the event?

Novels in multiple voices offer challenges to readers, and obstacles to writers. But when the form, characters, and story come together, and when the voices are all engaging and truly well developed, the multiple-voice novel can be among the most satisfying of books to read and to write.

Life as Story, Story as Life: Short Stories for Ages 6 to 12

By Paula Morrow

Joan Didion said, "We tell ourselves stories in order to live." From cavemen scratching on rock walls to the epic poets of ancient civilizations, from Chaucer's pilgrims on their way toward Canterbury to the guests on Jerry Springer or Dr. Phil, every human being is born with an urge to tell his or her story. Putting our experiences into words is how we ponder and make sense out of those experiences.

Listening to or reading stories widens our world and lets us share vicariously in adventures beyond our own experiences. This is as true for children as it is for the old man telling his grandchildren and great-grandchildren what life was like when he was a boy. Just as the grandfather's stories express his feelings for a time that was meaningful to him, the grade school student who relates a frightening event and adds, "I was so scared, I cried," is coming to grips with the emotion of fear and her own response to it. Reading a ghost story or retelling urban myths at a sleepover can meet the same psychological need.

We are all storytellers and story receivers.

Venturing Out

Children between the ages of 6 and 12 are in a special middle ground. No longer preschoolers, they are venturing into a world increasingly broader than home and preschool or child care center, yet they have not reached the independence of the teen years. Early childhood specialist, Sally Nurss, who also writes *The Well-Centered Child* newsletter, explains, "A cognitive shift occurs around age seven that enables a greater understanding of time and a better ability to organize the details of what children see and hear. They are now more able to understand others' viewpoints. Play interests involve games and fantasizing to self about being competent and adult." Children in grade school, she continues, "want to be part of a world of others their age, to be like their friends in skills, abilities, appearance."

The stories we tell and the stories we hope to sell are of different cuts of cloth.

Stories can be especially meaningful to readers in this age group, who are sorting out their own identity and place in the world. As a child gives a blow-by-blow account of his day at school or a video game he has played, he isn't just talking; he's working through and reinforcing narrative concepts such as beginning-middle-end and cause and effect. Unfortunately, the tale that so mesmerizes the ten-year-old teller may leave a listener yawning.

The stories we tell and the stories we hope to sell are of different cuts of cloth. Our daily stories tend to be ground-bound, drifting along at eye- and ear-level at best. The stories we submit to publishers have to rise above the mundane. They must soar in language and emotion and in the image-triggering recesses of our minds. This is what editors seek.

Word by Rhythmic Word

Marileta Robinson, Senior Editor at *Highlights for Children*, says, "In a good story, the writing has personality, rhythm, sensitivity, and life, but not in an intrusive way that draws attention to the author. If you have watched master storytellers, you have seen them disappear as they become the story they are telling."

Robinson touches on an essence, not only of literature, but of life: rhythm. Ursula K. Le Guin, in her excellent book, *Steering the Craft: Exercises and Discussions on Story Writing for the Lone Navigator or the Mutinous Crew* (Eighth Mountain Press), says the fiction of Virginia Woolf is "wonderful in itself and useful to anyone thinking about how to write." Le Guin quotes a letter in which Woolf said, "Style is a very simple matter; it is all rhythm. Once you get that, you can't use the wrong words. But on the other hand, here am I sitting after half the morning, crammed with ideas, and visions, and so on, and can't dislodge them, for lack of the right rhythm. Now this is very profound, what rhythm is, and goes far deeper than words. A sight, an emotion, creates this wave in the mind, long before it makes words to fit."

Ah, words. Would that they were always at our fingertips alongside the coffee and candy dispensers. Put in two quarters and a dime, get a 1.5-ounce snack of words. Well, to a writer, they may not always be at our fingertips, but they're between our ears. We just have to coax them out into the light.

Robinson notes, "In a good story, it's clear that the author has thought hard about each word. There are no words or sentences that can be taken out without diminishing the whole. And the words used are the right words, not just any old word. Mem Fox, a popular children's author from Australia, said in an interview, 'It is about the language, not just about good story. It's about where the words are put.'" ("Memorable Mem: Author and Peace Activist." August 2007. *Reading Today*, 25(1), 22.)

Deborah Vetter, Senior Contributing Editor of *Cricket*, offers an eloquent overview of what she looks for in a short story, then comments on the use of (what else?) language. "What gives me pleasure when reading or editing a short story is when I know the author has wandered his or her landscape and knows all its nooks and crannies. I want the author to share the most startling and memorable details with me so I can live in this world, too—even if it's a world of the past or a world of the imagination."

Read to Write

You've heard it before.

"For every word you write, read a thousand," lyricists Alan and Marilyn Bergman have said. Newbery-winning children's book author Linda Sue Park advises, "Read a thousand books in a genre before you try to write one." This good advice applies to short stories, too. How many have you read this year? Here are two excellent anthologies to add to your list.

➤ *Celebrate Cricket: 30 Years of Stories and Art*, edited by Marianne Carus (Cricket Books, 2003). Among the reminiscences, articles, anniversary greetings, and poems in this gladsome collection are some of the best short stories that have graced the pages of *Cricket*. Study the stories for the craftsmanship they evince, and don't overlook the authors' essays: James Cross Giblin on the need to revise until a manuscript is just right; David Wiesner on exploring inspiration; Eric Kimmel on the rewards of knowing how stories touch children's lives through generations.

➤ *But That's Another Story*, edited by Sandy Asher (Walker, 1996). Twelve stories introduce and illustrate twelve different genres, from humor to horror, from contemporary realism to time-travel fantasy. The successful and respected author of each story also provides a short essay explaining that genre. Asher has compiled two other excellent anthologies for ages eight and up:

— *DUDE! Stories and Stuff for Boys*, co-edited with David L. Harrison (Dutton, 2006).

— *On Her Way: Stories and Poems About Growing Up Girl* (Dutton, 2004).

Every library will have a different collection of short story anthologies you can browse. Pick out a few that appeal to you and take them home to study at leisure. If you like a story, figure out why. If you don't like a story, figure out why. Enjoy the process!

Note, however, that many books being sold as "short story collections" are not; they contain excerpts from novels. While some of these excerpts are fine writing, they aren't reliable models of the short story because they do not develop the characters, setting, or context, relying instead on the reader's acquaintance with the characters from the novel as a whole.

As examples, Vetter says, "What about a pair of Choctaw boys traveling by moonlight? Does the author say, 'The new moon rose,' or does she say, 'The bright moon rose as a curved slit in the sky. A star twinkled so near it seemed to sit in the moon's lap.' The latter is how Josephine Rascoe Keenan describes this particular moment in 'Ohoyo Osh Chisba: The Unknown Woman' (*Cricket,* November 2007). What about a young man stumbling down the dark, narrow streets of a medieval French town? He reaches out to steady himself. Does he say, 'The window bars were cold to the touch,' or does he say, 'The touch of cold window bars . . . startles the man like the touch of a toad'? This is Robert Louis Stevenson writing in 'The Sire de Malétroit's Door.'"

Read and ponder this line: "The first week of August hangs at the very top of summer, the top of the livelong year, like the highest seat of a ferris wheel when it pauses in its turning." It's the first line of Natalie Babbitt's *Tuck Everlasting,* and succeeds not only rhythmically, but in imagery as well. Do you remember "the man in the yellow suit" from that same book? Critics and pundits have squeezed that line and poked at it, trying to ferret out what sort of symbolism might be inherent in a yellow suit. Babbitt cleared up the matter quite concisely, saying, "For the rhythm of the phrase, I wanted a two-syllable word, and purple was out!"

Finding the Substance

Words are the foundation, of course, but any short story, just like a novel, needs structure and substance: it needs a beginning, a middle, and an end. It needs a strong and believable (and likable) main character, an age-appropriate problem for the main character to confront and resolve with his or her own wits (no adult intervention here), and it needs satisfying closure. And in every successful short story, there's an underlying value or message that the main character takes away at the end. It might be a theme of honesty, valor, compassion, friendship—it really doesn't matter. What matters is that the message is subtle. It's enough that the main character "gets it" in the end. Never, never beat a reader over the head with a moral. This is perhaps a moot point, because an editor will see to it that you don't have the opportunity.

Sometimes it's hard to separate ideas from plots, and it's hard to pin down exactly what your story is about. Ideas can bounce around and take you in many different directions. What you need is a way to sort through those ideas to come up with a plot, or a plan, for a story.

Barbara Seuling, former editor and author of more than sixty books for children, as well as *How to Write a Children's Book and Get It Published,* third edition, shares a tip for clarifying what a story is about: "I write it down in 25 words or less. That forces me to get rid of all the extraneous stuff and see my plot clearly. A plot is the road map that shows how to get where you want to go, but it is seriously bound up with cause and effect—one thing happens because of another. The 25 words reflect that relationship, showing the problem, what your hero does about it, and how it ends up.

"Example: A boy wants a dog but can't have one, so he adopts one at the animal shelter and gets to visit him every day. That's twenty-five words. Originally, I had the reason why he couldn't have a dog, but when I ran over the word limit, I cut that out. I still have the plot. It may be done in three short statements as well, but it should still be done in no more than twenty-five words. In that case it would look something like this: (1) Boy wants dog. (2) Boy can't have dog. (3) Boy gets dog."

Seuling points out that the list is devoid of detail; you can see through your story to the bare bones of your plot. "This is a lot harder than it looks," she continues. "Be patient and play with it until you get the hang of it. Practice with a familiar story like Jack and the Beanstalk or Cinderella, because they are tried and true and have to work with this exercise. In the future, you can use it on your own story to find out whether you have a plot that works or you have only an idea."

Beginnings and Endings

It's the rare author who can latch onto a word or a phrase and spontaneously write a delectable story around it. That's why the best advice is to tease your idea, outline it, feed it, stroke and pamper it until individual pieces, characters, and situations begin to emerge into a whole. Author Marion Dane Bauer in *What's Your Story? A Young Person's Guide to Writing Fiction* (Clarion) suggests "discovering the beginning in the ending." According to Bauer, "Knowing how your story will end also helps you know exactly where it must begin. That is because the ending you intend will tell you what is important for the rest of the story. It will let you know what you want your reader to pay attention to from the first line on."

The late author Mary Francis Shura apparently felt that the best ending for a story is simple and straightforward. She offered this anecdote during a cocktail party at the American Library Association convention in 1985. Her daughter called one evening and asked, "Mom, how do you end a story?" Shura replied, "You need 'Oh,' and 'Of course!'" The daughter said, "Thanks!" and hung up. She knew exactly what her mom meant: surprise followed by a sense of rightness.

What grounds a fantasy and gives even the wildest comedy staying power is heart.

Lasting Value

Christine French Clark, Editor of *Highlights for Children,* quotes the esteemed magazine's co-founder Dr. Garry Cleveland Myers, who sought stories that left a "moral residue." What is residue—besides the lint in your dryer's exhaust trap? It's what's left when the rest is gone: The dry clothes have been hung in the closet; the book has been returned to the library; the magazine is on a shelf. The residue of a story is what lingers on in the mind of the reader. But Aesop notwithstanding, it's not a good idea to state the moral. Allow your readers to discover it through the events and interactions within the story. By participating in the story, they will have more investment in the message and it's more likely to stay with them.

Bruce Coville, author of nearly a hundred children's books, was asked if there's a single element that has made his work so popular, especially with middle-grade readers. He replied, "I had to think about this for a while. My books go in a lot of directions, from wacky science fiction comedy like *My Teacher Is an Alien* (Aladdin) to some pretty serious fantasy, as in *Into the Land of the Unicorns* (Scholastic). Finally, I realized that I do think there is one thread that connects them all, something I will call, for want of a better word, *heart.* I think what grounds a fantasy and gives even the wildest comedy staying power is an underlying heart, a willingness to see the emotional truth of the characters, and

155

Short Story Checklist

➤ **Point of View**
 — appropriate for age group
 — consistent throughout manuscript
➤ **Main Character**
 — likable
 — flawed
➤ **Problem**
 — age-appropriate
 — manageable by protagonist
 — introduced early
 — clearly defined
➤ **Background Information**
 — spare but sufficient
 — introduced without interrupting or intruding
➤ **Dialogue**
 — natural
 — believable for character's age
 — purposeful to plot or character development
➤ **Behavior**
 — believable for character
 — logical from character's perspective
➤ **Show, Don't Tell**
 — scenes shown through protagonist's senses
 — transitions concise
➤ **Language**
 — age-appropriate vocabulary & sentence structure
 — appropriate to mood of story
 — verbs active
➤ **Tone**
 — respectful of reader
 — nondidactic
➤ **Resolution**
 — main character's initiative
 — learning or growth
 — applicable to readers' lives
➤ **Conclusion**
 — surprising
 — solves original problem
 — satisfying closure
➤ **Final Check**
 — grammar, spelling, mechanics
 — fact checking (even for fiction!)
 — fits chosen market's needs & guidelines

to openly and honestly express it. Walking the fine line between heart and sentimentality can be tricky, of course, and I can't claim that I always manage it perfectly myself. The guiding principal in that regard is to go for the truth of the character, not in order to manipulate the reader's emotions, but to honestly express where the character is."

Coville gives an example from his work: "In *Jeremy Thatcher, Dragon Hatcher* (Harcourt), it's the joy of having and raising a dragon that draws the reader in, but it's Jeremy's painful decision when it comes time to let the dragon go that gives the book its deeper resonance— its heart."

No Skipping

It's no secret that the best writers are voracious readers. Unfortunately, many aspiring authors echo the memorable line by Princess Buttercup in the movie *The Princess Bride*. When the hero, Wesley, rescues her in the midst of her enforced nuptials with the slimy villain, he asks whether she said "I do." She hesitates. "Well, we sort of skipped that part."

Don't skip that part. Read as much as you can. Subscribe to magazines, visit your library, ask the librarian to recommend the best of the best children's short story authors. You will discover that just like ice cream, each author offers a unique flavor, and many will leave you with rhythm and words you can savor.

It's important not to gulp. Francine Prose, who penned the bestselling book *Reading Like a Writer: A Guide for People Who Love Books and for Those Who Want to Write Them* (HarperCollins), advises,

> With so much reading ahead of you, the temptation might be to speed up. But in fact it's essential to slow down and read every word. Because one important thing that can be learned by reading slowly is the seemingly obvious but oddly underappreciated fact that language is the medium we use in much the same way a composer uses notes, the way a painter uses paint. I realize it may seem obvious, but it's surprising how easily we lose sight of the fact that words are the raw material out of which literature is crafted. (HarperCollins, 2006, p. 16)

Author, playwright, and anthologist Sandy Asher has published a variety of short story collections featuring the works of top-notch children's authors. According to Asher, "No two stories are alike. That's because no two writers are alike. Everyone sees the world in a unique way; everyone has unique tales to tell."

In the end, the crafting of a successful short story comes down to your own experiences, your own imagination, your own world view, and your own unique voice. Call upon these elements as you show your story through carefully chosen words and skillfully constructed sentences. Measure your short story manuscript against the ideal provided by Robinson: "In a good story, the beginning makes me care, the middle makes me worry, and the ending makes me sigh with satisfaction."

Read and revise, read and revise. When your story is the best it can be, send it out to travel the long but rewarding route through editor and publisher into the eager hands of middle-school readers. Your story may be just the one some child needs to help him make sense of something in his own life.

Spice Up Your Writing with Vivid Images

By Darcy Pattison

"Vivid imagery makes a story world come alive," says Stacy Whitman, Editor at Wizards of the Coast. A writer's ability to create images in readers' minds is integral to fiction—to transporting readers to new worlds, whether the stories are fantasy, realistic, historical, or any other. Imagery also enlivens nonfiction. It is the essence of poetry.

We all speak in images, from clichés (pigheaded) to colors (pea soup green) to conveying our feelings (sick with grief, over the top). Good writing intensifies or focuses human experience and understanding, and imagery is one of the strongest tools in the writing arsenal.

Broadly, imagery can be defined in two ways. One is writing that appeals to the senses with specific physical experiences that we have in common. The other involves figures of speech such as metaphor, personification, and symbolism. In either definition, imagery connects with the reader, who can picture, feel, and know with personal immediacy what is happening and who a character is. Or, they can intellectually comprehend more about the nonfiction truths being told.

Come to Your Senses

Imagery dwells in details, but when used best it reverberates through character, action, and theme. Sensory details are what a character sees, hears, feels (temperature, texture, kinesthetics), tastes, and smells. We all understand our world through the senses; fiction writers build their worlds on those fundamentals of human experience.

Tiffany Trent's *In the Serpent's Coils,* the first of a ten-book fantasy series called Hallowmere (Mirrorstone Books/Wizards of the Coast) features six girls from around the world. They come together to rescue missing schoolmates and struggle to prevent a war between the natural and supernatural worlds. Whitman, who edited the book, cites the following short scene because its vivid nature imagery sets a dreamy, magical tone while emphasizing the connection of the vampire Fey to nature:

> But then she saw a dark shimmer by the hemlocks again. The tall man turned, as though he felt her gaze. He wore shadows deeper than twilight, and, as before, she couldn't see his face. But she felt his gaze, felt it through the swift gasp of her heart, the seizure in her knees. The Captain raised his hand to her, and she saw, despite the dusk, that his hand was shiny and scarlet, as though wet with blood.

Sight is the strongest sense in this excerpt both in what the girl can see and in what is shadowed, or what she can't see. The paragraph contrasts what only can be imagined as gray: shadows, twilight, shimmer, and dusk. Then comes the sudden appearance of scarlet and the comparison to blood. Here, the sensuous imagery touches on metaphor and symbolism in a novel about life and death. Also powerful in the imagery is the kinesthetic—the gasp of her heart, the seizure in her knees, and even the instinctive sixth sense in feeling the Captain's gaze.

Alan Gratz creates a different mood in the award-winning historical fiction *Samurai Shortstop* (Dial Books). He does so through imagery that he calls "stark and direct description." In a highly emotional scene set in the nineteenth century, *Samurai Shortstop* opens as the protagonist Toyo helps his Uncle Koji perform the Japanese ritual suicide *seppuku*.

> Now Toyo sat in the damp grass outside the shrine as his uncle moved to the center of the mats. Uncle Koji's face was a mask of calm. He wore a ceremonial white kimono with brilliant red wings—the wings he usually wore only into battle. He was clean-shaven and recently bathed, and he wore his hair in a tight topknot like the samurai of old. Uncle Koji knelt on the tatami mats keeping his hands on his hips and his arms akimbo.

While Gratz's visual details are clear and precise, he also gives us the damp grass and the kinesthetics of how Uncle Koji holds his body.

Nonfiction Alive

Sensory details can be assets in nonfiction writing, but often writers must infer from given facts what it would feel like for a person to be in a particular situation. Carla McClafferty, author of the award-winning *Something Out of Nothing: Marie Curie and Radium* (Farrar, Straus and Giroux), pays careful attention to these details as she researches a topic. "I don't want the information I share to be dry and boring as if it came out of an encyclopedia. I want it to be alive with details so the reader can visualize what is happening," says McClafferty.

While researching Curie's story, McClafferty paid attention to any facts that could help create a sense of place and experience. For instance, at Curie's Polish school, officials rang a bell to warn teachers when Russian inspectors came to make sure that only Russian history and language were being taught—no Polish.

> Two long rings, two short—the dreaded warning bell cut through the classroom noise. Four schoolgirls launched into action. Forbidden Polish books and papers were gathered with speed and precision into aprons and hidden. The girls slipped silently back into their seats just before the door opened to reveal the enemy.

Readers can hear the bell ring, four times, long and short, and the intensity of the school experience becomes immediate. The aprons vividly suggest the urgent hiding required. All the images help readers understand the atmosphere in which Marie Curie was educated and

161

something about the world in which she lived, contributing to the portrait being painted of the woman and scientist Curie was to become.

As a nonfiction writer, McClafferty's use of imagery begins in the universal, but with a difference. "Some things are common to all people. Everyone knows what it feels like to be hot, cold, afraid, or hungry," she says. "As a writer you can take what is common human experience and use it to flesh out a scene. You can't make up any facts in nonfiction, but you can add details that make it read like fiction."

McClafferty's process in creating the opening scene above illustrates: "I knew that the Russian inspector was fat. But I don't say that. I mention gold-rimmed glasses perched on his round face and that he squeezed into a chair. That gives you a visual of him without saying outright that he was overweight. In my research I didn't see a sentence that said he squeezed into a chair, but I know he was overweight, and I know what kind of chairs usually fill classrooms, especially a classroom for young girls. And I've seen overweight men sit down in a chair in a child's classroom and noticed how they seem to sort of squeeze down in them, and then have trouble getting up from them. I felt it safe to say this overweight man squeezed into the chair because it's a common human experience. You get the information about this man, but in a way that seems natural to the nonfiction narrative."

Selectivity

To less sophisticated writers, it might seem that loading up on adjectives and adverbs is the way to create vivid imagery, but Gratz and McClafferty offer different advice.

McClafferty believes strong verbs and specific nouns are the core of writing. Adjectives, adverbs, and metaphors in whatever form should only be added as needed. "It's like cooking with cayenne pepper: You want to give writing some spice but you don't want to overpower the whole thing."

In magazine stories and articles, writers don't have the luxury of excess words. Katy Duffield, author of *Farmer McPeepers and His Missing Milk Cows* (Rising Moon) and articles in *Highlights for Children, AppleSeeds, Clubhouse*, and many other magazines, says, "One strong verb can replace several weak words. I concentrate on fun action words kids will enjoy. It may sound boring, but a neat exercise is to take an old manuscript and change every verb. Often, the tone changes dramatically, making the story more vivid, more accurate, and especially, more fun."

Gratz says his first drafts are overwritten. To strengthen his imagery, he next concentrates on simplifying. He illustrates with *Samurai Short-stop*. "Since seppuku is already a startlingly graphic thing, I knew that to overplay it would ruin it. I used the occasional metaphor *(his body*

> # Using imagery is like cooking with cayenne pepper: You want some spice but you don't want to overpower.

deflated like a torn rice sack) but for the most part I presented the ritual steps in almost a clinical fashion. I wanted to show the suicide in the simplest, most direct means possible."

This mantra of "simplify, simplify, simplify" extended even to the dialogue Gratz wrote between the father and son that ends the ritual suicide chapter. In the end, only five lines and twenty-three words spoken by the characters remained:

> "Did you watch carefully?" his father asked.
> "Hai," Toyo said.
> "You observed precisely how it was done?"
> "Hai, Father."
> "Good," Sotaro Shimada said to his son. "Soon you will do the same for me."

Authors make choices, selecting the right details and the right places to use images. Whitman says, "Improving imagery doesn't just mean becoming more and more observant of the sensory world around you. It also means knowing how to express that imagery. An author can even use too much imagery, muddying the intended effect."

Mel Boring, author, with Leslie Dendy, of *Guinea Pig Scientists: Bold Self-Experimenters in Science and Medicine* (Henry Holt) and other nonfiction titles, says the audience is the ultimate touchstone for the imagery. "For me, it's how the scene affects the reader, and how he or she interacts with the scene. I try to dissolve any barrier between the reader and the scene being described. I want the reader to feel as if they are acting a part in the story."

The key is to select and focus. "Get to the core of the scene," Whitman says. In the Hallowmere selection below, the first draft focused on the main character's point of view, but it wasn't working. Whitman explains, "It pulled the reader away from what Corrine saw, and too much was happening. The core of the scene, the man with the red hand lurking in the shadows, was lost. The revision picked fewer images to narrow in on, allowing those images the strength they need to evoke the mood."

Compare this original draft to see how the final version is focused:

> She could see the very edge of the hawthorn if she leaned out far enough. Ghostly light from the hedge flashed in re-sponse to the sky above. In one of the flashes, she saw a tall figure standing in front of the hawthorn, and although it was man-shaped, she had the distinct feeling that it wasn't en-tirely human. She also was quite sure it was looking at her. The being raised its hand toward her. Its outstretched palm glistened in the uncertain light.

Imagery and Character

Use of imagery doesn't come into play on the first draft for all writ-ers. Candie Moonshower, author of *The Legend of Zoey* (Delacorte), says she is a character-driven writer who tends not to begin with the senses. "I have to remind myself to not forget sensory details. My first draft is always a huge info dump. I write fast and furious, spelling out the plot for myself, a bare-bones plot often, but at least I have the story from which to hang the details. I then go back through and cut all the unnecessary verbiage. On the third draft is when I start asking questions about sensory details and also the psychology of the scene and character."

Moonshower wants to put the reader into the mind and emotions of her character. In the excerpt below, Zoey is looking for her mule, King George.

> I took off my shoes and stepped into the creek. The water
> was frigid, but that didn't stop me. I desperately wanted to
> catch King George before he ran away again. He still wore his
> bridle with the reins dangling in front, though his packs had
> disappeared . . .
>
> In answer, the mule nudged me, hard. I threw my arms
> around his broad chest and cried into his mangy coat. He
> was skinny and he stank a bit, but no animal had ever looked
> as dear to me as King George.

Moonshower explains, "I focus on showing how the mule's appearance let Zoey know that he'd been through a lot to make it back to her, so I used details such as his ribs showing, his mangy coat, and his stinky smell. I also wanted to evoke Zoey's real emotion at seeing her mule-friend again—how very much it means to her that in the midst of her topsy-turvy flight into a chaotic and frightening past, King George the mule can be counted on."

Jennifer Wingertzahn, Editor at Clarion Books, agrees that vivid writing can open up a scene and reveal character. "Showing us a scene—fleshing it out with dialogue, perspective, voice, and language—opens up characters and lets the readers see them interact firsthand. Suddenly these characters feel more real because we can hear their voices and see the drama between them for ourselves." She points to Deborah Davis, and her YA novel *Not Like You* (Clarion), as one who uses vivid writing to peel back the layers of characters. Here's an excerpt:

> It was midmorning, as our duct-taped car rattled across
> West Texas, when my grandmother Esther rose from the
> dead. Up until then, I thought we were leaving Dallas much
> the way we'd left Ashland and St. Louis and Wichita—
> aimlessly and in a hurry, a trail of broken appointments and
> head-shaking teachers behind us—with one big difference:
> Mom wasn't nursing a Texas-sized hangover.

Wingertzahn says, "These two sentences convey so much in so few words. Each detail and metaphor adds another layer to the scene—the voice, the setting, the duct-taped car, naming the different cities they've lived in—and come together to create a cohesive image. And it's done without lengthy paragraphs of description or exposition."

On the Main Narrative Path

Imagery makes scenes come alive, but it must not be a story's nerve center. "The images must not overbear the narrative, so that the images become side trips away from the narrative," Boring says. Narration ties story together, and consists of (1) scenes with information (including sensory or metaphoric images) that interprets the action of the story, and (2) transitions between scenes. Boring points to Christopher Paolini and his Inheritance trilogy. "Not only are his images sharply vivid, but the narrative transports you to a fantasy setting with scene touches and descriptions that dissolve any barrier to being transported to that fantasy."

Whitman succinctly reinforces this idea: "Vivid images are at the service of narration." She offers these examples of narration, first poorly done and then well-supported by sense images:

Clunky: Corrine felt rough hands at the back of her smock tying the laces.
Smoother: Rough hands turned Corrine and tied the laces at the back of her smock.

Clunky: Corrine felt that Mara eyed all of them, especially her, with a piercing disregard.
Smoother: Mara eyed all of them, especially Corrine, with a piercing disregard.

Shun complexity for connection in imagery for children. "I'm a big fan of purity and simplicity," says Moonshower. "If I can write imagery in such a way that it speaks to some experience a child has had—whatever that experience might be, and it could be different for each child—and that imagery is intrinsic to the scene and the characters, then I feel I've done my job. When I first started writing for children, I tried to write beautifully and lyrically, but when it is forced, it is often a lot of beautiful lyricism that says nothing to the child reader. Now I try and say it in a way that speaks to the child in me, and I hope that it speaks to other children, too."

No Cheap Theatrics, Please! Avoid Cliché and Melodrama

By Katherine Swarts

Recipes for successful fiction come in many flavors, but certain ingredients should never be allowed into the writer's pantry. Foremost among them are stick-figure characters acting in skeleton plots.

Bad enough apart, together these components are fit only for amateur stage melodramas. Add moldy metaphors and stale dialogue to produce unappetizing character types in an unsavory plot. Unless you want to write a hackneyed, maudlin, or just plain unbelievable story that editors have tasted countless times, toss out all such ingredients.

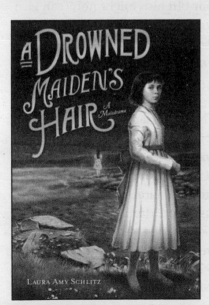

Still Surprising

But while adults may choose cornish game hen from the menu, the tastes of children run to chicken fingers with ketchup. They have limited exposure to the more elaborate—food or writing—and sometimes old standards can work well for them.

"We should be able to read drama and think, 'That could be me.' Melodrama means that we don't really believe what is happening," says Catherine Mackenzie, Children's Editor at Christian Focus Publications. Of course, "what might be a cliché in an adult book can still hold surprise when you are just learning about life and personalities. With child readers, clichéd characters are not always as clichéd as they would be in a more mature book."

Editor of Journey Stone Creations, Patricia Stirnkorb, agrees: Elements that hint of "cliché and melodrama must be used in moderation. But with children's books, authors have a wider path, since many readers are new to old clichés."

When used well, some elements of melodrama can be satisfying; that's why it has remained popular in some form for so long. "Melodrama and cliché represent poetic justice, everything tying together in the end with no questions remaining," says Mackenzie. "There is a place for that sort of literature; sometimes kids want a straightforward read with no strings attached. However, the real gems in writing are the ones that leave readers thinking things over after they leave the book behind. These are the books that get under your skin." These are the stories that become classics.

"A melodramatic happy ending is very clean-cut," Mackenzie explains. All the problems are solved, the villain will never bother the good guys again, and that's that. Fiction that is a little ambiguous, that "makes you think this might end happily but also might not," can give the story a deeper reality. Such writing creates such a powerful suspension of disbelief that the reader "almost thinks that the story goes on, that it's working itself out—happily or otherwise—in real life somewhere." A first-rate story will "take the reader out of present-day reality, but not completely."

"Good" melodrama does exist, and Melissa Manlove, Assistant Editor of the Chronicle Children's Group, offers examples. She calls *A Drowned Maiden's Hair: A Melodrama* (Candlewick), by Laura Amy Schlitz, straight melodrama. Lemony Snicket's amazingly popular A Series of Unfortunate Events (HarperCollins) mixes melodrama with humor, and Stephenie Meyer's *Twilight* (Little, Brown) is a combination of melodrama and fantasy.

Even with children's stories, however, silly plots are easy to find and clichés easy to fall prey to. Mackenzie remembers a manuscript where "two boys were in a rowboat that capsized at sea. They were rescued by dolphins and taken to dry land, only to come across smugglers on their arrival. Having two crazy things as major plot elements is taking it too far."

Where's the Plot?

Manuscripts that comprise a series of crazy events often have no central goal or theme. Melodrama is traditionally defined as having more action than character depth, with theatrical extremes and little thematic development. Writing with what is, in essence, too much plot—too much going on—ultimately bores.

> # Popular books have mixed melodrama with humor or fantasy to great success. But plot lines lifted from bestsellers are as dull as a blurred photocopy.

"A melodrama without a beginning, middle, and end—with no highs and lows—is doomed to fail," says Richard Mousseau, owner of Moose Enterprise Book and Theatre Play Publishing and publisher of Moose Hide Books. "I have received manuscripts that ramble on with no plot or conclusion."

One theory of writing holds that only so many plots exist, and that it is the way those basic story lines are used, embellished, and developed through character, theme, and language that creates originality. Some writers rely too much on traditional plot structure without adding enough extra into the plot pot. Editors increasingly complain that too many writers wrongly see the imitation of successful authors (the next J. K. Rowling, anyone?) as a sure way to bring in the money—and they lift their genres and plot lines from current bestsellers. The result is usually as dull as a blurred photocopy.

"We publish fantasy for children," says Nina Hess, Senior Editor of Mirrorstone Books, "so we get hundreds of manuscripts with wizarding schools as central settings. We also see many fantasy quests with elves, warriors, or other typical fantasy characters in medieval worlds.

Another common thread is fairy tale retellings featuring princesses or knights."

Mousseau agrees: "I'm becoming tired of fairies, little people, hobbits, underworlds, the hunt for the golden ring, witches, and sorcery. I want writers with the courage to be different, to search their imaginations for topics no one else is writing about."

"The greatest cliché we see is the overuse of popular themes," says Stirnkorb. "We receive hundreds of manuscripts each month that are take-offs on well-known stories or common plot and character elements. While we realize there are no *new* ideas, only old ones rewritten from fresh perspectives, it becomes boring to see story after story written 'just like Dr. Seuss' or 'a Chinese fable.' The world has those already! Rather than more of the same, we need new insights and themes."

Perhaps more than any other quality, *melodrama* evokes black-and-white characters and plots. The heroines are pure and innocent; the villains are devoid of any redeeming qualities; and good triumphs decisively over evil, leaving no hint of regret or of further struggles to come.

Characters should seem like real people, even if they're elves or wizards or anthropomorphized animals such as those in the classic *The Wind in the Willows*. "All characters should be multifaceted and three-dimensional," says Mackenzie. A villain who arouses no sympathy or understanding might as well be a nameless force of bad luck, and— even more—a flawless hero or heroine is boring, nearly impossible for readers to identify with.

On Its Head

To learn more about overcoming cliché and hackneyed habits, Manlove recommends reading M. T. Anderson's *Whales on Stilts* or *The Clue of the Linoleum Lederhosen* (both published by Harcourt). "Those are almost guidebooks to literary clichés. And Anderson is a genius." The books take on the stereotypes and commonplaces of series fiction, and with great humor (irony, absurdity, simple silliness) breathe new life into them and create a wholly original feel.

If you do catch yourself slipping into a cliché, or if in revision you recognize that you've walked that road, regroup. "When writing isn't going well," says Mackenzie, authors "often fall back on comfortable and non-taxing clichés at the expense of creativity. The best thing is to go back to the beginning and look at your initial outline. Get back to the foundation of your story and make sure the key elements work. Melodrama and cliché are often signs of deeper problems by a writer who hasn't thought things through and planned properly."

Even with careful planning, you may still be attracted to a well-used situation or character type and may really want to include it. In that case, concentrate on making it distinct from the ones used by other writers. "Stretch the stereotypes a little and twist the clichés a bit," suggests Mackenzie. "The most effective way to use a cliché is to turn it on its head. The reader, recognizing a character or situation, thinks he knows what is going to happen—then discovers that the author has other plans."

For Mirrorstone Books, says Hess, "Try taking just one element of fantasy—character, plot, or setting—then place it in an original, surprising, or unusual context. Once you start turning clichés on their heads, you never know what you might come up with."

"Concentrate hard on your own voice," advises Manlove.

Because one weakness of traditional melodrama is being so plot-driven that the characters are little more than props, always make sure to develop your characters thoroughly. Many fiction writers make a habit of getting to know the major figures of their stories better than readers may realize. The authors prepare a résumé or background sketch for each significant character, listing the imaginary person's family history, primary fears, nervous habits, physical idiosyncracies, even favorite foods and colors. Though few of these details make it into the published material, they help the writer see each character as a real person—and it shows in the story.

"Good melodramas aren't about sensational events," says Manlove.

"They're about people's reactions to those events. Make sure your reader can experience strong reactions through your characters."

Hess suggests, "Focus on developing multilayered characters, and give your setting a convincing twist that makes it stand out. I recently got a proposal for a fantasy quest, but instead of using the same old medieval setting, the writer had fashioned a very unusual and creative world. The characters had fascinating backstories. This is the kind of manuscript that catches my eye."

Mousseau articulates an important truth of the publishing industry: "Everyone wants to be the next famous writer." Unfortunately, few

The path to fame cannot be navigated by signs that say "Bestseller 25 Miles This Way."

understand that the path to fame cannot be navigated by signs that say "Bestseller 25 Miles This Way." Everyone has to blaze a separate trail. Aspiring authors are always "basing their stories on the same ideas and characters as current writers. New writers need to be themselves and try to be different."

If your individual talents include a gift for satire or spoof, you can use melodrama to poke fun at literary clichés themselves, especially those situations and characters you're personally sick of. Anderson's Thrilling Tales series is an example of that.

Mackenzie makes the point, "Melodrama can work effectively in comedy or farce, where the sentimental and conventional become things to laugh at. If a writer has an unconventional idea that he or she wants to draw attention to, a backdrop of ultra-conventionality may be needed."

The Bare Bones

The larger structure and characterization of fiction isn't the only place where writers can slip into the overused and pedestrian. Even if an overall story is good, clichéd phrases, images, dialogue, and other basic writing elements can surface frequently.

Most writers wouldn't consider using phrases like "a stitch in time,"

Cover Letter Cliches

Banalities may have been edited out of your manuscript, but they can still catch up with you in other writing—cover letters, proposals, or queries. Approaching editors melodramatically can scare them away before they read the first sentence of your manuscript.

Patricia Stirnkorb, Editor of Journey Stone Creations, receives many a proposal full of "overly dramatic or theatrical phrases: *the greatest, the most important, the best ever, inspired by God.*" The last phrase is the bane of virtually every religious and inspirational publisher. It is no exaggeration to say that letters come in professing, "This book has been inspired by God and I know that you will be excited [or, worse, honored] to publish it."

It's a paradox. Those who write such words claim greatness, when what they are saying is commonplace. In addition, such claims don't reflect the qualities associated with religion at its best—humility, patience, and respect for others. If you're a firm believer in divine inspiration, consider the following statements from Jerry B. Jenkins, co-author of the blockbuster Christian apocalyptic Left Behind series:

> The words you choose, regardless of how completely you have surrendered yourself and your work to God, are not sacred. . . . An inside joke among editors in inspirational publishing is that God is the worst literary agent ever. . . . I never think of submitting a piece of writing that I think I can still improve upon. (*Writing for the Soul: Instruction and Advice from an Extraordinary Writing Life.* Writer's Digest Books, 2006.)

That comes from a man who takes his faith seriously—and who has been writing for more than 30 years; has authored or coauthored more than 150 books, including several bestsellers; and teaches writing professionally. Don't brush aside his advice until you can claim equal experience.

Stirnkorb paraphrases another cover letter cliché that smacks of melodramatic arrogance: "Although you don't generally do this type of fiction, this book is so well done that you will love every word in it." That remark is an equal-opportunity offender; virtually every editor in every genre hears it far too regularly, and virtually every one is frustrated, if not infuriated, by it.

The writers who do their publishing research thoroughly, who have true professional understanding and courtesy, and who know better than to expect special consideration before they have even been published, simply would not be so rudely melodramatic.

"flat as a pancake," and "don't count your chickens before they hatch" anymore. Such aphorisms were fresh and colorful when first used, decades or even centuries ago. They were so good that everyone repeated them until they mutated into pandemics of dull reading. That writers still catch the virus is evident in the quip, "Avoid clichés like the plague," which has itself been used to the point of clichéhood. Recognize too that many turns of speech and ideas that have a more modern provenance have quickly become clichés.

"We receive many manuscripts filled with overused, worn-out adverbs and adjectives," says Stirnkorb. "There is an abundance of difference between 'Caroline asked her teacher the same question a thousand times' and 'Caroline's question to the teacher was so well-known that the students mouthed the words in unison as she asked it.' Exaggeration is a wonderful way to emphasize a particular event, phrase, or character—when used correctly, with outstanding and creative words. The verbal outcome should surprise and delight readers. When the same words are used again and again, it just gives people a chance to nap. So get creative; be original; use the thesaurus. In fact, get several word books so you can learn to use new words in different settings."

"Going overboard with clichés, trying to hold a story together with a single spoof or exaggeration, and repeating things over and over again" does nothing for a story, says Mousseau, or for gaining "the approval of the reader. Show restraint. Tease, if necessary, but do not offend the reader's intelligence."

Stirnkorb advises, "Don't always pick the same phrases when you describe a character." Don't be flat in your descriptions, either: "His nose is big" isn't as effective as "He should have received a prize for the most humongous nose known to man." Stretch! Use comedy when possible, and engage the reader. A writer is a wordsmith. Keep learning your craft.

What applies to narrative also applies to the dialogue. Let your characters speak realistically, but don't overload their talk with worn-out clichés (unless that's an important part of establishing a character's personality—and even then, don't let monotony dominate). Be extra careful with newly coined clichés—aka slang. "The current fashionable lingo does not make for good writing," says Mousseau. "Words are important, and should not be reduced to gibberish." Besides, overuse of "the current fashionable lingo" often means that interest in your work will be as fleeting as the fad.

A Real Life Happy Ending

Clichés tend to go with other weak writing. New writers may tell instead of show or rely more on plot than integrating character or paying attention to theme. But even well-published writers need to be self-aware and avoid the well-worn grooves of past writing. "Generally, other problems raise their heads before melodrama and cliché," says Mackenzie. Read good books and stories; study prizewinners and best-sellers. All good writers learn much by absorption. But do not copy or even echo, except with your own real, fresh, and well-crafted voice.

Chances are, once you start reading, you'll find that many writers have broken one or more of the principles discussed here and used a cliché or a melodramatic element and still succeeded. Don't use these principles as excuses. Do let them encourage you to be original, even when your instinct urges you to try something usually associated with melodrama or cliché.

"Do something well," says Manlove, "and it won't matter how many times it's been done badly."

In Transition

By Leslie J. Wyatt

A story you're reading is unfolding through a scene firmly planted in the here and now. The next thing you know, the characters have apparently leapt backward or forward in time. Just how that happened is pretty hazy, and how the next scene connects has you wondering if you blinked and missed some vital information. Or perhaps you're reading a science article and in one paragraph the author is talking about swimming with sharks and in the next, curiously, you think, is swinging with baboons.

Maybe what you missed was a good transition. Though not as visible an element of writing as characterization nor as exciting as plot, transitions have an important part to play. "Good, smooth, logical transitions are an inherent part of good writing when considered as a whole," says Greg Leitich Smith, author of *Ninjas, Piranhas, and Galileo* and *Tofu and T. rex* (Little, Brown).

Sue Alexander, author of more than two dozen books, provides a basic definition: "Transitions are connectors that lead from one thing to another in a logical manner." Whether a couple of words or several

177

Transitional Words & Phrases

➤ **Addition:** additionally, also, again, and, and/or, another, as well as, besides, both...and, coupled with, equally, first...second, etc., finally, further, furthermore, in addition, in the second place, likewise, moreover, not only, similarly, together with, too

➤ **Cause and effect, consequence:** accordingly, as a result, consequently, for this reason, for this purpose, hence, otherwise, so then, subsequently, therefore, thus, thereupon, to this end, wherefore, with this in mind, therefore, thus

➤ **Contrast and comparison:** after all, although, at the same time, but, by comparison, by the same token, by the way, compared to, comparatively, contrarily, conversely, correspondingly, despite, however, incidentally, in contrast, in spite of, instead, likewise, nevertheless, notwithstanding, on one hand, on the other hand, on the contrary, rather, similarly, still, up against, vis à vis, whereas, yet

➤ **Emphasis:** above all, again, also, besides, certainly, chiefly, especially, furthermore, indeed, in fact, in truth, particularly, of course, really, singularly, specifically, surely, with attention to

➤ **Exception:** although, aside from, at any rate, barring, besides, despite, even though, except, excepting, excluding, exclusive of, granted that, in spite of, maybe, nonetheless, other than, outside of, perhaps, save, sometimes, still, yet

➤ **Generalization or summary:** accordingly, after all, all in all, all things considered, as a result, as a rule, as usual, because, briefly, by and large, consequently, finally, for the most part, due to, for this reason, generally,

sentences, transitions move your work along. They link what has gone before to what is still unfolding, and cue the reader that new information is forthcoming.

In nonfiction, transitions move primarily from thought to thought and bolster an argument or help structure the information conveyed. In fiction, that logical movement is also present with the added task of supporting the believability of an imagined world. Vicki Grove, author of *Rhiannon* (Putnam), puts it this way: Fictional "transitions keep the dream you're creating in the reader's mind continuous, with no breaks opening the curtain to show that is all done with smoke and mirrors."

Transitional Words & Phrases

generally speaking, hence, in any case, in any event, in brief, in conclusion, in short, in the final analysis, in the long run, in other words, in summary, on balance, on the whole, ordinarily, so, to summarize, to sum up, usually, therefore, then, thus

➢ **Illustration:** as an example, as an illustration, chiefly, especially, for example, for instance, for one thing, illustrated by, in detail, including, in particular, markedly, namely, in this case, particularly, specifically, such as, thus, to explain, to illustrate

➢ **Reiteration:** in essence, in other words, namely, that is, that is to say, in short, in brief, to put it differently

➢ **Spatial:** above, alongside, along the edge, around, at the back/front, at the left/right/top/bottom, at the top, behind, below, beneath, beside, beyond, close, far, here, in the center, in the forefront, in the foreground, in the distance, in front of, in the front/back, near, nearby, on the side, on top, opposite, out of sight, over, near, nearby, nearly, next to, straight ahead, surrounding, there, under, within sight, out of sight, across, under, nearer, adjacent, in the background

➢ **Time:** after, afterward, at first, at the same time, first of all, before, to begin with, concurrently, currently, earlier, for the time being, formerly, for now, immediately, in the first place, in the meantime, in the morning/afternoon/evening, in the spring/autumn/etc., in time, in turn, later, meanwhile, next, the next step, once, on Monday/Tuesday/etc., rarely, simultaneously, soon, subsequently, then, while

Anchorage

Whether the metaphor is smoke and mirrors or verbal tinker toys, connections are made from sentence to sentence, paragraph to paragraph, scene to scene, and in books, chapter to chapter. Terry Davis, author of *Vision Quest* (Delacorte) and *Mysterious Ways* (Viking), explains that transitions connecting paragraphs are tighter than those connecting scenes, and "transitions exist between sentences, too. Although these are usually more subtle, they're vital to coherence."

Transitions keep readers firmly anchored by providing that coherence, and continuity. They express relationships in time (first this happened, then that) or between ideas (logic, thoughts, purpose), or between

179

Simple Mechanisms of Transition

➤ **Pronouns:** The most common transitions are those in which a pronoun of some form refers to a preceding noun. *Personal pronouns* are I, me, you, he, she, it, him, her, we, they, me, us, and them. *Possessive pronouns* are my, mine, yours, his, hers, its, ours, and theirs. *Demonstrative pronouns* are this, that, these, and those.

- The forest is primeval. It is full of ancient pines.
- Daffodils have multiplied everywhere. What a delight to see them.
- Shelties come in various colors. These include sable, tricolor, and blue merle.

➤ **Adverbs:** Adverbs can act conjunctively to transition between ideas. They join independent clauses, or lead from one complete sentence to another. Among these are: *accordingly, also, anyway, besides, certainly, consequently, finally, furthermore, hence, however, incidentally, indeed, instead, likewise, meanwhile, moreover, nevertheless, next, now, otherwise, so, still, then, thereafter, therefore, thus.*

- Fiction and nonfiction transitions are the same in principle. In nonfiction, however, they may be more formalized.

➤ **Repetition:** A mirroring or repetition of words or phrases also connects sentences, paragraphs, and potentially even chapters.

- Mark Twain was known for mischief throughout his sickly childhood. Mischief became the stuff of *Tom Sawyer.*

➤ **Synonyms:** The thesaurus is arguably a writer's best friend, and in no small means when it comes to continuity without boredom. Too many uses of the same words in transitions can make the writing staccato and dull. Look for alternative words—though don't end up sounding like the thesaurus either. Select the right words and use them well.

- The pharaohs were Mike's favorite subject in school. He imagined himself living as one of the great Egyptian kings.

people, places, things, or events. The connection may take the form of similarity, contrast, addition or deletion, summary, temporal or spatial change, examples or exceptions, echoes or recapitulations, intensification, logical proof, disputes or concessions.

Some transitions are made through expressly connective words or phrases: *in addition, however, meanwhile, similarly, at the same time, instead.* Pronouns, possessive pronouns, demonstrative pronouns, adjectives, adverbs, and synonyms and antonyms can all be mechanisms of transition, as can repetition.

> # Transitions are like the small but essential parts of an engine. If missing or not working well, you won't get very far down the road.

These methods of moving forward operate on the micro scale of sentences, but they build toward macro transitions. In fiction in particular, an entire paragraph can move a story forward by providing essential information at a different pace.

Greater Movement

Transitions are like the small but essential parts of an engine: If they're missing or not working well, you won't get very far down the road. Besides preventing "reader whiplash as you leap to the next scene," says author Sue Bradford Edwards, transitions "keep the reader reading by compressing lengthy narrative passages that are unimportant to the story into brief transitional passages. Instead of detailing a walk to school, I might simply write, 'When he reached school, he ran through the door and to Mrs. B's classroom.' Unless it is important to the story, the reader doesn't need to know that a character crossed three streets, said hello to the crossing guard, and narrowly dodged a piece of gum on the sidewalk."

Grove offers this perspective: "I probably don't recognize a difference in the transitions used in different parts of the structure within a story or book. I would classify differences by what you're trying to accomplish with a transition." Are you moving from one event to another? Maybe the setting changes, or you need to show the passage of time. Sometimes that may be as simple as using the phrase *three days later.* "Because you're presenting time as a continuum, as it is in real life, you have to make the reader perceive that three days have actually passed, but you have to do it quickly," Grove says. She gives this example:

> It rained so much that weekend that I stayed inside, bored to tears, mostly helping my little brother Charlie with one of his humongous puzzles. On Monday I just kind of moped around, doing all the junk my mother makes me do on school holidays, dusting and stuff. I went to bed that night nearly sick with nerves because it was suddenly almost Tuesday, the day of Staci's party.

Just how fundamental to the reading experience transitions are is expressed in printing conventions—like indents for new paragraphs and new pages for chapters. "The transitions connecting paragraphs or scenes are meant to make the reading logical and smooth; the transitions between chapters have a very specified purpose—to lead the reader to go on to the next chapter," Alexander says.

Leitich Smith explains, "A paragraph-to-paragraph transition needs to refer more closely to what's gone before. Indeed, the reader expects it because it isn't as dramatic as a scene or chapter transition, which usually involves a change of page or other printer's marking denoting the change."

Chapter stops and shifts might seem more definitive, but Edwards says, "Transitions between chapters can be tricky." Most readers don't read a book cover to cover in one sitting, and chapter breaks are an obvious place to pause. It may be hours or days before they open the book again. "You need to make it clear from the first line of the chapter where you are, when you are, and what the characters are doing."

With chapters in particular, strong transitions are formed by making use of foreshadowing and echoing. As one section ends, the final sentence or sentences foreshadow the next.

Time Transitions

Whether a writer hones transitions during initial writing or in the revision and polishing stages, transitioning brings certain challenges. One of these is transitions of time. Chapter breaks naturally lend themselves to time changes, but author Sue Alexander notes that "within any given chapter" the passage of time "can be a thorny problem."

One way of handling this is to condense the timeframe of your story into as short a period as possible. Readers have less of a tendency to lose track of time if the action takes place over a two-week period, for example, or during summer vacation. That way, transitions can be "short, sweet, and unobtrusive," says Alexander.

But sometimes the scope of a story is much broader than a week or a month. The judicious use of flashbacks can be a solution. Yet of all transitions involving time, flashbacks can be the most fraught with risk. "I try to avoid flashbacks if I can, because coming out of a flashback will always involve an especially treacherous transition," author Vicki Grove says, quoting advice she received from a respected editor. "For me, a story strung over months and months with lots of flashbacks is going to be a transition nightmare, period."

Grove uses a chronological outline created at some point during her novel, usually after the book has gained some momentum. "I make a timeline—Monday morning, Monday afternoon, Monday night, Tuesday morning, etc. I leave a few lines after each of these and jot down what will happen. Most writers I know have written a book or two where they got 'lost in space,' forgetting which day it was in the book, or even which week. It seems easier to figure out smooth time transitions when you absolutely have to put something in each blank, account for each little section of time the protagonist is experiencing."

Nonfiction Bridges

Whether you're writing fiction or nonfiction, each paragraph has its own center—a topic, theme, point to make, or other purpose. While holding to that center and its own integrity, a paragraph should interlock with the next and pull the reader along on a clear train of thought. That next paragraph may provide a related topic, or expand, or contrast, and so on.

Alexander thinks the connections made in nonfiction and fiction are much the same in principle, since they do the same job. "However," she says, "in nonfiction, sometimes you need a different sort of transition—one that leads the reader to a new topic smoothly."

Nonfiction often contains more formal transitions that function much like bridges, leading readers into the next topic while remaining connected to what has gone before, according to Leitich Smith. "While the nonfiction writer usually has a narrative, he's also often trying to drive the reader to a particular conclusion. Also, paragraphs tend to be longer, so there is more room, if you will, for transitions."

Davis agrees: "Transitions in exposition or even personal narrative, and certainly biography, are nearly always more formalized than in fiction." He calls a transitional word such as *moreover* "almost elegant in its simplicity and connection to rhetoric throughout history."

Fiction has a greater proportion of action than nonfiction, explains Leitich-Smith, which makes some difference in how transitions and forward movement take place. A series of actions in a fictional narrative takes on a life of its own and may not need formal transitions. In nonfiction, if passages move by logical cause and effect, fewer transitions may be needed other than the paragraph breaks.

Edwards says, "I don't think that the differences between well-written fiction and well-written nonfiction are as great as many writers assume. Clear poetic writing is just that, whether it is fiction or nonfiction. That said, many writers are tempted to do an information dump when writing nonfiction rather than writing skillful transitions. We don't need every detail! Give us what's interesting and then compress the rest so that the article or chapter keeps moving forward."

Processing

As important as transitions are, perhaps they deserve a high level of attention as we write. Not necessarily. Some writers don't specifically consider them when writing a first draft. Alexander says she doesn't "at all—unless I get to one that isn't working. That can get me stuck for days!" In her first drafts of fiction, says Edwards, "I generally leave transitions out completely. When I finish a scene, I simply enter several blank lines and then go on to the next scene. It is generally as I rewrite that I create transitions."

Other writers are very aware of connections from the beginning. They spend time creating segues that are neither wordy nor confused, that move the discussion or the story from one topic, time, or place to the next without slowing the pace. "I'm acutely aware of transitions when I write anything," says Davis. "I want to be subtle—not call attention to myself as the writer—but I want to be clear in the transition. I don't want to subtle myself out of clarity."

Another pitfall to avoid is wordiness. "You have to balance carefully the need for information with the temptation to go on for too long. Duck in, duck out, and get the job done. As with writing in general, it is a matter of balance, and practice makes perfect," says Edwards.

Grove agrees. "I have to say I think I've gotten better at transitioning, from long practice. I used to overwrite transitions, and my book editor at Putnam would cross out whole paragraphs that she said were overkill. I trust myself more now to pick a few good details or a snappy sentence or two of dialogue to paint the required small scene that should move a reader in a very few words from action point to action point. For instance, I wanted Carly, my protagonist in *Reaching Dustin* (Putnam), to go from a nerve-wracking school scene to a scene where she talks privately with her brother some hours later. After trying a few overloaded and cumbersome paragraphs, I ended up with, simply: "'What did you creepy sixth graders do to Dustin Groat today?' Noah asked as we started our chores in the barnyard that evening.'"

Less is more applies here, and that *less* should be interesting and intentional. Long, rambling transitional sections are somewhat like taking a greyhound bus cross-country—they stop at every little doghouse and gas station along the way. You do eventually reach your destination but, whew, it takes a lot of effort. Tight and specific transitions make the journey more like a plane ride: They allow the reader to reach the next scene with ease and enough energy to keep reading. Akin to convoluted transitioning is a tendency to reiterate, just in case we didn't make it clear enough the first time. If the transition needs to be restated for clarification, perhaps the passage needs tightening instead.

Davis has this to say about weak transitions: "The greatest pitfall—aside from being clumsy—is to call attention to the writing. Fiction is about the story you're telling; nonfiction is about the argument you're making or the subject you're writing about. You never want the writing to call attention to you."

A String of Pearls

The universal advice to read widely in good writing, to read your own writing aloud as part of your process, and to let your work sit and then come back to it is highly applicable for improving transitions.

Davis advises "reading fine work and reading it so hard it yields the secrets of its fineness in the area of transitions or any other aspect of composition."

Leitich Smith echoes this advice. "Read, read, read. Read so you can develop an ear for what works and what doesn't." He also advises reading your work out loud. "You'll often catch a bad flow that you gloss over when reading to yourself." And finally, "Work on writing as a whole." He points out that he's never heard anyone comment that a book was terrible, but its transitions were awesome.

Let your writing cool at least a day, or even a week or more if possible, Edwards advises. "When it is no longer in the forefront of your mind, you will read it with a fresh eye. You will see places that you have used transitions where they are not necessary because the step from point A to point B is so obvious as to need no explanation. You will also be able to spot the places where you have left the reader glancing from side-to-side thinking, 'How in the world did I end up here?'"

How indeed? Whether between paragraphs, scenes, or chapters, in fiction or nonfiction, transitions—like the almost invisible string of a pearl necklace—are essential in good writing. With some careful attention, avoiding wordiness and a tendency to reiterate, they can function as they are meant to. Sometimes you want sharp transitions, dramatic breaks. Sometimes a clearly visible and logical progression, step by step, strengthens a work. Sometimes your writing calls for invisible movement, flowing seamlessly from one topic to another, leading readers straight to an ending that satisfies.

Cooking Up a Theme

By Virginia Castleman

It has been called the thread that runs through a story, the harmony, the glue that holds writing together. Theme is one of the five main elements of story and it is a consideration for editors acquiring manuscripts. Yet some editors, agents, and writers are hardpressed to define theme clearly.

Picture for a moment a stove with five elements on it, each with a label: *character* at the center and around it, *plot, theme, setting*, and *point of view*. Each element can be adjusted to a different heat, but all together they cook the meal.

Revelation

Authors Judith Ross Enderle and Stephanie Jacob Gordon, who sometimes write under the pseudonym Jeffie Ross Gordon, say that among those elements, character ranks first, but theme is what you leave the reader with.

"What a character does drives the plot," says Enderle. "Authors should know their characters as well as they know themselves. Plot ranks next because it's what happens in your story. Your main character and the conflicts that surround him or her drive the plot. Setting grounds the characters, and the setting can even be a kind of character in itself. An interesting exercise is to take a favorite story and think of different places to set it. Point of view is important, especially for younger readers, where a single viewpoint helps the reader stay right inside the main character."

Character often drives theme, even if theme precedes a full-bodied character. "Sometimes the character reveals the theme to you," Enderle points out. "Most likely, the theme of your story was in your subconscious all the time, but you didn't see it at first. It helps, however, if you know ahead of time what you want to say." Theme, she continues, "will take care of itself if you know what you want to say to your readers before you start writing. It can come out of how your character acts, reacts, and solves the problem or reaches the goal of the story."

"The trick," Enderle and Gordon explain, "is not to hit the readers over the head with your message, but to keep it part of the plot shown through the action and reaction or growth of your main character."

Their books provide examples. "While *Two Badd Babies*, illustrated by Chris L. Demarest (Boyds Mills), is about twins who travel around town in their crib when they are supposed to be napping, the underlying theme is sharing. Though it's not quite as visible, we treat the same theme in *Hide-and-Seek Turkeys*, illustrated by Teresa Murfin (McElderry), when ten turkeys try to escape a fox and find the perfect hiding place. This book contains other threads, though not true themes; it's a counting book and also introduces colonial clothing. Our short chapter book, *Will Third Grade Ever End?* (Scholastic) deals with being the new kid in school with the theme of what it means to be a friend and make a friend." Their newest title together, *Smile, Principessa!,* illustrated by Serena Curmi (McElderry Books), "shows the struggle Principessa faces when she has to share her world, and especially the photos Papa takes, with a new baby brother."

Tracey Adams, of Adams Literary, agrees about the meeting points of theme and character. "As an agent, I can't think of a theme I wouldn't care to read about, as long as it's meant for children's books. But for me, theme falls somewhere in the middle of the five story elements. When I love a manuscript, it's most often because I've fallen for the characters. If the characters are real to me and I care about them, I become invested in their stories and whatever themes surround the work."

Discovery

Adams has seen writers work with theme in different ways. "Some of the authors I represent begin a manuscript with a theme, an idea, and then create characters around that. Others have a character in mind from the start. They know that character very well, and want to tell her story. That theme will develop with the plot."

Suzanne Williams, author of historical and multicultural nonfiction and regional advisor for the Sierra Nevada chapter of the Society of Children's Book Writers and Illustrators (SCBWI), says that sometimes themes must evolve.

"Nonfiction books begin with a subject but, when I work, themes only appear after doing the research. For example, in *Made in China, Ideas and Inventions from Ancient China* (Pacific View Press), the major theme became how inventions changed history and how changes led to more inventions. I had to do a lot of reading before I realized that this was the idea that excited me about Chinese inventions."

Williams says, "In a nonfiction book, a theme moves the book from a collection of facts that might simply be a report to a book that grabs your attention and gives you something broader to think about. A strong theme helps to organize your book, too. I know some authors keep theme in mind from the beginning of their writing. My process is more one of discovery. The day I find the real theme is the day I can't stop writing."

The theme that emerges can sometimes surprise her, Williams says. "When I wrote *The Inuit* (Franklin Watts), I expected the main theme might be about people creating a culture in an extreme climate. There is plenty of that threading through the book, but after spending time with Inuit and southern people in the Canadian Arctic, I knew that the other strong theme had to be how people cope, change, and respond when two very different cultures (traditional Inuit and European/North American) meet."

Themes often have a universal appeal, but at the same time some seem to speak to young readers in a given culture at a given time. As an

agent, Adams always looks for timeless themes. "When I think of my favorite books from childhood, it's those same themes that speak to children today: family, friends, siblings. These classic themes can help a book stay in print longer, since children will always identify with the characters' issues."

Samantha McFerrin, Editor of Harcourt Children's Division, says, "Though I look more for a strong voice, character, and plot, there are some themes that interest me, such as family, siblings, adventure, friendship, love, mystery, and different cultures. The more universal the theme, the better." As examples, McFerrin says, "Tony Johnston's picture book *The Worm Family*, illustrated by Stacy Innerst, has strong family and self-love themes. Harcourt released a restored edition of *The Hundred Dresses*, by Eleanor Estes and illustrated by Louis Slobodkin, and it has a wonderful friendship theme. And one of my favorites, *A Northern Light*, by Jennifer Donnelly, explores themes of romance and history."

Penguin Editor Susan Kochan is not drawn to moody or precious manuscripts, but says, "I am interested in tension-filled themes of childhood that are approached in unique ways with strong characterization —sibling rivalry, moving, first day of school, fights between friends, cheating, lying, bullies, and group dynamics." Of the books she's edited, Kochan says, "*The Whispering Road*, by Livi Michael, is a fantastic survival story. *Cowboy José*, written by Susan Middleton Elya and illustrated by Tim Raglin, about the importance of friendship, and *Where I Want to Be*, by Adele Griffin, dealing with a sibling's death, reflect strong themes."

Other editors, like Jennifer Weiss of Simon & Schuster, say themes aren't that important. "I'm looking for edgy, contemporary young adult. But really, I'm looking for strong writing—voices that ring true. I'm looking to discover the next Jacqueline Woodson or Chris Lynch."

The Measuring Cup Method

At writers' conferences, editors often ask writers to give them one word, or at the most one sentence, to tell what their stories are about. One way to do this is to define the theme of your story or book by the measuring cup method. Let's say your story focuses on one strong character, has plenty of spellbinding action (plot), a clear point of view, and a sense of place (setting), but you're not sure how to put into one word or phase what the story is about (theme). Draw a measuring cup and fill the cup with words that describe qualities of the protagonist or the main concepts of your story. When you're done drawing, figuratively swirl the measuring cup. Picture opening the cup at the bottom, knowing only one word can spill out onto the plate. What will that word be?

The following example is based on a story written for *Highlights for Children*.

Story Title: "Rabbit and Tiger"
➤ *Character qualities:* passionate, scared, insecure, fearful, sensitive, confident, daring
➤ *Story concepts:* bravery, heroism
➤ *Theme:* Courage

Here's how the theme was then incorporated into the opening paragraph of a cover letter:

> Dear Editor:
>   "Rabbit and Tiger" is an 800-word story about a courageous rabbit that outsmarts the king of the jungle and wins the admiration of all the other jungle animals.

Look at all the elements that this sentence contains: character (rabbit), plot (outsmarts tiger/wins admiration), theme (courage or bravery), setting (jungle), and point of view (rabbit). One word says the theme. One sentence says it all.

Next time you're struggling to define what your story's really about, get the elements ready, take out the measuring cup, and see what themes you can cook up.

Messages, Subtexts, Insights

Theme can be much closer to the surface in magazine writing, since quite a few children's publications operate with theme lists as the basis of their editorial calendars. A designated theme can be very helpful in developing stories, though the lists are perhaps more accurately seen as subject lists than as directives for a particular idea or orientation in composition. Each of the pieces written on the designated subject should have its own well-developed internal theme.

Marileta Robinson, Senior Editor at *Highlights for Children,* says, "*Highlights* doesn't have monthly themes. We do use seasonal and holiday material, which we accept any time of the year. I view theme more as an underlying idea, rather than as a topic. Any well-written story has a theme, an underlying idea of some kind. This is not the same as a moral, which spells out the lesson of a story and detracts from the story's appeal to kids and editors."

Enderle's perspective differs a little: "Theme is the substance of your story; some might define it as the message or moral. It's what you want to leave with the reader when the book has been read. Some themes can be expressed as adages: Be careful what you wish for, a stitch in time, too many cooks spoil the broth. Theme should be the subtext, not the upper level of your story." Williams says, "If I had to narrow theme down to one word, the word would be insight."

Robinson thinks story qualities are inseparable. "I don't think you can separate story elements. If the theme is overcoming fear, for example, you need a character who has a fear to overcome and a plot that allows her to overcome it." As for differences between them in magazine stories and books, Robinson says, "It depends. I think a novel may have a major theme that relates to the larger story and minor themes that relate to individual characters' subplots. A novel's theme may be weightier than a short story's theme because of its larger scope."

"Don't let theme drive you crazy," Enderle and Gordon caution. "Write the strongest story you can. Trust yourself as an author. But when you hunker down to revise, you'd better be able to identify the theme. If it's missing, your story won't have enough depth." Enderle names *The Recess Queen,* by Alexis O'Neill (Scholastic); *Max and Felix,* by Larry Dane Brimner (Boyds Mills); *Bloody Jack,* by L. A. Meyer (Harcourt); and *Escaping Tornado Season,* by Julie Williams (Harper-Teen), as notable books with strong themes.

"We like to think of theme as the chocolate filling hidden inside the cupcake," Enderle concludes. "Sometimes you don't know it's there until you've taken a big bite."

The Light Dawned: Improve Your Character Epiphanies

By Darcy Pattison

"And then, it suddenly dawned on her."

That phrase is the ultimate cliché for a character epiphany. *Epiphany* literally refers to the physical manifestation of a deity, but in fiction it has come to mean the point at which a character recognizes a truth, coming to learn or understand something.

"The epiphany is the moment of self-realization; it's when the character's change and growth hits him or her, even if the character doesn't fully understand it," says Elaine Marie Alphin, author of fiction from early readers to young adult novels, and several nonfiction books.

Alphin looks to her novel *The Perfect Shot* (Carolrhoda) for an example. "Brian is a high school basketball player who has always believed what you do on the court, you do in life. However, as he approaches a major game he knows he's hiding important information in a murder investigation, information that could save an innocent man's life. He's been threatened to stay silent, but as he goes into the game he doesn't feel good about himself, and his play on the court reflects his confusion." In this excerpt from the half time scene, Brian refers to Amanda, his former girlfriend, who is also one of the murder victims:

> But I don't buy it—because when we play like a team,
> when we're there for each other, we're unstoppable.
> As I say the words, I know what I'm going to do. I'm not
> living scared of that flat, dead voice forever, thinking I don't

stand a chance against [the murderer]. I'm going to be there for Amanda, not keep her from getting justice by keeping my mouth shut . . . . I'm going to talk to [that reporter]. . . . Knowing the decision is made, and it's right, I know I'm going to lead the Warriors back onto that court looking like a different team.

Brian's realization that he can't live in fear is the epiphany that puts him on the path toward catching the murderer.

Epiphany Versus Climax

An epiphany may seem like the high point of a story, but it is not synonymous with the climax. Janni Simner, author of the middle-grade novel *Secret of the Three Treasures* (Holiday House), says, "I tend to think of the epiphany as part of the character's internal arc, while I think of the climax as external—even though, of course, internal and external arcs really tend to be intertwined in various ways."

The epiphany demonstrates the growth that a character experiences as a result of story actions. Structurally in a narrative, this means that the epiphany is near the climax since the internal and external arcs usually coincide. In practice, though, stories have variations.

Simner uses Madeleine L'Engle's classic *A Wrinkle in Time* (Farrar, Straus and Giroux) as an example of a book in which the epiphany and climax happen together. "On Camazots, Meg Murry realizes that 'like and equal are not the same thing,'" says Simner, "and that it's okay for people to be different from one another. This is the point where she believes it, and that belief and acceptance allow her to love and accept —and rescue—her brother Charles Wallace."

Sometimes, the epiphany precedes and causes the climax. In Mary E.

Pearson's *A Room on Lorelei Street* (Henry Holt), Zoe has been trying to separate herself from her family and their troubles. But in a tight spot for money, she spends time at a local motel with a generous customer. Carlos sees her getting out of the customer's car.

> He smiles. A quick, jerky smile she hasn't seen before . . .
> "Carlos—"
> "You don't need to explain."
> She doesn't. She is floating, hovering somewhere outside herself. A hollow distance that can't be measured. Far, but as close as skin to skin. She looks at his eyes.
> She reads them.
> She recognizes them.
> They are her eyes. Her own eyes. Her own eyes looking at Mama.

Pearson says, "This is a turning point for Zoe, a realization that she is following in the very footsteps she had sought to avoid. From here a climax follows, which spawns further epiphanies, and Zoe is pushed to a final decision."

By contrast, *Secret of the Three Treasures* places the epiphany after the climax. In a climactic scene, Tiernay West has just taken her place in the world as a famous explorer, with one adventure behind her and many more ahead. But she must accept her mother as a non-adventurer. Tiernay demonstrates her acceptance by inviting her mother to have dessert with her and a fellow adventurer—a small, but important gesture that is an epiphany. Looking at her mom, Tiernay thinks:

> I wondered whether one day she would understand better about adventuring, if I was patient like Jane Grey said. Adventurers aren't good at being patient—but if T. J. Redstone could wait six months to translate a single coded missive, if Dad could wait five years for the first T. J. book to sell— maybe I could wait, too.

Simner says, "I think that's the point, very close to the end, where Tiernay decides that she can make the effort to live in a world filled with non-adventurers, at least when those non-adventurers are people who are important in other ways."

In relation to the climax, then, epiphanies can come before and trigger the climax; during, to spin it in a different direction or move it along; or after, as a grace note in the denouement.

Wider Enlightenment

While stories have high points and low points, they have a single climax. They may have multiple epiphanies, however, as one character grows and grows and has different moments of enlightenment, or the epiphanies may be experienced by more than one character.

Pearson says that Zoe's epiphany in *A Room on Lorelei Street* is followed by further epiphanies. How many epiphanies is enough? As many as your story needs. Evaluate a character's arc to see when and where it's appropriate for characters to experience a turning point or come to some realization. In fact, Pearson points out that not every main character has an epiphany. "There are exceptions, especially where the main character is an unreliable narrator. In that case, the epiphany may still occur, except that it is the reader who experiences it and not the protagonist."

In *The Perfect Shot*, the secondary character Julius realizes the importance of the team effort at the same time that Brian does. Alphin explains, "Julius, Brian's best friend, is the high-scoring, star player and also one of the few black kids in their small, white Indiana town. When he's pulled over by city policemen, he calls on Brian for help. The police encounter makes Julius bitter, turns him against everyone (even his white teammates, who used to be his closest friends), and makes him into a ball hog.

"Trust me," I tell them. "I'll be there for you the rest of the game. I trust you guys to be there for me."

They crowd around me, hands stretching into the center of our circle, gripping hard. Julius's hand comes down last, crowning the clasp.

"Team!"

Julius holds onto us for a long moment. Then he whispers, "Team."

Moments Gone Wrong

Writing about a pivotal point in a character's understanding can be tricky. It needs to be right for the character and story, integrated yet truly illuminating. Here are some common obstacles and how to hurdle them:

➤ *It suddenly dawned on her.* A sudden revelation where the experience is told rather than depicted rarely works because it doesn't allow the reader to experience the epiphany. Use action and imagery to reveal a truth, and build to that truth throughout your writing.

In my fantasy novel, *The Wayfinder* (Greenwillow), Win has traveled through the depths of grief over losing his sister, Zanna, and emerged stronger. But he has to deal with his grief one more time, as Paz Naamit, the giant eagle, flies him back over the Rift (a deep canyon) to his home.

Win rose and helped Lady Kala climb onto the broad back of the eagle. When they were both seated, the eagle gave a mighty leap. Her wings spread majestically, and they sailed out over the Rift. Far below, the shiny ribbon of water was still in deep shadow. . . . Win's right hand crept into his pocket and pulled out the white rock from Zanna's cairn. He had traveled through the depths of the Rift and fought his way to the top and across to the black sand of the Well of Life, then back across the prairie to the Rift again—and Zanna was in none of those places.

Instead she was with him and in him. . . . For as long as there were memories or words, Zanna would live. For a moment he hefted the bone white stone in his hand, then

reared back and threw it into the Rift, back into the depths
from which it had come. It fell soundlessly, and he didn't
know when or where it landed. Paz Naamit caught an up-
draft and spiraled higher and higher. Win laid a hand on
Lady Kala's warm back and turned toward G'il Rim and home.

The symbolic white rock and the giant eagle spiraling higher demonstrate that Win has moved to a higher plane of understanding.

➤ *Let me tell you the truth.* A character's moment of revelation often
demonstrates some eternal truth, but it's a mistake just to state that
truth as fact. Instead, allow the reader to follow the process of learning
or understanding. We tell stories because the actions of the story illustrate the principles. In *The Wizard of Oz,* Glinda asks Dorothy, "What
have you learned?" Dorothy doesn't simply state, "There's no place like
home." Because of everything that has happened, she feels it with all
her heart, and so does the reader.

➤ *Suddenly golden light washed over him.* Overblown language can
ruin an essential moment. Stick to solid actions, strong verbs, and concrete images. In Alphin's *The Perfect Shot,* the team finally starts working together. Brian calls to a teammate to give up the ball to Shooter,
who is in a good position to take a last shot, the shot that will determine if they win the game. What's implied here is that the winning is
not just about this particular basketball game, but about the teamwork
needed to succeed in life.

> But Julius gets the message. In the first half he would have
> forced the shot, but now he flicks the ball behind his head, a
> blind pass to Shooter. Shooter takes the pass and, in a single
> motion, shoots up into the air from just behind the three-
> point line, his arm muscles flexing as he launches the ball
> into space. The buzzer sounds as all eyes watch the ball, now
> falling back toward earth, heading for the target: a small
> round hole hovering in the space between it and the floor.
>   Swish—the perfect shot!

➤ *I haven't mentioned this before, but . . .* An epiphany has to be a natural outgrowth of the story and not tacked on. Build in cause and effect. The story's events and growth within the character should lead ultimately to the epiphany.

In Katherine Paterson's classic *Bridge to Terabithia*, the epiphany comes a few pages before the ending. Here, Jess reflects on his friendship with Leslie, who has drowned.

> He thought about it all day, how before Leslie came, he had been a nothing—a stupid, weird little kid who drew funny pictures and chased around a cow field trying to act big—trying to hide with a mob of foolish little fears running riot inside his gut.
>
> It was Leslie who had taken him from the cow pasture into Terabithia and turned him into a king. He had thought that was it. Wasn't king the best you could be? Now it occurred to him that perhaps Terabithia was like a castle where you came to be knighted. After you stayed for a while and grew strong you had to move on. . . . Now it was time for him to move out. She wasn't there, so he must go for both of them. It was up to him to pay back to the world in beauty and caring what Leslie had loaned him in vision and strength.

This epiphany sets up the last scene where Jess takes his little sister, May Belle, and introduces her as the new queen of Terabithia. Everything, including the epiphany, has led up to this poignant moment.

➤ *I'm so wonderful to understand this.* When your first-person narrator is ready to experience an epiphany, it could be tempting to make the character have a moment of self-congratulation. A true-to-life moment of understanding, one the readers can share, often should have humility. The narrator may also report on someone else's epiphany. Alphin handles this well in *The Perfect Shot*, where the narrator both has internal dialogue and demonstrates the epiphany through his actions.

➤ *I had an epiphany, didn't I?* Sometimes the epiphany is too obscure or its expression is, well, boring. Instead, carefully word the moment of personal revelation so that the reader grasps its importance and knows more about character and story. Find a path between the fireworks of overblown language and the quicksand of an understatement.

Planned Epiphanies

A single experience of illumination may not be the germ with which many stories begin, and yet epiphanies are at the heart of growth in characters and stories.

Simner rarely knows what revelations the characters may have in the planning stage of a novel. "I write the story and I listen to my characters, and usually at the crucial moment, my main character will tell me what he or she has realized. I find I can plan out other things, but epiphanies—for me—have to arise out of the writing process itself."

Pearson says the same. "Let the epiphany grow naturally out of the story." While writing *A Room on Lorelei Street,* she explains, "I realized about the same time as the main character what she needed to do in order to have her deepest need met. I didn't write toward that epiphany. It just finally all added up to the character and consequently added up to me, so it was there for me to write down."

Knowing upfront what a character will come to understand can be tricky. Alphin says, "Probably the biggest pitfall is that the writer knows what the epiphany is and what it means, but the main character is just discovering it, so the writer tends to explain beyond what the main character yet understands. Because the epiphany is so obvious to the writer, the element of stunned realization that the main character experiences tends to be underplayed and the reader is told about the significance of the epiphany instead of experiencing it along with the character."

Epiphanies are emotional high points of a character's arc. Writers who consciously carve an epiphany for maximum impact can create stories that tug at the emotions of their readers even more powerfully.

Who Said That? Using Dialogue and Idiom to Define Character

By Sue Bradford Edwards

"**D**o not write in dialect. Don't even think about it."
When you started writing for children, putting words into your characters' mouths, this was probably some of the first advice that you heard. It makes sense. Dialogue needs to move the story forward. If the reader spends too much time deciphering tricky turns of phrase, they will stop reading.

Once you're advanced in your craft, you may choose to ignore this advice because dialogue gives voice to your character, in addition to propelling your story. Debby Edwardson's Amiqqaq sounds like a boy in a modern Alaskan village in *Whale Snow* (Talewinds/Charlesbridge). Tracy Barrett's Anna leaves no doubt that she is a Byzantine princess

in *Anna of Byzantium* (Delacorte). Listen to Joyce Moyer Hostetter's Ann Fay in *Blue* (Calkins Creek) and you won't be able to picture her anywhere but in her Carolina home. In each case, where and when these characters live is critical and shapes how they speak.

"I want, in all of my books, to give the reader a strong sense of place and culture. To do this the characters must speak the way real people speak," says Edwardson. Before you can create this type of dialogue, you, as the writer, must talk the talk.

Firsthand Knowledge Pays Off

It isn't enough to know that your character must use the phrases of Warring States China or speak with an accent that could only come from Massachusetts in 1795. Before you begin to craft dialogue, you have to know the rhythms and patterns of the speech as intimately as you know your own language.

Authors do often begin with their own heritage. "My family moved to the South when I was a year old, about ten years after *Blue* would've

taken place. So from the time I learned to talk, I was in the presence of folks who spoke like the characters in *Blue*," Hostetter says. "Of course, I still hear those speech patterns around me. I didn't have to think them up. It was more like I had to listen—to stop and ask myself 'How would Ann Fay say this?' Or 'What would Junior say in response to what Ann Fay just said?' When I did that, the answer was usually nearby."

Edwardson is similarly fortunate in that she has lived in Barrow, Alaska, much of her adult life. Daily, she hears Village English. "It has grammatical characteristics that are derived from the Inupiaq language and includes the use of some Inupiaq words in place of English words and some English words that are given Inupiaq sounds and endings—like *sigaaq* for *cigarette* or *manik* for *money* or *computaaq* for *computer*," she says. The cues that Edwardson needs to write her stories are available every day.

This level of familiarity isn't necessary only for characters who are fluent in a language, but also for those communicating in a language imperfectly mastered. Three years' residence in Italy helped prepare

Kristin Wolden Nitz to write *Defending Irene* and *Saving the Griffin*, both set in Italy (and both published by Peachtree Publishers). Nitz portrays characters from the United States who are learning to speak Italian, as well as Italian characters learning to speak English. "I had a couple of advantages. First of all, I knew lots of people who spoke English as a second language. Secondly, I'm conversant in Italian. I knew which words can get mixed up in translation," she says. "For example, Italians will *take* a decision and *make* a photo instead of the other way around."

If you don't speak your character's language, serious research will be needed. Sometimes your gap in knowledge may be the result of the passage of time. Hostetter may hear Carolina English daily, but she doesn't hear the language as it was spoken in the 1940s. She performed research to correct possible errors in memory. "I listened to old radio programs and read newspapers and magazine stories of the era as well as books that were written during that time period."

The more exposure you give yourself to the language you want to duplicate the better, even if you are writing the briefest picture book. "Read letters and speeches to get a feel for speech patterns," advises Jane Yolen, who did this and more when researching *My Brothers' Flying Machine: Wilbur, Orville, and Me* (Little, Brown). Syntax, even of your own language, changes over time.

Kirby Larson did similar research for her Newbery honor title, *Hattie Big Sky* (Delacorte), about an orphaned 16-year-old Iowan girl who goes to homestead in Montana. "I read dozens of journals and diaries, as well as newspapers—including every single issue of the 1918 *Wolf Point Herald* to get a flavor for how people spoke in that time," says Larson. Although she didn't quote dialogue word for word as she would have done in writing nonfiction, she learned the phrasings and patterns of the language of that time period.

Flavoring

Mimicry, not duplication, is the key. "Dialogue is designed to appear real when, of course, it is nothing of the sort, nor would we want it to be," says Edwardson. "When real people talk, they hem and haw and waste space with purposeless small talk. In writing dialogue, the best we can do is to pay scrupulous attention to speech patterns, giving fictional conversations the illusion of reality."

This is one reason why beginning writers are told to avoid dialect. Many beginning writers follow spoken language too closely in their attempts to write dialogue. Especially when recreating a dialect, this gives your reader more than they can decipher.

Instead, create a skillful adaptation. "You are not trying to transcribe every single sound and inflection, but rather to give the flavor of the dialect so strongly that in the end readers can hear it clearly and feel as if they could speak it themselves," says Edwardson. "This is an art and it is not at all easy."

What aspect you choose for flavoring depends on the story you are writing. For a picture book, a few words in the original language may be enough. "The characters in *Whale Snow* don't really speak Village English, but I did want to make sure that the little boy who is the main character

uses words a contemporary Inupiaq child would use, instead of the English equivalent, such as *aaka* for *grandmother*," says Edwardson.

Idioms also give a strong feel for the culture that produced them and thus the character speaking them. This is largely because idioms do not translate literally. Spanish-speaking Guillermo would call his studious sister a library rat instead of our bookworm. Zulhanif from seaside Malaysia wouldn't apologize for butting in, but he might realize that he had been walking like a crab. Why use an English phrase when an idiom from the appropriate culture or language says so much more?

You can also give a taste of another culture or language by using the title of a movie or book, because they seldom translate word for word. Nitz used this technique in *Saving the Griffin*. "Fabio compared his griffin sighting to seeing something from the 'island that isn't there,' which is how Italians translated Peter Pan's Never-Never Land."

Period slang worked well for Hostetter in *Blue*. "Several people have asked me about Ann Fay's use of the word *dope* for *soda* or *soft drink*. I

Spanish-speaking Guillermo would call his studious sister a library rat. Malaysian Zulhanif wouldn't butt in, but might walk like a crab.

never hear this usage anymore, but when I was a little girl I heard it often. In fact, I can't remember what else people would have called soft drinks unless it was by the brand name," she says. "When I was writing *Blue*, I wanted to be sure about the use of the word *dope* so I called an older friend and said, 'When you were a little girl and you wanted a soft drink what would you ask for,' and she said, without hesitation, 'A dope.'"

Although using individual words and phrases can help, more needs to be done to duplicate the feel of a language. This is especially true if your character would be speaking something other than English, the language in which you are telling the story. In *Anna of Byzantium*, Barrett obviously couldn't tell Anna's story in the character's Greek language, but she could create English with a similar feel. "I aimed for a rather formal way of speaking, avoiding contractions and obvious modernisms. I tried to make it sound like a good, literary translation of some nonexistent Byzantine Greek original," says Barrett, whose day job helped her create this facsimile. "Since I'm a language teacher, my ear is pretty well trained to hear linguistic subtleties."

Observe whether a language is poetic or direct, whether sentences tend to be long or very short. Duplicate these traits to recreate the syntax of a non-English language. Just don't go beyond what your reader can take in.

Written Dialect 101

Still not sure you can write successful dialect? "Study the masters," says author Debby Edwardson. "Read Mark Twain, who mastered a number of dialects, portraying them with such precision that T. S. Eliot characterized it as, 'a new discovery in the English language.' Read Amy Tan, who conveyed a Chinese dialect almost entirely through the use of syntax. Read Rita Williams-Garcia, Harper Lee, and Sherman Alexie: They all found ways to successfully convey very specific dialects in very realistic and understandable dialogue. Then read M. T. Anderson's *Feed* to see how a writer uses the rules of dialect to invent a new dialect and make it real. If you study what you read closely, you will discover lots of tricks that different writers have used. Borrow them freely."

Your research into the language itself should have revealed words, phrases, and patterns you can borrow. If not, go back and read some more with this in mind. "Look for sound bites, not long speeches," says author and editor Jane Yolen. "Search for an iconic moment out of letters or journals or newspaper accounts or speeches." This will give you the syntax you need to duplicate.

Edwardson agrees. "Don't try to transcribe every single sound," she says. "Pick a few characteristic sounds and use them consistently to give the reader a strong sense of the flavor of the language."

Use these techniques together and you will create a believable voice. This voice, in turn, will give readers a look into your character's soul.

Excuse Me?

In writing dialect or any non-standard English, you must strike a balance between the language itself and what the reader can comprehend. "Some of my characters, including the narrator, use improper grammar," says Hostetter. "Of course, incorrect English doesn't read smoothly. I was constantly balancing the characters' use of language with the reader's need to comprehend. There were some misuses of the language and local expressions which I simply didn't use because I didn't want them to get in the way of the story."

When including non-English vocabulary, such as Edwardson does, weigh each word carefully. This is what Nitz did when her character in *Saving the Griffin* discusses Peter Pan. "Si, si, si. And the *coccodrillo* with the clock." Why didn't she translate *coccodrillo* for the reader? "I bet that American readers could figure out that *coccodrillo* was *crocodile*," she says. Used sparingly, this technique works.

When numerous non-English words and phrases are used or when they aren't likely to be deciphered by the reader, include a glossary. "I used both Italian and Etruscan words in *On Etruscan Time* (Henry Holt)," says Barrett. "I included a glossary of both in the book. I did try to use these foreign words sparingly and to make them as clear as possible in context, since it's annoying to have to flip to the back of the book when you're at a tense point in a story!"

Even when you are sure that readers can figure out each word, remember that your dialogue has to flow just like spoken language. "Read it aloud," says Barrett. "I think reading aloud is important for most writing, but crucial for dialogue."

Keep It Respectful

Finally, when creating dialogue in non-standard English, make certain the language isn't demeaning in any way. "One of my biggest concerns was the speech of Imogene Wilfong. I wanted her to sound like a southern black girl but I didn't want to stereotype her," says Hostetter. "Since I was teaching school when I wrote the first draft, I listened to the speech patterns of my black students and tried to incorporate what I heard, the parts that were not trendy or modern in any way. Then I submitted the manuscript to an African-American writer friend for review. I counted heavily on her feedback to let me know if I was getting Imogene right." Sometimes it takes firsthand knowledge to avoid stereotypical, demeaning dialect.

It can be especially difficult to write English as spoken by characters struggling with a new language. Nitz solved this problem by demonstrating the parallel difficulties that English-speaking characters had in their new language. "I showed how my characters would have been completely lost if they'd had to speak Italian," says Nitz. "They had picked up a few words, but not enough to carry on a conversation. They had a great deal of respect for someone who could communicate with them in English because they knew just how hard it was to learn a second language."

In Nitz's "Soccer in Any Language" (*Highlights for Children,* April

The One and Only

Not only does a character's speech reflect their time and place, it also reflects who they are, from age to individual personality traits. "I have a friend who begins every response to a question with '*So*,'" says Kirby Larson, author of *Hattie Big Sky*. "An acquaintance who name-drops. My mother-in-law answers the phone by saying, 'Yell-oh?' People have different speech patterns, habits and tics. Fleshed out characters do, too. I thought about who my character was and how he or she would talk based on life experience, personality, beliefs, etc. The better you know your characters, the easier it is to write natural, believable dialogue."

Still stumped? Think of someone you know who speaks much as your character would. "I'm afraid the mother in *Saving the Griffin* is a very thinly disguised version of myself," says Kristin Wolden Nitz. "I also used modeling. I wrote the first draft when my son was seven, just like the younger brother in the story. My oldest daughter was just about the age of my main character."

With help from her editor, Joyce Moyer Hostetter carefully crafted the individual voices in *Blue*. Thus, each character's dialogue reflects something about them and shows the variety possible through fairly simple adjustments to word choice. "Bessie Bledsoe regularly says 'Have mercy,' which simply reflects her big heart—her desire to relieve pain and discomfort in general. And I think it reflects her faith in God, too," says Hostetter. "Even before I knew who my protagonist would be I knew this would be a survival story. I knew my character would have to be tough. When Ann Fay Honeycutt emerged, her speech reflected this. She said things like 'I tell you what's the truth' and 'If you think.' Her bluster was her way of convincing herself that she could do hard things, and of warning others not to get in her way!" Hostetter also worked to make each of Ann Fay's parents unique rather than presenting them as a matched pair. "Ann Fay's parents are simple folks and yet I felt that her mother was maybe slightly more refined than her daddy was," says Hostetter. "She used correct grammar while he was more likely to slip into the wrong tense or use a particularly southern colloquialism."

Look carefully at individual word choice. A simple phrase can give a feel for the time or place in which a story is set, as well as tell the reader something more about the character who is speaking.

2006), "My main character couldn't understand Italians speaking at top speed," says Nitz. "A few words would pop out of the torrent of words. He and a friend had agreed to help correct each other's language mistakes." Showing the problems of both English as a Second Language (ESL) characters and native speakers, as well as creating a cooperative bond, allowed Nitz to approach both the reader and her characters with respect. Knowing exactly how to do it enabled her to break the rule.

Do not write in dialect—unless you absolutely must to bring your character to life.

Coming of Age—Again!

By Sharelle Byars Moranville

Ask a group of editors, agents, and writers their favorite coming-of-age stories and Louisa May Alcott's *Little Women* will likely make the list. There's an unforgettable, principled sweetness to the world of Jo and her sisters. The girls struggle with poverty, help their mother, and await their father, who is a chaplain with Union troops in the Civil War. Despite the conflicts and changes in the world, at the end of Alcott's story, the little women have come of age safely.

But then read Geraldine Brooks's Pulitzer Prize-winning novel, *March*, in which Brooks extends the world of *Little Women*. She makes their father, Captain March, the main character in a novel about the war. Captain March, too, comes of age—with the dismaying discovery that the worthy principles he has instilled into his daughters are, in fact, worthless, perhaps even harmful. By implication, his story shines a harsh light on the world of the little women. They are not yet through coming of age.

Perhaps we're never through coming of age. And perhaps that's why bookshelves are crammed with coming-of-age stories.

Inevitably

"To some extent, you could categorize most children's books as coming-of-age stories, in the sense that most fiction for young readers (and even picture books) is on some level about a young person learning something new about him or herself, and about life, coming to terms with it, and growing up as a result," says Caroline Meckler, who was Editor at Henry Holt Books for Young Readers and more recently became Assistant Editor at Random House's Wendy Lamb Books.

Tracey Adams, of Adams Literary, echoes this when she says that "looking at the middle-grades and YAs on our shelves, it's honestly hard to say that any of them are *not* coming-of-age stories. In most fiction for young readers, the main character grows up in some way, whether it's in a fantasy, an edgy YA, or a work of historical fiction."

Traditionally, however, coming-of-age books are most associated with the passage from adolescence to adulthood, not merely the growth throughout childhood. Liz Waniewski, Editor at Dial Books for Young Readers, says, "Young adult characters tend to grow and mature throughout the story and learn something new about themselves, gain a broader world view, or come to a new understanding of the world and people around them that is different from how they thought at the beginning of the story. Isn't this what coming of age is all about?"

In literature and in life, people come of age more or less constantly—gracefully, messily, happily, miserably, willingly, unwillingly, humorously, and tragically. Sometimes they refuse to come of age. An example is young Nick Adams in Hemingway's famous short story "The Indian Camp." This growth and change (or resistance to it) is universal and endlessly fascinating, creating a steady market for coming-of-age stories.

Believability

Meckler says that while she was editing at Holt, the company welcomed coming-of-age stories that appealed to both girls and boys. "The challenge is that, according to traditional thinking, boys don't want to read books with female narrators, and vice versa. With coming-of-age stories, I think this holds even truer, as young readers tend to appreciate these stories for their insight into another person's experience and world, to which they can somehow relate."

Whatever the audience, Meckler looks for good books that cover a critical moment in the main character's life. "The qualities that make me want to buy a book include an individual voice, strong setting details, and a well-constructed story that compels you to find out what happens." Meckler refers to the truism that there are only seven or so possible plots in all of literature, and says, "The best stories convey those plots in a fresh, believable, and interesting way. The more specific and concrete details a story offers, the more believable it is for the reader." The reader has to buy fully into the story: "You don't want your willing suspension of disbelief to be broken by discordant moments that cause you to question the believability of the story."

Many coming-of-age books are also literary novels. Meckler explains that the authors of these books stay very attentive to language as they describe "in a unique way, the universal feelings of what it's like to grow up. Specificity breathes life into a coming-of-age story, and we usually categorize as literary the strong voices and descriptions that make a story feel specific."

A literary story can also be humorous, Meckler believes, and she cites Margo Rabb's *Cures for Heartbreak* (Delacorte). This is the story of a ninth grader facing her mother's death from melanoma only 12 days after the diagnosis. The narrator's life is consumed by her father's chronic and terrifying heart condition, a very small extended family of holocaust survivors, a stepmother with lung cancer, and a boyfriend with leukemia. Yet, as Meckler says, the novel is "surprisingly humorous, which is, to me, a literary achievement. I think it's very challenging to write successfully about a tragic situation in a humorous way. As a reader, you almost feel uncomfortable laughing when you should be crying, and you probably end up doing both, but that's what life's all about, isn't it?"

As a young reader Meckler loved fantasy, mystery, and adventure stories, and she admits she sometimes read coming-of-age stories reluctantly. But once she was nudged into trying them, she enjoyed them. "I remember really liking Katherine Paterson's coming-of-age novels: *The Great Gilly Hopkins; Bridge to Terabithia;* and *Jacob Have I Loved.* I also loved classic books, such as *The Secret Garden, Anne of Green Gables,* and *Little Women*." Now she includes Lois Lowry's *The Giver* (Delacorte), Stephanie F. Tolan's *Surviving the Applewhites* (Harper-Collins), and Dodie Smith's *I Capture the Castle* (St. Martin's) among her favorites.

Evolutions and Revolutions

The passage into adolescence and then to adulthood is a natural field for cultivating fictional conflicts. At Knopf, Editor Cecile Goyette looks for the proverbial coming-of-age journey, "with fits and stumbles along the way as the lead character figures out at least a little part of who he or she is, or might become. Characters also have to be up against something of real significance (as opposed to just whining about something)."

She continues: "There's also a nice intimacy with coming-of-age in that these stories chronicle an inner evolution, or sometimes even a revolution! I like to see the struggle from without and within, and some real vulnerability. If a character doesn't have some openness, however reluctantly, they can't credibly evolve. In younger stories, it's nice to see a character with some enthusiasm. Wanting something spurs you on, makes you reach, gets you into all sorts of enjoyable trouble, allows for progress."

Goyette gives clear warning to anyone who might consider showing her a manuscript with this type of one-dimensional character: "If the story features a surly teenager (a totally tiresome cliché), I like to see the cracks in the veneer—and to see them very early, please. For me, ultra-whiny or constantly sardonic characters need not apply (a personal professional peccadillo)."

As a child, Goyette read Dorothy Canfield Fisher's *Understood Betsy* "umpteen times" and now cites among her favorite coming-of-age stories Tony Earley's *Jim the Boy* (Little, Brown), Jerry Spinelli's *Wringer* (Joanna Cotler), Francesca Lia Block's *Weetzie Bat* (Joanna Cotler), Avi's *The True Confessions of Charlotte Doyle* (Scholastic), and Richard Peck's *A Year Down Yonder* (Dial).

Young adult novels are by definition coming-of-age stories, says Wendy Lamb, Vice President and Publishing Director of her own imprint at Random House. Whether they are literary or commercial, fantasy, realistic fiction, or historical fiction, young adult fiction is "about the protagonist going out into the world in some way and learning to be independent." A criterion for coming-of-age stories that interest Lamb is that "the ending should be truly earned, and readers must truly share the adventures that inspire growth in the protagonist."

Lamb lists classics, modern classics, and contemporary novels among her favorites: Charles Dickens's *Great Expectations,* Esther Forbes's *Johnny Tremain,* and the more recent title by Sarah Dessen, *Someone Like You* (Viking).

Dessen's novel is about Halley and her best friend, Scarlett, who has become pregnant by a boy who is subsequently killed in a motorcycle crash. The story resonates with the truth of being a teenager facing such a crisis. It's about parent-child relationships, sex, romance, self-worth, grief, peer groups, and comets. But mainly it's about friendship. It's a story of laughter and tears.

Another of Lamb's personal favorites is a book she edited herself: the Michael L. Printz award-winning *How I Live Now,* by Meg Rosoff. This is a contemporary story about an American girl, Daisy, who is sent to England to live with an aunt and cousins because her new stepmother wants her out of the way. While Daisy's aunt is away, a fictional war breaks out and England is occupied by enemy forces. Daisy and her four cousins are alone in the countryside as the horrors of occupation come ever closer. They begin as children having adventures, clever and imaginative as they make their survival plans. But as the reality of war bears down on them, they're forced to make decisions that, in a saner world, would fall to the adults. Daisy's journey through this chaos is terrible and damaging. She has to make adult decisions. She does adult things. Ultimately, she does one understandable, but cowardly, thing.

How I Live Now is not a *Little Women* story. It's more a *March* story. But, as is true of most YA novels, a measure of hope is offered at the end. Daisy muses on the closing page, "fighting back is what I've discovered I do best."

Wider and Well-Rounded

Someone Like You and *How I Live Now* are coming-of-age stories in the strict sense of the adolescent journey to maturity. The lead characters are truly young adults. But in the Agnes Parker books for younger readers, the characters only begin to come of age. Goyette talks about editing two of those novels while she was at Dial Books for Young Readers. "I'm proud of what Kathleen O'Dell achieved in her Agnes Parker books. Agnes doesn't really come all the way of age (the stories take place over just a few weeks' or months' time), but she always discovers worthy stuff about herself and life, and moves herself forward throughout the plot. The plots feature what I call regular kid material (a big fight with a best friend, the unsettling realization that your parents are human, discovering a window into another family's troubles, going to camp, having a crush, etc.), told with a great voice and a keen eye."

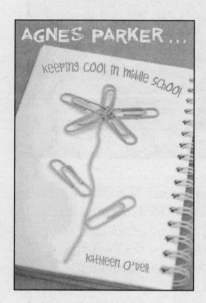

Goyette acknowledges that she "worried a little bit about the story material not being extreme or unusual enough—no one's in rehab, nobody goes to jail or gets pregnant, parents actually like each other, etc. But Kathy has rendered Agnes and her scenarios both relatable and memorable, and showed a strong faith that regular kid stuff can offer great reading experiences. Oh, and the books are quite funny. Yep, I like some humor! For me, Agnes reads as the type of girl I'd like to follow through all her coming-of-ages."

In *Agnes Parker . . . Happy Camper?* soon-to-be-seventh-grader Agnes goes to camp with her best friend Prejean. Through an administrative snafu, they are separated—Agnes becoming a resident of the Mallard cabin and Prejean becoming a Fawn. They are, in fact, also separated by Prejean's sudden, blooming adolescent beauty. Their story is true. It's the way girls are, the way camp is, and the way it feels to finally go home at the end of summer—a little bit the same and a little bit changed. And it's funny. Agnes comes only slightly of age. She never has to make a truly adult decision or play the role of a parent. But the total thrust of the book is still about growing up.

It's not the age of the characters, or whether they are realistic, historic, or fantastic—coming-of-age fiction is about the movement from one stage of life to another.

Perhaps this is the ultimate hallmark that separates full blown coming-of-age stories from other kinds of stories. It's not the age of the characters or whether they are realistic, historical, fantastic, or science fiction—it's the emphasis on movement from one stage of life to another.

Most good books have well-rounded characters who grow in maturity because they overcome obstacles. But the emphasis may not need to be on the protagonist reaching maturity. Though their heroine is a bit young to come fully of age, the Agnes Parker books are still about that growing up. They are quiet, sweet, funny books as opposed to Rosoff's raw and gripping *How I Live Now,* but still about a character's interior and exterior movement.

Contrast both of those books to another great read, Caroline B. Cooney's *Code Orange* (Delacorte). This is a grip-the-pages-with-damp-fingers story about a teen boy in Manhattan who finds a smallpox scab tucked into an old book. The compelling question becomes whether or not another wave of smallpox has been unleashed on the world by this charming, guileless boy. He's a rounded character in the sense that he does stupid things that he later regrets (but that drive the plot) and he gets the girl in the end. But we don't really care about his character growth; we just want to sit on the edge of our seats, turning the pages until one in the morning, praying he saves the world from germ warfare. *Code Orange* is not a coming-of-age story—though the protagonist does face his own flaws and strengths and the audience is young adults—because the book is not primarily about growing up.

Let's Hope

It may be easier to define coming-of-age stories by example than by discussion, but everyone, from very young Agnes Parker readers to adult readers of Ernest Hemingway and Alice Munro, finds them compelling. Yet there is one important difference between coming-of-age stories for adults and for younger readers: hope.

In arguably the most famous American coming-of-age short story, Hemingway's "The Short Happy Life of Francis Macomber," big-game hunter and guide Robert Wilson witnesses Francis Macomber's bravery when three African buffalo charge their small hunting party. Macomber faces oncoming death like a man and is transformed by the ordeal. He is no longer the person who, the day before, ran from a wounded lion or who merely whined and begged when his wife cuckolded him. Wilson is very touched by the change in Macomber and muses to himself that he had seen men come of age before and it always moved him. But within minutes of Macomber's new footing, his wife shoots him to death.

There is no hope of a safe coming of age in Hemingway's story. But in Rosoff's young adult crossover novel *How I Live Now*, even with its horrors and the dreadful symbolism of a once lush, Edenic garden transformed to a frightening, hellish place, hope abides. Daisy, although scarred, has found a way to live.

Writers and editors still tend to protect young readers. Coming-of-age stories end with some hope, but otherwise, the form is universal. As Goyette says, "Writers are drawn to the coming-of-age story by its classic appeal and form. They know it's a genre that allows for a million different tellings since it centers on characters in all their permutations and various starting points."

The (New and Improved) Truth About Autobiography

By Christina Hamlett

"**B**ack when I was your age . . . "
As many a child or teen can attest, nothing invites these words faster than complaining within earshot of adults that life is too hard, too boring, or too lacking in creature comforts. While the recollections of walking miles to church on Easter Sunday, wearing hand-me-downs, or enduring an entire childhood without CDs or a computer may contrast the advantages of the present to the hardships of the past, such personal stories also reveal that the generation gap is often much narrower than either side may think.

The assimilation of autobiography into fiction and other forms of writing has a long heritage. James Boswell, Charles Dickens, Virginia Woolf, James Joyce, Richard Henry Dana, Lorraine Hansberry, Ernest Hemingway, James Baldwin, Nora Ephron, and Neil Simon represent only a handful of successful authors whose memorable creations were drawn from the pages of their past.

Spinning personal anecdotes and insights into a framework for young readers takes more than translating reminiscence into prose. The real challenge lies in finding a way for the life experiences of adults to resonate with a generation that, like every other before it, maintains that its feelings, fears, and dreams are unique.

Keeping It Real

The level of abstraction from the specifics of personal experience depends on genre—memoir, advice, how-to, first-person account, short story, novel.

Autobiographical Nonfiction of Childhood

➤ *Anne Frank: The Diary of a Young Girl.* Anne Frank (Bantam). Originally published in 1947 and written by the now famous 13-year-old Jewish girl hiding with her family in Nazi-occupied Amsterdam. For all ages.

➤ *Boy: Tales of Childhood.* Roald Dahl (Farrar, Straus and Giroux; Puffin paperback). The eccentric boyhood that formed a classic writer. Middle-grade.

➤ *Celia's Island Journal.* Celia Thaxter (Little, Brown). Picture book based on a nineteenth-century poet's childhood journal. Ages 4-8.

➤ *Hotel Kid: A Times Square Childhood.* Stephen Lewis (Paul Dry Books). Growing up as the son of the Taft Hotel manager in the 1930s and 1940s. YA and adult.

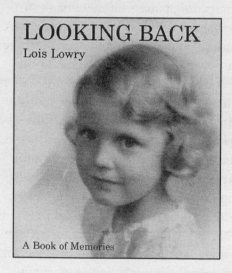

LOOKING BACK
Lois Lowry

A Book of Memories

➤ *Knots in My Yo-Yo String.* Jerry Spinelli (Knopf). Childhood reminiscences of life in Pennsylvania in the 1940s and 1950s. Middle-grade.

➤ *Looking Back: A Book of Memories.* Lois Lowry (Walter Lorraine Books/Houghton Mifflin). Memorable moments, dreams, imaginings, family and friends from childhood, all told in relation to Lowry's career as a writer. YA and adult.

➤ *Too Close to the Falls.* Catherine Gildiner (Viking). The humorous coming-of-age memoir of a "hyperactive" girl who grew up in the 1950s in western New York, near Niagara Falls. YA and adult.

➤ *When I Was Your Age: Original Stories About Growing Up.* Edited by Amy Ehrlich (Candlewick). Two volumes in an anthology of memoirs from children's book authors, including Avi, Francesca Lia Block, Paul Fleischman, Karen Hesse, E. L. Konigsburg, Norma Fox Mazer, Mary Pope Osbourne, Katherine Paterson, Walter Dean Myers, Jane Yolen, and others. Tween and teen.

In nonfiction, reflections about coping with bullies, dealing with illness or death, adjusting to a new school, or going on a first date tie directly to what young readers are going through themselves. The level of personal detail may be high, and the themes relatively obvious. Because young readers specifically seek out autobiographical books or articles for help handling the awkward transitions from childhood to puberty, the tone of the writing is likely to be one of reassurance, encouragement, and inspiration.

Nonfiction based on life experience may also educate by broadening a young person's view of the world or enhancing respect for diversity. Journal accounts of living overseas, surviving a disaster, or participating in a historically significant event open windows of awareness and reveal perspectives that readers might not glean from textbooks or the Internet. First-person accounts are popular in monthly young adult and middle-grade magazines. *Seventeen, Brio, Faze, Breakaway,* and *Girls' Life* typically address topical issues such as health, sexuality, peer pressure, substance abuse, dating, and mastering future employment skills.

Imaginary, but True, Tableaux

Autobiographical fiction, in contrast, generally poses questions and weaves more ambiguous interpretations. While remaining true at heart, these stories don't need to be based on empirical evidence, as nonfiction does. Authors ultimately create an imaginary tableau filled with traits such as loyalty, perseverance, courage, friendship, fearfulness, angst, and so on, through the device of characters who take a page from the author's own life. Plots may integrate timeless themes about overcoming obstacles, being popular, and achieving goals, in a setting with updated cultural elements that make the work appeal to a contemporary audience.

Updating, of course, is a crucial component in the process of adapting autobiographical content to a modern backdrop. Even if your readers know that an adult has penned the story, that fact shouldn't be made obvious to them through iconic references or obsolete phrases that only have meaning to an earlier generation. Describing a character as listening to his favorite band on an eight-track will only confuse the reader born at the turn of the millennium.

Novels can be carved from an entire life, but sometimes episodes, or individual experiences or people, or a even just a general quality of life growing up inspires a book or character. In works such as those in the sidebar on page 225, elements of the authors' past breathe life into fictitious personae. Paula Danziger used to say that *The Cat Ate My Gymsuit* was the book closest to her own life. In *Rules* (Scholastic), Cynthia Lord skillfully applies her experience as the mother of an autistic son to the

storyline. Cynthia Kadohata's family history is mined for the characters and events in *Weedflower* (Atheneum). *Penny from Heaven* (Yearling) was inspired by Jennifer Holm's Italian-American family. Among the classic American writers, Louisa May Alcott's novel about the plucky March family during the Civil War mirrored her own impoverished upbringing in Massachusetts with three sisters. Mark Twain not only tapped his intimate knowledge of slavery but also spun his Hannibal, Missouri, roots into the fictional hometown of St. Petersburg for his most famous juvenile pranksters, Tom and Huck.

Humor like Twain's is an effective delivery mechanism for making understated points about responsibility, resiliency, and society at large in autobiographical writing. In my upcoming *Movie Girl,* which is the launch title for a new teen/tween fiction series to be published by Hard Shell Word Factory, more than 75 percent of the characters and events were drawn from my junior year in high school. While there was certainly nothing amusing at the time about my fave heartthrob not even knowing I existed, its subsequent replay 30 years later through the eyes of my alter-ego heroine, Laurie Preston, is gently comedic and is meant to be as relatable to today's lovestruck teen girls as it was to the women of my own generation.

Romance, sports, historical fiction, and coming-of-age stories lend themselves most readily to autobiographical material for young adult

Autobiographical Fiction of Childhood

➤ *The Cat Ate My Gymsuit.* Paula Danziger (Puffin). An insecure thirteen-year-old girl meets an inspirational and unconventional English teacher. Middle-grade.

➤ *Little Women.* Louisa May Alcott. The classic story of four sisters during the American Civil War.

➤ *Rules.* Cynthia Lord (Scholastic). An adolescent's life with her autistic brother. Middle-grade.

➤ *Tom Sawyer, Huckleberry Finn.* Mark Twain. The American classics, and other stories by Samuel Clemens, are famously autobiographical.

➤ *Penny from Heaven.* Jennifer Holm (Random House). A girl growing up in 1953 Brooklyn learns the truth behind her father's death. Middle-grade.

➤ *Weedflower.* Cynthia Kadohata (Atheneum). A Japanese-American girl in the aftermath of Pearl Harbor. Young adult.

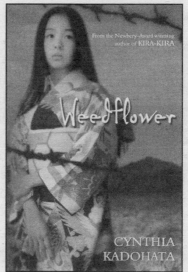

readers. But if you have a particular background in science, travel, adventure, or working with animals, you can work these topics into creative stories as well and accomplish a twofold purpose of entertaining as well as subliminally teaching. Experts beware, though! The frequency of factoids and chronological details you embed for the sake of accuracy should never dominate the plot nor take on the characteristics of a lecture.

Cathartic or Commercial

Composing out of somewhat distant memory can provide a sense of perspective that was probably lacking in real life. Circumstances that may have seemed devastating to our young egos—getting dumped by a boyfriend or losing a school competition—assume lesser significance

225

simply because we were able to move on to new relationships and opportunities. How many times, in fact, do we find ourselves breathing a huge sigh of relief that we weren't able to pry open some of those slamming doors?

The advantage of grown-up hindsight, however, can be negated if writing trivializes events that are painful or bewildering to the latest generation to experience them. A communication disconnect comes with condescending analysis or insensitive dismissal—which can be interpreted by young readers as a lack of respect for their fears or

Catharsis may be good for the soul, but it's not necessarily lucrative for a publisher.

expectations. No matter how much we affirm that first crushes are transitory or that not landing the lead role in *Our Town* isn't fatal, we can never forget that such losses may be a first for readers desperately trying to handle feelings of failure and insecurity.

An article, story, or book should empower a young person to make good decisions, usually by relating to a character's experiences. Don't vent personal frustrations or rewrite the past into what "should have been." Catharsis may be good for the soul, but it's not necessarily lucrative for a publisher. Airing feelings, defending mistakes, and vengefully turning the unlikable classmates of our past into even more unlikable characters doesn't often translate into marketable stories. Strive for creative, well-rounded intimacy, immediacy, and resonance.

Memories should not descend into a string of day-to-day vignettes in which nothing exciting or thought-provoking ever happens either. Commercially viable stories thrust ordinary individuals into extraordinary circumstances (the young protagonist in *Weedflower* is sent with her family to an internment camp on an Indian reservation in 1941). Alternatively, extraordinary individuals must function in an ordinary world that doesn't accept their unique viewpoints, talents, intellect, or physical appearance. For instance, *Raisin Wine: A Boyhood in a Different Muskoka* (Douglas Gibson Books) revolves around the author's childhood awareness that being of mixed race can be a blessing and a curse. It is the fourth in a series of autobiographical books by James Bartleman, who grew up to become Lieutenant Governor of Ontario.

Truth and Creative License

It's only human nature to want to embroider, embellish, and enhance the various chapters of our lives with each retelling. Whether to escalate our original level of participation, redefine past motives to accommodate contemporary perspectives, or perhaps just customize a message we think should be heard, the tendency to play revisionist is not inconsistent with a memorable narrative. Sometimes modifications are an innocent by-product of the passage of time. The cramped childhood home we were so eager to leave is later nostalgically recalled as a bastion of safety. Just as frequently, whatever joys and comforts that truly existed may be squelched in memory because of people who subsequently wronged us.

Time isn't the only culprit in manipulating our ability to deliver the truth. Adam Gopnik's "Angels and Ages" (*New Yorker*, May 28, 2007), discusses the debate over whether Edwin Stanton's words at Abraham Lincoln's deathbed were "Now he belongs to the ages" or "Now he belongs to the angels." Despite a roomful of mourners and a stenographer corporal who judiciously recorded the president's last moments, no one could agree on the exact verbiage. As Gopnik points out, "The past is so often unknowable not because it is befogged now but because it was befogged then, too, back when it was still the present." Our comprehension is influenced by what we want to see and hear.

Take the case of a colleague whose nonfiction specialty is first-person travel writing. She paints her journalistic pictures in a subjective frame of reference, a discovery I made when traveling with her. Not being a morning person, she leaned toward greater criticism of hotels, restaurants, and other venues that required our presence before 10 AM. In her write-ups, she stayed within the parameters of reality—history, geography, climate—but still, she worked with a subjective mindset based on past trips, expectations, interactions with others, and even her mood on any given day. So do we all.

There's the rub. Personal is good, but it has its pitfalls. We write because of who we are, because of what interests us, and because of what we've lived, autobiographical or not. If the pages of your diary are destined for a work of fiction, creative license—the selective tweaking of truth—is acceptable, even encouraged. If the pages of your diary are destined for nonfiction, truth is the starting point, but the other essentials are context, timeliness, authenticity, and if you're a writer for children or teens, connecting with that audience.

Your life, my life, everyone's life can be dull, and yet it can be the root of great stories. Don't let the drab enter your writing. Fiction or nonfiction, eliminate dull episodes to enliven pace. In fiction, manufacture relationships with full-blooded characters who can be sounding boards, and find straighter paths to reach epiphanies, all via the wisdom you have as an adult and as a writer.

Nonfiction, however, not only imposes limits on the creative license we can exercise with autobiography, but also calls for judgment and diplomacy in revealing information about third parties without their permission. A client of mine wanted to pen her memoirs about the early years of the women's movement for a readership of high school girls. Unfortunately, some of her best anecdotes either cast a negative light on public figures who have a reputation for suing their critics or telling the stories meant divulging confidential information my client had acquired as an attorney. Another writer I know wanted to share funny experiences he had as a costumed character for several summers at Disneyland. Even though his anecdotes about the Happiest Place on Earth were 100 percent favorable, he was firmly advised by counsel that an "unauthorized" book written for his own profit could potentially be subject to a lawsuit.

This again circles back to the rationale behind autobiographical revelations. If your trek down memory lane is meant to inform, enlighten, and amuse future generations, that's one thing. If it's meant to exact vengeance and settle a score, however, the trouble it could invite into your life may be more than you bargained for.

Value Perception

Everyone has a story to tell. Whether or not that story gets published, however, depends on an editor's perception of its value and insight. In analyzing autobiographical material for submission, editors consider the following factors to determine project marketability:

➤ What unique challenges does the protagonist have to overcome and how are these achieved?

➤ In what ways are the main characters similar to (and different from) the target readers?

➤ Are the concepts and language age-appropriate?

➤ What will readers learn about themselves as a result of reading this book or article?

➤ Is the pacing tight and even?

➤ Is it relevant to the fears, hopes, and concerns of today's youth?

Your chronicled life may not be for everyone. Its emotional essence, however, can still be conveyed through the medium of creative fiction or parsed out in the form of short stories, articles, or nonfiction books that focus on the resolution of one central problem. The secret is simply not to lose sight of your kinship with a generation that likes to insist you have absolutely nothing in common.

Taking Care of Business: Magazine Contracts and Payments

By Mark Haverstock

You're getting ready to pitch that new article to an editor. You've repeatedly heard editors say, "Know our market and our needs." So you look at sample magazines and market guides and decide which publications are the best matches for your piece.

But have you decided which publications are the best match for you as a writer, your writing business, and your finances? Make informed submission decisions by also researching magazine business policies — not just current editorial needs—and reviewing the items in the contracts you receive once your editor gives you the thumbs up.

Some questions you should consider are: What rights does the magazine want? Will you be able to resell your article later? Can you modify the terms of the contract? What are you likely to get paid and when?

Show Me the Money

According to a study by *Editors Only*, between 40 and 50 percent of the publications surveyed pay on acceptance, though the percentage varies with the market. Fifty percent of association publications generally pay on acceptance. Trade magazines are least likely to pay on acceptance—about 40 percent. Consumer magazines were right in the middle at about 45 percent.

Acceptance can be a somewhat nebulous term, but usually means when the article has passed muster with the editor and placement in a future issue is certain, or at least very likely. If the magazine pays on acceptance, consider yourself fortunate. No matter what happens to your article from that point on, whether it gets published or not, you've already been paid.

Like many publications in the religious market, *Pockets* pays on acceptance. Well-established publications with large circulations often

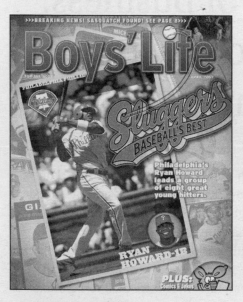

pay on acceptance as well. *Boys' Life* and *National Geographic Kids* are two examples. These publications are also usually conscientious about keeping authors in the loop. "We state in the agreement when we antici-pate publishing the article, with the understanding that things may change at the last minute, depending on the number of ads," says Catherine Hughes, Senior Editor of *National Geo-graphic Kids*. "I keep writers informed of when it's been rescheduled if that happens. All of our writers seem to be very understanding, especially because they've already been paid."

If magazines want to attract and to work with the best people, they need to be writer-friendly. Paying on acceptance is one way to accom-plish this goal. It's no wonder that most writers prefer to work with a pay-on-acceptance publication.

The Waiting Game

The remaining magazines in the *Editors Only* study, a little more than half, paid upon publication or shortly thereafter. These magazines typi-cally offer an assignment; accept the piece; edit and hold it until placed in an issue; publish; and finally, pay the writer. But payment on publica-tion may not mean the check will be in your hands exactly on the cover date. Posts on several writers' message boards suggest that payments from some magazines arrive 30, 60, or 90 days—and even longer—after publications hit the newsstands. In the worst case, pay-on-publication can mean no payment at all if there is a change in editorial focus or the publication suddenly folds.

Magazine editors who pay on publication offer several reasons for this policy. Some have tight budgets and need time to accumulate money to pay authors. Others wait for ad revenues, which are often invoiced at the time of publication and may not arrive for a billing cycle or two. At some, the accountants claim pay-on-publication is easier, since they can pay on a regular schedule instead of dealing with dozens of individual invoices throughout the month. They say it simplifies the process and limits mistakes. Finally, the policy provides an out for publications who don't want to pay in advance for something they may later be unable to use.

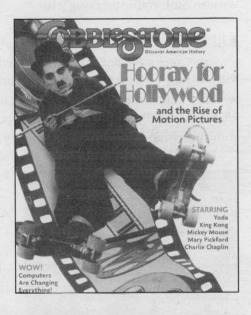

One way to minimize the downside of pay-on-publication is to try to get a commitment on the publication date; at least you'll have some idea when the check will arrive. Editorial Director Lou Waryncia says all the magazines in the Cobblestone Group pay on publication, but that they work with an established editorial calendar. "Unlike some other publications where they accept a piece and they don't have any idea when they will publish it, we do," he says. "If we assign an article for the May issue, it will likely be in the May issue."

Regular contributors in most markets can expect to earn more for their efforts, and receive more desirable assignments. "Our standard is one dollar a word, and we do have some columnists who have become regular contributors," says Hughes. "Over time, we've been known to give them raises. But in their case, it's often by the column rather than the word count."

J. D. Owen, Editor in Chief of *Boys' Life,* says that regular contributors are treated preferentially. "We often give them choice assignments and they tend to write the longer pieces for us, which pay more," he says. Distinguished authors who write for *Boys' Life*, such as Thomas Fleming or Gary Paulsen, earn top dollar. "We pay more for names and people we are comfortable working with."

Kill Fees

Sometimes assigned pieces are pulled for any of a variety of reasons. Kill fees may be paid to compensate authors for their time and effort when an editor ultimately chooses not to use an assigned article. Though kill fees are infrequently used by most publications, many contracts have some provision for them. Typically, they are 25 percent of the originally agreed upon fee, but they can range from 10 to 50 percent.

"We prefer the euphemism *assignment termination fee*," says Chris Lutes, Editor of *Ignite Your Faith*, when "the writer just wasn't able to follow the assignment, or they just weren't able to make it work." Occasionally, this happens with first-person stories. Lutes may decide to take a chance on a new writer and what looks like a good story. He assigns the story and believes it will work—but it doesn't. For whatever reasons, the writer doesn't have the skill to pull it off. "If they can't get it in two or three rewrites, that's when we'll make the decision to pay the kill fee," says Lutes. "But it doesn't happen very often because I really want to work with an author to make the piece successful."

Waryncia shares a similar philosophy, rarely paying kill fees. "We usually make that decision after a couple of steps. First the editor will try to work with the piece," he says. "If they feel that they can't edit, add, or subtract and make it workable, we generally send it back to the author

234

The Big Picture

According to the editors interviewed for this article, there is little difference between most writer and illustrator contracts, other than in the clauses related to art. Author/illustrator Melanie Hope Greenberg shares her thoughts about contracts that work in the best interest of illustrators.

➤ **What is your opinion on the purchase of rights from illustrators?**

"I am in strong favor of the artist owning all rights. Then an artist has a chance to reuse the art for something that is not in conflict with the original usage, and get an additional fee—like selling a magazine illustration to a greeting card company. Keeping the art as the property of the artist is only fair. If a magazine is earning money by reusing art in various ways, and the artist earns no extra income, I believe it's unfair. Typically, I ask for first North American rights, which means the magazine has the right to publish the art only one time and only within the U.S. or Canada."

➤ **What are the major concerns of author/illustrators regarding magazine contracts?**

"The artist/writer needs to: (1) own the copyright; (2) get their original artwork/sketches returned; (3) add in a kill fee (if there is none), in case the job is terminated by the magazine; and (4) get samples for their portfolio."

➤ **Have you found that contracts are carved in stone, or are editors generally willing to make allowances for reasonable requests regarding rights and terms?**

"Generally, editors I've worked with are flexible on the terms and have granted most of my wishes."

➤ **Do you have any additional advice for illustrators regarding contracts?**

"Do not give up your copyrights. That is the only way to fight back legally in the case of plagiarism, or reuse without permission—such as finding out your art for an article is now a famous poster, like what happened with the famous LOVE icon. Use the Graphic Artist Guild's 'Pricing and Ethical Guidelines' for contract forms and information, and determining how to price a job."

At Your Expense?

Sometimes writers incur expenses while researching articles, yet most contracts don't specifically state whether the author will be reimbursed. Often, it's just a matter of discussing the issue with your editor and getting prior approval.

"I tell writers that if expenses are an issue for them, to negotiate it. Sometimes editors will be aware of unusual circumstances, asking authors to send a list of expenses," says Lou Waryncia, Editorial Director of the Cobblestone Group. "We did that recently with someone. The article was going to require a lot of phone calls to central Asia, we knew they were going to be expensive, and we agreed to cover the cost. We will pay if we've discussed it with the author; for us it's never a problem."

J. D. Owen, Editor in Chief of *Boys' Life*, says, "If we send you to cover an outdoor event—you travel there, you have meals, and you drive back home—we'll pay you for all normal and reasonable expenses. When we make an assignment, we ask writers to document their expenses."

with a list of suggestions. Once we get it back, it will be evaluated again and go through an editing process." If at that stage the editor decides it still can't be used, or the expert—a consulting editor for an issue—gives the piece a thumbs down because the information is fundamentally inaccurate, then they decide either to reassign the piece or to go a different way.

Rights Issues

The steamiest hot-button issue in magazine contracts is the purchase of rights. In an effort to optimize multiple venues, many of them Internet-based (websites and e-letters, for instance), a significant number of magazines opt to purchase all rights. Unfortunately, this practice restricts an author's ability to generate income themselves through other venues. National organizations such as the Authors Guild and National Writers Union advise authors to hold onto as many contract rights as possible, avoiding the selling of all rights and signing work-for-hire contracts. Their recommendations: Sell first North American serial rights (FNASR) and negotiate more pay for any other rights.

Many of the large children's

publishers, such as *Highlights for Children,* Children's Better Health Institute, and Scholastic magazines, specify purchase of all rights. Carus Publishing Company follows different policies for its different divisions. Rights purchased by the literary magazines (*Cricket, Babybug, Ladybug, Spider, Cicada*) and nonfiction magazines (*Ask, Click, Muse*) of the Cricket Group vary according to the type of article. All rights are routinely purchased by the Cobblestone Group (*Cobblestone, AppleSeeds, Calliope, Dig, Faces, Odyssey*).

Analysis of the *Magazine Markets for Children's Writers 2008* Fifty+ Freelance list, which includes publishers in the children's market that purchase more than half of their materials from freelancers, shows that about 33 percent purchase all rights. The remaining 66 percent purchase first rights, one-time rights, or state that their policies vary.

One compelling reason for publications to buy all rights is to supply their content-hungry websites with articles. They also don't want the purchased material to appear in competing publications in substantially the same form.

Economics is another factor in choosing to purchase all rights, says Christine French Clark, Editor of *Highlights*. "Without advertising revenue, magazines such as ours operate on very slim margins," she says. "Quite simply, purchasing all rights is a part of the economic model that allows us to continue to publish, to continue to offer children's writers a venue for their work, and to continue to offer kids and families our brand of Fun with a Purpose."

Although rights are often an economic issue, author Natalie Rosinsky notes that they are an artistic issue as well, because writers may end up ultimately giving up control of content. "No one likes to sell all rights. The bit of extra income that a resale brings is nice, but I am more concerned about the future alteration of my work without my input," she says. "I have seen several of my articles reprinted without the sidebars that I wrote for them, and once saw one transmogrified for reprint in another venue. I would have been happier to lose that writing credit, and had my byline removed from that altered piece."

Sharing the Proceeds

Agreeing to sell all or a substantial part of your publication rights may not always be a bad idea, especially when your editor is willing to split

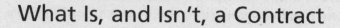

What Is, and Isn't, a Contract

What is a contract:

In its simplest form, a contract is a document that spells out the terms of a sale. These include:

> A boilerplate form, with blanks provided for author name, title of the article to be sold, and the payment.
> A letter of agreement which can be tailored for your particular article, or a standard form letter.
> A fill in the blank/check the boxes form.

What isn't a contract:

> A stamp on the back of your check indicating that your endorsement on the check transfers all rights to the publisher.
> Writers' guidelines, either printed by the magazine, published in a market guide, or published on a website.
> A notation on your manuscript indicating rights you are offering.
> A verbal agreement made over the phone (though legal, it is not always enforceable).
> An altered document where you've crossed out or revised unwanted clauses. Both parties must sign or initial any changes.

When you don't receive a formal contract:

Be sure to document what you and the editor agreed upon verbally—rights, payment, and other important issues. Type up the details you agreed upon and mail two signed copies to your editor with an SASE to return one of the copies. If you have e-mailed arrangements, keep and file the e-mails.

proceeds, negotiate on your behalf, or even let you negotiate your own deal. One example relates to the electronic rights agreement contained in the *Boys' Life* contract. "We have contracts with educational databases that take our articles—just the text, not accompanying photos or artwork," explains Owen. "They sell article access to schools and libraries and they pay us a royalty on that. The reason we initially put in the [relevant contract] language is so we'd have those rights to meet contract obligations."

But once the arrangement was successful, and the numbers made sense, Owen started sharing the royalties with his authors. Every fall, *Boys' Life* looks at the royalties for the preceding year, splits them 50/50, and gives every contributor to the magazine a share. "If you wrote for us once, we give you one share, four times would be four shares, and so on," he says. "At some point we may refine this process, but for now it works for us and our authors. It's the fair thing to do and it's set up such that there's not a big accounting burden on us."

Reprints are another angle, and what could be easier than just buying rights to an already edited piece? *Highlights* traditionally shares reprint fees with authors. Before *Guideposts Sweet 16* ceased publication, Editor Betsy Kohn did as well. "Say Chicken Soup for the Soul Enterprises wanted to include something of ours in their next book, which happened several times," says Kohn. "We negotiated a price with them and then split the fee with the author. In some cases, I felt we could · negotiate a higher price for the story that an individual author could do on their own." Because these were usually ghostwritten stories, the split was a little different. Fifty percent went to the publication, 25 percent to the ghostwriter, and 25 percent to the narrator of the story. Articles that were not ghostwritten yielded a 50/50 split.

"Anytime an outside company contacts us and expresses an interest in reprinting, either in whole or in part, something that appeared in the magazine, we make our best attempt to contact the author, who we consider to be the copyright holder, and put them in touch with that company," says Owen. "It's great publicity for the author, and good publicity for us, so we do make that effort." He notes that *Boys' Life* gets these requests frequently, often for use with state proficiency testing or other educational materials. In this case, the author has the opportunity to cut the best deal with the buyer, independent of the original publisher.

Contracts: Carved in Stone?

Most editors would rather do what they do best: edit. "I do as little with contracts as possible," says Hughes. "I print them out, send them, get them signed, and turn them in for payment. Our contract is what it is. I can't think of any circumstances where we've made exceptions." Does this mean there's no room for questions or negotiations? The

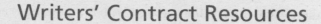

Writers' Contract Resources

Description of rights purchased by magazines:
> "Rights: What They Mean and Why They're Important," by Marg Gilks, *Writing World,* www.writing-world.com/rights/rights.shtml
> "Rights 101: What Writers Should Know About All-Rights and Work-Made-For-Hire Contracts," www.asja.org/pubtips/wmfh01.php
> The Publishing Law Center, www.publaw.com

Payments/Questionable Markets
> "How to Make Sure You Get Your Check," by Felicia Hodges, *Writing World,* www.writing-world.com/rights/hodges.shtml
> "What to Do When Clients Don't Pay," by Melissa Brewer, *Writing World,* www.writing-world.com/rights/brewer.shtml
> "Whispers and Warnings," *Writers Weekly,* www.writersweekly.com/whispers_and_warnings.php

answer often depends on the editor, magazine policies, and the request. It doesn't hurt to ask, especially if you have an established relationship. At worst, you'll still have your original offer.

"Editors are real people on the other side of the contract, just like you," says Kohn. "If anyone has questions about the language or doesn't understand something, they should talk with the editor." She notes that issues with *Sweet 16* were rarely over article payments, though she went back to her editor in chief on a few occasions for authorization to offer more money. Mostly, the questions involved rights policies and bylines. "There's often a way to work things out, but if there isn't, just move on."

Writers sometimes call Clark with questions about their contracts. "Ninety-nine percent of the time, they just need clarification. Rarely do we have to agree to disagree and stop the sale," she says. "In my experience, most children's writers experienced enough to sell to *Highlights* have done their homework ahead of time." It's easy to research *Highlights* rights and payment policies in advance of submitting. They're widely known in children's writers circles, posted in industry market guides, and explained in their writers' guidelines.

Lutes rarely makes adjustments for rights in the contract at *Ignite*

Your Faith. "It's a company policy, so we try to live by it." Does the magazine bend on certain issues? Sometimes. It has granted requests from authors asking to post work on their private websites or sell reprint rights to another publication before the specified contract limits. "Sure, we've made some exceptions with issues like these, especially if it doesn't involve a competitive market," he says.

As Waryncia likes to tell writers, even though the Cobblestone Group buys all rights, that does not preclude it from returning some rights back to the writer at a later time. "If they were writing their own book and wanted to include that material, it's okay with us because it's going to be in a different form. We just ask that they request permission from us and credit the magazine where the text originally appeared," he says. "Generally, all a writer would need to do is change a small portion of the work they've submitted to make it a different story." He cites the example of an author who submitted a piece a few years ago on the Dust Bowl. The author started doing more research and decided he could write a book on the subject, and he got a deal for one. "There are snippets of that original article in the book, but he expanded upon it to create a whole book," says Waryncia. "We both benefitted from it."

Market Smart

Whether it's payment amount, payment policy, or rights issues, one size doesn't fit all. Be market smart. Prepare before submitting. In addition to knowing editors' needs, know what your potential markets pay, when they pay, and what rights they routinely require. In this way, you won't be faced with surprises or second thoughts when an editor decides to send you a contract.

Never sign a contract you don't understand. Ask an editor for specific details. It doesn't matter whether you're a relative newbie to writing or a seasoned professional. If they don't know an answer, ask them to direct you to someone in their organization who does. Some contracts are short and straightforward, such as Cobblestone's one-pager. Others are like the *National Geographic Kids* contract, with nine pages of heavy reading.

If you choose to negotiate contract terms, seek reasonable and achievable goals. It's unlikely you'll get double the offered price for your article, but a modest increase, a few extra author's copies, or an okay to sell to noncompeting markets are well within the realm of possibility.

Rosinsky suggests contract negotiations should also be considered in a broader context, looking toward the future. "As one negotiates terms for a particular article, the author is also establishing the dimensions of what will hopefully be an ongoing professional relationship," she says. "So, suggesting the potential for further sales would be one of my goals in such exchanges. This is the time to mention possible spinoffs from this piece and other articles or ideas you have that would suit the publication's content and style. Think outside the contract!"

After the sale, don't hesitate to follow up by e-mail or phone about important issues: The check wasn't in the mail, the article didn't appear when it was supposed to, or your author's copies didn't arrive. It's part of being a writing professional, as long as you don't overdo it. It's also an indicator of the kind of editor and publication with whom you're working. If you get timely responses and actually get that check in a week or two, you'll know this is someone you'll want to work for in the future.

When it comes to the choice between getting paid on acceptance versus on publication, the obvious first choice is going to be payment on acceptance. Agreeing to sell first North American serial rights has more advantages than selling all rights. But just like building an investment portfolio, you're likely to take on some risks that may yield returns in the form of career status and future sales.

The Questions, Quandary, and Quest for an Agent

By Judy Bradbury

"**N**o agent necessary." That was a common and comforting declaration made for decades in children's publishing. But in the 1990s that statement evolved into a question: To agent or not to agent? Around 2000, the debate intensified. Now, before the turn of a decade later, a quandary seems to have evolved into a quest: How do I get an agent?

Children's writers have witnessed more and more attention paid to agents. Agents are present at writers' conferences, and more publishers' submissions guidelines list them as requirements. Children's authors increasingly consider retaining the services of an agent to represent their work. From online chats to cozy critique groups, there's buzz about agents.

Deciding if an agent is right for you, and then obtaining the services of a good match, takes time, honest appraisal, a bit of soul searching, and a clear sense of the goal.

Appraising Your Need

Children's writers often have a special attachment to their work. They are literary people, whether they write fiction or nonfiction, and they care about their audience of children. Agents are in business and their purpose is selling literary property for profit. Some writers, even those with some success, remain skittish about the divide between literature and business, and so, skittish about agents.

According to the Association of Authors' Representatives (AAR), "Literary and dramatic agents are engaged in the marketing of rights

What an Agent Can Do

➤ Market literary material.

➤ Establish contacts with editorial staff who wish to acquire rights to literary material.

➤ Negotiate and review contracts and licensing agreements.

➤ Offer advice on current trends, conditions of the contract, and contractual language.

➤ Monitor the marketing of your work.

➤ Review royalty statements.

➤ Offer editorial and career guidance.

to literary properties." Their task is to "serve as their clients' representatives with respect to the clients' literary work. They review their clients' work and advise them about its quality and potential marketability, and the possible strategy for securing its publication. An agent's relationship to a client is fiduciary and includes fiscal responsibility for funds collected on the client's behalf."

Most agents agree that an author should demonstrate professional commitment and a track record before seeking representation. That doesn't mean you must be published before approaching an agent, though the majority of clients have at least some publishing credits before an agent signs them. It does mean they exhibit ability, talent, commitment to craft, and a professional approach to writing. For an unpublished writer, it may be more difficult to snag an agent than a book contract.

Remember, however, that although children's book editors increasingly rely on agents to be first readers or gatekeepers, editors still do read at least some unagented, unsolicited work. So, at this point in your career, is your time better spent honing your craft or seeking representation?

Not all children's authors choose to seek representation from agents. As one author of 30 children's books, who asked to remain anonymous, explains, "Too many agents feel that part of their job is to offer a critique of their writers' manuscripts. Frankly, I am not interested in reworking a story until it meets an agent's liking, because the agent is not going to buy the story. What makes a story salable is subjective: More than once I've had one editor say no to a manuscript that another editor has accepted. I don't feel I need the extra step of trying to please an agent." This author has other reasons for reluctance. "I have heard writers talk about how they love their agents, extolling their good qualities, but when I've been told something the agent suggested, I've thought, 'I don't think that's a wise decision.' At other times I think to myself, 'I don't see this agent doing anything for this writer's career.' I guess I'm not ready yet for an agent relationship, and maybe I never will be."

Editors are clear-eyed about agents. "There are definite advantages and disadvantages to having a children's book agent, many of which depend on who your agent is and their strengths and weaknesses," says Abigail Samoun, Project Editor at Tricycle Press. "One obvious advantage in having an agent is being able to get your work into the hands of editors who don't accept unsolicited manuscripts. Another advantage is having someone who knows the business negotiate the publisher's contract on your behalf. However, if your agent doesn't know the children's book business, doesn't have a Rolodex full of editors to contact, or doesn't have experience in negotiating contracts, you certainly might be better off managing your relationships with editors and publishers on your own and keeping the 15 percent commission for yourself." At Tricycle Press, says Samoun, an author can be published without an agent. "Roughly a third of our authors and illustrators are unagented."

Karen Wojtyla, Executive Editor of Margaret K. McElderry Books, agrees. "Agents do get material directly into the hands of senior staff," but she is quick to point out that "although that may be useful, I don't believe it's crucial." Wojtyla explains a procedure common in editorial suites: "In our office, junior staff meet regularly to go through unsolicited manuscripts and queries looking for promising manuscripts." With policies such as this in place, Wojtyla maintains, "I don't think agents are necessary for children's authors."

Shopping for an Agent

If you're still itching to go agent shopping, various reliable sources can help you find one. AAR lists members on its website (www.aar-online.org). Literary agents are also listed in many book sources, including *Literary Market Place*, which is available at most libraries, and the annual Society of Children's Book Writers and Illustrators (SCBWI) *Publications Guide*, available free to members. Your primary sources, though,

What Agents Look For

Agents, of course, size up the qualities they seek in prospective clients. Here's what several agents reveal.

➤ **Jennie Dunham, Dunham Literary:** "Professional writers who understand the business and are open to an agent's guidance. Authors who write strong stories with memorable characters."

➤ **Emily Sylvan Kim, Prospect Agency:** "Someone who knows the market," an author who writes "a concise, exciting query letter" as well as a "captivating" first chapter. "The writing more than the subject matter" grabs Kim's attention.

➤ **Daniel Lazar, Writers House:** "Terrific writing and vibrant ideas. A professional manner, and passionate but realistic expectations. A good sense of humor helps too."

➤ **Erin Murphy, Erin Murphy Agency:** "Solid and unique writing, and story concepts that make me catch my breath. Professionalism, but not to the point that personality and individuality are stripped. Confidence that comes from knowing the business and trusting one's craft. Openness to feedback and a desire to have a partnership."

may be recommendations from fellow writers, editors with whom you have a relationship, writing instructors, and information from writers' conferences you attend.

Samoun believes, "The right agent can make all the difference in the world to your professional career. An agent can provide encouragement, direction, and professional savvy, making the author-agent partnership incredibly powerful. Getting there, though, takes responsibility on the author's part." Samoun advises authors seeking representation, "Find the right agent for you and your work; have reasonable expectations; be clear with those expectations; trust your agent's suggestions to make your work more publishable; and provide your agent with projects she can sell."

The Quest

Just as with editors, find out what forms of communication prospective agents prefer. Many agents will not accept queries by telephone, fax, or e-mail, although there are exceptions. Emily Sylvan Kim, owner of Prospect Agency, actually requires e-mail submissions (www. prospectagency.com). For Daniel Lazar, an agent at Writers House, e-mail is also preferable: "Initial submissions by e-mail are usually faster, but regular mail is fine, too." Lazar asks that authors include the first five pages of the manuscript. Paste the pages into the e-mail; don't attach. This is to help avoid viruses and application conflicts. "Remember," cautions Lazar, "the *first* five pages, not the middle five pages, even if your middle five pages are 'more exciting.' If your manuscript isn't exciting until page 100, there's a big problem!"

Jennie Dunham, of Dunham Literary, prefers "a query letter first that has one paragraph of no more than five sentences about the book and one paragraph about the author of no more than five sentences. This allows me to tell quickly if the author might be a match for me. If I think so, I can request the manuscript." The complete process for submitting to Dunham Literary is outlined on its website (www. dunhamlit.com).

Agent Erin Murphy, who founded her eponymous literary agency in 1999 and currently represents about 60 authors and author-illustrators, is not open to unsolicited submissions or even general queries. "I only consider new clients who come to me by referral (as from current clients, editors, other agents, and so on), and I am also open to queries from people who attend conferences and workshops where I speak and teach. This is not to foster an air of exclusivity that writers have to penetrate. It's because I'm a one-person operation and I have a lot of clients, and they always come first. This submission policy means that when a writer asks me to represent her, she already knows something about me and has a sense of how I operate and what I like (and thinks she and I would mesh well, accordingly). If she comes by referral, she has been vetted a bit by someone who knows me and has a sense that the author and I would be a match, and that the author is accomplished enough to be ready for representation."

Generally, to contact a prospective agent, write a brief letter that describes your work and lists your prior publications, if any. Include a self-addressed stamped envelope (SASE) for reply. It's fine to approach several agents at the same time, but submit material only when an agent requests it. Honor the wishes of those agents who ask you to inform them when you are submitting to more than one agent simultaneously. Materials should be neatly typed and double-spaced, of course, and always keep a copy of your manuscript.

The Questions

Once you have an agent interested in representing you, take a deep breath. Before you join forces with an agent, you'd be well advised to compile a list of questions. Think hard about what you are looking for in an agent and an agency.

Lazar, who represents literary and commercial fiction, narrative nonfiction, young adult, middle-grade, pop culture, and humor, believes, "Authors should ask about the agency agreement's basic terms. Is the agreement per book or for all the author's books? What is the duration of the contract? Does the agency charge expenses for copying, messengers, and overseas mailings? Ask how the agent communicates with clients. Does he or she prefer phone or e-mail?" In Lazar's opinion, most agents don't mind chatting on the phone with clients, especially when making important decisions, but e-mail is often "much faster than getting on the phone to discuss little details along the way."

He encourages authors to interview the agent. "Ask agents to pontificate about why they loved your book—let them puff up your ego, tell you why they want to work with *you!* Ask agents if they have any thoughts on ways to make the book stronger." Ask agents about the way they work, too. "Ask how they submit projects—exclusively to one editor at a time, or in a wide round of submissions. It's certainly fair to ask if you can speak with one or two of their clients if that makes you more comfortable in getting to know the agent and his work."

Dunham has been a literary agent since 1992 and started her own firm in 2000 to represent authors of children's and adult books. She advises authors to be direct. "Ask, 'Why do you like my work?' It's important for an agent to *get* an author's work, and be able to verbalize it, because this is how an agent makes a pitch to an editor." This is not easy to answer off the cuff, Dunham cautions, so she recommends authors "give the agent some time to think about it."

Authors should be proactive. "Ask what you can do to help sell your work. The agent may give a variety of suggestions from being patient, to asking the author to bolster his or her credentials, to putting together a marketing plan," says Dunham. Also helpful is finding out how an agent got into the business. "This gives the author an opportunity to get to know the agent better and to see if personally they're a match." Finally, Dunham says, don't forget to ask an agent "the terms of the contract—what the services and the costs are."

Murphy focuses on middle-grade and YA fiction, and some picture books and trade nonfiction. She suggests authors ask a prospective agent, "If I were your client, what should I expect of you and what

An agent should *get* an author's work and be able to verbalize how they can pitch it well to an editor.

would you expect of me? It's useful to find out if the agent has a written agreement, and if so, is it for a set period of time. What is required to end the agreement if the agent and author aren't happy with each other?" Murphy encourages authors to ask questions of the agent that are "particular to your needs and situation as a writer."

Emily Sylvan Kim opened Prospect Agency in 2005 after working with Writers House. Her focus is fiction, and she is especially interested in YA and middle-grade, although she represents a small number of picture book authors. Kim suggests authors ask agents about their track record. "How many books have they sold? What is their training? Are they willing to answer questions their authors may have? Are they a good fit for your personality?" Specifically, Kim says, "How does the agent handle subsidiary rights? Does the agent have the resources to negotiate these? How large is the agent's contact base of editors?"

Kim also believes questions related to the author's career goals are essential. "Share your expectations for communication. Ask about the level of support you can expect. If you have a special need to share your personal life, for example, or if you have a specific preference an agent ought to know about, be sure to explore those with a prospective agent before sealing the deal."

Do you have clear ideas about what you should reveal to agents you are interviewing? "Briefly discuss other projects you're working on. Be sure to let the agent know if you've made submissions directly to publishers on your own. If you're related to Oprah, that's relevant too," quips Lazar. Dunham suggests authors "gather any relevant credentials that increase their profile in that particular field, such as work as a children's book librarian or as a book reviewer for a magazine." She also encourages authors to "have a clear goal of what you are trying to accomplish and what areas you want to build your career in." Finally, think about and discuss "ideas of how you'd like to promote the book once it is published." Murphy suggests that authors simply "tell the agent about your hopes and dreams—briefly stated and reasonable."

Can We Work Together?

Among the skills of a good agent are a mix of business ability, personal communication, and a true feel for writing and publishing.

"Good agents are real networkers," believes Samoun. "They attend conferences, they regularly correspond with editors from an array of publishers (corporate and independent alike), they know the tastes and preferences of individual editors, and they keep current with news of the publishing biz, such as the formation of new imprints or changes in publishing staff. The children's book publishing world is vast, with many different options for writers. A good agent will know which arena best suits your writing, whether that's trade, institutional, or mass-market." But like the authors they represent, agents are individuals, with different philosophies, communication styles, and expectations.

Getting a sense for how an agent prefers to work is paramount to developing and maintaining a successful relationship. According to the AAR, "The specifics of the relationship between an author and agent will vary depending on the nature of the work in question, the author's needs, and the agent's policies and practices." Lazar, at Writers House, thrives on involvement. "I'm very hands-on throughout the process—from helping to shape a project from its inception to the selling and negotiating process, putting in my two cents on the jacket, helping secure endorsements, and doing what I can to help with the publisher's promotion. And that's just Monday!"

Kim, too, describes herself as "hands-on." She admits to spending "hours and hours doing editorial work," as well as spending time "studying what the market calls for, what editors are publishing," and

Caution

Abigail Samoun, Project Editor at Tricycle Press, cautions authors, "There are unscrupulous agents out there and writers should do their homework when choosing where to submit their work. Luckily, some websites keep track of agents to avoid. Talking to fellow writers and attending Society of Children's Book Writers and Illustrators (SCBWI) conferences are also good places to start your research." For more on incompetent or irreputable agents, for example, see the Science Fiction and Fantasy Writers of America website (www.sfwa.org/beware/agents.html).

Authors can access information about members of the Association of Authors' Representatives (AAR) on its website (www.aar-online.org). The AAR formed in 1991 with the merger of the Society of Authors' Representatives (founded in 1928) and the Independent Literary Agents Association (founded in 1977). AAR is a "not-for-profit organization of qualified literary agents and dramatic representatives of authors, dramatists, and other creators and owners of intellectual property."

AAR prohibits its members from charging reading fees, stating that the practice "reflects adversely on our profession." The SCBWI agrees, noting in its materials on agents that they "should make money from selling your work, not from charging fees." If an agent asks for a reading fee, run.

maintaining strong relationships with editors so she's not "shooting in the dark" when there's a manuscript ready to be shopped.

Dunham characterizes her role as more business-oriented. "My job is to sell the manuscript or proposal, negotiate the contract, and handle the money related to it." But she finds that "often authors benefit from a critical agent's eye before the manuscript is submitted" and she relishes that part of her job as well.

"Communication-driven" is how Murphy describes herself. "I like being in regular touch with my clients. I like the big-picture career thinking, and I do work editorially on my clients' manuscripts before they go out to editors."

Building and Maintaining a Solid Relationship

Once you have entered into a relationship with an agent, be sure to work on maintaining good feelings. As in all relationships, there's a balance. Kim believes authors who respect that agents have other clients and projects go a long way toward strengthening the bond. "Pick and choose how to communicate. Respect your agent's level of activity and maintain professionalism." Kim appreciates clients who "honor contracts and allow me to do my job."

Along those lines, Dunham says, "Give the agent time to sell the work. Listen to the agent's advice and follow it. Be professional, meet deadlines, and promote your books once they are published."

"Be patient," says Lazar, "but certainly expect your agent to return your calls and e-mails in a timely manner. An agent should update you when you ask, but again, patience is very important. I'd also encourage you to discuss your ideas for future books before sitting down to write the entire thing. Your agent can usually help steer you in the right direction—encourage your idea or warn you about its possible hurdles —and give you a better sense of the market outside of your purely creative efforts." As an afterthought, Lazar says, "Be sure to thank your agent in the acknowledgements when the book is published!"

Murphy is reflective about the agent-author relationship. "It always helps if an author has a sense of forward momentum—catching hot news reports on subjects related to what the author is writing about in a work-in-progress, finding the local independent bookstore has championed the author so much that sales have shot up in the region, writing a particularly interesting blog entry and getting comments from several high-profile folks and being mentioned on other industry blogs. These kinds of activities show the agent that the author is hardworking and self-sufficient, and give the agent more things to say about the author to editors. I'd think an occasional update along these lines wouldn't be unwelcome, even with agents who don't like to be in touch as often, so long as it doesn't get out of control."

Successful agents work hard to maintain relationships with their clients, as well. "I make a big effort to be there when needed and to promptly address concerns," notes Kim. She does follow-up such as checking on advances and related work that many authors find distasteful or are uncomfortable doing.

Dunham tries "to be clear with a client about what I need them to do. I give the author feedback about their work. I send responses to submissions. But that said, this is actually an individual process, one that is not the same for any two clients. It really depends on what each client needs."

Murphy likes to be in touch fairly often. "I mass e-mail my full client list every time I have a sale or a big review or some such, so my clients can cheer each other on. It also gives me a chance to let them know what's on my schedule, like when I'll be away. Many of my clients also participate on a listserv that is exclusively for my clients, and I chime in when I can. They've planned a retreat in the past. I have a *reading week* every month, and my clients set deadlines for themselves based on that, which gives us a reason to be in touch about their works in progress." Murphy admits that it's difficult sometimes to meet her author relationship goals. "Lately I've been aware that I've been so busy with the day-to-day and week-to-week tasks that I've lost track of a lot of big-picture thinking. I've been making an effort to reconnect with individual clients and think in terms of what our big goals are and how things are coming with them."

Lazar also considers communication important. "I try to keep my authors regularly updated on what's going on. Checking in to say hello helps them know I haven't forgotten. I try to check in to make sure their writing is going well. I try to give as much feedback as humanly possible on their ongoing drafts or proposals. I offer fashion advice, too, if need be, though, sadly, it's not usually solicited."

The Gamut of Professional Organizations

By Veda Boyd Jones

For 17 years, I've met with a select few writers each Wednesday for lunch. We are not exactly the Algonquin Round Table, but we are working writers. Is this a professional writers' group? We don't pay dues. We don't have bylaws, we don't have officers, and we don't have programs. We exchange market information, share successes, and commiserate over rejections. We discuss which editors are easy to work with and which are ridiculous, and who has moved to another publishing house or a different magazine. We talk money—what editors pay and when the checks arrive.

All of us also belong to big professional organizations with conferences and newsletters and such. Which is more beneficial, my local group or the national ones?

At one Wednesday lunch, my colleagues and I talked about writers' groups we belong to, their benefits, what we want out of a group, and why. Networking, professional development, and friendship opportunities head the list. A community of writers who are knowledgeable and generous with markets is central to our dream writers' group.

Our group wants face-to-face meetings for the social factor: Only other writers understand why we're in this wonderful crazy business. In the Internet age, another component to networking and marketing exists in the form of online writer newsletters and groups. Large, national professional groups have websites with some of the same features as subscription services, but no longer do the national groups have a monopoly on career or marketing or other information. Each group, big or small, offers a unique slant on the writing business.

Society of Children's Book Writers and Illustrators

Most children's writers belong to the Society of Children's Book Writers and Illustrators (SCBWI), which started small in California in 1971 and today claims more than 19,000 members worldwide. The organization is open to anyone with an interest in children's literature, and members range from published and unpublished writers and illustrators to librarians, editors, agents, and educators.

Two big conferences, in February in New York City and August in Los Angeles, help make this the premier group for introducing children's writers to editors and agents face to face. SCBWI is divided into regional groups, each with an advisor who spearheads a state conference. Here again, writers can hear editors, agents, and successful writers give pointers based on their expertise. Many times at state events, writers can pitch projects to attending editors or agents. Regional SCBWI groups may also offer critique groups and social events for members.

SCBWI publishes a bimonthly newsletter that contains helpful articles on the craft of writing, news on current submission needs, and updates on which editors have jumped to other jobs. In addition, SCBWI has publications on markets, agents, educational publishers, contracts, and more. This information is also provided on the group's website in the members' only section. The discussion boards are well-used and give a sense of belonging to members writing from their isolated computers.

The national organization recognizes outstanding writing achievement with magazine and book awards in fiction and nonfiction. It also administers several grants for works in progress. Some SCBWI chapters award mentorships to writers and illustrators.

An additional perk of this organization is that some publishing houses that are closed to unsolicited submissions will make an exception and remain open to SCBWI members. Editors at those houses recognize membership in the organization as the sign of a professional.

American Society of Journalists and Authors

The American Society of Journalists and Authors (ASJA) is group of about 1,300 nonfiction writers who must meet rigid requirements for membership: publication over a sustained period of time with bylines in national magazines or big newspapers, or at least two books released by established publishers. Although the majority of members write for adult publications, some specialize in children's writing. The annual conference in New York City includes a panel of children's book and magazine editors.

Members receive a newsletter that includes printed versions of Paycheck Reports, also available on the website. In these reports, members reveal anonymously how much they were paid per word for a specific magazine piece, how long it took to get paid, what rights were sold, and if revisions were required. This valuable section lets other writers know the going rate for a magazine; it is particularly useful because market directories often indicate only that payment rates differ. ASJA members also post payments from book publishers.

Another member benefit is the deep discount in rates for magazine subscriptions, including many children's magazines. Writers know they must study a magazine before writing for it, and this perk cuts the steep cost of buying magazines on newsstands.

The online forums are busy, busy. Even if a writer doesn't want to post a note looking for an expert to interview or for an editor's e-mail address—which other writers answer quickly—a member can lurk and read and learn. Also online is a writer search, where editors in need of a writer can post a job.

The Authors Guild

Membership in this prestigious group requires a published book by an established American publisher, or three articles or short stories in magazines with general circulation. Roy Blount Jr. is the Guild's high-profile president; famed children's and adult novelist Judy Blume is one of two current vice presidents.

The Authors Guild has long advocated actively for writers, in the last decade most notably in the arena of copyrights, fair use, and electronic publishing. It has also made news over censorship issues. The Guild keeps track of payment rates and policies, mediates in contracts and other author disputes, and has been involved in litigation concerning opening government archives to researchers, the use of historical archives as source material, and the right to parody.

The Guild also holds informative seminars, including one not long ago on big profits in children's books and how authors can share in increased publisher earnings. Benefits of membership include website building, contract review, a quarterly bulletin, reports on job changes, and other publishing and member news. Members are also eligible to join a health insurance plan.

Novelists, Inc.

Writers must have two published books—in print, not electronically —to join this professional organization, but the average for its 700+ members is 16 books. The monthly newsletter targets seasoned pros with helpful articles on promotion, taxes, contract rights, and more. Novelists, Inc. offers its members networking opportunities, a national conference on the business aspects of a writing career, a legal fund, and directories of agents, editors, publishing lawyers, and more.

Although most members write for adult markets, the professional business information Novelists, Inc. provides on subjects from copyright to plagiarism to book industry trends is helpful to children's writers, too. An online forum is well-used by members.

Freelance Success

Freelance Success (FLX) is an online community of editors and writers that offers a weekly subscription newsletter. Every Thursday members receive by e-mail a detailed market listing for a magazine, complete with an interview with the editor. Although this is what subscribers sign up for and expect from FLX for the $89 subscription, the real deal for this site is the helpful members, who make frequent use of the forums.

Have a rejected piece that needs a new market? Post that information online, and it's likely that you'll have five suggestions from other members within an hour. Stuck on a query letter? Head to the Query Letter forum where members post letters that netted them assignments. Read all the letters and you will have a crash course on writing queries. One forum title, "The Juggling Writer," says it all. What writer doesn't struggle with life issues while trying to write an article or story? This is the place to ask advice on how to find time to write with preschoolers underfoot. This is the place where any subject that takes a writer's time, but isn't particularly related to writing, is posted. This is the place where writers make virtual friends with other writers.

FLX has a list of magazines with addresses, names of editors, and e-mail contact information. Although not many children's magazines make the list, many family and parenting magazines do. Writers can sign up for a free week's trial before deciding to pay the annual subscription rate.

Other Online Services

At one time, writers' organization bulletins and writers' magazines were the keepers of industry news and new markets lists. The Internet now bursts with sites that provide more up-to-date publishing information than any print publication could—some for a fee and some for free, some accurately and some less so.

➤ Publishers Marketplace is an excellent website for keeping track of which agents are selling what to whom. Deals for children's picture books, middle-grade books, and young adult novels are in separate lists. The site's daily newsletter, *Publishers Lunch*, is read by 30,000 publishing professionals.

➤ Agent Query is a free online searchable database of agents, including agents for children's book authors. The site relies on users (you and me) to send updates if we know of new agents or changes in a listed agent's e-mail or other relevant information.

➤ PEN American Center offers a subscription to Grants & Awards, a database listing more than 1,000 opportunities for writers in the form of grants, literary awards, fellowships, and residencies.

➤ The Children's Book Council (CBC) is a trade association whose website posts listings of member publishers, with their specialties, needs, information such as whether that house is currently accepting unsolicited submissions, and valuable links to the publishers' websites.

Organizations to Help Book Promotion

Although many writers belong to writers' organizations to network with other writers and editors, they also belong to literacy and education organizations to help them promote their books and learn of speaking opportunities.

➤ The International Reading Association (IRA) presents author programs at its annual convention, which was in Toronto in May 2007 and in Atlanta in May 2008. Many publishers exhibit at this conference and at the IRA's regional conferences. In addition, many local chapters

Organizations & Resources

➢ **Agent Query:** www.agentquery.com

➢ **American Library Association:** 50 East Huron St., Chicago, IL 60611. www.ala.org

➢ **American Society of Journalists and Authors:** 1501 Broadway, Suite 302, New York, NY 10036. www.asja.org

➢ **Association of Booksellers for Children:** 62 Wenham St., Jamaica Plain, MA 02130. www.abfc.com

➢ **Authors Guild:** 31 East 32nd Street, 7th Floor, New York, NY 10016. www.authorsguild.org

➢ **Children's Book Council:** 12 West 37th Street, 2nd Floor, New York, NY 10018. www.cbcbooks.org

➢ **Freelance Success:** 32391 Dunford St., Farmington Hills, MI 48334. www.freelancesuccess.com

➢ **International Reading Association:** 800 Barksdale Road, P.O. Box 8139, Newark, DE 19714. www.reading.org

➢ **Mystery Writers of America:** 17 E. 47th Street, 6th Floor, New York, NY 10017. www.mysterywriters.org

➢ **National Council of Teachers of English:** 1111 W. Kenyon Road, Urbana, IL 61801. www.ncte.org

➢ **National Writers Association:** 10940 S. Parker Road, #508, Parker, CO 80134. www.nationalwriters.com

➢ **Novelists, Inc.:** P.O. Box 2037, Manhattan, KS 66505. www.ninc.com

➢ **Publishers Marketplace:** www.publishersmarketplace.com

➢ **Romance Writers of America:** 16000 Stuebner Airline Road, Suite 140, Spring, TX 77379. www.rwanational.org

➢ **Science Fiction and Fantasy Writers of America:** P.O. Box 877, Chestertown, MD 21620. www.sfwa.org

➢ **Society of Children's Book Writers and Illustrators:** 8271 Beverly Blvd., Los Angeles, CA 90048. www.scbwi.org

➢ **Western Writers of America:** www.westernwriters.org

sponsor young authors' conferences, where students write books that are displayed at an awards ceremony. In my local area, awards are presented by a children's book author who is the featured speaker, and a copy of one of that author's books is given to each of the 300 young authors.

➤ The annual conference of the American Library Association (ALA) also features writers as speakers. Meeting librarians from across the country is a great way to introduce them to your books. A division of the ALA, the American Association of School Librarians (AASL), can provide valuable contacts with librarians who work on literature festivals or schedule author visits to their schools. Another division of ALA is YALSA, the Young Adult Library Services Association. It too has an annual conference, and it also offers online courses, a student interest group network, and more.

➤ The Association of Booksellers for Children (ABC) links independent children's booksellers. Authors may be non-voting members, but may request unlimited ABC mailing labels to publicize their books.

Genre Organizations

Many writers' organizations specialize in one genre and, while they may be primarily geared to writers for adults, also have members who focus on children's writing. Several of these organizations offer annual awards.

Mystery Writers of America presents the Edgar Allan Poe Award in adult, young adult, and juvenile categories. Western Writers of America gives Spur awards for juvenile books in fiction and nonfiction categories. Science Fiction and Fantasy Writers of America gives one of its Nebula awards to a young adult novel.

Non-members may enter the award competitions of these groups, but self-published or subsidy-published books are not allowed. Romance Writers of America, however, gives a young adult romance award to one of its members for an unpublished manuscript.

Be Active

Several members of my Wednesday group belong to book clubs. While these are not professional organizations, the members are readers, and where would writers be without them? I belong to two book clubs, and although that means I must read two books a month that I didn't pick out on my own, I gain insights into what resonates with readers, even if we're reading adult books instead of children's. In my groups, we've read both—from Leo Tolstoy's *Anna Karenina* to Lois Lowry's *The Giver*.

Belonging to a writers' group is helpful, no matter the size, and becoming active in the group can increase your knowledge of the business exponentially. Not only will you get to know more members and therefore enlarge your networking field, you may get to pick up conference speakers from the airport, introduce them, and dine with them. I met my first editor at a dinner the night before a conference, so I highly recommend getting involved in an organization by serving in a leadership position or on a committee.

Keeping up with publishing industry news, networking, learning tips that can help perfect writing skills, and socializing with other writers are reasons writers join professional groups. Writers' organizations, whether big or small or online, are important to a writer's career.

Into the Readers' Hands: How the Book Distribution Process Works

By Christina Hamlett

For many authors, and small emerging publishers, the challenge of making sure that every book finds its target audience and sells well can seem bewildering. Traditional sales and distribution channels have also been challenged in recent years by computer downloads, the recycling of used books via media such as eBay, and a generation of young people who often spend more time text messaging, watching streaming videos, and playing electronic games than reading novels.

An author begins with a book concept that aims at a particular readership—an age range, fans of a genre, educational—and researches markets to identify the right publisher to get the book to that audience. Next come promotion, marketing, sales, and distribution. Large publishers have marketing staffs to create promotional plans. They have sales staffs that go out in the field to bookstores—or to wholesalers. They have accounting staffs. But if you're an author working with a small press, or thinking of self-publishing or even starting your own small company, you'll need help navigating the circuitous waters of book distribution. We've tapped the expertise of Davida Breier, Sales and Marketing Director for Biblio Distribution, and Laura Moriarty, Deputy Director of Small Press Distribution (SPD).

Services and Customers

The terms *distributor, wholesaler, wholesale distributor,* and even *bookseller* are often mistakenly used interchangeably.

A *distributor* may buy a publisher's books, but more often its function as a go-between involves a consignment relationship. The distributor sells the books to bookstores, other retail stores, schools, libraries, or to wholesalers. For a fee arrangement, a *wholesaler* maintains inventory and fulfills orders (but does not promote or sell) to bookstores, individuals, schools, and other customers.

Moriarty clarifies operational differences: "Generally, wholesalers order books on a case-by-case basis rather than carrying all of the books by any one publisher. They don't operate on consignment. Distributors carry all or most of the titles of the publishers they represent and offer more services, including marketing and sales representatives."

The field is dominated by two large companies with considerable clout getting books on shelves—wholesale distributors Ingram and Baker & Taylor—but many other companies offer their distribution and/or wholesaling services, sometimes to special niches such as small presses, international markets, religious publishers, and so on. A distributor can bring several small to medium presses under one umbrella and maximize their respective exposure. It also takes on the responsibility of storing, shipping, and billing, and these tasks can impact the cost of the book and its profit margin. A wholesaler can offer tight control over inventory and be less expensive, but the money saved may actually be negligible for a self-publishing author or a small press that has to do its own promotion, sales, and order processing.

Biblio is a distributor that specializes in warehousing, sales, fulfillment, accounting, and collection for independent and small presses. "We have a sales force that tries to function as an emissary among publishers, wholesalers, and booksellers," says Breier. "Our job is to promote books to the wholesalers and booksellers in order to help both entities meet consumer demand. Our main fees are a $50 title set-up fee and a penny and a half per book, per month storage fee. It is a consignment relationship, so authors are paid 40 percent of retail price; Biblio keeps 10 percent; and the accounts generally buy at a 50 percent discount."

Launched in 2001, Biblio is the sister company of National Book Network, which is currently the largest distributor of independent publishers in North America. Biblio carries all types of books, representing approximately 550 publishers and 2,000 active titles.

SPD is unique, identifying itself as a nonprofit literary arts organization that helps "under-represented literary communities to participate fully in the marketplace and in the culture at large through book distribution, information services, and public advocacy programs," according to its mission statement. The organization, says Moriarty, "is something of a hybrid. We carry all of the books of the publishers we work with, as well as retain a large number of backlist titles. However, we operate on a consignment basis and, while we have three in-house sales people,

A distributor can bring several small presses under one umbrella and maximize their exposure.

we do not have sales reps in the field. As the only nonprofit distributor and the only purely literary distributor, we are able to offer distribution to much smaller publishers than commercial distributors, and to subsidize these services by fundraising. We pay publishers 50 percent of whatever we get for the book. Discounts to booksellers are standard and are listed on www.spdbooks.org in Booksellers Resources, and in our print catalogue. We also offer discounts to Friends of SPD and to our publishers."

Friends of SPD make membership contributions, or volunteer, to promote community-centered literature. SPD's area of expertise is in literary titles: poetry, fiction, and writing about art, culture, and politics. "We carry 450 publishers and approximately 13,000 titles," Moriarty says.

Breier and Moriarty both receive new submissions daily. They scout new publishing houses and stay abreast of marketing trends by attending trade shows, book fairs, industry seminars, and national conferences such as those of Associated Writing Programs and the Modern Language Association.

Legs

Much of what dictates the legs of a new book's journey at a large publisher is a combination of a company's overall marketing plan and the number of titles it has already published. Presses that turn out only a handful of books each year have a harder time getting their books noticed than major houses with sales and marketing staff, and deals with companies such as Ingram and Baker & Taylor that can help get placement on national bookstore shelves.

Unless a publisher has the marketing wherewithal to generate a strong buzz, the promotion onus can fall hard on the author. Many of the smaller houses now ask upfront how involved the writer plans to be in hyping a book, before offering a contract. Even if a small press's book is well-reviewed, many bookstores are reluctant to order when no major distributor is involved because of hassles dealing with book returns.

Both Biblio and SPD encourage writers and publishers to hawk their wares as much as possible. "Authors are always free to sell direct to consumers and to sell outside of our territory (through special sales, corporate sales, library sales)," explains Breier. "We are exclusive to the trade, however, so sales to bookstores and wholesalers need to go through us in order to protect publishers and our reps from miscredited sales and returns." Though many distributors operate on the basis of exclusivity, Moriarty says that SPD does not. "We encourage authors and publishers to do as much marketing as they can to sell books through alternative channels or directly from their websites or blogs."

Neither organization deals directly with authors in negotiating deals for their books, though Moriarty points out, "We do have a lot of contact with writers since many of our staff members are very active members of the writing community we serve." Breier explains that a distributor may be "tied to the publishers, and can't contract individually with authors."

Changing Routes

Increasingly, writers who have been rejected by traditional publishers are going the route of e-books and print-on-demand (POD). Could a successful track record of website sales, seminars, and word-of-mouth publicity on a self-published title nudge a distributor to change the methods by which new books are introduced to the mainstream?

"Whether a book is POD or printed offset," says Breier, "we usually don't see a crossover correlation from those [self-published] markets to the trade market. Word-of-mouth can be a bit different, but seminars and workshops usually don't cross over for us at all if that is the genesis of book sales." But that may shift, she admits. "We are in a period of tremendous change right now. We can look at how the TV industry has changed in the last 25 to 30 years from a few networks to hundreds of cable channels, and how the record industry changed from LPs to iTunes, to see that books (while a much older medium) will inevitably change to suit reader needs. I think we will see more niche titles and that more technologies will be used to suit reader demographics. We can even look at the rise in audiobooks to see that how people 'read' has changed and that a demand has been met. People will always want information and want to be entertained. We will see more POD and electronic books, but there is something about the hand-feel of a bound book that can't easily be replaced for many readers. E-books and PODs have not impacted us much, but Biblio was formed to handle all the micro-presses that Ingram ceased dealing with directly in 2001."

For SPD's customers, "POD tends to be more of a printing option than a distribution method," says Moriarty. The niche literary market "publishers who have signed with us tend to be very active in searching for the most economical ways to print books. While these publishers often have active websites, we have not seen a lot of e-books or other non-book formats. As a general criteria at SPD, we also don't carry self-published writers."

The fact that today's young people are reading fewer books is a concern not lost on Moriarty and her staff. "SPD is now doing a project called New Lit Generation. It is a program of events, publications, Web material, and other activities to encourage high school and college students to read SPD books. We are very much aware that the next generation of readers needs to be cultivated if literature is going to prosper. Young writers (and savvy older writers) are already actively using all available technologies to get their work out. We anticipate that trend will continue. One of SPD's strong points is our knowledge of the whole spectrum of literary activity by new, emerging, innovative, and even well-known writers whose work is not commercial. There is so much of this kind of activity that SPD's role has always been to select and present what is essential in the contemporary writing put out by independent publishers to booksellers, libraries, and individuals. No matter what format literature ends up taking, this

A Time-Space Continuum

The traditional paper-and-ink, printed-and-bound format still leaves booksellers, distributors, and publishers with space and time challenges in the form of remaindering and returns.

"Remaindering is essentially selling off excess stock at a deep discount," says Davida Breier, Sales and Marketing Director for Biblio Distribution. "This is often used when frontlist books move to backlist and the sales just aren't there to sustain the book in print. It's a good way to get books in front of readers and at least recoup some expenses." The practice is more common in trade than in literary publishing. Laura Moriarty, Deputy Director of Small Press Distribution (SPD), explains, "Independent literary publishers tend not to remainder titles but to retain backlist, often for many years."

As for returns, authors are sometimes naively alarmed to discover that bookstores won't keep their titles on the shelves indefinitely. Brick and mortar facilities, unlike online resources such as Amazon, have limited space and a constant influx of new works to sell. Publishers operate under the expectation that roughly 30 percent of the books that make it through a physical front door will subsequently become returns.

While Biblio, SPD, and many other distributors allow returns up to one year, small presses often have shipments returned within weeks if the initial consumer reaction doesn't register as a significant blip on a book-store's radar screen. "At SPD," says Moriarty, "all books are sold as returnable unless an account is specifically set up as non-returnable, for a deeper discount. Any returned books received in salable condition are restocked. Damaged books are either resold as hurts or destroyed." As for the pervasive myth that trade paperback covers are always stripped off to save returning shipping costs, this only applies to magazines and to mass-market paperbacks.

kind of filtering and selecting will continue to be important, and SPD plans to be there to help get the word out."

The Look of Success

It's a reality of our times that many an author dreams of appearing on *Oprah* or becoming the next author to scribble a chapter in a coffee shop that within a year or two will underwrite the purchase of a castle in Scotland. From a distributor's viewpoint, do some writers have a better chance of success based on the genre in which they choose to express themselves?

According to Breier, "From what I've seen at Biblio, nonfiction is usually a safer path. While you can hit big with fiction and children's titles, the books that make the bestsellers list represent an extremely small fraction of the titles published in those genres. Authors writing fiction should be prepared to work very hard marketing their books. Often, nonfiction books are found by an existing audience, but fiction is usually driven by word-of-mouth and name recognition."

"What makes SPD unique in answer to that question," replies Moriarty, "is that books of poetry surprisingly are our bestsellers. In fact, we even provide a bestseller list to the Poetry Foundation site. While the books we carry sustain themselves in that publishers are able to continue publishing literary titles, not much money actually makes its way to the writer. This is not a new phenomenon. Poets and writers of innovative fiction have long found teaching, awards, grants, and other jobs to be their main source of support."

Moriarty and Breier also volunteer some wisdom to individuals who want to start up their own publishing companies. "Don't reinvent the wheel!" warns Moriarty. "Find publishers who are the size you hope to be and talk to them. SPD and our sister organization, Council of Literary Magazines and Presses (CLMP), are good places to start. In traveling, it is often said that you should take half the luggage and twice the money. Unfortunately in publishing, the rule tends to be that it takes twice the money and twice the time that one had ever hoped to get a book into a reader's hands. The results can be very satisfying, but it is important to find out in advance what success looks like in today's small press world."

Breier agrees wholeheartedly. "Decide early on if [starting a publishing company] is a dream fulfilled or a business or a bit of both. If it is a dream, be prepared to do it as a hobby and not expect to make a profit. If it is a business, treat it as a business and do at least six months' worth of research before printing or acquiring a title. Publishers should understand multiple markets and not assume that books will be stocked in bookstores just because they are published. Far from it! Work with experts and get consumer feedback before committing to print. For example, a bad cover can kill a good book. Don't scrimp on editorial work or design work, as that will stand out. Make sure your marketing plan shows an understanding of your target audience. If I see a submission with *audience* indicated as *everyone who reads*, it usually becomes an automatic rejection because the writer or publisher doesn't understand who their readers are and thus how to reach them."

Passionate as you are about what you've written, the distributor's reality is that every new client is a risky proposition; a smaller press can translate to an income stream that may not be worth their while. Commit to being your own best salesperson. Even if your publisher uses a distributor with an enthusiastic marketing arm, the amount of hoopla you can stir up yourself through bookstore signings, talks, blogs, websites, book fairs, and workshops will make the distributor's job that much easier in keeping your product visible.

Making a Career Splash

By Chris Eboch

Every author would like to be a bestseller. It's not just about the money—it's about reaching readers and building a career (the money would be nice, too). But authors quickly learn that their publisher's busy publicity department can only do so much for them. With thousands of new books on the market every year, authors must help their books stand out from the masses.

According to book marketing consultant John Kremer, "The book will only sell in most cases if the author gets behind the book and does speaking engagements, Internet marketing and interviews, makes PR contacts, etc., in support and in coordination with his or her publisher."

Several authors shared their experiences working through a variety of traditional and original means to make a splash in the crowded ocean of children's books.

Doing it All: Marketing Plans

➢ *Kirby Larson:* Larson's historical fiction, *Hattie Big Sky* (Delacorte), was a Newbery Honor Book and made the *New York Times* bestseller list.

"My picture book, *The Magic Kerchief* (Holiday House), had fallen into that horrible purgatory of 'out of stock indefinitely.' I didn't want *Hattie Big Sky* to suffer the same fate. Six months before the publication date, I began a marketing plan. I filled a huge notebook with every tip I could glean—from the Internet, from friends, from books on marketing. A group of local authors met several times to share what we'd

Supportive Editors

Editors love finding authors who are so fully committed to their books that they will take on marketing tasks with energy and innovation.

Liz Waniewski, Editor at Dial Books for Young Readers, says, "I try to acquire books based on the quality of the writing first and foremost. But it is always a huge bonus to find out that authors are willing to do self-promotion for their books. Authors who are willing to introduce themselves to their local librarians and booksellers, perhaps offer to do a stock signing for a bookstore, speak at schools and libraries, and set up a website are doing great things for self-promotion. Nothing can beat going out there and interacting directly with your target audience. Giving a presentation at a school or a library puts you in direct contact with the kids who will be reading your books. Remember how much it meant to meet the author of your favorite book?"

Michelle Poploff, Vice President and Editorial Director at Bantam Delacorte Dell Books for Young Readers, says, "It's terrific when an author helps seed the marketplace for her book by making herself known to local booksellers, schools, newspapers, media, etc. Find out if there are book festivals in your area or other local events where you can make an appearance to promote your book and make yourself known in a positive way. Sometimes authors create bookmarks, postcards, or other giveaways that provide publication date, price, website information. If an author sends us these to use in mailings or at conventions, we will try to do so. Many

learned about marketing. I participated in an Authors Guild phone seminar on marketing. I made a month-by-month plan to implement the marketing ideas I felt I could do.

"I had a mini-website made for *Hattie Big Sky*; people could download the first chapter of the book and listen to a video-podcast of me talking about the research process. I printed off several hundred chapbooks that included the first chapter, a letter from my editor, and a letter from me and sent it to independent booksellers all around the country. I also handed these out at the Pacific Northwest Booksellers Association trade show, when the advance reader copies ran out.

"Because I was a marketing novice, I hired people to help me. Sara Easterly of Sara Easterly and Friends designed the mini-website, including

Supportive Editors

authors have done their own bookmarks, postcards, or brochures that are visually pleasing, but booksellers are inundated with these materials. An author may have a leg up if she creates something unique that ties into the theme of her book."

Author Kirby Larson found such a twist for *Hattie Big Sky*. "I had packets of sunflower seeds made up with a letter to the reader from Hattie on the back of the packet. I paid for them myself, but my publisher handed them out to sales reps and other folks, which helped generate interest. The more I stretched, the more they were willing to come alongside me."

An author's willingness to do marketing is so important to Miriam Hees, Publisher and Managing Editor at the small publisher Blooming Tree Press, that she says, "I ask an author when I am offering a contract of their willingness to promote. I like to see an author be a book's own best cheerleader—from websites promoting the book to author visits, book signings, and most important, word of mouth. I'd have to say word of mouth is the most effective. Next would be to be a member of writing organizations that can help spread the word. And then just getting out there to schools, libraries, and bookstores, shaking hands and talking about their book. Anything that gets their face and the book to the public. If you are shy about face-to-face meetings, then begin with Internet exposure, newsletters, and e-mails. Then progress to phone calls. In no time you will feel comfortable talking to anyone about your masterpiece."

podcast, and my promotional materials. Illustrator Jaime Temairik designed the chapbook. Web designer Aaron Hedquist designed my [regular] website. I spent nearly 50 percent of my advance on marketing. My original goal was to tell as many people about HBS as possible. To that extent, I think my efforts were effective."

See Larson's efforts at www.kirbylarson.com and at the linked mini-website, www.hattiebigsky.com.

Getting the Word Out: Mailings

➤ *Alan Gratz:* Gratz's first novel, *Samurai Shortstop*, sold out the first print run within six months.

"*Samurai Shortstop* was my first big shot at establishing myself as an

Focus Your Marketing

John Kremer has edited the *Book Marketing Update* newsletter for more than 20 years, and is the author of *1001 Ways to Market Your Books* (Open Horizons), and other books on publishing and marketing.

To publicize their books, Kremer says, authors should "create a list of the top 100 media they want to be featured in and work to create relationships with the decision makers (editors, producers, hosts, etc.) for those media. It is the most important list for anyone marketing a book. Focus 90 percent of your attention on mailing, e-mailing, phoning, and meeting these key people in person. Create a relationship with them where they will want to interview you, review your book, have you write a column, etc.

"Get book reviews, interviews, articles, columns, etc., with media that reach your core audience. For children's books, that would mean magazines such as *Parents, Parenting, Family Fun, Cookie,* and *Child*, plus mothering magazines, newspaper lifestyle sections (don't expect book reviews from the book review section), radio interviews, and some TV if you are good on TV."

Kremer also recommends "Internet marketing, especially creating relationships with the top 30 websites for your key search terms (the words people might type into a Google search box to locate your book, you, or your website). Offer these top websites content: A book to review, a great idea for an interview (either via e-mail, podcast, or teleseminar, depending on what that site currently does), an excerpted article from your book, a blog post, interview, or comment. All content should end with a credit to you and a link to your website or book sales page."

author, so I wanted to pull out all the stops. I had finally gotten my foot in the door, and I was ready to do anything I could to kick it open.

"Booksellers have been my greatest allies, and just letting them know that I and my book existed among the mountains of new titles that season was half the battle. To do that, I mailed out postcards announcing the publication of my book. My greatest expense by far was postage. To compensate, I was selective with my address lists, targeting those who had some particular interest in me, my book, or young adult fiction in general. That made the creation of the mailing list time-intensive, but the payoff was palpable—I got galley requests from booksellers, saw selected media coverage, and garnered enough popular opinion to get *Samurai Shortstop* listed in the *Booksense 76* newsletter. Dial Books has been great. When I asked for money to cover the cost of postcards and baseball cards they happily agreed.

"It's important to remember that a publisher's publicity focus on your book—or lack thereof—is nothing personal; it's a business decision, based on potential earnings versus expected expenses. The more I can do to promote and sell my book on my own—and thus increase its earnings—means the more Penguin [Dial's parent company] will do to promote it. I put in a lot of that initial work, and Penguin has been great responding in kind." Learn more about Gratz at www.alangratz.com and at http://gratzindustries.blogspot.com.

On the Road: Book Tours

➤ *Naomi C. Rose:* Rose wrote, illustrated, and designed *Tibetan Tales for Little Buddhas* (Clear Light), which sold out its first printing within a year and was a bestseller in several independent bookstores.

"*Tibetan Tales for Little Buddhas* took me ten years to complete and get published, so I wanted to launch it well. I organized book tours to several areas where I had friends, family, or professional contacts. For each tour, I scheduled a variety of public appearances (children's museums, libraries, bookstores, schools, Buddhist centers, churches, and galleries).

"Bookstore appearances informed booksellers about my book. However, school and library visits tended to draw the biggest crowds and sell the most books. The libraries bought books for all their branches. Many schools bought books for their libraries, and I sold many books to the students. Museum appearances were good for sales, too. The bookstore at the San Francisco Asian Art Museum ordered 50 books.

Blog Bonus

Lisa Yee, author of *So Totally Emily Ebers* and *Millicent Min, Girl Genius* (both from Arthur A. Levine/Scholastic), estimated that 95 percent of the people visiting her Live Journal website are other authors. She found MySpace better for connecting to kids. Also, she found that bookstores and libraries were "friending" her on MySpace. Now, she writes on Live Journal and pastes it into MySpace.

"I also sent press releases to the area's media and followed up by e-mail or telephone. I got some good articles in the press, and bookings on radio shows and local television. Even when attendance at my appearances was low, I knew many people had heard about the book from the media.

"Occasionally, I hired publicists to help. This paid off some of the time. One publicist arranged for a small review in the *San Francisco Chronicle*. Another booked me on a TV show that drew people to my appearances.

"I devoted a solid year of my life to promotion and I continue to do it whenever I can. Promotion is the hardest work I've ever done, but I felt I owed it to my book. My efforts built support and interest in my book from the ground up. I made contacts that I can use for my next book, and I'm much more comfortable making public appearances. With the contacts I've made and the confidence I've developed, promotion for my next book should be easier." Rose's website is www.naomicrose.com.

Connecting Online: Blogs

➤ *Gregory K. Pincus:* On April 7, 2006, Pincus's blog about poems based on a mathematical sequence called the Fibonacci sequence was featured on Slashdot (http://slashdot.org). That day, his blog got more than 32,000 hits. On April 24, he closed a two-book deal with Arthur A. Levine Books at Scholastic. The first will be *The 14 Fabulous Fibs of Gregory K.*

"I've always loved the connected nature of the Web, and that is something that matters in marketing. On the Web, people can find you. You can find people. It's all good.

"In general, I try to limit myself to 20 minutes on my own blog a day, but to participate fully in the blogosphere (which is the whole point!), I spend another 30 minutes most days reading and commenting on other blogs. I have forged great friendships and business relationships, and have had many wonderful things happen—like being in an article in *School Library Journal*— all because of my blogging.

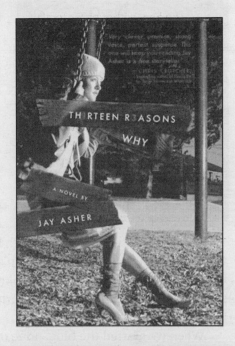

"I have daily readers who will see any news (appearances, reviews, whatever), plus I've built a small mailing list. I have people who will naturally talk about my book or any other news I have, much as I talk about their news. But I wouldn't ask them to promote me, and they never ask me. Other than talking about my book and appearances, etc., I won't be doing much different on my blog than I've done up til now: talking kids books with a bunch of folks who love them.

"For me, the joy of blogging is being a part of the online kidlit community. I love celebrating the success of my blogging friends and colleagues. If by mentioning them, I help market them—yay! But it's not intentional networking so much as the very basis of what makes blogging fun and satisfying for me."

Find Pincus at http://gottabook.blogspot.com.

Attention Grabbing: Blogs for Buzz

➤ *Jay Asher:* Asher's first novel, *Thirteen Reasons Why* (Razorbill/ Penguin), sold at auction. Two editors told Jay they'd heard librarians and other editors talking about his Disco Mermaids blog before seeing his manuscript.

"I started the Disco Mermaids blog with my two writing partners. We saw the idea of short but creative blog posts as a nice way to break up the daunting novel writing experience. And yes, we also thought of marketing. We especially wanted to attract a librarian readership. When

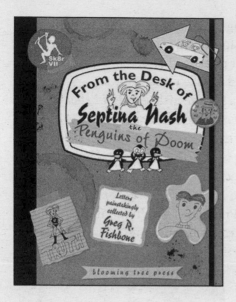

a New York City children's librarian featured our series of posts called The dePaola Code on her blog, things exploded.

"We spend no money and less time blogging than most bloggers. We post every other day, so we each post about once a week. But we also do group posts, such as the Internet's first game of Blog or Dare!

"For my first book, *Thirteen Reasons Why,* we have fun contests to give away autographed copies. But in general, we keep the blog itself interesting so people will keep reading it. We started the blog ten months before I sold my first book and people seemed to enjoy following the process. So we'll stick with the format of honestly portraying the ups and downs of trying to make it in this business.

"When we started the blog, none of us were agented. Now, we all are. One of the Disco Mermaids signed with an agent who approached her because her posts were always so funny. Because of our blog and the attention my book has been receiving, some editors have told us they'd like to publish the next Disco Mermaid."

Find Asher's blog and other information at http://discomermaids. blogspot.com and www.ThirteenReasonsWhy.com.

Working Together: The Class of 2007

➤ *Greg R. Fishbone:* Fishbone founded the Class of 2k7, a marketing coalition of children's book authors with their first novels out in 2007. As "class president," Fishbone is the group's main spokesman.

"After I sold my first book, I discovered that most publishers expect authors to help out with marketing. There was so much to learn, so much to do, and so little time! I figured that other debut authors were probably facing the same issues, and thought it would be easier for us all to promote all our books as a team.

"I passed the word around through author mailing lists and message boards to find people interested in forming a marketing collective. Over about six months we developed our plans and added new members until the publishing industry started to take notice.

"So far, the Class of 2k7 has had a feature article in *Publishers Weekly*, a nice write-up in *School Library Journal*, a feature in the *SCBWI Bulletin*, links from a whole bunch of great kidlit blogs, an interview on the Just One More Book podcast, and a feature in the *2008 Children's Writers and Illustrators Market*—which will also feature a few 2k7 books in individual author profiles. My book, *From the Desk of Septina Nash: The Penguins of Doom* (Blooming Tree Press), has gotten mentions.

"The group has been wildly successful in bringing 2k7 authors and our debut books to the attention of librarians, booksellers, and teachers. But the most useful part for me has been the close-knit community of authors we have created in the process. It was a lot of work, but also fun because we got along well as a group."

See the websites at http://classof2k7.com, http://gfishbone.com, and http://septinanash.com.

Building Buzz: The Book Launch

➤ *Jon Lewis* and *Derek Benz:* The coauthors of the Grey Griffins series (Orchard Books) launched the second book, *The Rise of the Black Wolf*, at Changing Hands Bookstore in Tempe, Arizona, with nearly 300 teachers, parents, and children. They provided raffle prizes that included an iPod nano, lunch with the authors, a $50 Toys "R" Us gift card, and a signed manuscript page.

Lewis: "We put in less than a thousand dollars."

Benz: "And probably about 20 hours of work. Kids were having a

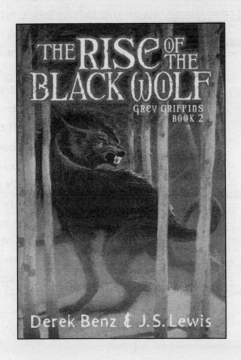

ball as prizes were awarded over the course of the event, keeping their attention zoomed right in on every word. From the artwork to the signed manuscripts, everything kept building as we worked our way toward the Rainforest Cafe lunch and the personalized Grey Griffins iPod, containing the *Revenge of the Shadow King* audiobook."

Be innovative with marketing. One way is through viral marketing.

Lewis: "I spent quite a few years as an advertising executive. The sentiment is that mass-marketing through traditional channels is all but dead, so we need to be innovative. One way to do that is through viral marketing: Word of mouth is the most effective marketing tool. We'll continue to invest in promotion where it makes the most sense. We have a budget, and we're careful not to spend outside of it. It's key to success, but it could mean time and sweat equity as much as financial investment."

Benz: "We're still kids at heart, which makes doing things like this not only very natural, but also a whole lot of fun."

Find out more about the authors at www.greygriffins.com and www.myspace.com/greygriffins.

Up Next

The Class of 2k7 and the Grey Griffins book launch attracted extra attention because of their novelty. Future classes may benefit from working together, and authors who provide valuable prizes at their book launches may draw more people to the events. But the media is likely to lose interest in these methods as well, and go searching always for the next new thing.

A combination of old and new publicity techniques will help any book reach readers. If you can come up with a brilliant new idea, your book is sure to make an extra big splash.

Software to Simplify the Writer's Life

By Christina Hamlett

For 400 years, William Shakespeare has reigned as one of the world's most prolific authors. Not a bad reputation, considering that the tools of his trade were limited to a quill pen and parchment paper. If the Bard had been born in the age of technology, he would be the proverbial kid in a candy store with a tantalizing array of writer software for summoning the muse, creatively composing, flawlessly formatting, perfectly pitching, and tenaciously tracking sales.

Forsooth! Yon felicitous fortune beckons in boundless bytes . . . .

Such Stuff as Dreams Are Made On

For writers who have ever lamented that their idea streams have run dry, the days of sitting in front of a blank computer screen and whimpering are over. The volume of software products designed to kick-start the imagination can actually leave consumers dizzy. These applications range from modest to pricey in cost and include registration, which allows access to online assistance and system upgrades. Many of the writer software programs also have downloadable demos on their websites so you can try before you buy.

➤ *Storybase:* This entertaining plot-generator program developed by film and television veteran Tom Sawyer is replete with thousands of linked story ideas, characters, and surprise twists that enable users to build a complete fictional framework in just a matter of keystrokes. Compatible with standard word-processing applications, Storybase not only constructs a working outline from beginning to end but can also reverse engineer a premise for those who know what they want the outcome to be but can't, for the life of them, figure out exactly how to get there. (www.storybase.net. Available for Windows. $69.)

➤ *Dramatica Writer's DreamKit:* Has your alarm clock ever gone off in the middle of a promising dream? Furiously you thump the snooze bar to go back and pick up where you left off. But it just never works, leaving you to wonder how the story might have ended. A similar frustration can occur during waking hours at your keyboard when you dis-

Alarm clock go off in the middle of a promising dream? Thump the snooze bar, return to the dream, and grab those ideas.

cover that you've either lost your train of thought or perhaps a smart finale was never on board. Dramatica Writer's DreamKit predicts a variety of outcomes based on the development choices you have made. It also helps determine which character represents the strongest—and most commercial—point of view. The same company also sells Story-Weaver, story development software. (http://dramatica.stores.yahoo. net/dramwritdrea.html. Windows and Macintosh. DreamKit, $49.95; StoryWeaver, $29.99.)

➤ *StoryCraft Pro:* If you're like many writers, you have a plethora of half-finished projects that you haven't been motivated to complete. StoryCraft Pro intends to be an over-the-shoulder collaborator that can tell you what genre is the best fit and whether your hot idea is destined to be a novel, short story, or screenplay. The software also juxtaposes your work with themes from classic myths and literature to produce an outline according to story type. It also helps in character development and encourages brainstorming in each step along the way. (www.storycraftpro.com. Windows. $79.)

➤ *Writer's Blocks 3:* Who would have thought that writer's block could be a good thing? This visual outliner is a brainstorming tool that enables writers to organize random thoughts into cohesive and compelling plots. Instead of jotting down fleeting moments of inspiration on scraps of paper, writers can use this software program to embrace the power of association. Writer's Blocks claims to facilitate access and organization, give writers a bird's eye view of where their thoughts are taking them, and increase productivity. A split-screen function allows authors to view and edit simultaneously, and a time-saving autotype feature replicates any word that already exists in the current document. (www.writersblocks.com. Windows. $149.)

➤ *QuickStory 5:* Whether your writing forte is fiction or theater or film, QuickStory 5 aims to assist authors who already have a general concept in mind but are looking to flesh out their characterizations and plot points. Its companion software, Character Pro 5, marries technology and psychology. It uses an interview format to produce detailed profiles based on classic Enneagram archetypes, and generates advice on how your fictional personalities should think, talk, and interact. (www.quickstory.com. Windows. $69.99.)

What's in a Name?

➤ *Muse Names:* Stymied by clever monikers for your key players? This database provides more than 40,000 names from 70 ethnicities, including Celtic, Egyptian, Rumanian, and Thai. Searches can be conducted by first names, last names, or any combination. If you're into numerology and the psychic meaning of specific names as a clue to psychological traits, the software has a function which addresses that as well. (www.inklinksoftware.com/musenames. Windows. $84.)

Speak the Speech

Solitary a craft as writing is, there's probably no shortage of writers who would like to have a personal assistant who could jot down our brainstorming notes, take flawless dictation, and efficiently respond to e-mails. Even better, of course, would be an assistant who was available 24/7 and didn't mind working for free. While the following software programs can't refill your coffee or make you a date for indulgent pampering at the spa, they're fast, accurate, and compatible with Microsoft Word, Excel, WordPerfect, Corel, and other applications. If you like to compose your thoughts while wandering around the house in your bathrobe, you can even dictate into hand-held devices or use the microphone on your Bluetooth.

➢ *Dragon Naturally Speaking 9:* Most people can talk much faster than they can type. Voice recognition software can capture your brilliant thoughts and commit them to paper three times faster than fingers flying over a keyboard. In addition to dictating book chapters, letters, articles—or even recording random musings—you can surf the Internet via verbal commands, reconfigure your desktop, and casually chat through your e-mails instead of writing them. Dragon Naturally-Speaking 9 could be a huge time-saver for authors whose typing style is hunt and peck; its 99 percent accuracy rating is also a bonus for bad spellers. Those accustomed to mumbling, however, may need to focus on their diction skills, since this technology can only transcribe what it actually hears. (www.nuance.com. Windows. $99.99.)

➢ *ViaVoice*: Developed by IBM and available in multiple editions of complexity for PCs and Macintoshes, ViaVoice was initially targeted to office workers and typists suffering from carpal tunnel syndrome. It has since found a widespread fan base among writers who enjoy the convenience of being able to dictate their material, then go back and do edits. The system will even learn new words (unusual character names, sci-fi realms, etc.) and store them in its electronic dictionary. In addition to creating custom macros, select editions also carry specialized jargon (business, finance, cuisine, legal) to speed the flow of creative juices. (www-4.ibm.com/software/speech. Windows, Macintosh. $45–$70.)

A Dish Fit for the Gods

If you pulled together the most mouth-watering ingredients in the world for a gourmet meal, would you really want to slop it onto a paper plate and hand your guests plastic utensils and cheap napkins? Suffice it to say, many of the manuscripts that editors and writing consultants are given to read have been thrown together in either ignorance or defiance of the industry's precise rules for formatting—rules that exist to accommodate strict timeframes and uncluttered readability.

Earlier generations of writers had to endure the tedious preliminaries of setting tabs and margins on their typewriters or word processors and had to be mindful of widows and orphans (words or lines that are detached and free float at the bottom or top of a page). Today, a bounty of formatting software can automatically set up your screen, novel,

Formatting Scripts & Screenplays

➤ *Final Draft:* This product's tag line says it all: "Just add words." Whether your style is to experiment with story cards or type FADE IN and go straight to your first master scene and dialogue, Final Draft 7 formats your screenplay to industry standards; creates PDF files, which can be opened by collaborators, agents, and producers even if they don't have Final Draft themselves; and supply male and female voices to read the lines you create. Included in the package purchased is the Writers Guild of America (WGA) *Creative Rights Handbook,* online assistance by stage and screen pros, and direct access to WGA's website for registering your script upon its completion. (www.finaldraft.com. Windows, Macintosh. $229.)

➤ *Movie Magic Screenwriter:* This software is another popular favorite with aspiring scripticians. In addition to its easy-to-use templates for movies, TV, and stage plays, Movie Magic Screenwriter also addresses the growing field of multimedia presentations. It imports material from a variety of different formats into products that are used in education, corporate training, and marketing. There is also a versatile function that allows users to import and export scripts that have been created by other screenwriting software applications. Like Final Draft, it has an on-screen script notes feature that allows you to post reminders and comments throughout the text as you work (i.e., "Was Anna of Cleves Henry's fourth wife or his fifth?"). (www.write-bros.com. Windows, Macintosh. $229.)

story, article, script, query letter, proposal, or anything else. The finished product will be picture-perfect and look as if you labored for hours over a hot keyboard.

➤ *The Wizard of Words:* If you've ever been daunted by how to format a book proposal, arrange chapters, set up a query letter, orchestrate an index, or properly cite resources for a scholarly dissertation, The Wizard of Words can make problems vanish faster than an incantation by Merlin. The software package includes Book Writer, Essay Writer, Novel Writer, Short Story Writer, Thesis/Dissertation/Term Paper Writer, Article Writer, Book Proposal Writer, Query Letter Writer, and Mass Mailer. As is often said, we never get a second chance to make a first impression. It is critical to the pitching process to win decision-makers over with a professionally tailored product that is structurally sound and error-free. The economical price of this software also makes it a must-have addition to every writer's computer. (www.inklinksoftware.com. Windows. $75.)

➣ *StyleWriter:* "The Plain English Editor," this software focuses on usage and grammar, offering to improve clarity and break writers of bad habits. The software includes Writer's Organizer, Essayist, Technical Writer, Letter Writer, Résumé Writer, Business Plan Writer, Writer's Dictionary and Thesaurus, Typing Tutor, and Writer's Calculator. (www.inklinksoftware.com/stylewriter. Windows. $150.)

Wherefore Art Thou?

Do you know where your (fictional) children are? When I first began my career as a writer, I had an unsophisticated method of tracking which projects were where. Specifically, I scribbled their *out* date in a notebook and wrote myself a reminder to check up on them three months later. That was in an era when the pace of publishing moved much slower than now, but I would often find myself accidentally querying the same house twice or—in the case of different articles sent to the same magazine—getting rejection letters that didn't reference which one of my proposals had merited a no. Today, software not only makes it easy to track a project's immediate whereabouts, but also lets you make notations regarding feedback or invitations to submit future ideas.

➣ *Write That Down:* This electronic tickler system shows you at a glance which projects are pending and gives you an overview of their submission history—like many writers, you probably have an A, B, and C hierarchy of markets targeted in the submission process. Detailed contact information can be generated, along with follow-up correspondence on those projects that are past the date you expected a response. Want to grade your experience with each editor, agent, or producer for future reference? In my own work, for instance, I am often asked if I have heard of a particular editor and what my experience was. If it was two or three years ago, who can remember all the particulars? Write That Down also has spreadsheet capabilities to track how much money you've made, and reminders about those markets that are overdue on their payments. (www.writerssupercenter.com)

➤ *Power Tracker:* Available only in a downloadable format, this file management and submission tracking software has easy-to-use menus that keep records of all contacts, pitches, associated expenses, and responses. Project information can be accessed by title, subject matter, media, or any other category that applies to your field of endeavor. Users can also sort data for a one-glance tally of how many screenplays, novels, or articles are currently in circulation, as well as review the method of delivery (in-person, e-mail, U.S. mail, Federal Express, etc). (www.write-brain.com/power_tracker_main.htm. Windows, Macintosh. $29.95.)

Exeunt

There is no question that technology has streamlined our lives. We can download thousands of tunes on our iPods as we surf the Internet, share experiences via chatrooms, and Google topics that we might otherwise have spent hours trawling for in city libraries. The insular nature of these endeavors, however, is perhaps robbing us of the one thing that makes writers a unique breed—the ability to go mingle with the masses, eavesdrop in sidewalk cafes, and connect on an interpersonal level with those who will eventually comprise our colorful collection of characters.

The time has already arrived when an author need never leave his or her keyboard and yet have access to everything under the sun that he or she needs to assume the prestigious title of Writer. Everything, that is, except the most precious component—the ability to observe the mirth and foibles of the human experience firsthand and to spin them into an entertaining finished product that will endure the test of time.

"The play's the thing," dear William wrote. In turning over the process of creation to a marvelous machine, let us not forget the joys of skipping through life totally unrehearsed and enjoying its spontaneous wonder.

Create an Author Website

By Mark Haverstock

A uthor websites used to be a novelty, something that those of us with some artistic flair or computer skills might attempt to post, or convince someone to post for us. But in 2008, websites have become the virtual equivalent of a business card, fan club, information center, and sales force for the serious writer.

"They've become de rigeur. The majority of readers, educators, and librarians head to the Internet to find more information about a book or author, so it makes sense to

have a site available, giving readers and book buyers more knowledge about you and your books," says website designer Vicki Palmquist, whose company is called Winding Oak. "It's also an effective way to reach your current and future readers, and for them to reach you."

Websites are also there when you can't be. "Making a website for myself was one of the smartest things I ever did," says author Dan Gutman. "It's like having a TV station blasting 'DAN GUTMAN DAN GUTMAN DAN GUTMAN' 24 hours a day!"

Website Marketing 101

Unless you have an advertising firm on retainer or a personal marketing department, a website is the next best marketing tool for an author. "It saves me a ton of time, because anytime somebody asks me for information about my books, myself, or my school visits, all I have to do is point them to the site where the information is waiting," says Gutman, whose books include *Getting Air* (Simon & Schuster) and *Satch & Me* (HarperCollins). "Schools I visit print out the information on my site and display it in the hallways. Also, having a good-looking site gives you credibility. You look like a professional. Hey, I probably wouldn't even be part of this article if you hadn't found me through my site."

Science writer Vicki Cobb says websites offer a great way for potential clients to contact her. "In general, people e-mail me to find out my speaking fee," she says. "I answer all queries instantly, giving my fee and my phone number. If people can afford it, they usually call me." In addition, her site features a catalogue of her current books and provides links to Amazon and Barnes & Noble. Her scores of titles include the Robert F. Sibert Honor book, *I Face the Wind* (HarperCollins).

When author Dian Curtis Regan checks her website stats, she's

by Vicki Cobb Illustrated by Julia Gorton

amazed how many hits the site receives from all over the world. "Whether or not any one hit leads to a sale, it at least means one more person is aware of my books. It's all good," she says. "Many of my author friends are also starting to sell autographed books from their sites. I am interested in doing this in the future, so am looking into it." Among Regan's titles are the middle-grade Princess Nevermore books, including *Cam's Quest* (Darby Creek).

Selling Yourself

A website can also be a great place to showcase your work to editors, through sample chapters from published books. Though some editors still prefer to see printed clips with a proposal, others will explore a website to see posted copies or links to articles, if they're interested in your work. "Because my website includes all my written texts and scripts as well as info on all my books, I've gotten a number of rights requests from various publishers," says Aaron Shepard, author of many picture books, such as *One-Eye! Two-Eyes! Three-Eyes! A Very Grimm Fairy Tale* (Atheneum), as well as books on self-publishing. "The most lucrative have come from foreign publishers wanting to reprint my picture books, many of which have had the rights reverted to me. I've made several thousand dollars this way, though it's not as common as it was a few years ago."

Will you get writing assignments as a result of posting a website? It's possible, but most likely if you've already been published. Editors generally don't have time to browse the Internet, but they will likely find you if there's something you have that they need. "One editor I used to work with at Scholastic e-mailed to say she found me through my site and asked if I would interested in writing for her now that she'd moved to Simon & Schuster," says Regan. "We did five books together at Simon & Schuster. She's recently returned to Scholastic and wants me to do a project for her there." Regan mentions other offers she's received through her website, including an invitation to write a piece on immigrant students, and a movie option.

"Recently, I got an e-mail from a TV writer who wants to turn the My Weird School series into a TV series," says Gutman. "We have already completed the first draft of the script, and we are about to pitch it to the networks. He might have been able to track me down if I didn't have a website, but it made it a lot easier for him."

Web Addresses

Authors

➤ **Vicki Cobb:** www.vickicobb.com

➤ **Dan Gutman:** www.dangutman.com

➤ **David Lubar:** www.davidlubar.com

➤ **Dav Pilkey:** www.pilkey.com

➤ **Dian Curtis Regan:** www.diancurtisregan.com

➤ **Aaron Shepard:** www.aaronshep.com

Designers

➤ **Karin Bilich:** www.smartauthorsites.com

➤ **Theo Cobb:** www.vickicobb.com/theocobb.html

➤ **Vicki Palmquist:** www.windingoak.com

➤ **Neil Kozlowicz:** www.booksandwires.com

Connecting With Readers

Your publisher might have printed a brief biography of you in your books, but it's likely your readers will want to know more about you: your hobbies, how you get your ideas, your next title, and other personal information you're willing to share. Typically, an FAQ (frequently asked questions) section satisfies the curiosity of most visitors to your site.

"I've found that my site serves much better as a source of information than as a marketing tool," says David Lubar, author of *Hidden Talents* (Starscape/Tor) and *Sleeping Freshmen Never Lie* (Puffin). "In other words, I don't get school visits because people stumble upon my site. But if people are specifically looking for me, my site tells them what they need to know. I think, to a large extent, it's the same for book sales. I suspect the greatest impact is on people who intentionally visited my site to see what's new, as opposed to those who found me during a search for lumbar support."

It's a good idea to provide contact information for website visitors to reach you, but avoid phone numbers and addresses. Cobb suggests that you use your website as your business e-mail address, and have your website host forward any fan mail to your personal e-mail address for two reasons: It protects your privacy and, if you change your personal

Internet service provider (ISP) for some reason, you can still keep getting your fan mail.

Of course, you'll hear from wackos from time to time and receive your share of spam, but you'll also get to see those priceless pats on the back and heartfelt thank you's from readers who enjoy your work. Sometimes you'll get requests—some doable and some not. "I get lots of fan mail but most says something like, "I need help with my science fair project . . . do you have any ideas?" Cobb says. "I politely send them to read my books. Here's one example (mistakes and all) of a request I got."

Hello Mrs. Cobb,
I have one of your book, its called, science experiments that you can eat, Can you please help me on FRUIT AND TEA PUNCHES!!! Its in that book! Im going that for a science fair and I want to know how I do it! I want to win 2nd place this year, can you Please help Mrs. Cobb if you do it will be my pleasure
Thank You,
Marry

The ultimate tribute is a fan site, a virtual fan club, designed and maintained by one of your devoted readers. Regan explains, "Last fall, a fan contacted me through my site, which led to her putting up a fan site for one of my books. (http://princessnevermorefansite.com). She and her friends recently added a forum for discussion of my fantasy novels."

Content

Every author website is as different as the writer it represents. "Everything you create reflects your personality," says Gutman. "I like to think my books are funny, entertaining, and informative at the same time, and so is my site. I am also seriously concerned about the environment, and have a section on that issue titled 'Nothing to do with Dan.'"

In addition to being uniquely you, you should consider certain essentials when building a website. "The basics for a website include book pages with review excerpts, information about the author that isn't available on your book jacket or author blurb, specific details about your speaking presentations, and other things that you can uniquely offer to your readers," says Palmquist.

Web designer Neil Kozlowicz of Books and Wires agrees with the value-added angle, giving your readers something they won't find anywhere else. "For example, if you go to the J. K. Rowling site, you'll be connected to the author, who gives updates on her writing progress and editing choices. You'll see various extras not found in the books." Kozlowicz also emphasizes that content should be well-organized and easy to navigate.

A list of your current as well as past titles, perhaps with book jacket photos, should figure prominently on your home page. Don't forget some free samples: Let potential readers peek at a couple of pages or even a short chapter. Think about the way you normally choose books. Most book buyers don't just look at a title and a cover picture. They open it up, read a few paragraphs, look at a table of contents or index, and may even find a chair and continue reading before they decide to purchase the book. Give your potential readers the same opportunity online. If you're paranoid about having your work copied to another site, lock it up inside a read-only PDF file.

Are your books likely to be part of a school curriculum? Consider posting downloadable activities, worksheets, or discussion questions. Teachers, who are always short on time, appreciate easy-to-find supplementary materials of good quality they can use with book units and literature circles.

Interactivity

Once you've finished with the basic introductions, such as a biography, picture, book descriptions, and FAQs, you may decide to take your website—and relationship with your readers—to the next level. "You can increase the value of that relationship by allowing readers to submit

The Case for Professional Design

There's a good reason why writers should consider choosing a Web design professional to build their site, especially one who caters to writing professionals. "Writers should write their next book, which is best for their long-term career," says website designer Vicki Palmquist. "Unless they plan to support themselves by designing websites, writers should hire a professional who will understand color psychology, current website usage, navigation design, children's literature, and marketing strategies."

According to Web marketer Karin Bilich, having a well-designed website can improve an author's image with the general public, publishers, and literary agents. It therefore can play an important role in jump-starting any future books published.

What kind of creative and technical work is involved in designing a website? Designer Theo Cobb makes creative decisions regarding colors, fonts, graphical icons, and many other artistic considerations, as well as organizational decisions—what links to what, where links are found, what the viewer sees or doesn't see.

On the technical side, it's important that any bells and whistles, such as games, chat, downloads, or other features, are user-friendly and work properly. "A design/hosting company, especially one that deals only with authors, is up to date on current technology and knows how that technology can best serve authors," says designer Neil Kozlowicz. Additionally, the company may offer book marketing services or recommend services beyond what the author's publisher provides, he says. An author-dedicated company also regularly works with publishers and booksellers to integrate book marketing.

Website design is only one piece of the puzzle. "While it is certainly important that the website's design be professional and reflect the look and feel of the author's books, many other elements are involved in creating a successful website," says Bilich. "To implement a content plan and marketing strategy in the most successful fashion, a level of experience in the book publishing field is required. A standard Web design or hosting company does not have the depth of understanding of book marketing and promotion that we do."

questions that the author can answer online, inviting them onto a message board to chat with the author, or writing an author blog that people can follow," says Karin Bilich, Web marketer and founder of SmartAuthorSites. "All of these elements begin to build a relationship between author and reader."

➢ *Web logs*, known as *blogs*, are a combination personal diary, pulpit, soapbox, and breaking-news outlet. They are an attractive addition to your website, provided you have the self-discipline to update them weekly (preferably more often). They'll give your readers the inside scoop on your latest books, articles, and book signings. But if you begin to procrastinate and skip posts, people will begin to drop you from the list of blogs they read regularly.

➢ *Message boards* are online bulletin boards where readers can exchange messages or just read the posted comments, presumably about your published books and articles. You can find examples of these at many websites, including the Writers Weekly Forum (http://forums. writersweekly.com) and at humorist Dave Barry's site (www.davebarry.com). Special software is available that provides discussion board capability for a website from a host company or Web designer.

➢ *Activities*. Those who are really ambitious or have the resources of a good Web designer might consider interactive features—games, puzzles, music, or videos—to entertain as well as inform visitors. "That's what young audiences like, so it enhances the appeal and is par for the course these days," says illustrator and designer Theo Cobb, son of Vicki Cobb.

An example is the website of Dav Pilkey, author of the enormously popular Captain Underpants series. Among the website features you'll find games and videos. They start with simple paintbox and matching activities for younger readers and progress to full-featured video games based on Pilkey's characters, such as "Ricky Ricotta's Mighty Robot vs. the Stupid Stinkbugs from Saturn" and "Hamster Highway." Playable and downloadable music and videos are found in the Junk, Stuff, and Thingies link, including some weird and wacky productions starring Koji Matsumoto, a sushi chef and friend of the author who transforms himself into Captain Underpants.

Is the Effort Worthwhile?

Whether a website is worthwhile depends on your approach and your goals. Certainly some Web presence is beneficial to writers, even in a small way. "I think nowadays that just about any author has to have at least a simple website to provide basic information," says Shepard. "Anything more elaborate (and my own site is an extreme example) can become a serious diversion from writing and selling books."

Search Engine Registration & Submission

➤ **Quick Register:**
www.quickregister.net
➤ **Submit Express:**
www.submitexpress.com
➤ **Search Engine Optimising:**
www.searchengineoptimising.com
➤ **Words in a Row:**
www.wordsinarow.com

Lubar agrees with the minimalist approach. "I think a writer has to have a website because everyone expects writers to have websites," says Lubar. "But a simple site—even a single page—is probably enough. I have more than that just because it's fun to tinker."

Websites can show that you've arrived in the writing business. "I absolutely think every author should reserve his or her name as a domain, and put up a site as soon as that first book is published," says Regan. "It's like setting up shop and hanging an Open for Business sign in the window. Everyone knows where to find you."

To be sure you're found, market your website address. "Be sure to hand it out whenever you make a public appearance, have it printed on your book jackets, and mention your website features when you speak," says Palmquist. Make sure to add your name to the major search engines, so they can help readers find you. Register yourself on individual sites via the sites listed in the sidebar above. To save time, a free auto-registering service can put you on multiple Web search engines at one time.

Create enough new and interesting content on a regular basis to keep people coming back. "A website should be updated with new information at least quarterly or it becomes a *cobweb* site, static and unvisited," says Palmquist. "Plan how you'll update your site when you design your site. It will make your Web designer's job much easier."

DIY Websites

If you're on a budget or would like to exercise your own creativity, the do-it-yourself approach to developing a website might be the way to go. For starters, go to some of the writers' website links listed below. Look at content, page layout, graphics, and overall appeal. Assess the strengths and weaknesses of each site. Draw up your own plans based on your research, tastes, and personality.

Many Web hosting sites have ready-to-use templates that will make your site building experience a little easier. If you have FrontPage, DreamWeaver, or another commercial product available, you can create your own pages on your computer and upload them to many hosting sites using FTP.

Website Links for Children's Authors
➢ **American Library Association:** www.ala.org/ala/alsc/greatwebsites/greatwebsitesauthors.htm
➢ **Children's Book Council:** www.cbcbooks.org/contacts
➢ **Children's Literature Web Guide:** www.ucalgary.ca/~dkbrown/authors.html
➢ **Index to Internet Sites:** http://falcon.jmu.edu/~ramseyil/biochildhome.htm
➢ **The Purple Crayon:** www.underdown.org/topsites.htm

Inexpensive Web Hosting
This is a sampling of Web hosting companies that charge minimal monthly fees for your website. Most have templates and website tools to help. Plans and features vary significantly, and prices may vary due to promotions and the nature of this very competitive market. Be sure to get all the details before you sign up.

➢ **Authors Guild:** www.authorsguild.net. $3-$9. Requires membership in the Authors Guild ($90 a year).
➢ **Go Daddy:** www.godaddy.com. $4-$15. Domain name registration additional $2/yr.
➢ **Host Papa:** www.hostpapa.com. $8. Discount for multi-year sign-up, blog, and multimedia features.
➢ **1 & 1:** www.1and1.com. $4-$20. RSS and blog features included.

DIY Websites

➤ **Yahoo:** http://smallbusiness.yahoo.com/webhosting. $12-$40. A $25 setup fee (sometimes waived, along with discount promotions).

Free Web Hosting

Yes, there can be a free lunch (or launch) when it comes to establishing your website. However, be prepared to endure limited features, as well as banner ads, in exchange for a freebie. You can upgrade features, remove ads, and obtain your own domain for a monthly fee on any of the sites.

➤ **Tripod** and **Angelfire:** www.tripod.lycos.com; www.angelfire.lycos.com. Upgrade, $5-$20.
➤ **Geocities:** http://geocities.yahoo.com. A free version of Yahoo web hosting. Upgrade, $5-$12.
➤ **Freewebs:** http://members.freewebs.com. Upgrade, $4-$21.
➤ **Zoomshare:** www.zoomshare.com. Upgrade, $10; premium site is www.digitalwork.com.
➤ **Free Hosting Now:** www.freehostingnow.com. Upgrade, $9.95-$75; discount coupon available.

Prime the Pumps and Start the Ideas Flowing

By Sue Bradford Edwards

Take a look at the publications of a career writer to find a clue. Jane Yolen has written about pirates and ballet, historical fiction set in the British Isles, and humorous science fiction featuring a talking toad. Patricia McKissack's books span baseball and whaling, George Washington Carver and the wind. Gary Blackwood has covered Shakespeare and paranormal powers, written an alternate history of the American Revolution, and created a variety of rogues.

In addition to honing their craft, career writers do something else essential: generate numerous ideas. "To be honest, I'm constantly besieged by ideas, because practically everything seems like a potential story idea to me," says Blackwood. "I have a bulging file folder full of them, some of them quite good, and will never get to them all if I live to be 200."

To sustain a writing career, prime the creative pump and get the ideas flowing. Here's how.

Start the Stream

The natural first place to look for ideas is someplace you know well, but the pivotal point will be moving past generalities to the new, by tapping into your creativity.

"Sometimes it's as simple as making a list of all the things you know a lot about, or want to know a lot about, places you've lived, jobs you've done," says Blackwood.

Take a look at your list. Most of the items are probably rather broad. My own list includes local history, archaeology, gardening, horses, cats, and carnivorous plants. While these categories are too loosely defined to be good story ideas, they produce more possibilities when I combine them.

➤ Archaeology plus gardening could yield a piece on gardens in a Mississippian village or medicinal plants in Hermann, a historic Missouri town.

➤ Coupling cats and archaeology could lead to a piece on cats in the earliest human settlements, neolithic cat burial sites, or archaelogical evidence for domesticated cats in Cyprus.

➤ Local history and gardening add up to a possible article on Glebe House, in Woodbury, Connecticut, where the acclaimed twentieth-century English garden designer Gertrude Jekyll created gardens at the Revolutionary-era home that was the birthplace of the Episcopal Church.

➤ Horses and gardening bring to mind equine-inspired garden statues and fountain ornaments, ranging from centaurs to gentle foals.

➤ Link horses with archaeology and you may very well find yourself working up an article on the horses that accompanied Emperor Qin's terracotta army.

➤ Carnivorous plants and gardening might lead to a piece on creating a bog garden complete with pitcher plants, sundews, and Venus flytraps.

Try combining one, two, or even three items on your own list and see what happens. You have just started priming your creativity.

Drift with the Printed Page

You're producing a trickle of ideas but you can do better. Focus now on your reading. Blackwood believes, "Nonfiction books can be a goldmine of ideas, and when you read the number and variety of them that's required for research, it's hard not to stumble on a dozen fascinating ideas." In his own experience, he says, "The nugget of information that formed the basis of *The Shakespeare Stealer* (Puffin) I stumbled upon while reading a newspaper. The idea for *Second Sight* (Jove) came to me while I was researching the Secrets of the Unexplained series."

Use anything in another piece of work that sparks your imagination. It might be a person, place, or concept or even a single word that catches your eye.

Make notes on these things as you find them. What thoughts do they trigger? What questions do they lead to? The ideas should be flowing heavier now but you can do even better.

➤ Reading a book on mid-twentieth century New York City brings the idea of profiles of the many famous students who graduated from Stuyvesant High School (James Cagney, Ben Gazzara, Lucy Liu, Thelonious Monk, Lewis Mumford, Paul Reiser, Tim Robbins, and numerous scientists, mathematicians, as well as four Nobel laureates) or how specialized schools—in science, math, performing arts—succeed, or don't.

➤ Conn and Hal Iggulden's *The Dangerous Book for Boys* (HarperCollins) may lead you to brainstorm things to do with a pad of paper that range from folding paper airplanes or cranes to simple games such as tic-tac-toe or hangman to making a paper ball for a quick game of table football. Remember all of the things you used to do during indoor recess?

➤ A national newspaper reported on sixteenth-century family records preserved in Timbuktu: Is there a story about the trail of ancient manuscripts in Africa? A young character who finds lost pages and journeys into his family's past?

➤ Following today's erratic business news suggests a history on some aspect of the stock market (its origins? important figures? technology?) for teens, or articles making concepts like hedge funds or futures understandable.

➤ Flip through your son's Cub Scout manual and you'll find yourself listing a variety of magazine article ideas, from exploring local history to putting on a top-notch skit.

➤ Read the reports of environmental change that are to be found almost daily in the newspaper, and you may find yourself looking into historical customs or events behind improvements, such as U.S. agricultural practices that led to

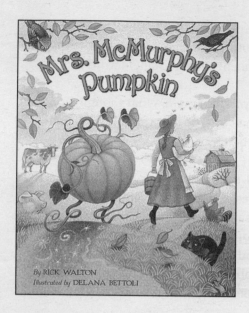

By RICK WALTON
Illustrated by DELANA BETTOLI

the Dust Bowl and how those were addressed in later years.

The Tide of Prompts

Whether you start with your own interests or facts discovered while reading, you are using something that many writers employ to generate ideas: a prompt.

"I just start with anything that can be part of a story," says picture book author Rick Walton, "and everything can be part of the story. I start with nouns, actions, characters, conflicts, plot shapes, titles, first lines, emotions, catch phrases, anything. I'll pick something at random, and then I'll start asking questions. As I ask questions and answer them, the story fleshes itself out. For example, *Mrs. McMurphy's Pumpkin* (HarperFestival) began with a letter of the alphabet. I picked one at random—P. What begins with the letter P? Pumpkin. What kind of pumpkin is it? A jack-o'-lantern. What kind of jack-o'-lantern? An evil jack-o'-lantern. What's it doing that is evil? It's threatening an old lady. What's he threatening to do? He's threatening to eat her. How does she respond? I keep asking and answering questions until I have the whole story in my head."

Author Darcy Pattison was inspired by prompts from illustrators and developed the Friday Ideas Group. Pattison's online explorations had led her to IllustrationFriday.com. "Illustrators visit this website each Friday to get a key word and then they produce a piece of art and link it to the IF site. It's a way for them to showcase their art, and work to expand their portfolios, and hopefully have some fun," says Pattison. "If illustrators can do it, why not writers? I wanted to play! I invited a group of seven other writers to join me, and we created a Friday Ideas mailing list. Each week, we take the key word and try to generate at least one unique, different, never before seen in the marketplace, viable idea."

Hints and Nudges

Explore the world online for a collection of prompts that stimulate your imagination.

➤ Like many writers, my ideas come from all over: my reading, museum displays, and working with the Cub Scouts. Sometimes I use prompts I find online. As part of the Friday Ideas Group, discussed in the accompanying article, I develop several ideas a week with the IllustrationFriday.com prompt. If I'm having problems using a prompt, I check out what the illustrators created from it.

➤ Dictionary.com sends out a word of the day. The word for June 12 last year was *fulminate*. On August 7, it was *levity*. The October 15 word was *purblind,* and November 8, *ameliorate.* Other words have been *celerity, furtive,* and *disconsolate*—all potential character traits.

➤ For a more elaborate list, I use Reference.com's On This Day (www.reference.com/thisday/). One daily listing last year included a Fact of the Day on amino acids; six holidays from various nations worldwide; 14 events ranging from anniversary dates and political events to inventions and natural disasters; and the birth or death dates of 11 famous people including Anne Frank and civil rights activist Medgar Evers.

➤ The Quotations Page publishes a series of quotes each day (www. quotationspage.com/qotd.html). Just think what you could do if your villain loved this Gore Vidal quote: "It is not enough to succeed. Others must fail."

➤ Sometimes I want to know what the market will be before I start generating ideas. That is when I turn to magazine theme lists as prompts. Theme lists for *Hopscotch, Boys' Quest,* and *Fun For Kidz* can be found on their website (www.funforkidzmagazines.com), as can those for the Cobblestone family of educational magazines. (Check the site map at www.cricketmag.com.)

How you work with a prompt is up to you. Some writers follow a set path. Pattison says, "I look up the prompt word in my unabridged dictionary and photocopy it and put it into my notebook. Sometimes, I look it up on Rhymer.com and tape the rhyming words into the notebook," says Pattison. "Then, I play. I let my brain noodle around with ideas. Or

"It's like a meditation. Clear away all the distraction and focus on one bright image."

sometimes, I force myself to write down 20 specific ideas complete with character names, specific settings, etc., in 30 minutes. In the end, when I work with a topic for several days, I wind up with oodles of ideas!"

You may need a less structured approach. "It's like a Buddhist meditation," says Friday Ideas member Lynnea Annette. "Instead of following instructions to do something, your task is to clear away all the distractions and focus on just that one bright image. Then, from that single focus, all these unknown stories bubble up."

Using a prompt may influence how you collect ideas. "I find I carry the word through the week," says group member Susi Gregg Fowler. "If the word is *green*, I'm noticing everything green I see and wondering if it has a story. When I see the new word, I often groan at first and think, 'Impossible,' but then find that actually it's fun to have so much freedom—after all, it's a single word. There are many ways to mine a single word. It just takes stretching."

This stretch to develop unique ideas from a prompt takes patience and time. "The longer I can sit, the more I'll come up with," says Friday group member Dori Hillestad Butler. "One week I made a goal of coming up with 25 ideas. It took me the whole week, but I did it." Start with a simple goal, such as one workable idea per prompt.

Even this may be difficult at first, whatever your method: Flow of consciousness. Word association. Brainstorming. Doodling. All of these can help pull ideas from a prompt. But your creative muscles may be flabby. Give yourself time to tone them up, but stick with the exercising.

Other times the problem is your internal editor. "Don't worry that your answers might not be interesting. Just brainstorm. Turn off the editor, and anyone else who wants to judge the ideas," says Walton. "Brainstorm a lot. Coming up with ideas is like turning on a faucet that hasn't run for a while. You need to let it run to get all the dirt and rust out. Then the clear water starts flowing. The more you actively brainstorm ideas in this way, the more you get, the better chance there is that at least one of them is going to grab you, and the more conditioned your subconscious will be to start recognizing ideas and miraculously get them to you."

A Transformative Tide

Once your ideas are flowing well, you can share them with a respected colleague or friend, or with your critique group, or writers like those in the Friday Ideas Group. "Part of the feedback we give is just that this or that idea really stands out," says Pattison.

Because sharing ideas with Pattison's group means sending them through a listserv, participants must first write out the ideas. This alone can help. "I'm noticing that often by the time I've written two or three or four sentences about an idea, I've already found its central flaw — sometimes unfixable. While just carrying an idea around in my head, which I have often done, I tend not to be aware of an idea's shortcomings," says Fowler. If an idea has an irreparable flaw, let it go. If it simply isn't fresh enough, there may be help.

Blackwood knows it takes ongoing work to take ideas to a fresh, new level. "Obviously, there are no new ideas or themes; it's all been done. It's the approach that makes it fresh. Even boy meets girl seems new when it's set in a very specific time and place, and the boy and girl are specific, unique characters. By the same token, even the most original idea can fall flat if it's not fleshed out with vivid, specific settings and detail and characters," he says. "I'm glad that people think the plot of *The Shakespeare Stealer* is new and fresh, but it's basically just the old familiar orphan-finds-a-home plot; only the specific nature of the time and place and details make it seem new."

One way that Blackwood freshens a timeworn idea is to play *what if.* "Boy meets girl is blah," he says, "but what if the girl used to be a boy? What if they can't really meet because one of them is dead? What if they meet only by e-mail and can't stand to meet in person?"

Look at the reading you are doing and you'll spot what-if results that arose from tweaking old ideas. Fairy tales provide strong examples. The story of the three billy goats gruff becomes *The Three Silly Girls Grubb* (Houghton Mifflin/Walter Lorraine), by John and Ann Hassett. The tale of the boy who cried wolf becomes Bob Hartman's *The Wolf Who Cried Boy* (Putnam).

It doesn't matter how you choose to practice generating ideas, just do it—that is the necessary priming of your creative pump. "One thing I've learned is that generating lots of ideas—enough to sustain a career—takes discipline," says Pattison. But as you practice more, you will open up to the possibilities more. Ideas are all around you, ripe for the taking. Butler points out, "Orson Scott Card says that everybody walks past a thousand story ideas every day." Learn to see them and you'll soon be swimming in a stream of ideas.

Backstory: Life's Breath of Frontstory

By Sharelle Byars Moranville

Backstory gets characters to page one, fully realized and stepping lively. It makes connections, enriches plots, and creates universes. If some of the backstory never makes it explicitly onto the page, it still informs the story in subtle, wonderful ways.

Bebe Faas Rice, author of more than 20 novels for children and adults, says she always creates backstory for her characters because "fictional characters must be as intricately and wondrously made as their real life counterparts. Their backgrounds of nurture, nature, character, personality, and life experiences are what inspire and predicate the story."

The techniques for developing backstory are as many and as varied as the writers of fiction. Some authors just *think* their characters into existence, holding the backstory in their minds; others write out pages and pages of biographical detail. Some authors use structured exercises to get started. Others, like Carolyn Lieberg, author of *West with Hopeless* (Dutton), uses more free-flowing methods.

"I begin with a strong cup of coffee after a good night's sleep," says Lieberg. "I select a character, wind the clock back in their lives and begin daydreaming—truly staring into space—while my fingers fly. (Sometimes I set the font so small I can barely read it, so that I will give no attention to the prose, and simply write.) I think about stories that many of us have regarding siblings, pets, getting lost, wanting something and getting it or not. I begin by considering big issues and before I know it, I'm writing about one particular event in the character's life."

Whatever method a writer uses to start the flow, backstory is a powerful inspirational tool that can create flawlessly motivated characters; make connections between characters that enrich conflict; build up layers of emotional texture; foster strong and dramatic beginnings; breathe life into biographical characters (who sometimes tend to go flat); and create the universe through which the characters are moving when we catch them mid-stride on page one.

Defining Moments

Fully motivated characters act in ways that strike readers as inevitable. In a good book, readers are lulled into a sense of trust. They relax into the fictional world, comfortable and happy there—caring about the characters and investing in the uncertainty of their lives. But

Let motivation get a bit shaky and suspect, and the whole edifice begins to quiver and crumble.

let motivation get a bit shaky and suspect, and the whole edifice begins to quiver and crumble. Suddenly readers get nervous. They don't trust the story anymore. They don't care about the characters. They want out.

Jan Blazanin relates an anecdote about how lack of backstory caused her writers' group to lose interest in the characters in a YA manuscript she'd written, which she later went on to revise at the request of an editor. The story is about a teen beauty queen, Oribella, who at the zenith of her modeling and movie career is stricken with alopecia, an autoimmune disease that causes severe hair loss. This horror for a beauty queen undoes Ori and her backstage mother, Rhonda, and puts them at terrible emotional odds.

When she took the first 30 pages of the manuscript to her writing group, Blazanin says, "They set me on my ear. They told me they couldn't care about Ori as readers until they knew what Ori's life was like before it fell apart. I muttered under my breath for two or three weeks, but eventually I scrapped most of those pages and started over. But this time I started before the beginning and looked back into the fourteen years of Ori's life before the reader meets her.

"When I wrote Ori's backstory, I realized I couldn't tell her story authentically without writing her mother Rhonda's backstory as well. As I wrote Rhonda's history, I discovered the defining moment of her life—the boating accident that killed her parents and destroyed her beauty. Then I was able to understand why Rhonda couldn't bear it when, in her mind, Ori lost her beauty as well. If I hadn't written the backstory for both those characters, they'd lack the sense of history that makes all people, real or imaginary, who they are."

The importance of knowing what has happened to the characters before we meet them on page one is reiterated by Dori Hillestad Butler, author of more than a dozen books for young readers, including *My Grandpa Had a Stroke* (Magination Press). She uses backstory in every novel she writes. "If I don't know my characters' backstories, I can't move them forward," Butler says.

She keeps characters' backstories in her head and sprinkles enough detail so her readers can understand character motivation. For example, in *Sliding into Home* (Peachtree), Joelle, the protagonist, wants to play baseball on her school baseball team, but she can't because in this community softball is considered the girls' alternative to baseball. The backstory is that Joelle was a star player at her old school. Readers need to know that so they can understand what motivates her.

Lieberg discusses how she used backstory as a way of bringing out motivation in the book she's completing, *Lost*, which is about a mother who disappears: "That was my initial idea. I knew nothing else. All I could imagine is that her family and the whole town would wonder what's happened. Kidnapped? Murdered? Amnesia? Would she possibly have run away? As I wrote her story, I learned what happened to her and why. The entire plot of this book hangs on the discovery process of the backstory."

Carol Gorman, author of the Dork series (*Dork in Disguise, Dork on the Run,* published by HarperCollins), creates would-be cool guy, Jerry Flack, who readers love precisely because of his past life (backstory) as a hopelessly dorky kid. Gorman says, "I think backstory provides opportunities for a character or characters (or towns or other groups of people)

to demonstrate something in their past that helps to illuminate their present condition. In my Dork novels, Jerry Flack occasionally remembers what it was like when he was a dork in elementary school. One time, he remembers standing with a group of geeky kids when a popular student walks past with friends and points them out, saying, 'Hey, look, it's a Dork convention!' Remembering how he was an outsider in elementary school motivates him to act totally different now."

Historically Speaking

For historical novelists, backstory is equally important in creating motivation, plus it is enriched by records of real people and events. Delia Ray's *Ghost Girl: A Blue Ridge Mountain Story* (Clarion) is an example. *Ghost Girl* is tied closely to historical fact, and recounts the story of a one-room schoolhouse that President Herbert Hoover and his wife built for impoverished children near their summer fishing camp in the Blue Ridge Mountains of Virginia. Ray was inspired by a collection of letters at the Hoover Presidential Library, which were sent from Christine Vest, the teacher of the school, to the White House.

Ray says, "While the letters contained fascinating details about day-to-day life at the President's mountain school, there was almost no written information about individual students, who would become my most important characters in the novel. There were three photographs of the students in Miss Vest's classroom and these became the inspiration for conjuring the personalities, physical traits, and backstory for my characters.

"As I examined the faces in the old black-and-white photographs, I noticed that the same girl, with light eyes, pale skin, and blonde hair, stood close beside Miss Vest in each of the pictures. Immediately, I knew this was my character! Yet something major was missing—a story for this mysterious, wistful-looking girl. After months of floundering for a believable history to match with the face in the picture, I made a trip to the Shenandoah National Park Archives, near the spot where the events in my novel took place. It was there that I found a transcribed interview with a former student of the President's mountain school.

"A few lines in the 30-page interview caught my eye and haunted me for days to come. They had to do with a young sibling who had died when her nightgown caught fire as she passed by the open fireplace in the family's log cabin. Before the accident, the girl had begged her father to order a victrola. It arrived after her death, but no one in the family could bear to play it because the music brought back too many painful memories of the lost girl." This family tragedy becomes the motivation for the uneasy relationship between April Sloane and her mother that drives the needy feelings April has for her new teacher, Miss Vest.

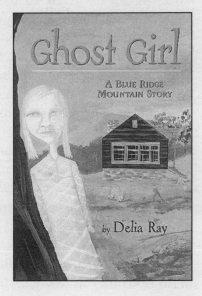

Ray says she finds herself "turning to this tactic again and again—sometimes it's an act of blind faith—waiting for snippets from historical photographs, letters, and other documents from my chosen time period to reveal backstory for important characters." Whether the backstory grows solely from the writer's imagination or whether it leaps out from an old picture or letter, backstory gives integrity to the motivation of characters.

The universe created by backstory is especially complicated in historical fiction. Rice, author of several historical novels, points out, "historical fiction requires a second level of backstory, the grinding of yet another facet on the face of the diamond. It is the raison d'etre, the primary cause for the tale's inception. Without it there would be no story. It enriches the narration, like more eggs in a cake, because the character's backstory and front story are told within the context of another era, another time. In the telling, the reader is enriched and made familiar with that era.

"I'm always painfully aware," Rice says, "that most children resist being taught history, so I try to sneak the historical backstory in under the petticoats of the action, culture, place, dress, behavior, and speech of the time."

Even so, Rice admits to times when only literal backstory narration works—when she needs "to inject a section of bald narration to explain tersely and accurately what is or has gone on historically in that second level of backstory. It must be done as briefly as possible, and must seem to be a part of the story. In *The Place at the Edge of the Earth* (Houghton Mifflin), a novel dealing with the infamous American Indian schools of the late nineteenth century, I had to sum up the history of what was called the Indian Problem—a difficult endeavor indeed—in little more than one and a half manuscript pages. I finally did it as a school research project written by my thirteen-year-old female protagonist and a friend, with a little dialogue thrown in to break the narration.

"In my recently completed *Bleddingwoode*, which takes place in fifteenth-century England during the Wars of the Roses, I handled the problem of explaining a period of enormous complexity by telling the story in two alternating voices—one an 18-year-old boy fighting for the House of Lancaster, and the other a 15-year-old girl who is fiercely loyal to the House of York. Since each is told in the first person, I could take the liberty of having my characters describe the backstory of people, events and battles in an impassioned you-are-there way, using incident, dialogue, and flashback with a vividness and excitement that I, as simply an author narrator, could not."

Real People, Real Backstories

A creative backstory can also breathe life into fictional characters who are autobiographical or biographical. Writers often use themselves and other people they know in their stories. While such sources can serve as wonderful starting points, if they are served up naturally, with no trimming, sauce, or spice, they often go flat.

Why? Perhaps because they are real instead of imagined, literal instead

314

of dramatic. But often they just refuse to spark and catch fire. This is where backstory comes in. By tossing a bit of fiction into the flames, writers can transform them into more lively and fully realized characters.

Ray talks about this in relation to Gussie Davis, the main character in *Singing Hands* (Clarion). "Gussie is modeled so closely on my mother's stories about her childhood experiences," Ray explains, "that every so often, I lose track of whether certain details in the novel are fact or fiction. Like my mother, Gussie grows up in Birmingham, Alabama, during the 1940s as a hearing daughter of deaf parents. Just like my mother as a child, Gussie has a persistent curiosity and a mischievous streak—not the most convenient traits for the daughter of a revered minister.

"But as soon as the novel began to take shape, I realized that in order to heighten tension in my story, Gussie would need to carry her mischief a few drastic steps further than my mother ever did. Fortunately, my mother was happy to give permission to let my imagination run wild. So in my finished novel, Gussie hums through her father's signed services for his deaf congregation. She sneaks into the room of one of her family's boarders and reads her treasured love letters. She uses her offering money for church to buy milkshakes for her friends downtown.

"In basing *Singing Hands* on my mother's childhood, I had the best of both backstory worlds: the ability to pick and choose from my mother's very real and intriguing catalogue of experiences and her permission to supplement with twists that would create a more potent plot line."

Connect to Conflict

Backstory can also make connections between characters that enrich conflict. In *Writing the Breakout Novel*, Donald Maass talks about complex connections and how they can take plot and conflict to a new level. He questions why a secondary character should serve only one purpose in a story and suggests that the plot texture will be richer if each character has multiple *nodes* of connection with other characters. He specifically suggests that writers can best work this out in back-story. He writes:

> Why should a wife's best friend be only her best friend? Cannot she also be the co-worker who is causing the wife's husband a problem at his office? Cannot the co-worker's own husband be the first wife's doctor, who must inform her that she has cancer? Can the two men be old army buddies? Can the women have an old high-school rivalry? (Writer's Digest Books, Cincinnati, Ohio, 2001, page 188).

While the specifics of this example may not fit novels for children, the point is still apt: Plots and subplots will have more depth and interest if characters are connected in some way to most of the other characters. This is the business of backstory: building those nodes of connection that allow energy to flow into the front story.

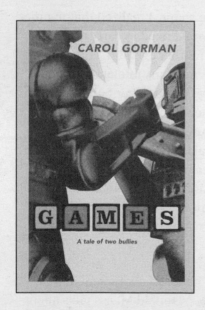

Gorman gives a good illustration when she discusses *Games: A Tale of Two Bullies* (HarperCollins). Gorman describes a scene where she wants the reader to understand how thrilling it is for one of the main characters, Mick, when Tabitha (every guy's fantasy) approaches him in the hallway. "Mick and his nemesis, Boot, who are always getting into fistfights, have been sentenced by the principal to play board games until they can figure out how to get along. Tabitha flirts and asks about their fights. Mick, who is totally inexperienced with girls, narrates: 'Little does [Tabitha] know that Boot and I came very close to fighting over her about two months ago.' He describes what happened when he ran into both Tabitha and Boot at the city pool that summer. The boys jockeyed for her attention and put on displays of toughness and bravado, hoping to impress her. The backstory gives the reader a peek into the boys' past competition and Mick's fantasies about this girl who has just been introduced." Thus, the backstory enriches the texture of the boys' macho encounter.

Some writers address the nodes of connection by making character maps. For example, if a novel has five significant characters, a character is placed in the middle with the other four characters arrayed around him or her, then the writer annotates the connections between the character in the middle and the other characters. If each character has significant connections with all or most of the other characters, the main plot and subplot will inevitably be enriched. On the other hand, if a set of character maps reveal that certain characters have only one or two nodes of connections, it may be a signal that a writer needs to devote more time to creating a cohesive backstory. Perhaps some characters can be eliminated; perhaps two characters can be morphed together. Thinking out the cast of characters, the work they will do in the plot, and the layers of conflict is time well spent.

Informed with Detail

Some of what's created in backstory is never expressly written into the manuscript. The real effect is on the writer who, post-backstory, has gotten to know the characters just as intimately as family members. With this kind of familiarity, very small details can invest the story with emotional richness and integrity.

"So much is divulged through posture and body language," says Lieberg. "I think I generally write fairly visually, and the backstory can sometimes inform a facial expression or a physical action by a character. If I can attach a memory from the backstory to the character that resonates with his or her current situation, the joining of the past and present can sometimes suggest a detail of physical movement that enriches the moment. Our current reactions to many things are determined by previous events, hopes, fears, or treatment we've received from others."

Lieberg cites a specific example in *West with Hopeless*. "Writing the backstory of my protagonist's older sister, who is the Hope in Hopeless, raised all sorts of issues. Her mother had died when Hope was very

317

young, but in the backstory I discovered or invented how that had happened—a car wreck in Nashville where she was trying to break into music—and found that I had a profile of a loving mother who adores music and wants to give her daughter full attention as well as the example of a woman who seeks her joy. Pieces of this entered the book. When Hope pawns a necklace that had been her mother's in order to buy gas and get out of the middle of Nevada, the decision carried more feeling than it would have without that background. Generally, even if the backstory details don't show up in the front story, I know I can write with more depth about the character, even in small ways."

An author's feeling for her own character is the genesis of the feeling that the character will awaken in the reader. If the pawning of a necklace triggers certain responses in the author because she knows the whole backstory, those same emotions are more likely to resonate in the reader.

Starting Off

Extensive, thoughtful backstories also make for stronger manuscript beginnings. Many writers say that the beginning is the hardest part of a manuscript; yet, paradoxically, it may be the most important. Writers sometimes dump entire first chapters. Butler says that she made a mistake when she first started writing novels. "I used to load up my first few chapters with backstory. Then I realized that the real story started somewhere in about chapter three, and that wasn't a good idea. Now I try to keep the backstory out of the story if at all possible, or limit it to just a few well placed details throughout the book, details that are important to the story."

Discussing her novel *Jennifer the Jerk Is Missing* (Simon & Schuster), Gorman says, "My editor told me that I'd started the novel too early, that it didn't get interesting until about the fourth or fifth page. She was right. I should have been hooking and drawing my reader into the story." Gorman made revisions so that the necessary backstory got woven in in bits and pieces rather than being presented in a indigestible chunk at the beginning.

Probably every author has produced a few beginnings of the kind Butler and Gorman describe: slow, telling rather than showing, tentative, and uninteresting. An antidote to such beginnings can be a fully developed backstory—either written out or carefully thought out—before even tackling the opening scene.

It's natural to want to begin by explaining that 14-year-old Lucy's mother died five years ago, and Lucy and her dad have struggled terribly with the business of taking care of the seven-year-old twins, Nate and Milly. That without the help of Gran and Pop, who drive over from Omaha every weekend, Lucy and her family would never have survived in the little town where she goes to high school with her best friend Candace, and where the twins play after school with the Miller twins two blocks down. But such backstory-heavy openings drag for the reader, who longs to be swooped up in drama and intrigue.

A stronger beginning could be a scene that catches Lucy in mid-stride dealing with the horrors of Nate's bloody baby tooth dangling by a tiny, white root—making the reader wonder what's going on, making the reader want to turn the pages to find out why Lucy's life is the way it is.

Without a backstory, a writer may find herself getting to know the characters as the opening pages are being written—which is too late. But with a backstory in place, she can begin with a quirky close-up where every gesture, word, and detail resonate with interest and promise.

A good backstory serves both writer and reader. The writer fills out each character from top to bottom, writing more confidently from page one on. The reader feels the full blown integrity of each character: sees, touches, smells, hears, and even tastes the sweat of these creatures who are, for a little time, real. When this happens, the work on the backstory has soaked through into the front story and the characters emerge fully realized.

The Fine Art of Brainstorming

By Katherine Swarts

O ne factor that separates serious writers from wannabes is that serious writers don't sit around waiting for inspiration to strike. Nor do serious writers work only when they feel like it. Serious writers stick to regular schedules, as they would with any job.

Still, sometimes even a serious writer finds him or herself staring into space with no idea what to write about or no clue where a story is going. When that happens, it may take a little serious brainstorming—jotting down ideas at random and at top speed—to open creativity floodgates.

The Basic Rules of Brainstorming

Brainstorming can help a writer over bumps in any stage of writing. But before looking at issues appropriate to specific stages, it's important to know the general principles of brainstorming:

➤ *Write it down.* Purely mental brainstorming is as foolish as fishing with an unbaited hook in a storm. If you keep the tempest confined inside your brain, nearly every idea will slip by unsecured, and you're unlikely to reel in anything worth keeping. The basic recipe for brainstorming is simple enough, though. First, set a time limit, such as 10 or 15 minutes. Ask yourself a basic question: What do I want to write about? What should my hero do next? Then, jot down every possible answer that comes to mind as fast as your hand can follow your thoughts. It doesn't matter whether you use pen and paper, computer, or display board. Just get everything into visible form. Having all those ideas before your eyes will help you pick out the best ones later.

➤ *Fast and furious is the rule.* Never dam up the free flow of a brain-storm by stopping to consider whether an idea is worth keeping. Don't even let your mind register the thought, "That will never work." Put down everything that comes into your head. There will be time after-ward to consider respective merits. Sometimes a "ridiculous" idea, when examined closely, turns out to be the best solution.

➤ *Free write.* If you're too stuck even to start brainstorming, begin with free writing. Take 10 or 15 minutes just to journal your frustration with the whole thing. That usually proves sufficient to unblock the flow of ideas and lead you into real brainstorming.

➤ *Join others.* When all else fails, ask for help. Schedule an informal brainstorming conference and invite your critique group, or a group of kids who read the kind of material you're trying to write. Have everyone call out ideas as fast as they come. You assume the role of the note-taker who records everything. Or if you're short on interested acquain-tances, check the library for titles on writing *and* brainstorming; many books provide exercises to assist in the process.

When you have a good-sized list of brainstormed ideas, scan it care-fully for the best answer (or answers) to your starting question. Now, on to how brainstorming can be used in different stages of a project.

Getting Started: Brainstorming What to Write About

One problem that plagues many a writer is knowing that you want to write but not being sure what to write about. You love reading, but you go blank at the thought of putting your own ideas into permanent form. This problem isn't exclusive to beginners. "In the early stages of my ca-reer, I didn't have writer's block as much; there were so many topics to write about," says Sandra Toney, author of *The Simple Guide to Cats* (TFH Publications), seven other books, and more than 500 articles. "Now, a project may involve something I have written about several times."

For beginners, the problem is often that they doubt they know enough about anything to write. They've never taken an exotic vacation, or they feel sure that nothing young readers would find interesting has ever hap-pened to them. They shelve the whole idea of writing, waiting until inspi-ration strikes. Successful writers can fall into a similar rut, fatigue, or block. Don't wait for the muse. Do brainstorm interesting angles:

➤ *Where you live.* Remember that not all stories are set on the Riviera, or even in Manhattan. What were your hometown's top local news stories of the past six months? How does your Chamber of Commerce attract tourists? What are the community's most popular kids' and family events? Who are your town celebrities or eccentrics? What does your state atlas say about your town? What have other local authors written?

➤ *What you do.* What attracted you to your career? Why did you take your current job? What products or services, or unique selling points, has your employer pioneered? What internships and training programs are available? Could you write a career guide for high school students considering the same field? Create a fictional character who is studying for a job similar to yours?

➤ *Who you know.* What unique family traditions did you grow up with? What interesting traits of your children or other relatives could be implemented into story characters' personalities? What makes your friends laugh? What problems do your kids complain about?

"I think part of being a writer is having a certain sensibility," says author Christine MacLean. "You realize that everything is grist for the mill. I frequently think, 'Hey, that would make a terrific essay,' or 'What a great idea for a short story!' It's a matter of seeing the world through a writer's eyes and having your ear cocked. For example, when my son was about three, he loved to play firefighter. One morning while he was pretending to put out fires with the vacuum cleaner hose, I said, 'How about a hug?' He said, 'Sorry, Mom, I am too busy putting out fires.' I said, 'Even firefighters hug their moms.' That incident turned into *Even Firefighters Hug Their Moms* (Dutton)."

"Ideas are everywhere," says Toney. "The key is being able to recognize them and turn them into articles. I am always looking for new material. I watch people and events around me to spark

Brainstorming Titles

Marcia Yudkin is a freelance writer and a creative marketer whose Named at Last (namedatlast.com) services focus on creating effective names and tag lines for businesses. The following ideas have been developed from her article, "Brainstorming Games for Naming Companies or Products," which was in turn, partly adapted from *Brand It Yourself* (Portfolio Hardcover), by Lynn Altman.

Sometimes the shortest part of a story or book—the title—is the hardest part to create. A good title must be memorable, clever, and descriptive—usually in one to six words. If you have trouble coming up with a title, try one of Yudkin's exercises:

➤ Imagine that your best friend just read your book or story and called you up to tell you how much he liked it. But the end of his message was cut off. All you heard was, "Gosh, that was great! No wonder you called it—" Reconstruct the missing part of the message.

➤ Choose one card at random from a set of playing or Tarot cards, or a group of scenic postcards; then say in what way the picture resembles the story you've written. Let that characteristic suggest titles. Repeat.

➤ Close your eyes and envision a fabulous signing for your book. Where does it take place? What is the color scheme there? Which refreshments would be served? What music is playing? Who is the Master of Ceremonies for the event? What titles does that ambiance suggest?

➤ Collect a stack of different kinds of magazines, and select a photo of someone who looks like a major character from your story or a big fan of your work. Imagine the titles this person would come up with.

➤ Hold an informal contest to see which of your friends can come up with the title the whole group agrees is the worst. Keep trying to outdo one another for ten minutes. Then look back at the list and see if any horrible titles can be nudged into good ones.

➤ Pretend that your book or story is a sequel to a well-known one, or a title in a well-known series. What would the publisher call yours? Repeat with several books or series.

ideas. I believe, first and foremost, that personal experiences help give each article that unique angle. I rarely write directly about my experiences, but having a place to start ('yes, that happened to me') has helped immensely through the years."

If you're really stuck for ideas, try clustering. "In the mid-1980s, I ran across a book, *Writing the Natural Way,* by Gabriele Lusser Rico," says

Personal experiences help give articles a unique angle—even when not writing directly about yourself.

freelance writer and editor Nanette Thorsen-Snipes, author of more than 500 articles, devotions, and stories, including Arch Books's *Elijah Helps the Widow.* "The technique that most caught my eye was clustering. You start with a word or phrase, such as *letting go,* and circle it. Then you draw spokes out from the phrase, linking other words and phrases such as *of children, of dreams,* or *of pain.* You circle each new word or phrase. This kind of brainstorming technique is a great way to break through a writing block."

Brainstorming New Angles on Old Topics

Clustering does require a starting point, but then, you may already know what you want to write about. You may want to add to the material on a topic you find interesting. You may have an assignment involving a specific topic. Or the research for your last novel may have turned up something so fascinating it deserves its own book. In any case, if you're writing about something that's occurred to someone before, brainstorming can save you from arousing a been-there-seen-that feeling in readers.

First learn what has been done. "Read books like the one you want to write," says Dale Carlson, President of Bick Publishing House and author of more than 60 books. "Note inspiration, technique, length, and construction." At the very least, read reviews. There's a reason book proposals include "competing titles" sections. Knowing what ground others have covered will help you spot the untrampled paths. Start your brainstorming from there.

➤ What questions did other titles leave unanswered?

➤ What topic areas do you wish they had developed further?

➤ How could the information in a nonfiction title be used in a fiction piece, or an article be expanded into a book?

If you're using past research and your own published writing in this brainstorming also ask the following :

➤ What material do you still own the copyrights to?

➤ What new markets would be interested?

➤ Do you want to resell your piece to a market where your earlier readers are likely to encounter it, or to a market with minimal reader overlap? (The more overlap, the more material you should change.)

➤ If you don't own the copyright, how can you recycle the information (as opposed to the form) without violating any contracts?

➤ What interesting material did you uncover but not use during the research for other manuscripts?

"Recycling already used material is often simple," says Toney. "After all, it is your work. If, however, you want to quote a source you interviewed for another article, contact them and ask permission to use those quotes. Be careful not to copy an original piece of your own; rewrite it with a new angle and add more or different information."

"If I'm genuinely interested in a topic," says MacLean, "I write about it in different genres. In the course of writing my novel *How It's Done* (Flux), which touches on faith, I realized I also wanted to explore the topic in an essay. Also, some thinking that went into 'Intentional Living' (www.jugglezine.com/CDA/juggle/0,1516,113,00.html) was later used in a 'how to find time to write' piece. I might narrow a topic down, or rewrite a nonfiction piece for a different age group."

Brainstorming Your Way Through Writer's Block

Even once you have your topic in mind—even once you're going strong—you may find yourself in front of the computer one day, drawing a mental blank. You don't know what your characters should do next;

you suddenly don't have enough chapter topics to fill your book. The dreaded writer's block afflicts every author at one time or another. It can be caused by fear of failure (or success), by lack of self-confidence, by a poor writing environment, or by mental distractions.

The most important remedy to remember: Show writer's block who's boss! Pretend you're in a salaried job where there is no leave for worker's block. You should already have a regular writing schedule—don't even think about letting up on it. "Plant self in front of suitable writing implements every day for several hours," says Carlson. That in itself can sometimes propel you past writer's block.

If your case proves tougher, brainstorming can help you write past the block. Attitude is key. If you see yourself as helpless, you will be. If you see this as something you can get past quickly, get past it you will.

"I don't call it writer's block," says MacLean, "because that makes it seem bigger than it is. I call it getting stuck, a transitory state."

Proven ways of getting unstuck include the clustering and free-writing methods already described. Even writing over and over, "I don't know where to go from here," can help. Writing to someone else can be even more helpful. "I might write an e-mail to a friend," says MacLean, "starting out just to complain, but by the end of the message, many times I've worked out the problem. I didn't talk about my works-in-progress for a long time because I worried the energy of the story would dissipate, but then I realized there was a difference between talking through a specific problem and talking out an entire story."

Much writer's block is due to fear—fear of being tried and found wanting, fear of being unable to cope with fame, fear of being asked for more and being unable to produce. MacLean remembers, "The magazine I used to work at hired a fact-checker to make sure all the information in the articles was correct. This involved near constant phone work. After a few months, I learned that the new fact-checker, who had been doing a great job, had phone phobia. She dreaded making calls; her hands got clammy, and her voice shook uncontrollably. We asked her why on earth she had taken the job. 'To get over it,' she said. I think the same principle applies to writing. The best thing you can do for writer's block is to take a writing job with frequent hard deadlines, such as writing for a newspaper or writing a weekly column or writing for a corporation. The deadlines force you to write—something, anything—and after a while, you develop confidence that words will always come to you. Even if they are lousy words, it's a starting point. I began my writing career by taking just such a position, and had similar jobs for the next ten years."

If you write fiction, try playing *what if*. "I help one children's author, an American missionary who has lived in Chile for 30 years," says freelance editor Erin K. Brown. "We use Instant Messenger to play what-if games when she needs to add a twist or create a difficult situation. Once, she was struggling with creating a surprise ending. I began the game with 'What if the boys went to get help? What if they found a cop? What if the cop turned out to be bad? What if the bad cop was only playing bad cop and was really a good cop involved in a sting operation?' That was all she needed to get her imagination fired up. This author has found that what-if questions stimulate her thinking in a fresh way."

Another fiction technique is to interview your viewpoint character. Picture him sitting in a chair across from you, and ask him directly what he thinks of the situation and what he would do next. This interview shouldn't be too hard if you've created real, believable characters that you *know* personally. Many experienced writers say that their characters plan as much of the plots as they do!

If you get stuck here, maybe you've been using cardboard characters with no real personalities. Try going back and writing detailed character profiles on one or two major characters. What's her favorite food? Where did his mother go to school? What does she do for fun? Who was his favorite teacher? Whether or not you use any of this in the story, it can help you past writer's block.

Finally, make sure your writing or brainstorming environment isn't contributing to the block. Be quiet and alone whenever possible, says Carlson. Make sure your chair and keyboard are ergonomically sound; if writing is physically painful, you're guaranteed to do less of it. Clear your work area of all distractions, maybe including the phone. Sit by a window that lets in natural sunlight without glaring off your monitor, and has a not-too-distracting view. Rest your eyes by blinking regularly and by glancing at a faraway object every 15 minutes.

When It's Time for a Break

If all else fails—if you've tried every brainstorming technique and come up dry—and if you've been writing consistently for several hours or weeks, the problem may not be with your creativity. Your mind and body may just be trying to tell you that you need a break. If you've accomplished a good deal today or over the past week or more, and can honestly say you aren't just looking for an excuse to procrastinate, then taking some time off can actually help your brain unleash a few storms.

"My favorite way of getting unstuck is to lie down for a nap," says MacLean. "This is counterintuitive, but I've found it amazingly productive. The trick is to keep thinking about where you're stuck, as you fall asleep; your subconscious can do terrific work if you let it. When writing *Mary Margaret and the Perfect Pet Plan* (Dutton), I knew that Mary Margaret needed to come up with an interesting way to raise money; a lemonade stand wouldn't do. I came up with the idea for Number Two Totes (cloth bags that cover the plastic bags that hold doggy droppings) while falling asleep. But you have to be willing to pull yourself out of that sleep state to write the idea down. Otherwise it's lost in the ether."

Toney says, "I find it best to sleep on it. Usually, the writer's block will disappear once I've had time to write in my mind."

Exercise is another means of unlocking the subconscious. "Sometimes I take a long walk," says MacLean. "The rhythm of walking sparks my imagination. Don't forget to take a paper and pen." Any serious writer should have paper, electronic notepad, or a recorder constantly on hand, to capture those stray ideas that pop into your head without warning. Forgotten quickly if trusted to memory, such ideas can, when saved in tangible form, make up a brainstorming file you can refer to when stuck.

Therein lies another key to successful brainstorming. Just as you can't pour water from an empty pitcher, an empty brain will produce few storms. So keep your brain as full as possible. Read all you can. Join clubs, take classes, volunteer for new assignments. Go where you'll meet lots of kids and parents. Travel when possible. And write down notes on everything. Follow many or all of the pieces of advice here and you may soon find you don't have to think much about formal brainstorming techniques. They'll come naturally when needed.

Writing Coaches: Help Getting to the Top of Your Game

By Suzanne Lieurance

It's no secret that top athletes in any professional sport work with a personal coach at one time or another during their careers. A good coach can help an athlete attain the peak performance needed to get to the top of his game. In today's highly competitive world of publishing, many writers are now turning to personal writing coaches to help them get to the top of their games, too.

Writing coach Lisa Gates has degrees in journalism and theater and holds a professional coaching certificate from the Coaches Training Institute. She says, "When you really look at it, heads of state, athletes, and corporate executives have relied on coaching for years, if not centuries. We are now, once again, seeing that seeking outside help in our lives is not a sign of weakness, but a sign of strength." One reason writers are turning to writing coaches these days is because of the explosion of on-line communication. "The whole landscape of business and marketing is forever changed as a result of the Internet. We now have online literary magazines, consumer and news magazines, business blogs and websites, and other commercial venues. With all this, business professionals are challenged more than ever to get their expertise into print, and are seeking out writing coaches to help craft their voices."

This explains why many business executives, who aren't necessarily skilled writers, turn to coaches. But why would professional writers need a writing coach? Anne Wayman, a freelance writer, writing coach, and a founding member of the International Association of Coaching

(IAC) explains it this way. "I suspect that a good writing coach can provide the information, support, and even hand-holding that we think editors and agents of the past provided."

Diane Eble, whose coaching service is called Words to Profit, agrees with Gates and Wayman and points out, "There are more options for writing and publishing than ever, so it can be confusing. Or, the writer may not even know the options available. A coach can open doors of opportunity the writer never dreamed existed. A writer may also have a number of different goals. One writer may want fame, while another

> ## A coach can open doors of opportunity a writer never dreamed existed.

writer may want to make a decent living from what he does best (write), while yet another writer may simply want to write a book to fulfill a dream of having a book on the bookshelves of a library. A good writing coach should help a writer unlock his deepest dreams for his writing, as well as help the writer overcome the fears that may be holding him back from attaining these dreams." Those aids are in part what distinguish a writing coach from a writing teacher.

Teacher or Coach?

"A writing teacher has the responsibility for delivering a curriculum that's geared toward achieving a set of objectives and uses a specific structure for measuring results (papers, grades, etc.)," says Gates. "A writing coach works one-on-one, generally, and focuses on the client's specific needs inside his or her writing project or niche. Whether it's a book, a short story, a proposal, or whether it's tackling grammar pitfalls or passive voice or point-of-view shifts, a coach-client relationship almost always runs head-on into a writer's business and life issues as well."

A writing teacher determines the content covered and the method of study in an instructional session, whereas a writing coach helps a client determine what aspect of a writing career or project will be covered in each coaching session, based on his or her own needs at the time. Wayman says, "Looking for a writing teacher is wise for gaining general knowledge, but a writing coach can help a person apply the knowledge and proceed in light of specific strengths and weaknesses."

The Perfect Coach

A writer searching for the perfect coach should first consider personal expectations. Many coaches prefer to work with writers of fiction, while others are more comfortable coaching on nonfiction projects. Some, such as Eble, specifically help with completing and submitting book proposals to publishers. But Eble can also assist writers in learning how to make a living from their books, a process that is quite different for authors today than it was in the past.

Be as specific as possible about needs before searching for a writing coach. In fact, Gates suggests that writers ask themselves these questions:

> ➤ Do you want a coach to read, critique, and analyze your writing and coach you to completion of a project?
> ➤ Do you want someone who can support you in building your livelihood as a writer?
> ➤ Do you need a coach to help reveal and remove blocks in your personal life to make room for your writing?

Once you've answered these questions, and have a starting point, Gates suggests you "look for a coach whose experience or niche complements your needs."

Wayman advises writers to look for a coach who can really listen: "A coach who can get what the writer is saying or trying to say, then feed back the information in a truly supportive way is probably ideal." She clarifies, "Working with a writing coach is an intimate relationship. The writer has to be willing to open up to the coach if the coach is going to help. The writer also has to make a financial commitment. And, I think the writer has to be willing to search for the coach who will work best for him or her. I can't successfully coach just any writer. We need a certain rapport that is hard to define. A couple of phone conversations and an assignment from the coach will usually tell both parties if the relationship is working. I would urge writers to give the coach a fair chance, but not hesitate to fire the coach if the relationship isn't working." Wayman

The Benefits of Working with a Writing Coach

No matter what type of coach a writer chooses to work with, the writer should expect to receive the following benefits:

➢ A good coach helps a writer stay motivated by providing constant feedback and encouragement. A writer not working alone, and accountable to the coach on a regular basis, finds it's easier to keep going until a project is completed.

➢ A good coach provides a system for success that the writer can stick with. It's often difficult for a writer to break down a project into smaller activities, and learn how to do this with any type of project. A good coach helps develop a system based on an individual's particular writing and working style, while taking other, non-writing responsibilities and commitments into account.

➢ A good coach helps the writer learn to set realistic goals and stay focused on them. This is perhaps one of the greatest benefits of a writing coach. Writers are creative people and may be easily distracted by other exciting opportunities and creative ideas that come their way. A writer can learn not to become distracted by other possibilities when having a tough time with a current project.

➢ A good coach helps a writer get going again when stuck or off-track. A good coach will see that projects no longer end up as unfinished manuscripts tucked away in drawers. They will be completed.

➢ A good coach offers a writer professional advice. This is why it is so important to work with a coach who is also a professional writer, someone who knows the ropes.

➢ A good coach helps a writer accurately evaluate progress. Writers can be impatient and dissatisfied with their progress because they think they should be farther along than they are. Publishing is a slow game and a good coach helps the client see realistically.

➢ A good coach keeps the process enjoyable. Let's face it. A writer who isn't enjoying the writing and publishing process isn't very likely to stick with it. A good writing coach knows this, and provides ways to keep the process enjoyable so the writer will attain set goals.

has been known to fire clients, gently, when she has sensed that they weren't getting what they needed from her. "There needs to be a good fit between writer and coach because this will be an ongoing relationship. The writer should be able to trust the coach, and believe that the coach knows what he or she is doing (is competent) and has the writer's best interests at heart. The writer should agree with the coach's underlying philosophy and feel comfortable with the coach's policies and procedures. The writer should feel able to bring up to the coach any uncomfortable feelings that arise as they work together."

Gates, Wayman, and Eble all suggest that a writer look for a coach who not only has successfully written and published in the past, but is still doing it, at least to some extent. "Things are always changing, and you want to make sure your coach is still in the game and can give you up-to-date advice," says Eble.

Probably the best way to start a search for the perfect coach is to go online and simply type *writing coaches* into a search engine like Google. All sorts of websites for writing coaches will pop up. Some coaching sites will be associated with universities, others will be the personal sites of published authors and other professional writers who have added coaching to their list of writing and writing-related services offered at their sites. Organizations such as IAC and the Coaches Training Institute have searchable databases that writers can use to locate a coach online. Another good way to locate a reputable writing coach is to ask around on various forums and listservs for writers. Find out about coaches other writers have worked with in the past and would recommend.

The Coaching Process

Once a writer has found the perfect coach to meet specific needs and writing goals, the coaching process can have different personalities. Gates calls herself a "completion catalyst" and her coaching company Design Your Writing Life. She says, "My ideal clients are people with some foundation in personal development who not only want to write, but crave to create a business, launch a project, develop a venue for the expression of the work, and call that part of it done!" She prefers working with the whole picture, the whole life. "I work one-on-one, on the phone, generally once a week through a variety of formats. I offer a

Coaching Sources

➤ **Coaches Training Institute:** www.thecoaches.com

➤ **Diane Eble:** www.wordstoprofit.com

➤ **Lisa Gates:** www.designyourwritinglife.com

➤ **International Association of Coaching (IAC):** www.certifiedcoach.org

➤ **Suzanne Lieurance:** www.workingwriterscoach.com

➤ **Anne Wayman:** www.writingwithvision.com

12-week program called the Architecture of Identity, plus two four-week programs called Identity of Motion. I will be adding teleworkshops and an e-book shortly."

Wayman says, "My coaching works exactly the way the client wants it to work." Writers who are stuck on a piece and have a looming deadline can e-mail her and she'll arrange a phone call to help the client get it sorted out. Or, some writers have a great idea, but don't know what to do with it. Wayman helps by giving writing assignments that prompt clients to clarify what they want to do. Once the assignment is completed she calls the client to give specific feedback and a second assignment. After a second phone call and more feedback, both Wayman and the client decide if they want to set up more coaching sessions.

When working with people who want to prepare a book proposal and submit it to publishers, Eble first helps writers start to develop a platform for themselves and their work by having them build a website and/or blog; write short articles for article directories, to establish themselves as a respected expert in their area of expertise; and take on other promotional activities. In today's competitive book markets, many publishers want writers to have some sort of platform—a strong online presence, a mailing list, a developing or established readership—because there's less risk in publishing this writer's work.

Not every professional writer will choose to work with a coach. Not every writer needs a coach. While it can be quite challenging to find the right coach, for those who do choose to work with a coach, the process will pay off over time. A good writing coach can be just the help many writers need to get to the top of their game.

Oh, the Places You Can't Go! Researching Place

By Lisa Harkrader

When writing about real places, whether in fiction or nonfiction, details about the setting must be exactly right. An accurate, vivid setting gives readers the best sense of a place and the people who live there. Readers familiar with the real locale will almost certainly call you on it if you get something wrong.

The best way to research a setting, of course, is to go there and poke around. But a research trip is not always possible. Sometimes we don't have the time or money to travel. Sometimes the places are simply too far away. I've written books about Cuba, India, South Korea, and the Civil War. Sadly, none of my publishers offered a travel budget. Or a time machine.

Fortunately, more and more research tools are available for writers who can't travel. Working with these tools, we can write with authority about places we can't go.

The Big Picture

Writers who are familiar with a real place because of having lived or spent considerable time there have stored up more information than they may realize. Writers who can't visit the place they're researching should aim for a similar store of knowledge.

"Before I start a novel, I like to immerse myself as much as possible in background and setting," says Melissa Wyatt, author of young adult novels that include *Raising the Griffin* (Wendy Lamb Books) and *Almost Heaven*, scheduled for publication by Farrar, Straus and Giroux in 2009. "I try to learn as much about the place as I can, even though I know probably 80 percent of the information will never go into the book. But having that knowledge gives me a confidence that helps the details emerge more organically as I'm working. I don't have to stop and think, 'Okay, it's time to drop in details about what kind of trees grow here.' Instead, if I know almost as much as my characters would know, then I'll know as I'm writing what they would say or think about the trees, what they would notice, and what they wouldn't. It not only helps the details feel more natural, it can sometimes keep me from making my characters sound like tour guides."

The coming summer rain carries the smell of the paper factory from the west.

Wyatt looks for ways to incorporate all five senses into her description of a setting. She also tries to find details that only people who live in a place would know or understand. "In the town where I live, for example, we always know when it's going to rain in summer because the moisture in the air carries in the smell of the paper factory from the west. The smell is faint and if you didn't live here you might not notice the change, or you wouldn't know that it meant rain was coming. A few details like that can really deepen the sense of authenticity and reality."

The Armchair Traveler

A good place to begin your research is the same place you would probably begin an actual trip: a travel guide. You can find travel guides for most countries, states, and regions, as well as many cities, in a library or bookstore. Look for up-to-date guides that include sections on history, culture, and daily life, plus plenty of color pictures.

Katherine Sturtevant, author of the award-winning novels *At the Sign of the Star* and *A True and Faithful Narrative* (both published by Farrar, Straus), advises writers to go one step further. "Use both travel guides and travel writing, which are not really the same thing," she says. While travel guides can give a very good overview of a country or region, travel writing—by authors such as Bill Bryson and Paul Theroux— is usually a first-person narrative that gives a more personal flavor of a place.

Sturtevant also suggests consulting field guides to research a setting's flora, fauna, rocks, and other landforms. Phrase books aimed at travelers can also improve understanding of a region's language and the way people use it.

Reach Out

Your library can be a great source of information about places all over the globe. It's often easiest to start in the children's section, where the nonfiction books can give a good overview of a place at a glance. Once you know the basic facts, you'll have a better idea which longer, more detailed books you'll need for research. But don't rely solely on books. Large libraries also carry detailed maps of various locales, as well as nonfiction videos and sound recordings that show the sights and sounds of a place and offer insight into the people who live there.

Your research isn't limited to items your own library offers. Sturtevant advises calling the library in the town or city you're researching. "They'll know if a local history or photograph collection has been published that might be available through interlibrary loan. If it's a big place, you can locate a title using a major online card catalogue, for example, U.C. Berkeley's Pathfinder (http://sunsite5.berkeley.edu:8000), then request that title through interlibrary loan."

Sturtevant also suggests reading magazines and newspapers published in the area you're researching. "These are the biggest sources of information on daily living, which is the novelist's greatest need. Look at real estate sections, living and lifestyle sections, arts and 'what's on,' and crime reports, to get a sense of the place. Look at ads—invaluable —and prices. You can often subscribe by mail for a few months to a paper from the area you're researching."

At Your Fingertips

The world is a big place, but the Internet is making it smaller. You can access many research resources from your computer without leaving home.

The World Factbook (Central Intelligence Agency) is a reliable source of current facts and figures about the world's countries. It is updated every two years, and its website includes data and statistics on each country's geography, population, economy, and government, as well as a brief section on the nation's background and major problems it faces. (www.cia.gov/cia/publications/factbook/index/html)

Information from other websites may not be as accurate or current. For any research source, it's important to corroborate information with another source. For Internet sites, that is doubly true.

"I never rely solely on Internet sources without finding at least one independent backup source," says Wyatt. "The Internet is more like a guide. It says 'Look here, this is pretty cool. Go look for more stuff about that.' But the Internet also provides access to some original sources, like contemporary newspapers. For my second novel, *RAW,* which is set in present-day West Virginia, I kept up with local news through a regional newspaper's website. For *Raising the Griffin,* I found a number of websites for expatriates from various Eastern European countries, which kept people up to date on what was happening in their homelands, and connected them to their culture and each other. I found those websites to be a fantastic source for the kinds of details that resonate because the cultural details those people clung to were the ones that meant the most to them."

Call in the Experts

Sometimes the details you need are not readily available in written form. Instead of tracking down print or Web sources, you must track down experts and ask questions.

You can often find an authority on a subject at a university or through a website that specializes in your subject matter. When I was writing a book set in Australia, I needed to know the kinds of houses today's aboriginal people live in. Sources detailed the houses they historically inhabited, but offered nothing on how they lived now. I contacted a professor of aboriginal studies at a university in Australia, who was happy to answer my questions through e-mail. Similarly, when I needed to know how to throw a non-returning hunting boomerang, an e-mail to a company in Australia that sells them promptly produced a return e-mail with step-by-step instructions.

An expert doesn't always need a Ph.D. Sometimes you just need a person who lives in your chosen setting. "I've depended on the kindness of strangers—and friends—to help me out with real, today places," says Jody Feldman, who called on the expertise of Ohio resident Kate Tuthill, former journalist and freelance writer, when Feldman was researching Cleveland as a setting for her work-in-progress, *The Golly-whopper Games* (Greenwillow).

Some of what Feldman needed to know to make her portrayal of the setting accurate was whether folks in Cleveland say *pop* or *soda*, *tennis shoes* or *sneakers*, the kinds of houses they live in, the look of yards and neighborhoods, the schools, and when summer vacation starts. "I just kept feeding questions to Kate, who was very wonderful about feeding answers back to me," says Feldman.

If you don't already know someone in the locale you're writing about, you can put out a call on writers' listservs, such as Children's Writers and Illustrators (groups.yahoo.com/group/childrens-writers). Writers are usually happy to answer other writers' research questions.

Back in Time

Even if you can travel to, say, Boston to learn about an actual place, you can't travel to Boston in 1776. Researching a historical setting is, by definition, researching a place you can't visit.

Luckily, the Internet offers many historical resources where you can begin the research process. Annette Curtis Klause, author of young adult novels such as *Blood and Chocolate* (Delacorte), *The Silver Kiss* (Delacorte), and *Freaks: Alive, on the Inside!* (Margaret K. McElderry Books), has

An Editor's Perspective

As Managing Editor of Enslow Publishers, David Dilkes has edited books about many far-flung places. Among the nonfiction series he has worked on are Middle East Nations of the World, Continents of the World, and Oceans of the World. He recently took time to share his own insights on how writers can better research and write about the places in their books.

➤ **Other than basic facts and figures, what information and details make a place come alive for readers and for you as an editor?**

"The details that I feel make a place come alive for readers are positive things that relate to everyday life. For example, the inclusion of a song native to that place. Or a recipe for a native dish. A short poem can be good as well. Also, if the author is able to get a quote from a person who is about the same age or slightly older than the target audience, that adds an interesting personal touch. In general, any discussion of how the people in that region go about their everyday life will hold the interest of readers."

➤ **What mistakes do writers make when describing settings or places?**

"One mistake some writers make in describing a region is to assume that the readers know where significant places are. It's been my experience that a lot of younger readers do not have a strong grasp of world geography. If a book has good maps, that will surely counter it, but writers need to be wary of including place names and assuming the reader will know where these places are or that they will look them up.

"Another basic mistake is to include a measurement of area or distance without giving the readers something to relate it to. For example, stating that a place is 265,000 square miles sounds impressive, but it is really just a number. Saying that it is slightly larger than the state of Texas is something that many students in the U.S. can relate to."

An Editor's Perspective

➤ **Enslow enlists experts to fact-check manuscripts before publication. Do the experts find common mistakes or misconceptions in the manuscripts when authors write about places they can't personally visit?**

"The main misconceptions they bring to my attention are things relating to culture and stereotypes. Many of the manuscript experts we've used have at least spent time in the country that was the subject of the manuscript they were reading. So, they would sometimes shed light on a sensitive issue in that land that the author may not have been able to grasp by reading mass media news articles. But we also have to keep in mind that experts may have their own biases, which is why we try to use experts on each side of an issue. I recently edited a book about Palestine using an Israeli advisor and a Palestinian advisor, which helped to keep the book balanced."

➤ **Do you have any suggestions for ways writers could improve research on the places they write about?**

"The best advice I could give to writers wanting to research a faraway place is to collect as many different types of research material as possible. Of course, get the latest reference books and articles from mass media outlets. Get good basic background information. But also use the Internet to find other sources. States and provinces all have their own websites, many in English. Contact a tourism department for a state, country, or province and you will likely receive huge packets of all sorts of information.

"To get a personal perspective, try to find a few bloggers. Google's blog search will turn up blogs from people living almost anywhere. Ask a few people the same questions to try to gain the views and character of the people native to that region. That gives a good personal touch when it may be otherwise difficult to find someone to interview. Another place to look is craigslist.org. Craigslist has a website in dozens of countries and every region of the U.S. and Canada. You would be surprised at how many people will respond to a query or ad."

found that many local libraries maintain historic records online. "I sometimes find good historical setting information from local historical societies that have an online presence—like what buildings were around the town square in a particular town at a particular time, who owned them, and what went on in them."

Klause also accesses the Library of Congress online. "The LOC American Memory site (http://memory.loc.gov/ammem/index.html) has great resources for historical settings," she says, "including old maps, documents, photos, and audio and visual recordings. I used the railroad maps while researching for *Freaks*."

Newspapers can be as valuable in exploring historic settings as they are in researching modern locales. "The Library of Congress has thousands of historical newspapers online," says Klause. "You can also ask for help from a librarian online."

Tuthill, who has written for many book and magazine publishers, including the Cricket Magazine Group and CTB/McGraw-Hill, recommends Newspaper Archive (www.newspaperarchive.com), an online subscription service that houses newspaper articles from 1759 to the present. "I've used it for several biographical nonfiction pieces," says Tuthill, "and it's amazing what you can find. I found a number of articles, for example, from a Fort Wayne, Indiana, newspaper dating back to the mid-1800s about a judge I was researching."

Newspaper Archive doesn't include big newspapers, such as the *New York Times*, because the large papers keep their own archives. It is a subscription service; the fee to access articles is anywhere from $25 for a seven-day pass to $9 a month for an annual membership. Tuthill believes it is worth the price. The Archive provides information she couldn't find any other way. "It has old advertisements for products long since out of production and the social news, which is a good way to get the flavor of the times."

A Whole New World

Intense research about locations isn't useful just for books set in real places. Writers often use information about real places to help them create authentic fictional settings. To make Rovenia, the fictional former Soviet republic in *Raising the Griffin*, as believable as possible, Wyatt did exhaustive research on real former Soviet republics.

"I knew it would be very easy for people to dismiss the story if the setting didn't feel absolutely real," says Wyatt, "so I had to make sure that the country I created fit not only into the geographical region but also into the history that still impacts what is happening in those countries today. My country had to be shoehorned into that history, using a patchwork of details about real countries and specific events that would feel authentic without being immediately recognizable."

Accuracy of place matters in science fiction: plants, animals, terrain, shelter, culture. Pay attention to orbits, gravity, atmosphere, planetary neighbors.

Since her protagonist is the newly restored teenaged prince of Rovenia, Wyatt had to research the palaces and places royalty would haunt. "I remember reading one line from an interview with Princess Diana where she said, 'Everywhere I go, I smell fresh paint,' because the people at the places she was scheduled to visit would always rush to spruce up before she got there. I thought, 'Wow. Now that's authentic detail that only someone in this position would know.'"

The settings in science fiction and fantasy stories are often visited only in your imagination. But these genres hardly get a free pass in the research department. "A good science fiction setting is soundly based on, or extrapolated from, fact," says Rebecca Kraft Rector, author of the science fiction *Tria and the Great Star Rescue* (Delacorte). "You need all the same details that make any story feel real: plants, animals, insect life, terrain, shelter and housing, culture, education, transportation, communication, etc. But in science fiction you also need to pay attention to the bigger picture: the influence of orbits, gravity, atmosphere, planetary neighbors. You need to be sure that every detail is believable within your created world, and believable based on today's science."

Research sources Rector finds helpful include the NASA website (www.nasa.gov) and the BBC's Science and Nature website (www.bbc.co.uk/sn/). She relies on experts—a physicist and an environmental scientist—to answer technical questions, and science fiction writer Patricia Wrede's online worldbuilding questions (www.sfwa.org/writing/worldbuilding1.htm) to help pinpoint what kind of real life setting research she needs. Rector says those questions "are useful to writers of any genre."

You may not be able to travel to other planets or to real places right here on Earth, but it doesn't mean you're stuck writing about your own neighborhood for the rest of your career. By tracking down the right sources and turning up details both accurate and revealing, you can write with authority about places you've never been.

Worth a Thousand Words: Photos for Nonfiction

By Lisa Harkrader

Writers write. They use words to convey ideas and paint vivid images in readers' heads.

That works well for fiction, especially fiction for older readers. But when it comes to nonfiction, words may not be enough. Often those words need pictures to help readers understand the ideas and visualize images accurately. Nonfiction writers who find good photographs to enhance their words make their books more enjoyable, more valuable, and more meaningful to the young people who read them.

Who's Responsible?

For trade publishers such as Houghton Mifflin or Scholastic, writers usually do their own photo research. Some school and library publishers, such as Enslow Publishers or Lerner Publishing, require writers to find—and buy—images, while others acquire photos themselves.

"This depends on the publisher and on the contract for the specific book," says Debra McArthur, author of eight nonfiction books for children, including *Raoul Wallenberg: Rescuing Thousands from the Nazis' Grasp* and *A Student's Guide to Edgar Allan Poe* (both published by Enslow). "My first four books required the author to find the photos, pay any fees, and obtain permissions. My later books, biographies of famous authors, did not require me to do any photo research or pay for permissions."

Tara Koellhoffer, who has been an editor at Enslow and Chelsea House and now works as a freelance editor for publishing houses including Pearson, Marshall Cavendish, Greenhaven Press, and Teachers College Press, says most of the school and library publishers she has worked with obtain photos themselves. "The only publisher I've worked with that required authors to research and pay for the photographs for their own books is Enslow."

Elaine Marie Alphin, whose nonfiction books for children and young adults include *An Unspeakable Crime* (Carolrhoda), as well as a series on vacuum cleaners and other household appliances, feels fortunate that her nonfiction publisher, Lerner, acquires the photos for her books. But she offers help when possible. "I keep my eye out for possible photos as I do my research for the writing itself, and pass along information to my editor."

Costs

Writers who are responsible for acquiring photos want to find the best images at the most affordable price. Fortunately, many good photos are available for low or no cost.

"If you can, you're best off using government sources; they are generally free," says Elaine Landau, author of more than three hundred nonfiction books, such as *Suicide Bombers* (Twenty-First Century Books) and titles in a historical series that bears her name, including *Witness the Boston Tea Party with Elaine Landau* (Enslow). "I've found that the most expensive photos come from famous photographers and some very high-end photo stock houses."

Many government sources, including the Library of Congress and NASA, offer high-resolution photos online that can be downloaded and used at no cost because they're in the public domain—they're not protected by copyright and can be freely used by the public. Other sources, such as the National Archives, do not offer downloadable photos, but allow authors to order prints. The writer must pay for the reproduction, usually $15 to $35 a photo.

"But be careful!" warns Susan Campbell Bartoletti, whose non-fiction books have won countless honors, including the Sibert Award for *Black Potatoes: The Story of the Great Irish Famine, 1845-1850* (Houghton Mifflin) and a Newbery Honor for *Hitler Youth: Growing Up in Hitler's Shadow* (Scholastic). "Just because you find a photograph [in government sources] doesn't mean that it's in the public domain. It's your responsibility to track down the copyright holder and clear permission."

Foot Soldiers of the Terrorist Movement
Suicide Bombers
Elaine Landau

For some nonfiction topics, a writer won't be able to find government photos and must turn to museums, historical associations, and other sources. Stock houses offer thousands of images that can be licensed for specific uses. A Google search of *stock photos* or *photo library* turns up companies such as Getty Images (www.gettyimages.com), Corbis (www.corbis.com), and hundreds more.

"Privately held photo collections can be expensive or free, depending on the choice of the owner," says Mary Dodson Wade, author of such nonfiction books as *C. S. Lewis: The Chronicler of Narnia* (Enslow) and the owner and publisher of Colophon House, a small press specializing in Southwest history. "Generally, black-and-white photos cost about half what color photos cost. For the C. S. Lewis book I paid $600 for five black-and-white photos, with one being cropped and used on the cover."

"The most expensive photo I ever had to buy permission to use was an image of Saddam Hussein that was copyrighted by the Associated Press," says McArthur. "They charged me $120 for just the one photo."

The price of a photo can vary depending on the size needed and where it will be used. "A picture that takes up a quarter of a page will not cost as much as one used in a double-page spread or on the cover of a book," says Landau. "Some stock houses and agencies also charge by the size of the print run."

A Handful of History

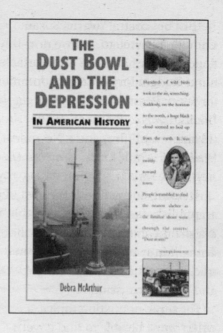

When Debra McArthur was writing *The Dust Bowl and the Depression* (Enslow), a friend introduced her to an elderly woman who had lived through the Dust Bowl as a child.

"I had already written the first chapter of that book, the story of a particularly bad dust storm that occurred on April 14, 1935, and later became known as Black Sunday," says McArthur. "The storm was one of the worst of the whole period, and it formed a giant wall of airborne dirt that traveled from the central states all the way to the east coast. The first letter I received from this lady included a black-and-white photo her sister had taken of a dust storm coming up over the back fence of their ranch in Syracuse, Kansas. On the back of this old photo was the faded, hand-lettered date: April 14, 1935. It was like holding a piece of history in my hands. The publisher used that photo in the opening chapter."

The woman provided additional information about the photographs she sent, which McArthur included in the photo captions.

A writer also needs to ask for the appropriate rights and permissions. "In some cases, it makes sense to clear world rights, all languages," says Bartoletti, "and in some cases, you're wasting money. If a book is completely Americentric in nature, you may not need to clear world rights since the book may never sell to a foreign country."

"No matter where the photos come from," says McArthur, "the author needs to document the source so that the publisher can properly credit the photos in the book."

Writers who must pay for photos can sometimes negotiate contract terms with their publishers that help offset costs. "You need to either get a photo allowance or a large enough advance to allow you to buy photos and still pay your mortgage," advises Landau. Bartoletti also negotiates a photo and permissions budget for her trade nonfiction.

But writers may not always get the terms they seek. "With one of my books, I was given an allowance, but it was then added as part of my advance, and I had to earn it out before getting more royalty," says Wade. "If I think I can supply photos at a minimal cost and effort, I will negotiate for a larger percentage royalty, usually two to three percent."

Helping authors with the cost of obtaining photos can be beneficial to publishers. Koellhoffer says that requiring authors to foot the entire bill can save the publisher money up front, but can also lead to problems. "Many authors would submit photocopies instead of prints or obtain only a bare minimum of images because they didn't want to spend their advance on photographs," she says. "As a result, the photos in the books weren't always as interesting or as good in quality as we might have hoped."

McArthur advises writers to keep records of their costs. "I do keep receipts, since this is a tax-deductible expense."

Choosing Images

Cost aside, authors naturally look for images that will best enhance their carefully crafted words.

"The best photos are those that add something to the text, rather than simply serve to break up the text," says Koellhoffer. "Too often, publishers, especially publishers of books for young adults, slap in gratuitous photos, just for color or to 'add interest.' If the book is about club drugs, they might use a random picture of kids standing around at a club, which doesn't really add anything to the narrative. It's always better to try to find photos or diagrams that can be used to add information that doesn't already appear in the text."

"I want the photographs to tell the story," says Bartoletti. "As a former teacher, I know the power that photographs have to pull nonreaders into the text—to trick them into reading." For *Black Potatoes*, Bartoletti used engravings published in contemporaneous newspapers from Ireland and England. "It was an unusual choice, but ultimately the best choice. The engravings provided a wonderful counterpoint to the text."

Landau looks for photos that offer readers a broad view. "If it's a historical subject, I look for a photo that reveals a wealth of historical details. These should show things like the types of cars people drove years ago, the clothing they wore, and the way the homes and streets looked. I make a point of avoiding headshots. I want the photo to at least show what the person is wearing and hopefully place that person in the context of the job he or she does."

In her biography *Marion Wright Edelman: Fighting for Children's Rights* (Enslow), Wendie C. Old explained that Edelman was afraid of dogs because her civil rights groups were attacked by police dogs. Old wanted a photo that helped readers connect with that fear. "Sure enough, I found a picture at the Library of Congress of police and their dogs attacking protesters. They might even have been the very dogs Marion Wright Edelman talked about!" Other nonfiction books Old has written include *The Halloween Book of Facts and Fun* (Albert Whitman) and *To Fly: The Story of the Wright Brothers* (Clarion Books).

Overexposed?

Writers often find photos that seem very familiar. There's a reason for that: They are. Some photos have been used so many times, in so many books and articles, they've become visual stereotypes.

"I have an editor who calls these photos 'done-to-death,'" says Landau. "When doing photo research, it's a good idea to look at the other children's books available on the same topic and avoid duplicating any photo already used in these books when possible."

Koellhoffer notes a few historical photos that are overused: images of slaves with scars from the pre-Civil War era; certain images of Thomas Jefferson, Abraham Lincoln, and other historical figures; the moon landing; the Kent State shootings; and several of Dorothea Lange's images from the Great Depression. "When a picture becomes this familiar," Koellhoffer says, "the reader doesn't even bother to pay attention to it, so it's a waste of space, and of money, if you've paid for permission to use it. Try to find pictures that are unfamiliar or unique in some way, which makes the reader stop and look at the photo, read the caption, and thereby pick up any additional information you may have placed there to supplement the text."

Old points out that some photos are so classic that a writer almost has to use them. "The photograph of the Wright brothers' first flight is a one-and-only. I got a copy of the best version I could find."

Sometimes the best photos—and those with the least chance of being overused—come from family photo albums. "If a writer is able to obtain childhood or family photographs from the subject's life, it really makes the book unique," says Koellhoffer. "It's often easier than you might think to get permission to use private photos. Many people are flattered to be the subject of a book and are willing to lend photographs to improve the final product."

For a biography Koellhoffer edited, *Isabel Allende* (Chelsea House) by Tim McNeese, she obtained many of Allende's family photographs free of charge by e-mailing Allende's assistant. Similarly, Wade borrowed photos for her biography, *Joan Lowery Nixon: Masterful Mystery Writer* (Enslow), from Nixon herself.

McArthur mined her own family's photos for her book about the Dust Bowl. "In my late grandfather's photo collection," she says, "I found a great photo that he took of a steam-powered tractor in about 1915. My mom was very excited that I was able to use his photo, and include his name in the photo credits for the book."

Do It Yourself

Sometimes the most thorough search does not turn up the photo an author needs. Many nonfiction writers then turn to another source: their own cameras.

Pat McCarthy, a photographer as well as a writer, took about half the photos for *Henry David Thoreau: Writer, Thinker, Naturalist* (Enslow) in Thoreau's hometown of Concord, Massachusetts, and at Walden Pond. McCarthy offers tips to authors taking their own photographs: "Get in close so your subject shows up well. Use a good camera, although most point-and-shoot digital cameras that have over three megapixels are fine."

For her biographies, Old has taken photos of the places her subjects lived. "I omitted modern people from the photographs or anything not invented when the person was living and working there."

McArthur needed a photo of a sod-busting plow for her Dust Bowl book. The only existing image she found would have cost hundreds of dollars to use. "I located two actual historical plows in museums in my

Photo Sources

Writers don't have to spend a fortune to find high-quality images for their books. In fact, some of the best sources offer photos either free or for a minimal cost. Often these images are catalogued online and can be downloaded directly from the website. Many of these photos are in the public domain and can be freely used—with credit given to the source. Some are not in the public domain, and writers may have to pay a fee to use them.

➤ **Library of Congress:** www.loc.gov/rr/print/catalog.html
The Library of Congress offers about half its images through the Prints and Photographs Online Catalog. Most of the images are in the public domain and can be downloaded in high resolution. Others can be ordered online for a fee.

➤ **National Archives:** http://aad.archives.gov/aad
Although only a small percentage of the Archives' holdings are catalogued online, the Access to Archival Databases (AAD) is a good place to search for images of historical documents as well as photos, most in the public domain. You cannot download the images directly, but you can order copies for a fee.

➤ **U.S. Holocaust Memorial Museum:**
www.ushmm.org/research/collections/photo
About 14,000 historical photos are listed in the Holocaust Museum's online catalogue. You cannot download the images directly, but you can order copies for a reproduction fee.

Government Agencies
These agencies offer high-resolution public domain photos that can be downloaded directly from their websites:

➤ **Department of Defense:** www.defenselink.mil/multimedia
In addition to downloading images, McArthur purchased, for $20, a CD set of more than 800 photos from the Department of Defense for her Gulf War book.

Photo Sources

> **Department of the Interior:**

www.doi.gov/photos/gallery.html

The website of the Department of the Interior also includes photo libraries from the Fish and Wildlife Service, U.S. Geological Survey, and National Park Service.

> **Drug Enforcement Administration:**

www.usdoj.gov/dea/photo_library.html

> **Federal Emergency Management Agency:**

www.photolibrary.fema.gov

> **National Aeronautics and Space Administration:**

www.nasa.gov/multimedia/imagegallery

> **National Oceanic and Atmospheric Administration:**

www.photolib.noaa.gov

> **U.S. Antarctic Program:** http://photolibrary.usap.gov

Other Sources

> **State and Local Governments**

> **Universities**

Universities often house collections of photos and documents related to specific subjects or historical figures. Author Pat McCarthy found several photos of Daniel Boone at the University of Kentucky. Author Wendie C. Old found photos of the Wright brothers at Wright State University.

> **Museums and Historical Societies**

McCarthy obtained photos free of charge from the Henry Ford Museum and the Thomas Paine National Historical Association.

> **Corporations**

Companies that have been in business for many years often have their own archives. McCarthy obtained photos free of charge from the Ford Motor Company. Author Mary Dodson Wade went to medical equipment companies for free photos for her book about amyotrophic lateral sclerosis (ALS), also known as Lou Gehrig's Disease.

area," McArthur says. "I took photos at both sites, and came up with one photo that was suitable for the book. I gave myself permission to use it, and it didn't cost me anything."

Alphin employed similar ingenuity for her biography, *Davy Crockett* (Lerner). Her publisher needed an image of a long rifle such as Crockett would have used. "They couldn't find one, so my husband loaned them [a long rifle] to use for the photo that's in the book."

Before popping into a museum to snap pictures, writers should make sure it allows photography. Many museums have strict policies regarding the use of cameras on their premises and often do not allow tripods or video cameras. Art museums usually don't permit flash photography, since the light can deteriorate the artwork, or photographs of special collections or artwork on loan. While most museums allow patrons to take photos for personal or educational use, many do not allow images of their structures, collections, or artworks to be used for commercial purposes—including book publishing—without permission.

Museums often list their photography policies on the visitor information page of their websites. "I always clear permissions and have my subjects sign a release," says Bartoletti.

Creative Captions

When nonfiction writers acquire their own photos, they often also write their own photo captions. "Creative caption writing is vital, to provide interesting facts or bits of trivia that don't already appear in the book and to connect the subject of the photo to the narrative," says Koellhoffer. Wade agrees. "I have used the caption for a photo to add information that I didn't have room to include in the text."

Captions can also help writers avoid misunderstandings. McArthur included an often used Dorothea Lange photo in her Dust Bowl book. "I did not try to imply that it was a photo of anyone I specifically mentioned in the book," she says, "but that it successfully illustrated the sadness and struggles of many people in the period. I was allowed to write the caption, so I was able to explain that."

In nonfiction, photos and words work hand in hand. A single dynamic picture can inspire, strengthen, and support those thousand already powerful words.

Add to the Writing Fun with Hands-on Research

By Mark Haverstock

When it comes to researching fiction or nonfiction, many of us find comfort in a trip to the local library or a quick search on our favorite search engine. But some authors go beyond cracking a book or perusing a website. They go out and do something, whether it's booking a trip to Africa, swimming with dolphins in Key Largo, or holding a handful of bees.

Hands-on research means getting your mitts dirty, gathering the kind of knowledge that can help you describe an experience in detail to your audience—the sights, the sounds, the smells. It means traveling, digging, and finding the missing pieces that breathe life into a book or article. This often involves doing something that's a little out of the ordinary, a little out of your comfort zone, and maybe even a little dangerous.

Australian science fiction and fantasy author Sean McMullen says he does hands-on research to write with authority, to create details not found in other books, and most important, to find empathy with his characters. McMullen practices what he preaches, spending several days in the Strzelecki Desert for his novel *Glass Dragons* (Tor Books), hauling 60 pounds of gear—shield, helmet, battle-ax, food, and water—while wearing chain mail and flat-soled boots.

Leading a Double Life

Travel writer Shannon Hurst Lane says she pinches herself every day to make sure she's awake and not dreaming. "Some days, I am mother, wife, and local fire service employee. I go to work, cook dinner, and

Paper Lions and Road Trips

Imagine yourself being sacked by a 220-pound linebacker or being demolished by a tennis pro. Getting into the game was something author George Plimpton took a long way. He was famous for competing in professional sporting events and then writing about them from the point of view of an amateur. In 1963, he joined the Detroit Lions at their preseason camp as a 36-year-old first-string writer trying out for third-string quarterback.

The Lions agreed to let Plimpton join them for four weeks of training camp. Wearing Number 0, he got his chance to show his stuff by calling a series of plays in an intra-squad game at Pontiac Stadium. Though he didn't make it as a football hero, this experience turned into a memorable, firsthand account of professional football in the book, *Paper Lion: Confessions of a Last-String Quarterback* (Lyons Press). Several of his books chronicled forays into other professional sports, including hockey, baseball, tennis, boxing, and golf. Plimpton noted, "The smaller the ball used in the sport, the better the book."

Jack Kerouac's classic novel, *On the Road,* grew from seven years of firsthand experiences gathered from spontaneous road trips with his friends, including frequent fellow traveler Neal Cassady. Contrary to the myth that he composed the book in a three-week marathon at his Manhattan apartment, much of this now 50-year-old title was written as it happened. Kerouac jotted down his accounts in the small notebooks that he always carried with him and wrote in during his spare time.

attend the children's functions," she says. "Other days, I am Shannon Hurst Lane, freelance travel writer and world explorer. It's a fantastic gig, and I wouldn't trade it for anything."

One assignment led her to the Outer Banks of North Carolina to write a historical article on the first flight at Kitty Hawk. Lane's local contact brought her to Kitty Hawk Kites to observe hang gliding on the dunes. "Next thing I know, I am harnessed into a glider being taught how to fly," she says. "It was my first flight at Kitty Hawk."

While attending a writer's conference in Fayetteville, she and some fellow writers had a day tour of Fort Bragg, where they were able to interview a few soldiers and see how they live. "Well, I ended up learning about the Airborne Division and what it takes to be a paratrooper," Lane explains. "I was the first of us to jump off the training tower, and boy was that scary. I now know that I have no desire to jump."

Magazine and newspaper writer Elise McKeown Skolnick also balances being an involved mom and doing the field research necessary to give that extra something to her articles. "I love meeting the people I interview for stories. Most are interesting, dedicated to, and passionate about the cause or industry they're involved in, and extremely knowledgeable about it," she says. "Many inspire me; I'm rarely bored."

One of her favorite interviews was with best-selling author Mary Higgins Clark. "I'd been reading her books for what seemed like forever, and she was easily one of my favorite authors," says Skolnick. "She was visiting town for a speaking engagement, and my editor at [the local newspaper] *The Vindicator* asked me to do a pre-interview with her. I called her at her home and we talked for half an hour. I don't think I've ever been that nervous or excited about an interview! Sometimes writing nonfiction means you get to research by meeting people you admire, but thought you'd never get to meet."

When it comes to fiction, you need to create characters and situations that keep your readers turning those pages. "To that end, I've found myself living the lives of dozens of people, all in the name of research," says author Jodi Picoult. "I've shadowed police chiefs and crime scene detectives, and learned how to speak Lakota Sioux. I've studied Wicca, held the hands of battered women and played Monopoly with pediatric leukemia patients. I've been to jail (but got to leave at night). I've been the only mom in my town to ride with the fire department and have my own turnout gear. Some of the research is heartbreaking and some is exhilarating, but all of it is eye-opening."

To fulfill a dream 25 years in the making, author Daniel Meyer rode from Dallas to Fairbanks, Alaska, on his motorcycle. "The purpose was to challenge man and machine, to test our limits, and to explore the world," he says. "Sometimes we have to journey far enough away from home so that we can learn who we are." Meyer tells his story about this and other road trips in a five-book series, Life Is a Road. The entire trip was life-changing for him. "My notion of *big* was ripped away and replaced with sheer wonder," he says. "I saw a forest fire a hundred

Can I Deduct It?

Hands-on research may involve out-of-pocket expenses. Some editors and publishers may reimburse you for part or all of these. If your expenses are not reimbursed, however, you may be able to deduct many of them at tax time on your Form 1040, Schedule C.

The IRS will let you deduct any unreimbursed expense that's considered "ordinary, necessary, and reasonable" for the pursuit of your writing business. In the case of hands-on research, the following may qualify:

➤ Travel expenses such as air, train, bus, and cab fare.
➤ Car mileage to travel to interviews or sites for research purposes, 48.5¢ a mile.
➤ Lodging and meals.

The key is to provide good documentation and make a clear connection between the research activity and your writing business. Keep tickets or receipts for the sites you visit for research, collect business cards from your expert sources, and log mileage connected with research activities. Use your common sense: Claiming you bought a new boat so you can write an article on fishing won't cut it with the IRS.

When in doubt, always contact a tax professional or visit the IRS site, www.irs.gov, and look under the topics *small business* or *self-employed*. Laws and amounts for deductions may change from year to year, so it's best to have accurate and up-to-date information.

miles long. I rode through smoke for a thousand miles. Want to see the world with wide-eyed wonder? Simply choose to. It's amazing what's out there."

Wild Kingdoms

Susan J. Tweit, author of ten books for children and adults, including *City Foxes* (Alaska Northwest), spends a good deal of time connecting with and writing about nature. Once she was visiting the research garden of Professor Gordon Frankie, University of California, Berkeley, when he plucked a black bee the size of a pill capsule off of a wildflower and dropped it in her hand. He'd already told her that, unlike European honeybees, most of the 4,000 or so native North American bees are not aggressive and rarely sting.

Many would be skeptical and somewhat terrified at this event, but Tweit seized the opportunity to watch and learn. "Was I afraid? Not exactly. I didn't have time to be scared. But I was startled," she explains. "The bee—it was a female—lived up to its billing. She wandered my hand, dusting my skin with a trail of pollen grains, and then flew off, headed back to the flowers to continue gathering pollen to provision the nests where she would lay her solitary eggs. Now when I see bees in my garden, I watch with interest: My skin remembers the delicate touch of one bee's feet, and their trail of bright pollen grains." Tweit incorporated these firsthand observations into "Creating Buzz: Native Bees," a feature she wrote for the May/June 2007 issue of *Audubon*.

Maybe your present circumstances won't permit you to go off into the wild or study exotic animals personally. Connect yourself with someone who can and does. "I actually knew about zoologist Kate Echeman's trip to Africa months before she left," says author Joelle Stebleton. "She was working as a waitress and told everyone that she was earning money to do field research with cheetahs in Africa. When she came home, she brought back all these pictures of the cubs (like a proud mama would) and passed the photo album around for everyone to see. I got the idea; wouldn't this make a cool children's article?"

Author Aline Newman has yet to visit the Serengeti, Kodiak Island, or any of a thousand fascinating animal havens. "But for the articles I write for *National Geographic Kids*, I've had the thrill of interviewing many top scientists and hearing firsthand their stories of work in the field," she says. "They include Jane Goodall, Marc Bekoff, Joyce Poole, Robert M. Sapolsky, Ben Kilham, Elizabeth Marshall Thomas, and science author Sy Montgomery. Goodall later wrote me a note, which included the understatement of the year, that she was 'glad to have been of use.'"

Setting the Scene

For author Jacqueline Winspear, visiting World War I battlefields played an important part in setting the scene and connecting with

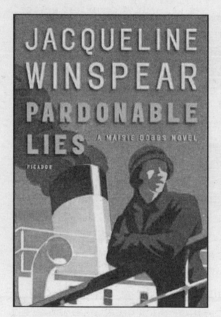

one of her characters in her novel *Pardonable Lies* (Picador). "I knew that Maisie had to go back to France, and I wondered what it might be like for her," Winspear explains. "Part of that imagining was to go to the Great War battlefields of France and Belgium. The journey was part research and part personal pilgrimage. My grandfather was badly wounded during the Battle of the Somme in 1916, and to walk those fields almost 90 years later, to reach down and pick up live ammunition from that bloody battle, to stand at the place where thousands died in hours was a deeply moving experience."

John Connolly enjoys many aspects of hands-on research. "At the very least, it allows me to travel and talk to people who lead far more interesting lives than I do," he says. "Frequently it throws up details that enrich the books. While researching my book, *Bad Men* (Pocket), I spent some time out on Peaks Island, which lies in Casco Bay just east of Portland, Maine. I wanted to set *Bad Men* in an enclosed, isolated community and an island seemed like the best bet, but I had no idea just how much material Peaks would yield." As it turns out, Peaks had a history that made it the ideal setting for a supernatural crime.

Digging Up the Past

Using her background in journalism and genealogy, Joyce B. Lohse looks to the past for hands-on research. She's written five nonfiction books with themes from the American West, four of them biographies.

"When possible, I start my research rounds at a cemetery, starting at the end and working backwards," she says. "Cemeteries sometimes provide more questions than answers, and can send you off on your chase in many directions. For example, one subject had a different cemetery listed on his death certificate and obituary than the place where I visited his gravestone. Turns out he was interred later, probably after the family settled up for the plot. Records from the other cemetery set the story straight."

Lohse's greatest finds have included love letters, receipts, photos, a passport, census records, and land deeds. "My specialty is finding newspaper articles that are contemporary to the life of the individual, and extracting quotations, photos, and artwork that may not have seen the light of day since they were published," she says. "This really paid off for my Molly Brown biography (*Unsinkable: The Molly Brown Story*, published by Filter Press). Although much has been written about her, I was able to pin down much truth about her life by focusing on primary evidence, and pulling some rare information from newspaper articles."

The mystery of well-known Colorado educator Emily Griffith's true age was solved when Lohse found a regional census listing the teacher's family, rather than relying on the statewide census. A silver-mine deed Lohse uncovered showed that in 1879, Colorado Governor John Routt paid only $1,000 for what he called his "hole in the ground"— rather than the $10,000 widely reported. "The huge deed book fell open in my hands to the correct page," she explains. "Serendipitous events like that often point me in the right direction. In the state archives, I found the governor's love letters to his wife buried in a file, and a receipt for payment of expenses for Ulysses Grant's funeral. This was news to Grant scholars when I contacted them. They were thrilled."

For more than two years, Newman has been researching a historical biography set in New York City. "This has required me to make several, multi-day research trips to Manhattan," she says. "My husband has taken vacation and gone with me every time, and we've shared some wonderful experiences, one of which is learning how to use one of the largest research libraries in the world—the New York Public Library. I had wandered through that library before but was far too intimidated to do anything but look." Now, thanks to this biography project, Newman has been granted admission to several locked rooms, including the Rare Manuscripts Division and the Print Collection. It was in the Rare Manuscripts Division that she found a handwritten letter containing an important clue to a mysterious episode in her subject's life.

"Besides the library, our investigations have taken us to the New York Historical Society, the Municipal Archives, the New York Society for the Prevention of Cruelty to Children, the NYC Tenement Museum, and the Museum of the City of New York," she explains. A little detective work at a variety of locations proved to be very beneficial to her project.

The Payoff

You never know who you'll meet or what influence your field research will eventually have on you or your writing unless you give it a try.

After nearly 20 years of writing nonfiction for young readers, author Kelly Milner Halls has hundreds of delightful experiences to share. "Tommy Smothers and I had so much fun he sent my daughter a yo-yo," she says. "A dolphin therapy expert offered me a longstanding chance to swim with dolphins in Key Largo. I even got spider web art from a man who harvests the fragile spinnings for a living. Researching is anything but dull or homework like. It's a treasure hunt, with hidden gems nearly everywhere you turn."

Sometimes your research will lead to an insider's view, with a few perks thrown in. When researching a nonfiction book on fireworks, I had the opportunity to visit a local fireworks factory and then go back that night for an employees-only test display. I also received an invitation to their fireworks technician school. A few months later, I attended their largest annual show in Louisville, Kentucky, with a spectacular view from the company's hospitality suite at a downtown hotel—about as close as you could get to the staging area on the Second Street Bridge.

Lynn Jones found a source who became her best friend. "I was researching whistling performers, past and contemporary, for an article on big band whistlers; my dad was one," she explains. "I happened upon the website of a particularly talented professional whistler, and noticed that he lived in a nearby town. We traded e-mails and phone calls, and two weeks later we met at a public botanical garden halfway between our homes. I knew this wasn't going to be a typical interview when ten minutes after we met we were holding hands and he was whistling love songs." It was a surreal experience, according to Jones. "Two months later we were engaged, but circumstances prevented a quick marriage, and the long-distance relationship didn't work out," she says. "We called off the betrothal but remain loving friends. I still feel that finding Whistlin' Tom was a major blessing in my life—and I'm still working on that article."

Become Expert at Finding Experts

By Christina Hamlett

My nephew was reading a mystery about a gumshoe detective "trudging through the snowy streets of another Sacramento winter." Snow? Sacramento? Having been born and raised in California's capital city, he was appalled by the writer's obvious lack of familiarity with its weather. "Couldn't he have just asked somebody who lives here?" he said. He not only never finished the book, but also never read anything else that author penned.

Nothing turns a reader off faster, especially a young one, than to stumble across a passage in a book that doesn't quite gel with his or her personal frame of reference. That frame is expansive today. While the Internet now gives us access to data we might once have had to travel great distances to find, it has also made it that much easier for others to catch us in a lie if our research is sloppy or nonexistent.

As writers, we are by nature curious. Through our fiction or non-fiction, we pursue subjects that appeal to us, or we find interest in the writing assignments that come our way. The process involves seeking out accurate information that gives our projects optimum credibility. Often, that takes the form of finding experts. As demonstrated by my nephew, it only takes one slapdash bit of guesswork to alienate a reader for life, a loss that can be avoided by simply knowing when—and where—to find expert help.

Start Local

Some of the best resources can be found right in your own community. Personal interviews with local experts often yield insights you might not gather from phone or e-mail conversations. When people are passionate about their jobs, their pastimes, or their life experiences, nothing flatters them more than to have an attentive audience.

➤ *Schools:* Let's say you're researching a science article targeted to teen and tween girls. Is there a junior college or university in your city? Professors (and even high school teachers) are usually enthusiastic to chat about their fields, especially if it will encourage eager young minds to follow a similar career path.

➤ *Businesses and professions:* Is your subject candy makers? Is your character a tree surgeon? An adoption counselor? A piano tuner? A trek through the business section of your city phone directory will give you a starting point. Find someone in the profession and frame questions for them. Local professionals can also vet your article or book for facts, or review your story to see that you have crafted scenes and dialogue realistically. The advantage of being married to a lawyer, for instance, has enabled me to script courtroom scenes that hold up to scrutiny; the friendships I have established through various law enforcement agencies have given me critical sounding boards for my depictions of how a fictional crime is committed, investigated, and solved.

Are you writing a historical YA novel and wondering what kind of clothing and footwear your characters would have? Odds are that the costume designer at your neighborhood playhouse or a local dressmaker who specializes in period styles will have the answers you need to ensure authenticity.

➤ *Newspapers:* Weekly newspapers routinely print human interest stories on local landmarks, organizations, and individuals who have done good deeds, lived through extraordinary events, or have unusual hobbies. Sometimes, these write-ups may gibe with topics you're already researching. At other times, they may provide you with ideas. Consider creating your own in-house version of a clipping service: Compile stories with names of potential contacts and file them according to themes you may want to pursue. If the contact information about the individual or organization is not included in the text, you may be able to follow up via the reporter's byline. While the reporter may not be at liberty to provide a phone number or e-mail, many will forward a message and leave it up to the interviewee to respond.

The Letters to the Editor section of the newspaper can also provide

Networking

When I began writing my first how-to book, *ScreenTeenWriters* (Meri-wether), targeted to aspiring high school filmmakers, I had exactly one expert who was also a personal friend. By the time the book was finished four months later, thirty industry professionals had contributed content and subsequently helped me promote the book.

That ripple effect came about for three reasons. The first was that, at the conclusion of each interview, I asked if my expert knew of anyone else who might have insights on the topic of breaking into Hollywood. Frequently, the expert would beat me to the punch by saying, "You know who'd be a really great person for you to meet?" The six degrees of separation theory is proven time and again; there's just no telling who you can end up talking to as a result of informal introductions.

The second reason was the book's target audience. Sharing expertise and providing encouragement to young people is an opportunity that few will decline. Getting experts on board for a project that directly benefits kids is fairly easy, especially if they are parents or were mentored themselves. Third was my offer of reciprocation. With a background in script consulting, media relations, and the performing arts, I had my own expertise to barter. I also emphasized that my offer was transferable to other people my experts knew. Over the years such offers have expanded my network of contacts across a wide range of occupations, time zones, and continents.

leads. The writers aren't shy about expressing their opinions, and often reveal their expertise about a topic they've chosen to comment on.

Go Global

Regional, national, and international resources for finding expertise are also almost as available as that clichéd click of the mouse.

➢ *Trade associations:* Take a moment to consider how many profes-sional publication subscriptions you currently have, as market resources and learning tools; how many memberships you hold in writers' organi-zations; how many writing-related websites you have bookmarked; and how many author chat rooms you routinely visit.

Most professionals and enthusiasts have similar forums to help them stay abreast of the latest news, techniques, products, and personalities.

These, too, are sources for locating experts. Regional chapters of national organizations offer a broad view of industry trends, while also encouraging local social interaction and networking opportunities. Troll the magazine racks at your neighborhood bookstore or newsstand for trade and specialty publications. Internet searches on topics as diverse as equestrian clubs, Civil War re-enactors, and autism will locate support groups, links to chat rooms, bulletin boards, speeches, e-letters, and articles.

➤ *Public relations:* Trade associations, corporations, nonprofits, and government offices generally have a public relations officer or media department that fields inquiries from the public. When you contact these organizations, introduce yourself, briefly describe the type of information you're looking for, and request a referral. If you plan to use direct quotes in your project, and especially if the topic is controversial, the PR liaison may request a copy of your questions in advance, and a preview of the finished product. Try PR Newswire (www.profnet.com) and Presswire (www.presswire.com) for experts who are especially receptive to reporters, freelance writers, and book authors.

In the case of high-profile interviews with celebrities, politicians, and so on, there's a good chance the entire exchange will be conducted through intermediaries. While some writers find this practice unsettling, it's important to understand that the objective is to protect privacy. Until a relationship of trust has been established, PR people are not going to give out unlisted phone numbers, addresses, or e-mails to anyone who calls up and claims to be an author doing research. For celebrities, two good places to start are Who Represents? (www.whorepresents.com) and the Internet Movie Database (www.imdb.com).

➤ *Directories and groups:* It's not surprising that the Internet has also given rise to sites specifically geared to finding authoritative sources. Websites such as Experts.com (www.experts.com) and Expertclick.com (www.expertclick.com) are great to bookmark for extensive articles and links.

Free registration with Yahoo Groups (http://groups.yahoo.com) or Linked In (www.linkedin.com) will broaden your circle of amateurs and professionals, who can point you in the right direction for expert advice. A cautionary note on forums, of course, is that you must confirm participants' credibility. Check the accuracy of all sources very carefully.

➤ *Media:* Thanks to the popularity of a PBS series called *History*

Detectives, writers and non-writers alike have become more expert on their own at uncovering clues through archives, architecture, genealogy, and journals. Visit the History Detectives website at www.pbs.org/opb/ historydetectives/techniques/experts.html for a beginner's guide to the kind of questions that should be asked during the investigative process.

➤ *Fairs and lectures:* Another excellent way to find experts is to attend conventions, book fairs, and lectures. Not only is this an opportunity to mingle and network with like-minded attendees, but also to take notes on speakers and authors with whom you would like to follow up. In my work as a script consultant, for instance, nothing endears me more than hearing from someone who refers to an anecdote I related at a recent conference, or jogs my memory about a brief chat we may have had during a book signing. On the flip side, of course, are the overzealous people who attempt to stuff scripts in my briefcase, monopolize my time, or follow me out to the parking lot in a quest to become my new best friend. Such maneuvers never bode well for future favors.

➤ *Writers' groups:* Do you belong to a local writers' group? As a twist on your regular get-togethers, plan an experts party. Invite the members to make a list of at least 10 individuals they know who are experts in any given field and exchange them with one another.

Ground Rules

Your initial contact with an expert—whether by phone, e-mail, or letter—should simply be to introduce yourself, briefly explain the type of information you're seeking, and ask the individual whether they have time for an interview. Soliciting assistance in person is an iffy proposition; people generally don't like being put on the spot, especially in earshot of third parties.

Never assume your chosen experts have all the time in the world to drop what they're doing and talk to you. As a courtesy, always give them the option of choosing the venue or medium (face-to-face or electronic) that best accommodates their timetable. Estimate how long you think the interview will take. The shorter the timeframe and the more convenient the conditions for the interviewee, the better your chances of getting a yes. Have your questions already prepared for those rare occasions when an expert says, "Actually, I can chat right now."

If you want to use a tape recorder in order not to miss anything, you must ask your subject's permission before you hit the on button. Not everyone feels comfortable being taped; recording can sometimes inhibit a conversation's flow. Once things are underway, don't be shy to ask for clarification if the jargon is confusing or a concept is difficult.

If you're in a crunch on, say, a nonfiction project, e-mail interviews can provide a distinct advantage. You can simply cut and paste an expert's replies into your piece and be assured of accurate quoting. If you and your expert reside in different time zones or your respective schedules aren't compatible for a live conversation, interviewees often appreciate the flexibility of being able to respond at their convenience.

Querying several experts at once? Resist the urge to send a global survey to multiple addresses in an e-mail. Recipients are more likely to answer if you personalize your request than if they see they're part of a herd. Include your deadline, prospective audience, and the name of the publication you're writing for. If you're unsure whether your target expert has the right background to participate in the survey, it's permissible to provide the gist of what you hope the finished product will accomplish.

As a deal sweetener, and to express appreciation for the expert's input, promise them a copy of the material when published. In the case of novels, where they have not been quoted but have provided useful content, ask if they would like to be mentioned on the acknowledgments page. Always send a thank you note on completion of the interview. It's a pleasant formality so few people observe these days that it will distinguish you as a class act and keep the door open.

Writing is a solitary craft but that doesn't mean you shouldn't be talking up a storm about your latest project at every opportunity. The payoff can be introductions you might not have made except through your regular social network. For example, in a casual conversation I had with a checker at the supermarket, she mentioned that her sister-in-law was an expert on Arthurian legend—the subject of a play I was writing—and also lived in my neighborhood. On other occasions, I've been referred to chemists (who helped me plot a fictional murder), an escape artist, a Broadway choreographer, and a woman whose grandmother survived the sinking of *Titanic* and had penned a detailed recollection of life aboard ship. Perhaps no words are better received than when a listener eagerly volunteers, "I know someone you've just got to talk to about this!"

Details Make the Difference at the Annual SCBWI Conference

By Judy Bradbury

The thirty-sixth annual Society of Children's Book Writers and Illustrators' (SCBWI) national conference in Los Angeles opened to the second largest gathering in its history: 964 participants (800 of them women) represented 45 states and 12 countries. Roughly half of the audience were published authors or illustrators.

The jam-packed event kicked off with its signature fanfare as the faculty paraded across the stage in what has become a tradition. They introduced themselves and offered a single word of advice. Emma Dryden chose *reaching*. Elizabeth Partridge's word was *doggedness*; Cynthia Leitich Smith posed *reinvent*; and Susan Patron, whose Newbery Award-winning novel *The Higher Power of Lucky* (Atheneum) has been the subject of much debate across the literary front, from blogs to *Publishers Weekly* and the *New York Times*, gamely offered the word found on page one of her book and around which heated censorship discussions swirl, *scrotum*. This set the stage for SCBWI Executive Director Lin Oliver's witticisms throughout the educationally stimulating, tip-filled four days.

Powerful Images

The first speaker to step to the podium was Walter Dean Myers, whose career in children's and young adult books spans 30 years and whose honors include the Coretta Scott King Award, Newbery Honor, and the Golden Kite Award. His novel *Monster* (Amistad/HarperCollins) won the inaugural Michael L. Printz Award. Myers challenged the audience to define story through detail and to refine those details so they go beyond simple information to creating powerful images in the reader's mind.

Myers sets goals for himself, writing a specified number of pages per day—ten pages daily when he wrote *Fallen Angels* (St. Martin's Press)— and on each page he strives to "make the story memorable through selection of detail." Myers heeds routine; his day begins when he is awakened at dawn by his cat, and includes reading his current work-in-progress to his family. He respects their feedback. In one instance, he knew he had sufficiently honed those details and hooked his audience when his wife left a note on the fridge begging him not to kill off a particular character. (He didn't.)

On the Road to Successful Picture Books

Ann Whitford Paul, author of *Fiesta Fiasco* and *Mañana, Iguana* (both published by Holiday House) among other books, outlined the details of picture book pacing in a breakout session in which she likened a picture book to a road trip.

The beginning should be quick, "like merging onto a highway." The author has a "narrow lane" of a few pages in which to let the young reader know who the main character is; what the story is about or what the problem is; establish the setting; set the tone; and provide a *wow* moment certain to grab the reader's attention. Next, "the wider lane of the highway" builds tension and involves action, as the main character endeavors to solve his problem. The action must be "cause and effect rather than incidental," and possess page-turner elements, escalating toward the conclusion. The "narrow exit lane" ought to be "quick, satisfying, and involve a twist or punch" that will make the reader want to jump on the highway and take the trip (read your book) again.

Paul offered several examples of "smaller roadways," such as repetitive phrases, suspense, and story within a story, that make the trip worthwhile. She highlighted common themes that work successfully in picture books, including counting, the alphabet, and seasons of the year. Paul concluded the hour-long session by reminding the audience that time and again a breakout picture book proves that "there are no hard and fast rules." The roads you lay before your character "offer great opportunities for change" and drive the success of a well-told story.

From the Basement to Memorable YA Fiction

Ellen Wittlinger, author of *Hard Love*, a Printz Award winner, and the new release *Parrotfish* (both from Simon & Schuster), as well as ten other novels for young adults, deals with tough, contemporary issues in her books. When searching for details that will make her work authentic, Wittlinger visits food courts, comic book stores, skate parks, high school drama productions, music and sporting events, and even the DMV to witness what she calls the "high drama" of this age.

Comically calling herself "just a teen without fashion sense or technical skills," the white-haired Wittlinger entreated those serious about writing for teens to "go back in time to your own adolescence." Even though styles and pastimes come and go (and come again), "emotions never change," she said. Citing Marc Aronson's book *Exploding the Myths: The Truth about Teenagers and Reading* (Scarecrow Press), Wittlinger believes a writer must be familiar with the "basement" and let the reader know that through honest writing. She describes the young adult's basement as the "foundation that's built upon . . . the depths of their being." Teens "don't know what's down there," said Wittlinger. "YA literature turns the lights on so they can look around." She advises writers of YA to rely on dialogue because it "exposes the character's inner life without using description. Often, a character says one thing but the reader understands what's behind it, even if the character doesn't know it." Although Wittlinger's books are often considered

controversial, she has found that "art can take you out of your small world. Art can save you." Reflecting on the subjects and details of her books, Wittlinger said, "If my book keeps one kid from jumping off the bridge, it will have been worth writing."

John Green, introduced to the group by Lin Oliver "as one of the guiding stars of our field," told the audience that he always wanted to be a writer. His debut novel, *Looking for Alaska* (Puffin) grew out of his experiences in a boarding school, but it wasn't until he "freed himself from the shackles of fact" and let go of actual people and events that his story took shape. What he did hang on to throughout the process, however, was the "recreated feeling."

Echoing Wittlinger's sentiments, Green said, "Writing is as much translation as it is creation." He then offered the audience four ideas. The first was, "Truth does not lie in the facts." He suggested that authors "never settle to catch small details when there are bigger truths in the pond." Second, Green has found, "Truth does not lie in artifice." He urged the writers to "Read lots of books . . . have a good ear . . . and always ask yourself: 'How will my writing convey emotional and intellectual truth?'" Third, Green believes, "Great books do not happen by accident. There is a measure of intent, thoughtfulness, and ambition. It doesn't just come to you." Green revealed that after a contract was offered on *Looking for Alaska*, "80 to 90 percent of the draft was changed." Finally, Green said, "The problem your characters face must reflect a universal truth."

Editorial Snapshots

Julie Strauss-Gabel, Associate Editorial Director at Dutton Children's Books and Green's editor, favors "playfulness and a lack of ego" in an author with whom she works; an author who is "ambitious in plotting, characterization, emotions, and structure"; and, one who exhibits "the power of commitment and energy to sustain the hard work of editing and revision.

"The joy of the editorial process is why I went into this business," says Strauss-Gabel, who considers herself a generalist but is partial to literary and contemporary fiction at the older end of YA (14 to 16 years).

She searches for stories that make her "behave better than I knew I was capable of behaving as a result of reading the book."

In her role as Vice President and Associate Publisher at Margaret K. McElderry and Atheneum Books, Emma Dryden oversees 10 editors and the publication of 100 books. She personally edits 15 books per year. To her, "story matters most." She looks for a tale that "wraps me in its arms" and offers "something with which I can relate." Dryden points to "love, family, and safety" as common themes and encourages authors to "write what you know, feel, and care about." She appreciates a

Writing is as much translation as it is creation.

sense of "spontaneity as well as planning in the story arc," looks for "text that allows room for art," and the use of "delicious words."

Dinah Stevenson, who describes her job as "triage," has worked at Clarion Books for 18 years. She is one of only six editors who have edited both the Newbery and Caldecott Medal winners of the same year. Stevenson characterized the imprint as the "smaller arm of a larger publisher" (Houghton Mifflin) that offers "creative, distinguished, award-winning books destined to be classics" and those that "ought to be on every bookshelf." Clarion's editorial office in New York City is staffed by nine full-time and three part-time editors who are open to fiction and nonfiction spanning all ages, picture books through YA novels. Clarion does not publish licensed characters, novelty, gadgets, stickers, series, or pop-up books. The office receives over 20 unsolicited manuscripts per day and remains "very committed to first-timers and those new to Clarion."

Stevenson reminded the audience that "All published writers were unpublished once." What Stevenson hopes for is "a story that can be shared and stands up to repeated readings." Yet, she said, "I am not looking for anything. The creative process starts with the author, not an editor's shopping list." She advises writers to "submit to publishers with books like yours," but be careful that your manuscript is "not in the same vein." Stevenson recalled receiving piles of historical fiction set in medieval times after she published Karen Cushman's acclaimed debut novel, *Catherine, Called Birdy.* "Look for a resemblance, not an identical twin, and don't package your manuscript too much!" (Later in the conference, both Stevenson and Allyn Johnston, longtime Editor in Chief at Harcourt Children's Books, showed the audience large, bright plastic fish they had received with submissions. They both kept the fish, but returned the work.)

Rachel Griffiths, formerly with the Scholastic imprint Arthur A. Levine Books and now Editor at Scholastic Press, also urged authors to submit to publishers whose lists consist of books that have "the sensibility and the same vision" as their project. "Go into bookstores and libraries and read critically to become a better writer. Analyze. Read to help fix your weaknesses and bolster your strengths. Research publishers' rules for submission. Polish your query."

On the subject of developing a query, Griffiths offered this advice: "Get in there with your best writing" and "give a sense of what the story is about. Read the books the editor has worked on and briefly comment on them. Write a description of your book in the voice of the character. Think flap copy, and offer intriguing, tantalizing bits that will hook a reader." Griffiths, who likes realistic stories, wants a sense of character and "some meat" in the first few pages she reads. Although she is "out there hunting for talent," her response time is so slow, she warns that she "looks for a reason not to request a submission" from a query. On the other hand, a fresh turn of phrase or a tidbit of interest will cause her to respond positively. She relishes "passion, a unique point of view," and a "peek into a fascinated mind."

Johnston specializes in books at the other end of the reading spectrum. Picture books recall the times that were "the coziest and happiest" of her childhood. When reviewing manuscripts, she looks for a story that "casts a spell around those reading it, and then makes them want to do it again when they're done." Johnston is editor to Mem Fox and Marla Frazee, among many other award-winning authors and illustrators.

A Critical Look

Stevenson also made the important point, "Publishing is a process, not an event." For many writers, an event in that process is a professional critique. One of the most valuable opportunities at the annual

SCBWI conference can be the individual critique sessions offered to full-time attendees who submit their manuscripts in advance. A half-hour one-on-one session allows authors to interact and discuss a specific piece of their work with a professional. Kim Turrisi, Director of Special Projects for SCBWI, coordinates manuscript and portfolio critiques. At this year's conference, 370 authors submitted work for review. "About half of those were picture books," Turrisi recalls, "and only one was nonfiction. The majority of the projects were YA, middle-grade, and chapter book series. There was a slew of fantasy and a couple of graphic novel ideas." According to Turrisi, "The critiques are designed to help SCBWI members move their manuscripts to the next level and encourage the writing process." Turrisi revealed that "at least one person, and usually more, gets discovered" as a result of participating in a professional critique at the conference each year.

Sara Pennypacker, the preceding year's winner of the SCBWI's Sid Fleischman Humor Award for her chapter book *Clementine* (Hyperion), fondly recalls her career-changing critique session at a New England SCBWI retreat. Amy Griffin, then Senior Editor at Orchard Books, loved the story Pennypacker submitted and made an offer on what would become *Stuart's Cape*. It was followed by the sequel, *Stuart Goes to School*. "If I had one piece of advice to give to writers, it would be to attend SCBWI conferences and pay the $50 or $75 to get a polished manuscript critiqued," says Pennypacker. "You have an opportunity for a one-on-one half-hour conversation about your work with a real, live editor! What better way do we have to meet and get to know an editor?"

Although sessions with agents and editors are most coveted, an author critique also can be valuable. "They're published, they can help make your work better by offering advice, and they may offer to introduce you to their editor or agent," Turrisi points out. "Three years ago a fledgling writer had a critique with an author who really liked her work. The author's agent was at the conference, and the author offered to introduce the two. The agent read the young writer's work, a contract to represent was offered, and eventually her book was sold."

In a panel entitled "Professional Criticism: How to Receive It and What to Do with It," Arthur A. Levine of Scholastic; Elizabeth Parisi, Executive Art Director of the trade hardcover division at Scholastic; Mark McVeigh, Editorial Director of Aladdin Paperbacks at Simon &

Promising Work:
The Sue Alexander Award

"Lin Oliver (Executive Director and co-founder of SCBWI) and Stephen Mooser (President and co-founder of SCBWI) conceived the award," says Sue Alexander, the author of more than 25 books for children, including *Whatever Happened to Uncle Albert?* (Houghton Mifflin), *Behold the Trees* (Arthur A. Levine), and *One More Time, Mama* (Marshall Cavendish). "The plaque they presented to me in 1996 says, 'To Honor Sue's Twenty-Five Years of Encouraging Excellence in Children's Books.' Lin said they felt it would give me an opportunity to be a 'fairy godmother' to some writers, and it has! I've been told by some of the recipients that receiving the award opened doors for them which they are sure would not have been opened otherwise."

Alexander notes, "Of the manuscripts I've selected since the award's inception, two have been published and a third has been contracted for and will be published in 2008 or 2009. In the case of two of the manuscripts, the authors were contacted by several publishers asking to see the project. Each one of these successes is a thrill to me."

Schuster; and Krista Marino, Editor at Delacorte Press/Random House Books for Young Readers, discussed the nuances of critique sessions. Levine posited that "criticism is best given and received between equals." He advised those who sign up for critique sessions to approach the meeting in such a way as to "get rid of the power dynamic." The panel unanimously agreed that behaviors they don't like to see in critique sessions include debating a "negative" comment, defensive responses, and overt emotional reactions. "Do your research on who you're meeting with," suggested Parisi, noting that biographies of the faculty members are included in each participant's packet. She also advised those whose work is being critiqued, "Listen and keep an open mind, and remember that my comments are just my opinion."

The panel's discussion led to the differences between a conference critique session and the editorial process on a project under contract. McVeigh offers comments in both situations, but composes in-depth editorial letters to authors whose work he edits for publication. In both instances, however, he chooses his words carefully. "I might phrase a suggestion with the opener, 'Would you consider . . . .'" In an editorial letter he identifies an issue and might ask, "How do you think we can fix that?" McVeigh believes authors don't need to do everything he suggests, "but at least address the comments and suggestions." All those on the panel agreed that a quick response to editorial comments is less appreciated than thorough, thoughtful revision. In editing projects with an author under contract, Levine relishes the "deep, playful back and forth" of a working partnership that feels as if "we're in it together." Levine, the U.S. editor of the Harry Potter series, claims he likes to feel as if he's helped an author.

Work-in-Progress

The Sue Alexander Most Promising New Work Award, named for the children's author and SCBWI founding member, is presented to the author of the best manuscript submitted for individual critique at the SCBWI Annual Conference in Los Angeles. There is no prior application process for this award, but only those manuscripts submitted by full-time conference attendees for formal critiques are eligible. Critiquers at the conference determine the finalists.

Alexander explains how it works. "Each manuscript consultant is told that if they find a manuscript that, after reworking, they feel will be publishable, they may submit it (one manuscript only) to me for consideration for the award." Alexander selects the winner after "reading and re-reading and reading again" throughout the month of September. "What I'm looking for in each of the manuscripts is not only good writing, but also for the manuscript to move me in some way—to make me laugh or cry or feel in awe. It must make me care deeply about the characters and want them to achieve their goal." Alexander expects to find these elements whether the work is fiction, nonfiction, or poetry. "When I've chosen the manuscript, I write a short summary of what the book is about and why I'm enthusiastic about it and send that to [SCBWI President] Steve Mooser, who sends it in a letter to all the editors in the SCBWI database, along with the author's contact information. And then I cross my fingers and wait." The annual recipient of the award receives an all expense-paid trip to New York City to meet with interested editors.

From plucking feelings remembered from personal experiences to personal critiques; from loitering at teen hangouts to designing an easy-to-access website; from choosing an editor to hashing out editorial comments—it's all in the details when writing for children. Bit by bit, we must do our best to make memorable books for children. As Kirby Larson, author of the 2007 Newbery Honor book *Hattie Big Sky* (Delacorte) suggested to an attentive audience, "There is nothing to be afraid of. Let's get writing."

Writers' Conferences

Conferences Devoted to Writing for Children— General Conferences

BYU Writing and Illustrating for Young Readers Workshop

348 HCEB, Brigham Young University, Provo, UT 84602

http://ce.byu.edu/cw/writing

Beginning to advanced writers are welcome at this five-day workshop, for full-day or afternoon sessions. Workshop highlights include writing and illustrating critique groups led by award-winning professionals, and seminars covering every aspect of children's fiction and nonfiction.

Date: June.

Costs: See website for cost information.

Central Ohio Writers of Literature for Children Conference

c/o Writers Director, 933 Hamlet Street, Columbus, OH 43201-3536

www.sjms.net/conf

St. Joseph Montessori School and a Columbus public elementary school coordinate this annual conference, which welcomes children's writers of all skill levels. Attendees may participate in writing and illustrating workshops and pitch sessions with an agent.

Date: April.

Costs: See website for cost information.

Highlights Foundation Writers Workshop at Chautauqua

814 Court Street, Honesdale, PA 18431

www.highlightsfoundation.org

In its twenty-fourth year, this annual workshop was created specifically for children's writers. Topics explore the range of genres, writing techniques, and the publishing business. Critique sessions with award-winning publishing professionals are available.
Date: July 12-19, 2008.
Location: Chautauqua, New York.
Costs: $1,785-$2,200 (includes meals).

The Loft Festival of Children's Literature

1011 Washington Avenue South, Suite 200, Minneapolis, MN 55415
www.loft.org

Children's book writers, illustrators, publishing professionals, and educators come together at this annual conference. It combines workshops, full-group sessions, and breakout sessions, and is also attended by children's book editors, authors, and art directors.
Date: TBA.
Costs: See website for cost information.

Oregon Coast Children's Book Writers Workshop

7327 SW Barnes Road, Portland, OR 97225
www.occbww.com

Designed for writers of all skill levels, this intensive workshop offers a high degree of one-on-one coaching from writers, editors, and literary agents. Participants learn to improve their writing through presentations, group manuscript sharing, and instructor consultations.
Date: July 14-18, 2008.
Location: Oceanside, Oregon.
Costs: $745.

The Pacific Coast Children's Writers Workshop

Nancy Sondel, Founding Director
P.O. Box 244, Aptos, CA 95001
www.childrenswritersworkshop.com

This three-day workshop is for middle-grade and YA novelists specializing in character-driven, realistic fiction. In a fast-paced seminar,

participants enjoy hands-on events such as writing critiques, Q & A sessions, focus groups, personalized pre-workshop readings, and worksheets to help polish novel submissions.
Date: August 22-24, 2008.
Location: Hilton Hotel, Santa Cruz, California.
Costs: $299-$599.

Pacific Northwest Children's Book Conference
PSU School of Extended Studies
P.O. Box 1491, Portland, OR 97207-1491
www.ceed.pdx.edu/children

Sponsored by Portland State University, this weeklong conference for writers and illustrators is known for its welcoming atmosphere. It covers all genres of children's writing and includes lectures, workshops, critiques by publishing professionals, first-page analyses, faculty readings, and open-microphone sessions.
Date: July 14-18, 2008.
Costs: See website for cost information.

Conferences Devoted to Writing for Children— Society of Children's Book Writers and Illustrators

<u>Alabama</u>
Southern Breeze Fall Conference
Regional Advisor
P.O. Box 26282, Birmingham, AL 35260
www.southern-breeze.org

Now in its seventeenth year, the Southern Breeze Fall Conference offers children's writers and illustrators 30 inspirational and educational workshops to choose from. Critiques of manuscripts, portfolios, or marketing packages are also available.
Date: October.
Costs: See website for cost information.

California
SCBWI Writing and Illustrating for Children
8271 Beverly Boulevard, Los Angeles, CA 90048
www.scbwi.org

This annual summer conference, sponsored by the largest children's writing organization in the world, offers writers the chance to network and learn from numerous publishing powerhouses. Events include workshop sessions, master classes, juried art showcases, manuscript/portfolio consultations, and a poolside gala.
Date: August.
Costs: $425 for SCBWI members; $485 for non-members. Additional fees for university credit, master classes, manuscript consultations, and participation in portfolio showcase.

North Central California SCBWI Spring Conference
Tekla White, Regional Advisor
P.O. Box 307, Davis, CA 95617
www.scbwinorca.org

Sponsored by the North Central California chapter of SCBWI, this spring event presents a full day of networking and educational opportunities for children's writers. It features workshops and presentations from industry professionals on all aspects of children's writing. Writers may submit one manuscript prior to the conference for a critique.
Date: March.
Costs: Visit the website for 2008 conference costs.

Ventura/Santa Barbara SCBWI Writer's Day
Alexis O'Neill, Regional Advisor
www.scbwisocal.org

The SCBWI-Ventura/Santa Barbara Region and the California Lutheran University School of Education present a day of activities related to children's publishing, including first-page critiques, manuscript/portfolio critiques, a writing contest, illustration displays, a book sale, and presentations by newly published authors and editors.
Date: October 25, 2008.

Location: Thousand Oaks, California.
Costs: $85 for members; $95 for non-members. Additional fees for manuscript and portfolio critiques.

Canada
SCBWI Canada East Annual Conference
Lizann Flatt, Canada East Regional Advisor
505 Highway 118 West, Suite 454, Bracebridge, Ontario P1L 2G7 Canada
www.scbwicanada.org/east/

This one-day annual writing conference offers children's writers the opportunity to hear from a variety of industry professionals, as well as the chance to participate in one-on-one manuscript critiques and first-page manuscript readings. A book sale features works by published SCBWI authors. Visit the website for complete conference information and 2008 speakers.
Date: June.
Location: Barrie, Ontario, Canada.
Costs: $85 for members; $100 for non-members. Additional fees required for manuscript critiques.

Carolinas
SCBWI-Carolinas Fall Conference
Stephanie Greene, Regional Advisor
www.scbwicarolinas.org

This annual event offers a dozen workshops to choose from as well as numerous opportunities to connect with editors, including an Editors' Evening, a buffet celebration, and first-page critiques. Complete manuscript and portfolio critiques are available for an additional fee. Visit the website for complete workshop list and conference information.
Date: September.
Location: North Carolina.
Costs: See website for cost information.

<u>Florida</u>
SCBWI Florida Regional Conference
Linda Rodriguez Bernfeld, Regional Advisor
10305 SW 127 Court, Miami, FL 33186
www.scbwiflorida.com

Attendees of this regional conference may participate in informal critique groups, first-page critiques, a dinner ball, a reception with authors and editors, and manuscript/portfolio critiques (for an additional fee). The conference is open to SCBWI members and non-members. Visit the website for complete conference schedule.
Date: January 18-20, 2008.
Location: Wyndham Miami Airport Hotel, Miami, Florida.
Costs: See website for cost information.

SCBWI Florida Mid-Year Writing Workshop
Linda Rodriguez Bernfeld, Regional Advisor
10305 SW 127 Court, Miami, FL 33186
www.scbwiflorida.com

This one-day workshop allows participants to focus on one of four tracks: picture book, middle-grade, young adult, and poetry. The day's events include first-page critiques, writing exercises, and market information for each specific genre. Informal critique groups and manuscript/portfolio critiques are also available.
Date: June 7, 2008.
Location: Disney Coronado Springs Resort, Orlando, Florida.
Costs: See website for cost information.

<u>Kansas</u>
SCBWI Kansas Fall Conference
Sue Ford
P.O. Box 3987, Olathe, KS 66063
www.kansas-scbwi.org

This conference was created to inspire writers of all skill levels, connect them with publishing professionals, and enhance their writing and marketing skills. Participants choose from a number of breakout sessions

covering all aspects of writing and publishing, and take part in a professional critique. It is open to SCBWI members and non-members.
Date: TBA.
Costs: See website for cost information.

Maryland/Delaware/West Virginia
SCBWI MD/DE/WV Summer Conference
Mona Kerby, Regional Advisor
www2.mcdaniel.edu/scbwi/

Open to writers of all skill levels, this regional conference offers attendees the chance to network with editors, authors, illustrators, and agents through a series of seminars, critiques, and informal gatherings. Conference scholarships are available for a limited number of participants; see website for information.
Date: July 18-20, 2008.
Location: McDaniel College, Westminster, Maryland.
Costs: See website for cost information.

Missouri
SCBWI Children's Writers Conference
Sue Bradford Edwards, Regional Advisor
www.geocities.com/scbwimo

This annual one-day conference covers all aspects of writing and illustrating children's literature. Participants must register and submit their work early to take part in manuscript critique sessions with editors.
Date: November.
Location: Cottleville, Missouri.
Costs: See website for cost information.

New England
SCBWI-New England Annual Conference
Marilyn Salerno, New England Regional Coordinator
www.nescbwi.org

Aspiring and experienced children's writers benefit from the range of workshops offered at this annual conference, which covers the craft of

creating books for children, marketing your work, and practical information. The day's events include an editor's panel and manuscript critiques.
Date: April 11-13, 2008.
Location: Crowne Plaza Hotel, Nashua, New Hampshire.
Costs: See website for cost information.

New Mexico

Handsprings: A Conference for Children's Writers and Illustrators
Chris Eboch, Regional Advisor
www.scbwi-nm.org

The annual conference of the New Mexico SCBWI chapter offers a day of information on how to break into the children's book business or advance your career. Attendees may participate in a 15-minute private critique with an editor, a first-page critique panel, or peer critique groups.
Date: April.
Location: Albuquerque, New Mexico.
Costs: See website for cost information.

Tennessee

SCBWI Midsouth Annual Fall Conference
Tracy Barrett, Regional Advisor
www.scbwi-midsouth.org

This weekend-long conference offers writers of all skill levels a chance to network and learn from well-known industry professionals. The conference program includes meet-and-greet sessions, manuscript critiques, and numerous breakout sessions. Conference participants may also attend group critique sessions.
Date: September.
Location: Nashville, Tennessee.
Costs: See website for cost information.

Texas

SCBWI-Houston Editor Day
P.O. Box 19487, Houston, TX 77224
www.scbwi-houston.org

This annual one-day event offers Houston-area SCBWI members access to editors from a variety of publishing houses. Conference attendees may participate in manuscript critiques, speaker seminars, and meet-and-greet sessions. Visit the website or send an SASE for current conference information and workshops.

Date: February.
Location: Houston, Texas.
Costs: SCBWI members, $90; non-members, $120.

Virginia
SCBWI-Mid-Atlantic Fall Conference
Ellen Braaf, Regional Advisor
www.scbwi-midatlantic.org

This one-day conference features a mix of keynote speakers, writing workshops, and a meet-and-greet with editors and agents. A limited number of manuscript and portfolio reviews are offered to members only. Early registration is recommended.

Date: October.
Location: Arlington, Virginia.
Costs: See website for cost information.

Conferences with Sessions on Writing for Children— University and Regional Conferences

Antioch Writers' Workshop
P.O. Box 474, Yellow Springs, OH 45387
www.antiochwritersworkshop.com

Organizers of this annual workshop strive to provide inspirational activities for professional and personal growth among writers of all genres. The weeklong program offers a mix of classes, lectures, intensive seminars, panel discussions, manuscript critiques, and more. Serious writers of all skill levels are welcome.

Date: July 12-18, 2008.
Costs: See website for cost information.

Arkansas Literary Festival
4942 W. Markham, Suite 1, Little Rock, AR 72205
http://www.arkansasliteraryfestival.org

Arkansas' largest literary event includes author readings and discussions, writing workshops, book talks, and a book fair to benefit literacy councils throughout the state. Writers can meet and talk with others who have had success in the industry, including best-selling children's authors. The festival also offers a children's breakfast, storytime, and craft centers, and writing workshops for teens.
Date: April 4-6, 2008.
Costs: TBA.

Aspen Summer Words
110 E. Hallam Street, Suite 116, Aspen, CO 81611
www.aspenwriters.org

Book lovers and writers alike find stimulation at this five-day retreat, which is a combination literary festival and writers' workshop. Literature appreciation classes, writing instruction, professional consultations, and daily writing exercises make up the educational aspects of this program.
Date: June.
Costs: See website for cost information.

Bear River Writers' Conference
Department of English Language and Literature
3187 Angell Hall, University of Michigan, Ann Arbor, MI 48109
www.lsa.umich.edu/bearriver/

With a focus on creative writing, this annual four-day conference offers attendees a chance to connect with nature while at the same time be inspired in their writing. Directed at writers of all levels, the program combines recreational activities with a variety of workshops, faculty readings, panel discussions, and free time for writing.
Date: May 29-June 2, 2008.
Location: Camp Michigania, Northern Michigan.
Costs: Check the website for cost information.

CanWrite! Conference
Canadian Authors Association
P.O. Box 419, Campbellford, Ontario K0L 1L0 Canada
www.canauthors.org

Sponsored by Canada's national writing organization, this yearly conference was created to support the Canadian writing community. Publishers, agents, and authors participate in writing workshops and readings, an annual short story contest, manuscript evaluations, and an awards banquet for presentations of the CAA Literary Awards.
Date: July 3-6, 2008.
Location: Edmonton, Alberta.
Costs: See website for cost information.

Cape Cod Writers Conference
P.O. Box 408, Osterville, MA 02655
www.capecodwriterscenter.com

This conference has been hosting distinguished writers and poets since 1963. It offers specific tracks in all genres from children's books to memoirs, and includes classes, workshops, and panel discussions. Manuscript evaluations are also available for a fee.
Date: August.
Location: Cape Cod, Massachusetts.
Costs: See website for cost information.

Central Coast Book & Author Festival
P.O. Box 12942, San Luis Obispo, CA 93406-2942
www.ccbookfestival.org

Created to celebrate "reading, writing, and libraries," this one-day festival provides a venue to meet authors, find out about new books, and participate in free author workshops. The family-friendly event also features musical entertainment and children's games and crafts.
Date: September.
Costs: Free.

Clarksville Writers' Conference
1123 Madison Street, Clarksville, TN 37040
www.artsandheritage.us/writers/

This conference offers two full days of writing workshops and presentations in historic Clarksville, Tennessee. In addition to the workshops, events include a bus tour of area writers' homes and related locations, manuscript evaluations, and a banquet.
Date: June 13-14, 2008.
Costs: See website for cost information.

Columbus Writers Conference
P.O. Box 20548, Columbus, OH 43220
www.creativevista.com

At the sixteenth annual Columbus Writers Conference, writers can "learn, network, and be inspired." The two-day conference includes presentations by writers, editors, and agents on a variety of topics, one-on-one consultations, agent/editor chat sessions, and panel discussions.
Date: August.
Costs: See website for cost information.

Far Field Retreat for Writers
English Department, Oakland University, Rochester, MI 48309
www2.oakland.edu/english/farfield

Writers of varying skill levels attend this four-day conference on the campus of Oakland University to study writing with a faculty of committed teachers and prominent writers. Attendees participate in workshops, readings, and craft/publishing sessions, and are allotted free writing time.
Date: May 8-11, 2008.
Costs: See website for cost information.

Georgia Writers Association Spring Festival of Workshops
1000 Chastain Road, Mail Stop 2701, Kennesaw, GA 30144
www.georgiawriters.org

Industry professionals come together for a full day of sessions on everything from agents and contract negotiation to publishing and the

writing life. Manuscript evaluations are available, as are writing resources such as magazines, market information, and publishers' guidelines.
Date: October.
Location: Smyrna, Georgia.
Costs: $75-$125.

Harriette Austin Writers Conference

Georgia Center for Continuing Education Conference Center & Hotel
University of Georgia, Athens, GA 30602
http://harrietteaustin.org/

Created in honor of Harriette Austin, a writing teacher at the University of Georgia Center for Continuing Education, this two-day conference is in its fifteenth year. Attendees participate in any combination of workshops, manuscript evaluations, Q&A sessions, and opportunities for networking such as informal dinners and book signings.
Date: July.
Costs: $75-$185.

Indiana University Writers' Conference

464 Ballantine Hall, Bloomington, IN 47405
www.indiana.edu/~writecon

This annual conference offers attendees a choice of taking classes in poetry, fiction, or creative nonfiction, or participating in manuscript-specific workshops. Staffed by prominent writers and teachers, the conference also features panel discussions, readings, and social events.
Date: TBA.
Costs: See website for cost information.

Iowa Summer Writing Festival

University of Iowa, C215 Seashore Hall, Iowa City, IA 52242-5000
www.uiowa.edu/~iswfest

Attendees sign up for the festival's series of weeklong or weekend workshops covering all genres, from memoirs to children's writing to poetry. Workshops are devoted to critiquing original work. Also offered are daily presentations on craft, the writing life, process, and publishing.

Date: Workshops begin on June 8, 2008.
Cost: See website for cost information.

Manhattanville College Summer Writers' Week
2900 Purchase Street, Purchase, NY 10577
www.manhattanville.edu

This weeklong writing program is for established and aspiring writers who want to create a work or revise a work-in-progress. Faculty members of editors, agents, and authors cover various aspects of writing and editing; additional activities include private conferences, readings, and social events. Participating writers can earn college credits.
Date: June 23-27, 2008.
Costs: See the website for cost information.

Maryland Writers' Association Annual Conference
P.O. Box 142, Annapolis, MD 21404
www.marylandwriters.org

Beginners and published writers alike attend this conference to hone their craft and learn more about the business of publishing. Book signings and networking opportunities are also offered.
Date: May 3, 2008.
Location: Linthicum Heights, Maryland.
Cost: MWA members, $100; non-members, $130. Additional fees for agent/editor consultation.

Mendocino Coast Writers Conference
College of the Redwoods
1211 Del Mar Drive, P.O. Box 2739, Fort Bragg, CA 95437
www.mcwc.org

This writers' conference is committed to writing for social change, because "honest words make a better world." It focuses on all genres for all age groups, and offers writing workshops (for work submitted prior to the conference), presentations, professional consultations, readings, and networking opportunities.
Date: July 31-August 2, 2008.

Location: Mendocino, California.
Costs: Check the website for conference costs.

San Francisco Writers Conference

1029 Jones Street, San Francisco, CA 94109
http://sfwriters.org

Designed to "Build Bridges to Better Tomorrows," this conference welcomes more than 100 agents, authors, and editors. Writers have access to publishing professionals through how-to sessions, panels, and workshops, including one-on-one "speed" sessions that provide a chance to pitch work directly to agents and editors.
Date: February 15-17, 2008.
Costs: See website for cost information.

Southeastern Writers Workshop

161 Woodstone Drive, Athens, GA 30605
www.southeasternwriters.com

Writers of all skill levels from around the country attend this annual workshop to hone their craft and be inspired. A new addition for 2008 is an intensive writers' critique workshop.
Date: June 15-19, 2008.
Location: St. Simons Island, Georgia.
Costs: Costs range from $359-$499. Lodging and meals are not included.

Whidbey Island Writers Conference

P.O. Box 1289, Langley, WA 98260
www.writeonwhidbey.com

Sponsored by the Whidbey Island Writers Association, this weekend conference combines an inspiring island atmosphere with a varied agenda of writing classes, workshops, "author fireside chats," and literary readings. Individual manuscript critiques are also available.
Date: February 29-March 2, 2008.
Location: Whidbey Island, Washington.
Costs: $320-$375. Additional fee for dinner with an author.

Writers Retreat Workshop

5721 Magazine Street, #161, New Orleans, LA 70115

www.writersretreatworkshop.com

Visiting authors, agents, and industry professionals present an intense week of workshops, meetings, lectures, writing exercises, and more for novelists. Writers attend in-depth morning classes on how to craft a novel for publication, focusing on their individual works-in-progress.

Date: May 26-June 1, 2008.

Location: Erlanger, Kentucky.

Costs: See website for cost information.

Yosemite Writers Conference

6737 N. Milburn #160, PMB 1, Fresno, CA 93722

www.yosemitewriters.com

Top agents and magazine and book editors share their expertise at this 2-day writers conference. The Yosemite Writers Conference includes lectures, social events, and workshops, as well as numerous writing contest opportunities. Visit the website for complete conference details.

Date: August 22-24, 2008.

Location: Fish Camp, California.

Costs: See website for cost information.

Conferences Devoted to Writing for Children—Religious Writing Conferences

Delaware Christian Writers Conference

6 Basset Place, Bear, DE 19701

www.delawarechristianwritersconference.com

Designed to help Christian writers of all experience levels to meet their publishing goals, this three-day conference features editors, agents, and authors as instructors. In addition to workshops, it also offers manuscript critiques, appointments with editors, and a writing contest.

Date: April 17-19, 2008.

Location: Newark, Delaware.

Costs: See website for cost information.

East Texas Christian Writers Conference
East Texas Baptist University
1209 North Grove Street, Marshall, TX 75670
www.etbu.edu/News/CWC/

Created to encourage Christian writers, this annual conference offers a variety of activities to develop the Christian writer's craft. Participants attend presentations and workshops, network with other writers, and consult with agents and editors.
Date: June.
Costs: See website for cost information.

Florida Christian Writers Conference
Billie Wilson, Coordinator
2344 Armour Court, Titusville, FL 32780
www.flwriters.org

Now in its twenty-first year, this conference is packed with opportunities for aspiring and published Christian writers. It offers 56 workshops, continuing classes divided by genre, a book/magazine editor panel, "Manuscript CPR," and after-hours special interest group meetings. A special Teen Track is also available.
Date: February 28-March 2, 2008.
Location: Bradenton, Florida.
Costs: Costs range from $410 (without lodging) to $930 (lodging included).

Glorieta Christian Writers Conference
2201 San Pedro NE, Building 1, Suite 225, Albuquerque, NM 87110
www.classervices.com

Classes, roundtables, and writing critiques are all part of this annual four-day conference set in the mountains of northern New Mexico. Geared toward helping Christian writers communicate their specific message, the conference helps writers fulfill their writing, publishing, and speaking dreams. Manuscript critiques are available.
Date: October.

Costs: See website for cost information.

Mount Hermon Christian Writers Conference

37 Conference Drive, Mount Hermon, CA 95041
www.mounthermon.org/writers/

Called an "exhilarating laboratory" for training writers of all skill levels, the Mount Hermon Christian Writers Conference offers five days of intensive writers' workshops. Participants can choose from specific genre tracks and take part in any of 70 individual afternoon workshops. Free manuscript critiques are included.
Date: March 14-18, 2008.
Costs: $364 for tuition only; see website for additional fees.

Oregon Christian Writers Conference

P.O. Box 20147, Keizer, OR 97307
http://oregonchristianwriters.org

This organization of amateur and professional Christian writers hosts several conferences each year. The one-day conference informs those who write for the ministry and other markets, and provides opportunities to meet with editors, agents, and other writers. The conference sets aside time for devotionals and prayer.
Date: February 16, 2008.
Costs: See website for cost information.

St. David's Christian Writers' Conference

87 Pines Road East, Hadley, PA 16130
www.stdavidswriters.com

For 51 years, this five-day conference has offered classes aimed at beginning, intermediate, and advanced writers. The agenda includes editor appointments, critique groups, meditation sessions, literary readings, and writing.
Date: June 16-21, 2008.
Costs: See website for cost information.

Writers' Contests & Awards

Jane Addams Children's Book Award

Susan C. Griffith, Chair
Central Michigan University, English Department
215 Anspach, Mount Pleasant, MI 48859
www.janeaddamspeace.org

Since 1953, the Jane Addams Peace Association and the Women's International League for Peace and Freedom have honored authors and artists of children's literature who reach standards of excellence while also promoting peace, the defeat of prejudice, equality of the sexes, and a unified world community. Books of fiction, nonfiction, or poetry for ages 2 to 12, published in the preceding year, are eligible.
Deadline: December 31.
Award: Winners, announced in April, receive an honorary certificate and cash award at a dinner in New York City.

Arizona Authors Association Literary Contests

Arizona Literary Contest Coordinator
P.O. Box 87857, Phoenix, AZ 85080-7857
www.azauthors.com/contest.html

Published and unpublished work for adults and children may be entered in this contest co-sponsored by AuthorHouse.com. Unpublished categories include short stories, poems, essays, articles, true stories, and novels. Published categories include children's literature, novels,

nonfiction, and short story anthologies. Entry fees range from $10 to $30 depending on category. Submit first 25 pages for novel entries.
Deadline: July 1.
Award: Winners in each category are announced at a November banquet, and receive $100 and publication in *Arizona Literary Magazine*. Winners in unpublished categories are published by AuthorHouse.com.

ASPCA Henry Bergh Children's Book Award
ASPCA Education Department
424 East 92nd Street, New York, NY 10128-6804
www.aspca.org/bookaward

This award recognizes authors whose work depicts humane treatment of animals and helps children understand the interdependence of humans, animals, and the environment. Entries are for children (to age 12) or teens (13 to 17), and may be fiction, nonfiction, or collections of stories, essays, or poems by one author.
Deadline: October 31.
Award: Winners are announced in May and honored at an annual ASPCA conference.

AWA Contests
c/o Julie Hale, Department of English
1350 King College Road, Bristol, TN 37620-2699
www.king.edu/awa/awa_contests.htm

Members of the Appalachian Writers Association may submit unpublished entries in the categories of poetry, essay, short story, and drama. No entry fee. Submit two copies. Word lengths vary for each category.
Deadline: June 1.
Award: Winners are announced in the fall. First-place winners in each category receive $100. Second- and third-place winners receive awards of $50 and $25, respectively.

Baker's Plays High School Playwriting Contest
45 W. 25th St., New York, NY 10010
www.bakersplays.com

High school students striving to become playwrights participate in this annual contest. Full-length plays, one-act plays, theater texts, musicals, and collections of scenes and monologues that can be produced by students in a high school setting are welcome. Entries should have a public reading or production prior to submission, and must be accompanied by the signature of a sponsoring English or drama teacher.
Deadline: January 30.
Award: First-place winner's play is published. Prizes ranging from $100 to $500 are awarded. Winners are announced in May.

John and Patricia Beatty Award
California Library Association
717 20th Street, Suite 200, Sacramento, CA 95814
www.cla-net.org

This award, co-sponsored by the California Library Association and BWI Books, recognizes children's book authors who promote an awareness of California and its people. Eligible books must have been published during the year preceding the contest. The winning title is selected by a committee of librarians.
Deadline: February 10.
Award: Winner is announced in April during National Library Week. Winner receives $500 and an engraved plaque, presented at the California Library Association's annual conference in November.

Geoffrey Bilson Award for Historical Fiction for Young People
Canadian Children's Book Centre (CCBC)
40 Orchard View Boulevard, Suite 101, Toronto, Ontario M4R 1B9 Canada
www.bookcentre.ca

This annual contest honors outstanding works of YA historical fiction by Canadian authors. Created in memory of Geoffrey Bilson, a respected historian and author, it is open to books published in the preceding year. Winners are chosen by a jury appointed by the CCBC. Picture books, short story collections, or plots involving time travel are not eligible.
Deadline: January 15.
Award: Winner is announced in November, and receives $1,000 and a certificate.

The Irma Simonton Black and James H. Black Award for Excellence in Children's Literature

Linda Greengrass
610 West 112th Street, New York, NY 10025
http://streetcat.bankstreet.edu

Created in honor of Irma Simonton Black, a writer and editor of children's books and founding member of the Bank Street Writers Laboratory, this award is given to a children's book that exemplifies an outstanding union of text and illustrations. A panel of authors, librarians, and educators choose 20 to 25 books as initial candidates. Copies are then sent to Bank Street and other schools, where students in grades one through three discuss the books and choose a winner.

Deadline: December 14.

Award: Winners are announced in May at a breakfast ceremony and receive a scroll designed by Maurice Sendak.

Waldo M. and Grace C. Bonderman Youth Theatre Playwriting Competition

Dorothy Webb, Contest Chair
1114 Red Oak Drive, Avon, IN 46123
www.indianarep.com/Bonderman

The Bonderman workshop, held every other year, encourages the creation of theatrical productions for young people. The competition is open to all writers who are able to participate in the development and presentation of their work in Indianapolis. Only uncommissioned plays are eligible. Plays for grades one through three should not exceed 30 minutes; grades three and up must be at least 45 minutes. Submit three copies, a synopsis, and a cast list.

Deadline: August 1.

Award: Winners are notified in January. The top four winners receive $1,000 and a staged reading of their play.

The Boston Globe–Horn Book Awards

56 Roland Street, Suite 200, Boston, MA 02129
www.hbook.com

Among the most prestigious honors in children's and YA literature, these awards recognize excellence in books published in the U.S. during the preceding year. Publishers submit entries, and judges appointed by the editor of the *Horn Book* choose a winner and up to two honor books in the categories of fiction and poetry, nonfiction, and picture book.
Deadline: May 11.
Award: Winners are announced in June. They receive $500 and an engraved bowl. Honor recipients receive an engraved plaque.

Ann Connor Brimer Award

Alderney Gate Public Library
60 Alderney Drive, Dartmouth, Nova Scotia B2Y 4P8 Canada
www.nsla.ns.ca/

The Nova Scotia Library Association and the Writer's Federation of Nova Scotia present this award to an author whose book constitutes an outstanding contribution to children's literature. Named for an advocate of Canadian children's literature, the award recognizes authors residing in Atlantic Canada who have written a book of fiction or nonfiction for readers up to age 15 during the preceding year.
Deadline: October.
Award: The winner, announced in May, receives $1,000 at a banquet.

Marilyn Brown Novel Award

Association for Mormon Letters, Administrator
P.O. Box 113, Vernon, UT 84080
www.aml-online.org/awards/mbna.html

The Association for Mormon Letters presents this award every other year at its annual meeting for the best unpublished novel submitted. No entry fee; one entry per competition.
Deadline: July 1.
Award: Winner receives a cash award of $1,000.

ByLine Magazine Contests

P.O. Box 111, Albion, NY 14411
www.bylinemag.com/contests.asp

Writers may enter their work in numerous contests held monthly at *ByLine*. Contest themes change monthly and include children's stories, fiction, poetry, nonfiction, creative nonfiction, humor, and memoirs. Entry fees and word lengths vary per contest; all entries should be unpublished at the time of submission.

Deadline: Deadlines vary by category.

Award: Winners are announced in *ByLine* and receive awards ranging from $10 to $70 and possible publication.

Randolph Caldecott Medal

American Library Association (ALA)
50 East Huron, Chicago, IL 60611
www.ala.org/alsc/caldecott.html

Named in honor of nineteenth-century English illustrator Randolph Caldecott, this prestigous medal is awarded by the Association for Library Service to Children, a division of the ALA, to the artist of the most distinguished American picture book for children. Open to citizens of the U.S., all illustrations must be original work published during the year preceding the award. Honor Books are also recognized.

Deadline: December 31.

Award: The winner is announced at the ALA Midwinter Meeting and presented with the Caldecott Medal at an awards banquet.

California Book Awards

595 Market Street, San Francisco, CA 94105
http://commonwealthclub.org

With the goal of finding the best California writers and spotlighting the quality of literature produced in the state, the Commonwealth Club annually awards 10 California authors with medals in recognition of outstanding literary works. Awards are presented in the categories of fiction or nonfiction for children up to the age of 10; fiction or nonfiction for children ages 11 to 16; and poetry. Submit five copies of entry.

Deadline: December 31.

Award: Winners are announced in May. Gold medal winners receive a cash award of $2,000; silver medal winners receive a cash award of $300.

Canadian Library Association's Book of the Year for Children Award
Jasmine Loewen, M.L.I.S., Assistant Librarian, Canmore Public Library
950 Eighth Avenue, Canmore, Alberta T1W 2T1 Canada
www.cla.ca

Any work of creative writing for children—fiction, poetry, retelling of traditional literature—is eligible for this award, which recognizes excellence in Canadian children's literature. Books must have been written by a citizen or permanent resident of Canada, and published in Canada.
Deadline: December 31.
Award: Winner is announced in the spring and presented with a leatherbound copy of the book and $750.

Canadian Writer's Journal Short Fiction Contest
Box 1178, New Liskeard, Ontario P0J 1P0 Canada
www.cwj.ca

Any genre of unpublished work not longer than 1,200 words is eligible for this contest, held in March and September by a journal that targets apprentice and professional writers. Each entry must be accompanied by a brief author biography. Entry fee, $5.
Deadline: March 31 and September 30.
Award: First-place winner receives $100; second- and third-place, $50 and $25. Winning entries are published in *Canadian Writer's Journal* and in a chapbook called *Choice Works.*

CAPA Competition
Connecticut Authors and Publishers Association
223 Buckingham Street, Oakville, CT 06779
www.aboutcapa.com

Open to everyone, this annual competition accepts entries of children's short stories (to 2,000 words), adult short stories (to 2,000 words), personal essays (to 1,500 words), and poetry (to 30 lines). Entry fee, $10. Multiple entries are accepted. Each entry must be accompanied by an official entry form, and four copies of the work.
Deadline: TBA.
Award: Winners are announced in October and receive $100; secondplace is $50. Winning entries are published in CAPA's newsletter.

Rebecca Caudill Young Readers' Book Award

P.O. Box 6536, Naperville, IL 60567

www.rebeccacaudill.org

Students in grades four to eight at participating Illinois schools choose the winner of this award for outstanding literature for young people. Sponsored in part by the Illinois Reading Council, the award was developed to encourage children to read for personal satisfaction. Participating schools nominate books for initial consideration. Elementary and middle-school students make their final selections from a list of 20 titles.
Deadline: Tallied votes must be received by February 28.
Award: Winner is announced in March and receives a plaque.

Children's Writer Contests

95 Long Ridge Road, West Redding, CT 06896-1124

www.childrenswriter.com

All writers can submit unpublished material to the two contests sponsored each year by *Children's Writer.* Contest topics vary and have included poetry, preK, seasonal, sports nonfiction, folktales, fantasy, science, historical fiction, and middle-grade adventure. The contests are judged by Institute of Children's Literature faculty. No entry fee for *Children's Writer* subscribers; $10 for non-subscribers (includes an eight-month subscription). Multiple entries are accepted.
Deadline: February and October of each year.
Award: Winners are announced in *Children's Writer.* First-place winners receive publication in the newsletter and a cash award. Second- through fifth-place winners also receive cash prizes.

Christopher Awards

The Christophers

5 Hanover Square, 11th Floor, New York, NY 10004

www.christophers.org

The Christophers is a nonprofit Catholic organization whose ministry is communications. The awards recognize artistic work in publishing, film, and TV that reminds people of their worth and power to create change. Profiles of courage, stories of determination and vision, and

chronicles of constructive action and empowerment are recognized. Only original titles published in the preceding year are accepted.
Deadline: November.
Award: Winners are announced in March. They are presented with bronze medallions at a ceremony in New York City.

CNW/FFWA Florida State Writing Competition
P.O. Box A, North Stratford, NH 03590
www.writers-editors.com

This annual contest, open to all writers, honors authors of nonfiction, fiction, children's literature, and poetry. Children's literature entries must be unpublished or self-published; poetry may be free verse or traditional. Entry fees vary by category, from $3 to $25. Multiple entries are accepted under separate cover. Word count should not exceed 5,000.
Deadline: March 15.
Award: Winners are announced by May 31. First- to third-place winners in each category receive prizes ranging from $50 to $100, and certificates.

Kimberly Colen Memorial Grant
Box 20322, Park West Finance Station, New York, NY 10025-1512
www.scbwi.org

Authors and illustrators aiming to publish their first children's book are eligible for this grant, established by the family of the late Kimberly Colen in conjunction with the Society of Children's Book Writers and Illustrators. Two grants are available for SCBWI members who have not published children's literature. Applicants must describe their work in fewer than 250 words; entries are judged on originality and creativity.
Deadline: Postmarked between September 15 and October 31.
Award: Grant winners are announced in January. Two winners receive $2,500 each, and publication in the SCBWI *Bulletin*.

Crossquarter Short Science Fiction Contest
P.O. Box 86, Crookston, MN 56716
www.crossquarter.com

Original short stories in the genres of science fiction, fantasy, or urban

fantasy that demonstrate the best of the human spirit are the focus of this contest sponsored by Crossquarter Publishing. $15 entry fee; $10 for additional submissions. Entries should not exceed 7,500 words.
Deadline: January 15.
Award: Winners are announced in the spring and are published in the *CrossTIME Anthology*. First place, $250. Second to fourth place, $125 to $50.

Delacorte Dell Yearling Contest
1745 Broadway, 9th Floor, New York, NY 10019
www.randomhouse.com

U.S. and Canadian writers of middle-grade novels are eligible for this annual award. Sponsored by Random House, the contest welcomes contemporary or historical fiction set in North America for ages 9 to 12. Entries should be between 96 and 160 pages and include a cover letter with a brief plot summary.
Deadline: Manuscripts must be postmarked between April 1 and June 30.
Award: Winners are announced in the fall and are given a book contract with a $7,500 advance against royalties and $1,500 in cash.

Delacorte Press Contest for a First Young Adult Novel
1745 Broadway, 9th Floor, New York, NY 10019
www.randomhouse.com

Intended to encourage contemporary YA fiction, this annual competition offers a book contract to a winning author living in the U.S. or Canada who has not yet published a YA novel. Manuscripts must be between 100 and 224 typed pages. Limit two entries per competition.
Deadline: Postmarked between October 1 and December 31.
Award: Winners are announced no later than April 30. They are given a contract with $7,500 advance against royalties and $1,500 cash.

Distinguished Achievement Awards
510 Heron Drive, Suite 201, Logan Township, NJ 08085
www.aepweb.org

This award, sponsored by the Association of Educational Publishers, recognizes the best in educational materials in many contest categories, including feature articles; poetry; plays; and editorials for adults, young adults, and children. Entry fee, $120 for AEP members; $240 for non-members. All eligible submissions must have been published in the year preceding the contest.

Deadline: January.

Award: Winners are notified by mail in April, and presented with a framed certificate at an awards banquet.

ECPA Christian Book Awards

9633 South 48th Street, Suite 140, Phoenix, AZ 85044

www.ecpa.org

The Evangelical Christian Publishers Association presents these awards to recognize books that exemplify the highest-quality Christian literature. Established in 1978, the competition considers eligible books based on content, literary quality, design, and significance of contribution in six major categories: Bibles; fiction; children and youth; inspiration and gift; Bible reference and study; and Christian life. Books must be submitted by ECPA member publishers in good standing. Entry fee ranges from $175 to $299 per title.

Deadline: December 15.

Award: Winners are announced at an awards celebration each summer and acknowledged with plaques.

Margaret A. Edwards Award

50 East Huron, Chicago, IL 60611

www.ala.org/yalsa

Established in 1988 by the ALA's Young Adult Library Services Association, the Margaret A. Edwards Award honors a living author for a body of work and special contribution to YA literature. The winner's writing will have been popular over a period of time and is generally recognized as helping teens to become aware of themselves and their role in society. Nominations are made by librarians and teens. All books must have been published in the U.S. no less than five years prior to the nomination.

Deadline: December 31.

Award: Winner is announced during the ALA Midwinter Meeting and receives $2,000.

411

Elixir Press Chapbook Competition
P.O. Box 27029, Denver, CO 80227
www.elixirpress.com

The chapbook contest is held every other year and accepts fiction and multigenre works. Entries should be between 18 and 70 pages. Entry fee, $20.
Deadline: May 31.
Award: Winner receives $1,000 and the entry is considered for publication by Elixir Press. Announcement is made in July.

Arthur Ellis Awards
3007 Kingston Road, Box 113, Toronto, Ontario M1M 1P1 Canada
www.crimewriterscanada.com

Canada's premier awards for excellence in crime writing, the Arthur Ellis Awards are sponsored by the Crime Writers of Canada. Categories include best short story, best nonfiction, best first novel, best juvenile novel, best novel, best crime writing in French, and best unpublished first crime novel.
Deadline: January.
Award: Winners are announced in June at the annual awards dinner and receive a handcarved, wooden statue.

Empire State Award
252 Hudson Avenue, Albany, New York 12210-1802
www.nyla.org

Each year the Youth Services section of the New York Library Association recognizes a living author or illustrator residing in New York State who has made a significant contribution to the field of children's literature.
Deadline: December.
Award: Winner is presented with an engraved medallion at the annual conference of the New York Library Association.

William Faulkner-William Wisdom Creative Writing Competition
624 Pirate's Alley, New Orleans, LA 70116-3254
www.wordsandmusic.org

To preserve the storytelling heritage of New Orleans and the Deep South, the Pirate's Alley Faulkner Society sponsors this national competition for writers striving to be published. Prizes are awarded in seven categories: novel; novella; novel-in-progress; short story; essay; poetry; and short story by a high school student. Entry fees range from $10 to $35.

Deadline: May 1. Do not mail entries before January 15.

Award: Finalists are announced in September; winners in November. Winners receive cash awards ranging from $250 to $7,500.

Shubert Fendrich Memorial Playwriting Competition

P.O. Box 4267, Englewood, CO 80155-4267

www.pioneerdrama.com

Playwrights who have not yet been published by Pioneer Drama Service qualify for this annual contest. Started in honor of the company founder, the competition encourages high-quality theatrical material for educational and community theaters.

Deadline: December.

Award: Winner is announced in June and receives a publishing contract and advance against royalties of $1,000.

Foster City International Writer's Contest

Foster City Parks and Recreation Department

650 Shell Boulevard, Foster City, CA 94404

www.geocities.com/fostercity_writers

All writers of original, unpublished fiction, humor, poetry, and children's stories are eligible to enter this annual contest. Word lengths vary for each category. Entry fee, $15. Multiple entries are accepted.

Deadline: December 30.

Award: Winners are notified in late January. First prize in each category, $150; second prize, $75. Honorable mentions receive a ribbon.

H. E. Francis Award

Department of English, University of Alabama at Huntsville

Huntsville, AL 35899

www.uah.edu/colleges/liberal/english/whatnewcontest.html

Original, unpublished short stories are judged by a nationally known panel of award-winning authors and editors for this annual award. Entry fee, $15. Manuscripts must not exceed 5,000 words.
Deadline: December 31.
Award: Winners are announced in March. First place, $1,000.

Don Freeman Memorial Grant-In-Aid
8271 Beverly Boulevard, Los Angeles, CA 90048
www.scbwi.org

Members of SCBWI who intend to make picture books their primary contribution to the field of children's literature are eligible for this grant. It is presented annually to help artists further their training and understanding of the picture book genre.
Deadline: Postmarked between January 2 and February 2.
Award: Winners announced in August. Winner, $1,500. Runner-up, $500.

Friends of the Library Writing Contest
130 North Franklin Street, Decatur, IL 62523
www.decatur.lib.il.us

Published and unpublished writers may enter this annual contest. It awards prizes in the categories of essay (to 2,000 words), fiction (3,000 words), juvenile fiction (3,000 words), and rhymed/unrhymed poetry (40 lines). Main judging criterion is salability. Entry fee, $3; limit five entries per person.
Deadline: November 1.
Award: Winners are announced in December. First place in each category, $50; second- and third-place, $30 and $20, respectively.

Paul Gillette Writing Contest
c/o Pikes Peak Writers
4164 Austin Bluffs Pkwy #246, Colorado Springs, CO 80918
www.ppwc.net

Writers looking for professional feedback, encouragement for producing a marketable piece, and the discipline of a deadline can find motivation through this contest open to unpublished authors of book-length fiction and short stories. Categories include children's books, YA books, romance, and historical fiction, among others. Entry fee, $30 for members; $40 for non-members. Critiques are available at additional cost. For books, include the first 15 manuscript pages and a synopsis; short stories must be no longer than 5,000 words and accompanied by a description of the target market.

Deadline: November 1.

Award: Winners are announced at the Pikes Peak Writers Conference awards dinner in April. Winner receives a refund of conference fee, or $100. Second- and third-place winners receive $50 and $30, respectively.

Danuta Gleed Literary Award

90 Richmond Street East, Suite 200, Toronto, Ontario M5C 1P1 Canada
www.writersunion.ca

This award, sponsored by the Writers' Union of Canada, celebrates the genre of short fiction. The prize is awarded to the best first collection of published short fiction by a Canadian author. Entries must have been published in the year preceding the contest. Submit four copies of entry.

Deadline: January 31.

Award: Winners are announced on Canada Day, April 23. First prize, $10,000. Second and third prizes, $500.

The Golden Kite Awards

8271 Beverly Boulevard, Los Angeles, CA 90048
www.scbwi.org

This is the only literary award presented to children's book authors and artists by their peers. The annual SCBWI Golden Kites recognize excellence in children's fiction, nonfiction, picture book text, and picture book illustration, as judged by fellow book authors and illustrators. SCBWI members are eligible for work published in the year preceding the contest. Editors and art directors of the winning titles are also recognized.

Deadline: December 14.

Award: Winners are notified by March 1. They are presented with cash awards in addition to Golden Kite statuettes. Honorable mentions receive plaques.

Governor General's Literary Awards
Canada Council for the Arts, Writing and Publishing Section
P.O. Box 1047, 350 Albert Street, Ottawa, Ontario K1P 5V8 Canada
www.canadacouncil.ca

Canada's national literary awards are given yearly to the best English-language and the best French-language books in the categories of fiction, literary nonfiction, poetry, drama, children's literature (text and illustration), and translation (from French to English). Publishers submit books that have been written, translated, or illustrated by Canadian citizens or permanent residents of Canada.
Deadline: Varies according to publication date.
Award: Finalists are announced in October; winners are announced in November. The winner in each category receives $15,000 and a specially bound copy of their book.

Lorian Hemingway Short Story Competition
P.O. Box 993, Key West, FL 33041
www.shortstorycompetition.com

This international competition was created in 1981 to support the efforts of writers who have not yet achieved major-market success. Writers of short fiction whose work has not been published in a nationally distributed publication (circulation of 5,000 or more) are eligible to enter. Original, unpublished fiction should be 3,000 words or less. There are no restrictions on theme, but only fiction is considered. Entry fee, $12 for entries postmarked by May 1, 2008; $17 for those postmarked between May 2 and May 15.
Deadline: May 15.
Award: Winners are announced by July 31 in Key West, Florida. First place, $1,000. Second and third place, $500.

***Highlights for Children* Fiction Contest**
803 Church Street, Honesdale, PA 18431
www.highlights.com

Highlights designated its 2008 contest theme as stories set in the future. Work from published and unpublished authors over the age of 16 is welcome. Stories can be any length up to 800 words. Stories for beginning readers should not exceed 500 words. Indicate word count in upper right hand corner of first page. All submissions must be unpublished. Clearly mark FICTION CONTEST on manuscript.

Deadline: Postmarked between January 1 and January 31.

Award: Competition is announced in September; winners are announced in May. Winning entries are published in *Highlights for Children* and three cash prizes of $1,000 are awarded.

Insight Magazine Writing Contest

55 West Oak Ridge Drive, Hagerstown, MD 21740-7390

www.insightmagazine.org

Inspiring, uplifting, and thoughtful writing with a strong spiritual message earns attention in this contest, in which Bible texts are encouraged. Categories include student short story, general short story, and student poetry. Unpublished, true stories are eligible. Entrants in the student categories must be under 22. No entry fee. Short stories should be no longer than seven typed pages, and one page for poetry.

Deadline: June 1.

Award: Winners are published in *Insight*. First- through third-place winners receive prizes from $50 to $250.

IRA Children's and Young Adult's Book Awards

800 Barksdale Road, Newark, DE 19714-8139

www.reading.org

This annual competition by the International Reading Association (IRA) supports newly published authors who show exceptional promise in the field of children's literature. Eligible works include an author's first or second published book written for children or young adults (to age 17). Works are divided into three categories—primary, intermediate, or YA—and may be either fiction or nonfiction. Books published during the year preceding the contest are eligible. Both authors and publishers may submit works for consideration.

Deadline: November.

Award: Winners are announced in January and receive a cash award of $500.

Barbara Karlin Grant

c/o Q. L. Pearce, 884 Atlantas Ct, Claremont, CA 91711
www.scbwi.org

The Barbara Karlin Grant is one of several grants offered by SCBWI, the largest children's writing organization in the world. To recognize and encourage aspiring picture book writers, this grant is given to SCBWI members who have not yet published a picture book. Works of fiction, nonfiction, or retellings of fairy tales, folktales, or legends are eligible. Length should not exceed eight manuscript pages. No entry fee. New applications and procedures are posted October 1 of each year.
Deadline: Completed applications are accepted between February 15 and March 15.
Award: Winners are announced October 1, and receive a grant of $1,500. Runners-up receive $500.

Coretta Scott King Awards

50 East Huron Street, Chicago, IL 60611-2795
www.ala.org

These distinguished awards are presented by the ALA to African American authors and illustrators for outstanding inspirational and educational contributions to children's and YA literature. Honoring Dr. Martin Luther King Jr. and his wife, Coretta Scott King, for their courage and determination, the award promotes understanding and appreciation of the many cultures that make up the U.S. All entries must have been published in the year preceding the contest.
Deadline: December 1.
Award: Winners are announced each January during the ALA Midwinter Meeting. They are given a framed citation, an honorarium, and a set of *Encyclopaedia Brittanica* or *World Book Encyclopedia*.

Magazine Merit Awards

8271 Beverly Boulevard, Los Angeles, CA 90048
www.scbwi.org

In recognition of outstanding original magazine work, SCBWI sponsors this annual award for magazine writing published for young people.

Categories include fiction, nonfiction, illustration, and poetry. No entry fee. Submit four copies of the published work, showing proof of publication date. Only SCBWI members are eligible.
Deadline: December 15.
Award: Winners, announced in April, receive a plaque.

Maryland Writers' Association Novel Contest
P.O. Box 8262, Silver Spring, MD 20910
www.marylandwriters.org

Promoting the art, business, and craft of writing, the Maryland Writers' Association sponsors this contest for aspiring novelists throughout the U.S. The contest's submission package is patterned on materials commonly requested by agents and editors. All entrants receive a detailed evaluation of their submission from two judges. Categories include action/adventure/horror; mainstream/literary; mystery/suspense/thriller; romance/historical; and science fiction/fantasy. Entry fee, $35. Submissions should be a minimum of 50,000 words.
Deadline: February 28.
Award: Winners are announced in June. The overall contest winner receives $100. First-place winners in each category receive $50.

Mayhaven Awards for Children's Fiction
P.O. Box 557, Mahomet, IL 61853
www.mayhavenpublishing.com

Mayhaven Publishing established this competition to encourage the writing of high-quality material for children. The competition is open to all writers and accepts entries written in English only. Entry fee, $50.
Deadline: December 31.
Award: Winners are announced in March. First-place manuscript is published by Mayhaven, which pays royalties. Second- and third-place, $200 and $100, respectively.

Michigan Literary Fiction Awards
839 Greene Street, Ann Arbor, MI 48104-3209
www.press.umich.edu

Open to writers who have published at least one literary novel or story collection in English, this program is sponsored by the University of Michigan Press. It welcomes original submissions of short fiction collections and novels. No entry fee. Entrants should include a copy of their published book and the manuscript. Entries should be 100 pages minimum.

Deadline: Postmarked between February 1 and July 1 only.

Award: Winners, announced in November, receive $1,000 advance and publication.

Mythopoeic Society Fantasy Award for Children's Literature

P.O. Box 320486, San Francisco, CA 94132-0486

www.mythsoc.org

This award honors outstanding fantasy books for young readers that are written in the tradition of *The Hobbit* or the Chronicles of Narnia. Picture books and early readers up through YA novels are considered. Books or collections by a single author are eligible for two years after publication.

Deadline: February 28.

Award: Winners are announced in August and presented with a statuette.

National Book Award for Young People's Literature

National Book Foundation

95 Madison Avenue, Suite 709, New York, NY 10016

www.nationalbook.org

One of the nation's foremost literary prizes, the National Book Award includes an award for outstanding literature for young people. Fiction, nonfiction, and collections of single-author short stories and essays are eligible; all books must be published in the U.S. in the year of competition, by U.S. citizens. Entry fee, $125. No translations or anthologies. Entries must be submitted by publishers.

Deadline: Entry forms due in June; books or bound galleys due in August.

Award: Winners are announced in October. In each genre, $10,000 is accorded for first place and 16 finalists receive $1,000.

National Children's Theatre Festival

280 Miracle Mile, Coral Gables, FL 33134

www.actorsplayhouse.org

The Actors' Playhouse at Miracle Theatre sponsors a yearly competition for playwrights. Submissions should be unpublished scripts, appropriate for children ages 3 to 12 and feature a cast no larger than 8 adults, who may play multiple roles. Works that have received limited production exposure, workshops, or staged readings are encouraged, as are musicals with simple settings that appeal to both adults and children. Entry fee, $10. Running time should be 45 to 60 minutes. Include sheet music and a CD of music with vocals for musicals.

Deadline: April 1.

Award: Winners, announced in November, are awarded $500 and a full production of the play.

The John Newbery Medal

50 East Huron Street, Chicago, IL 60611

www.ala.org/alsc

The ALA's Association for Library Service to Children gives its prestigious Newbery Medal to honor the year's most distinguished contribution to American literature for children up to age 14. Books are judged on literary quality and overall presentation for children. Eligible books are written by a U.S. author and published in the year preceding the contest. Genres include original fiction, nonfiction, and poetry. Nominations are accepted from ALSC members only.

Deadline: December 31.

Award: The Newbery Medal is presented to the winner at an annual banquet at the Midwinter Meeting.

New Millenium Writings Award

P.O. Box 2463, Room M2, Knoxville, TN 37901

www.newmilleniumwritings.com

This journal places no restrictions on style, content, or number of submissions for its annual contest. Entries are accepted in the categories of short-short fiction, fiction, nonfiction, and poetry, if published online or in a print publication with a circulation of less than 5,000. Entries should total no more than 6,000 words; short-short fiction, to 1,000 words; poetry, up to three poems, five pages total. Reading fee, $17. Simultaneous and multiple entries are welcome.

Deadline: November 17.

Award: Winners are published in *New Millennium Writings* and receive cash prizes ranging from $1,000 to $4,000.

New Voices Award
Lee & Low Books
95 Madison Avenue, New York, NY 10016
www.leeandlow.com

The New Voices Award was established to recognize new talent in children's picture books. It is open only to writers of color who have not published a children's picture book. The competition specifically looks for submissions that address the needs of children of color, ages five to twelve. Fiction and nonfiction entries are accepted, but folklore and animal stories are not considered. No entry fee. Entries should not exceed 1,500 words and must be accompanied by a cover letter with the author's contact information, and relevant cultural/ethnic information.

Deadline: Manuscripts are accepted between May 1 and October 31.

Award: Winners are announced in January, and receive a publishing contract from Lee & Low, plus $1,000. Honorable mention, $500.

NWA Nonfiction Contest
10940 S. Parker Road, #508, Parker, CO 80134
www.nationalwriters.com

The National Writers' Association established this award to recognize and encourage the writing of high-quality nonfiction. Unpublished works are eligible. Submissions are judged on originality, marketability, research, and reader interest. Entry fee, $18. Multiple entries are accepted under separate cover. Entries should not exceed 5,000 words.

Deadline: December 31.

Award: Winners are announced by March 31. First-place winners receive $200. Second- and third-place winners receive $100 and $50.

NWA Novel Contest
10940 S. Parker Road, #508, Parker, CO 80134
www.nationalwriters.com

This annual contest encourages creativity and recognizes outstanding ability in novel writing. It is open to all writers and accepts original, unpublished novels in any genre. Entry fee, $35. Multiple entries are accepted under separate cover. Entries should not exceed 10,000 words and must be written in English.
Deadline: April 1.
Award: Winners are announced in June. First place, $500. Second and third place, $250 and $150, respectively. Fourth through tenth place, a book and an honor certificate.

NWA Short Story Contest
10940 S. Parker Road, #508, Parker, CO 80134
www.nationalwriters.com

This contest looks for entries of well-written short stories. It accepts original, previously unpublished work only. Entry fee, $15. Multiple entries are accepted. Entries should not exceed 5,000 words.
Deadline: July 1.
Award: Winners are announced in the fall. First place, $250. Second and third place, $100 and $50, respectively.

Scott O'Dell Award for Historical Fiction
1700 East 56th Street, Chicago, IL 60637
www.scottodell.com

The Scott O'Dell Award is presented to a distinguished work of historical fiction for children or young adults. Named after a celebrated American writer of children's historical fiction, the award strives to encourage new authors to create historical fiction that boosts young readers' interest in history. Only books published in the year preceding the contest are eligible. No entry fee. Entries may be submitted by authors who are U.S. citizens or publishers. Stories must be set in the Americas.
Deadline: December 31.
Award: Winner receives $5,000.

Once Upon a World Children's Book Award
1399 South Roxbury Drive, Los Angeles, CA 90035-4709
www.wiesenthal.com

The Museum of Tolerance recognizes and rewards books that inspire positive change. Books written for ages six to ten that convey messages of tolerance, social justice, social and personal responsibility, effective communication, or diversity are considered. Fiction and nonfiction titles are eligible. No entry fee. All entries must have been published during the year preceding the contest.
Deadline: April.
Award: Winners are announced in June, and receive $1,000.

Orbis Pictus Award for Outstanding Nonfiction for Children
Literacy & Teacher Education, Husson College, School of Education
1 College Circle, Bangor, ME 04401
www.ncte.org

The Orbis Pictus Award recognizes excellence in children's nonfiction. Winning books are useful in K-8 classroom teaching, and are characterized by outstanding accuracy, organization, design, and style. Nominations may come from members of the National Council of Teachers of English, as well as the general educational community. Books must have been published in the U.S. in the previous calendar year. Textbooks, historical fiction, folklore, and poetry are not eligible. To nominate a book, write to the committee chair with the author's name, book title, publisher, copyright date, and a brief explanation of why you liked the book.
Deadline: November.
Award: Winners, announced in November, receive a plaque at the annual NCTE Convention. Five honor books receive certificates of recognition.

Pacific Northwest Writers Association Literary Contest
P.O. Box 2016, Edmonds, WA 98020-9516
www.pnwa.org

Open to previously unpublished writers, the Pacific Northwest Writers Association sponsors this literary contest that allows entrants to compete in one of 11 categories, including young writers, screenwriting, poetry,

mainstream novel, juvenile/YA novel, juvenile short story/picture book, and adult short story. Each entrant receives two critiques. Entry fee, $35 for members; $50 for non-members. One entry per category.
Deadline: February 20.
Award: Winners are announced in July. First place in each category receives $600. Second- and third-place winners, $300 and $150 respectively.

PEN Center USA Literary Awards
PMB 2717, 1420 NW Gilman Blvd, Suite 2, Issaquah, WA 98027
www.penusa.org

The Pen Center USA recognizes the literary achievements of writers living west of the Mississippi River. Entries are judged by a panel of distinguished writers, critics, and editors in the categories of children's literature, fiction, creative nonfiction, research nonfiction, poetry, translation, journalism, drama, teleplay, and screenplay. All entries must have been published in the year preceding the contest. Entry fee, $35.
Deadline: December.
Award: Winners are announced in late summer and receive $1,000.

PEN/Phyllis Naylor Working Writer Fellowship
588 Broadway, Suite 303, New York, NY 10012
www.pen.org

The PEN/Phyllis Naylor Working Writer Fellowship is given annually to a writer of children's or YA fiction to provide financial support for promising authors. Authors must have published at least two books but no more than five in the last ten years; likely candidates are those whose books have been well reviewed but have not achieved high sales. Nominations must be made by an editor or fellow writer via a detailed letter of support, accompanied by a list of the candidate's published work and reviews, and a description of the nominee's financial resources. Three copies of no more than 100 pages of a current work must be submitted.
Deadline: January 17.
Award: Winner is announced in May and is given a $5,000 fellowship.

Please Touch Museum's Book Awards
210 North 21st Street, Philadelphia, PA 19103
www.pleasetouchmuseum.org

Books that are distinguished in text, exceptionally illustrated, and that encourage a lifelong love of reading are recognized by this competition. Awards are given in two categories: ages three and under, and ages four to seven. Entries are judged by a panel of librarians, professors, and children's literature consultants.
Deadline: September 15.
Award: Winners, notified by December 1, receive a press release and are encouraged to hold a book signing at the museum. Awards are presented at the Early Childhood Education Conference in Philadelphia.

Pockets **Magazine Annual Fiction Contest**
P.O. Box 340004, 1908 Grand Avenue, Nashville, TN 37203-0004
www.pockets.org

Pockets sponsors this annual competition that is open to all writers. It accepts previously unpublished manuscripts. Entries must be between 1,000 and 1,400 words. Biblical and historical fiction are not eligible. No entry fee.
Deadline: Entries must be postmarked between March 1 and August 15.
Award: Winner is notified November 1, and receives $1,000 and publication in *Pockets*.

Edgar Allan Poe Awards
Mystery Writers of America
17 East 47th Street, 6th Floor, New York, NY 10017
www.mysterywriters.org

The prestigious Edgar Allan Poe Awards for mystery writers are presented for published work in categories that include best fact crime, best young adult mystery, best juvenile mystery, best first novel by an American author, and best motion picture screenplay. No entry fee. All entries must have been published in the U.S. during the year preceding the contest.
Deadline: November 30.

Award: An "Edgar" is presented to each winner at an awards banquet in April. Cash awards may also be given.

Michael L. Printz Award for Excellence in Young Adult Literature
50 East Huron, Chicago, IL 60611
www.ala.org/yalsa/printz

The ALA's Michael L. Printz Award recognizes excellence in YA literature. Fiction, nonfiction, poetry, and anthologies that target ages 12 through 18 are eligible; books must have been published during the calendar year preceding the contest. ALA committee members may nominate any number of titles. Entries are judged on overall literary merit, taking into consideration theme, voice, setting, style, and design. Controversial topics are not discouraged.
Deadline: December 31.
Award: Winners are announced at the annual ALA Midwinter conference.

San Antonio Writers Guild Writing Contests
P.O. Box 34775, San Antonio, TX 78265
www.sawritersguild.org/contest_sawg-annual.html

This multi-category contest is open to all writers in fiction, nonfiction, children's literature, and poetry. Each writer can submit unpublished entries in up to three categories. Word limits vary by entry: novels and nonfiction books, first chapter, to 5,000 words; short story, to 4,000 words; essay, memoir, or article, to 2,500 words. Up to three poems may be entered for one $20 non-member entry fee ($10 for members).
Deadline: October meeting of the San Antonio Writers Guild.
Award: First prize, $100; second prize, $50; third prize, $25.

Science Fiction/Fantasy Short Story Contest
P.O. Box 121293, Fort Worth, TX 76121
http://home.flash.net/~sfwoe

This contest from the Science Fiction Writers of Earth was established to promote short story writing in science fiction and fantasy. It is open to unpublished members. Entry fee, $5 for first entry; $2 for each additional entry. Manuscripts should be between 2,000 and 7,500 words.

Deadline: October 30.

Award: Winners are announced in February. First-place winner receives publication on the organization's website. First- through third-place winners receive awards ranging from $200 to $50.

Seven Hills Writing Contest

P.O. Box 3428, Tallahassee, FL 32315

www.twaonline.org

In this competition sponsored by the Tallahassee Writers' Association, awards are offered for short story, memoir, essay, and children's literature. Only unpublished material is eligible. Judging criteria include mechanics, technique, characters, dialogue, and use of language. Entry fee, $10 for members; $15 for non-members.

Deadline: Submissions accepted from January 1 through September 30.

Award: Winners are announced in December and published in the *Seven Hills Review*. First place, $75; second place, $50; and third place, $35.

Skipping Stones Magazine Honor Awards

P.O. Box 3939, Eugene, OR 97403

www.skippingstones.org

These awards were established by *Skipping Stones* to recognize books and films that promote diversity, peacemaking, environmental themes, and cooperation, and also serve as outstanding teaching resources for K-12 students. Entry fee, $50. Entries must have been published in the two years preceding the contest.

Deadline: February 1.

Announcements: Winners are announced in April. Cash awards are given to the first- through fourth-place winners. Winning entries are reviewed in the summer issue of *Skipping Stones*.

Kay Snow Writing Contest

9045 SW Barbur Boulevard, Suite 5A, Portland, OR 97219-4027

www.willamettewriters.com

This annual competition of the Willamette Writers encourages writers to reach professional goals. Original, unpublished material is accepted for adult fiction and nonfiction, juvenile short story or article, poetry, screenwriting, and student writing. Entry fee, $10 for members; $15 for non-members. Word lengths vary by category.

Deadline: April 23.

Award: Winners are announced in August. Finalists are notified by mail prior to the announcement of winners. Prizes range from $50 to $300 in each category. A Liam Callen award with a cash prize of $500 is given for the best entry overall.

Society of Midland Authors Awards
P.O. Box 10419, Chicago, IL 60610
www.midlandauthors.com

Authors and poets who reside in any of the twelve Midwestern states are eligible to enter this contest, sponsored since 1915 by the Society of Midland Authors. Awards for excellence are presented for adult fiction and nonfiction, biography, poetry, and children's fiction and nonfiction. Entries must have been published in the year preceding the contest. No entry fee. Book entries must be at least 2,000 words. Multiple submissions are accepted.

Deadline: January 30.

Award: Winners are announced in May. Winners in each category receive a cash award and a recognition plaque.

Southwest Writers Annual Contest
3721 Morris NE, Albuquerque, NM 87111-3611
www.southwestwriters.org

The Southwest Writers honor distinguished original and unpublished writing in a variety of genres: novel, short story, short nonfiction, book-length nonfiction, children's book, screenplay, and poetry. Entry fee, $44 for non-members; $29 for members. Multiple entries are accepted.

Deadline: May 1.

Announcements: Winners are announced in the fall and receive awards ranging from $50 to $150. First-place winners in each category compete for a grand prize of $1,000.

The Spur Awards

Deborah Morgan, Awards Chair
5552 Walsh Road, Whitmore Lake, MI 48189
www.westernwriters.org

The Spur Awards are presented for distinguished writing about the American West. Open to all writers, entries must be set in the American West, the early frontier, or relate to the Western or frontier experience. Categories include best Western novel, best short story, best juvenile fiction and nonfiction, and best first novel. Entries must have been published the year preceding the contest.
Deadline: December 31.
Award: Winners are announced in March and are awarded $2,500.

Stanley Drama Award

Wagner College, Department of Theater and Speech
631 Howard Avenue, Staten Island, NY 10301
http://leg.wagner.edu/stanleydrama/

Created to encourage and support aspiring playwrights, this contest accepts original full-length plays or musicals, or a series of two or three related one-act plays that have not been professionally produced or published as trade books. Entry fee, $20. Limit one submission per competition. Musical entries must be accompanied by an audiocassette.
Deadline: October 1.
Award: Winners are announced approximately 60 days after the deadline, with a first-place award of $2,000.

Peter Taylor Prize for the Novel

P.O. Box 2565, Knoxville, TN 37901-2565
www.knoxvillewritersguild.org

The Knoxville Writers' Guild created this award to identify and publish novels of high literary quality. The competition is open to published and unpublished writers across the U.S. Only full-length, unpublished novels are accepted. Entry fee, $25. Entries should be a minimum of 40,000 words. Multiple and simultaneous submissions are accepted.
Deadline: Entries must be postmarked between February 1 and April 30.

Award: Winners are announced in November and receive $1,000 and publication by the University of Tennessee Press.

Sydney Taylor Manuscript Competition

Association of Jewish Libraries
315 Maitland Avenue, Teaneck, NJ 07666
www.jewishlibraries.org

The Sydney Taylor Manuscript Competition is open to previously unpublished works of fiction containing Jewish content, but with universal appeal. Entries must be written for readers ages 8 to 11 and deepen children's understanding of Judaism. Manuscripts must be between 64 and 200 pages; short stories, plays, and poetry are not eligible. No entry fee. Limit one manuscript per competition.
Deadline: December 31.
Award: Winner is announced by April 15, and is given $1,000.

Utah Original Writing Competition

617 East South Temple, Salt Lake City, UT 84102
www.arts.utah.gov/literature/comprules.html

Honoring Utah's finest writers since 1958, this competition presents awards in categories that include YA book, novel, personal essay, short story, poetry, and general nonfiction. Only unpublished entries from Utah residents are eligible. No entry fee. Word lengths vary for each category. Limit one entry per category.
Deadline: Entries must be postmarked by June 29.
Award: Winners are contacted in September. Awards in each category range from $300 to $5,000.

Vegetarian Essay Contest

P.O. Box 1463, Baltimore, MD 21203
www.vrg.org

The Vegetarian Resource Group sponsors this contest that accepts personal essays highlighting any aspect of vegetarianism. Essays should be based on interviews, research, and/or personal opinion. There are three entry categories, determined by age: 14 to 18; 9 to 13; and 8 and under.

No entry fee. Entries should be two or three pages. Limit, one entry.
Deadline: May 1.
Award: Winners are announced at the end of the year and receive a $50 savings bond and publication in *The Vegetarian Journal* (all rights).

Jackie White Memorial National Children's Playwriting Contest

309 Parkade Boulevard, Columbia, MO 65202
http://www.cectheatre.org/

This contest is sponsored by the Columbia Entertainment Company to encourage the writing of scripts for children and families. Roles that challenge and expand acting talents are strongly encouraged. Entries should be full-length plays (60- to 90-minute running time) with well-developed speaking roles for at least seven characters. Only previously unpublished and unproduced material is considered. Entry fee, $10. Multiple entries are accepted. Include a cassette or CD of music, if appropriate.
Deadline: June 1.
Award: Winning entry is announced by August 31; playwright receives $500, plus possible publication or staged reading.

William Allen White Children's Book Awards

Emporia State University
1200 Commercial Street, Box 4051, Emporia, KS 66801
www.emporia.edu/libsv/wawbookaward/index.htm

This annual competition relies on children across the state of Kansas to vote for their favorite book from master lists chosen by the White Awards Book Selection Committee. Entries must have been published during the year preceding the contest, and are judged by committee members for clarity, factual accuracy, originality, and respect for the reader. Two books are honored: one for third- through fifth-grade students and one for sixth- through eighth-grade students. The contest is open to North American residents only. Textbooks, anthologies, and translations are not eligible.
Deadline: May.
Award: Winners, announced in April, receive $1,000 and a bronze medal.

Laura Ingalls Wilder Medal

50 East Huron Street, Chicago, IL 60611

www.ala.org/alsc

The ALA's Association for Library Services to Children (ALSC) presents this award every other year to honor an author or illustrator whose body of work has contributed substantially to children's literature. Only books published in the U.S. are considered; nominations are made by ALSC members. The winner is chosen by a committee of children's librarians.

Deadline: December 31.

Award: Winners are announced in January at the ALA Midwinter Meeting. A medal is presented to the winner at the ALA's conference in June.

Tennessee Williams One-Act Play Competition

938 Lafayette Street, Suite 514, New Orleans, LA 70113

www.tennesseewilliams.net

Playwrights around the world participate in this competition recognizing excellence in one-act plays. The winning script requires minimal technical support and a small cast of characters. Entry fee, $25. Multiple entries are accepted. Plays should be no more than an hour and must not have been previously produced or published.

Deadline: Entries are accepted September 1 through December 15.

Award: Announced in April, winning entries are granted $1,000 and full production of the play.

Paul A. Witty Short Story Award

Kate Schlichting, Chair, Awards Subcommittee

4000 Hounds Chase Drive, Wilmington, NC 28409-3274

www.reading.org

Sponsored by the International Reading Association, the Paul A. Witty Short Story Award is given to an author of an outstanding original short story published in the year preceding the contest. Fiction or nonfiction, the winning entry demonstrates a high literary standard and provides an enjoyable reading experience for children. Authors, publishers, and IRA members may nominate a short story. No entry fee. Limit of three entries per competition.

Deadline: December 1.
Award: Winner is announced in the spring and is presented with $1,000 at the annual IRA convention.

Carter G. Woodson Book Awards
National Council for the Social Studies
8555 16th Street, Suite 500, Silver Spring, MD 20910
www.socialstudies.org/awards

These awards honor distinguished social science books relating to ethnic minorities and race relations. The winning titles portray these issues with accuracy and sensitivity, and show respect for ethnic and racial differences. Entries should be informational or nonfiction trade books. All submissions must have been published in the year preceding the contest.
Deadline: February.
Award: Winners are announced in the spring. In November, commemorative gifts and a medallion are presented to two winners at the NCSS annual conference. Additional books receive Honor awards.

Work-in-Progress Grants
SCBWI, 8271 Beverly Boulevard, Los Angeles, CA 90048
www.scbwi.org

Each year SCBWI offers several grants to assist children's writers to complete projects not currently under contract. Grants are available to full and associate members of SCBWI in the categories of general work-in-progress; contemporary novel for young people; nonfiction research; and previously unpublished author. Requests for applications may be made beginning October 1. All applications should include a 750-word synopsis and writing sample of no more than 2,500 words from the entry.
Deadline: Applications are accepted between February 15 and March 15.
Award: Grant winners are announced in September and are given $1,500.

Writers at Work Fellowship
P.O. Box 540370, North Salt Lake, UT 84054-0370
www.writersatwork.org

Created to recognize emerging writers of fiction, nonfiction, and poetry, this fellowship is presented annually by Writers at Work, a non-profit literary arts organization. Writers not yet published in the genre of their entry are eligible to submit original works, though they may be self-published. Entries are judged by faculty members. Entry fee, $15.
Deadline: March 1.
Award: Winners are announced in May. They receive $1,500 and publication in *Quarterly West.* Honorable mentions are also awarded.

Writer's Digest Annual Writing Competition
4700 East Galbraith Road, Cincinnati, OH 45236
www.writersdigest.com

Writer's Digest sponsors this annual competition for entries in many categories, including children's fiction, short stories, screenplays, and plays. It accepts previously unpublished work only. Entry fee, $10. Multiple entries are accepted.
Deadline: May.
Award: Winners are announced in the November issue of *Writer's Digest.* The grand prize is $1,500. Other prizes and selections from Writer's Digest Books are given to winners in each category.

Writers' League of Texas Annual Manuscript Contest
1501 West Fifth Street, Suite E-2, Austin, TX 78703
www.writersleague.org

This annual novel contest accepts entries in the following categories: mainstream fiction; middle-grade; YA; mystery/thriller; science fiction; historical or Western; and romance. Only original, unpublished material is accepted. Entry fee, $50. Include a one-page synopsis along with the first 10 pages. Visit the website or send an SASE for complete guidelines.
Deadline: March 1.
Award: Winners, disclosed in June, are invited to a meeting with an editor or agent at the Writers' League of Texas Agents and Editors Conference.

435

Writers' Journal Writing Contests
P.O. Box 394, Perham, MN 56573-0374
www.writersjournal.com

Writers' Journal sponsors numerous contests year-round for writers of all experience levels and areas of interest. Categories include short story, ghost story/horror, romance, travel, fiction, and poetry. Word lengths and guidelines vary. All entries must be unpublished. Entry fees range from $3 to $15, depending on the category.
Deadline: Varies by category.
Award: Winners are announced in *Writers' Journal* and at the website after each contest deadline. They receive cash prizes and publication.

Writers' Union of Canada Writing for Children Competition
90 Richmond Street East, Suite 200, Toronto, Ontario M5C 1P1 Canada
www.writersunion.ca

Open to Canadian writers who have not yet had a book published, this competition helps discover and encourage new writers of children's literature. Multiple entries are accepted. Entries should not exceed 1,500 words. Fee, $15.
Deadline: April.
Award: Winner is announced in July and receives $1,500 and submission of their manuscript by the Writers' Union to three children's publishers.

Young Adult Canadian Book Ward
Jessica Cammer, Collections Coordinator, Regina Public Library
2311 Twelfth Avenue, Regina, Saskatchewan S4P 3Z7 Canada
www.cla.ca/awards/yac.htm

Given to a work of YA fiction by a Canadian citizen or landed immigrant, this award honors an outstanding Canadian book in English. It is bestowed by the Young Adult Services Interest Group of the Canadian Library Association.
Deadline: December 31.
Award: The winner receives a leather-bound book embossed with the award seal in gold.

Paul Zindel First Novel Award

Hyperion Books for Children
P.O. Box 6000, Manhasset, NY 11030-6000
www.hyperionchildrensbooks.com

Honoring bestselling author Paul Zindel, this annual award honors works of contemporary and historical fiction set in the U.S. Manuscripts should reflect the cultural and ethnic diversity of the country for readers ages 8 through 12. Submissions should be between 100 and 240 typed pages. Limit is two entries per competition.
Deadline: April 30.
Award: Winners will be notified after July 15, and receive a book contract with Hyperion Books for Children, including an advance against royalties of $7,500, and an award of $1,500.

Charlotte Zolotow Award

Megan Schliesman, Chair, Cooperative Children's Book Center
600 N. Park Street, Room 429, Madison, WI 53706
www.education.wisc.edu/ccbc/books/zolotow.asp

This award is given to the author of the year's best picture book text. Honoring the work of distinguished children's book editor Charlotte Zolotow, this award was established in 1998 and is administered by the Cooperative Children's Book Center. Picture books eligible for review must be written in English and may be fiction or nonfiction.
Deadline: December 31.
Award: Winner is announced in January, and is given $1,000 and a bronze medal.

Index

Abandon trilogy 134
Abbott, Tony 127
Abdel-Fattah, Randa 107, 109
ABDO Pub. 99, 100, 102, 131
Above and Beyond 139
Abrams Books 76, 77, 83, 89
The Absolutely True Diary of a Part-Time Indian 126
An Abundance of Katherines 126
Acadiana Moms 133
Activities 95, 115-124
Adams Literary 188, 189, 190, 214
Adams Media 137
Advance Pub. 131
Advances 252, 351
Adventure 13, 61, 77, 130, 135, 225
The Adventures of the Dish and the Spoon 128
The Adventures of Marco Polo 127
Afraid of Dogs 127
African Americans 15, 19, 131, 132, 209
After Tupac and D Foster 108
Agents 188, 190, 243-253, 259
Agnes Parker books 218, 219, 220
Aiken, Joan 83
Airhead trilogy 134
Aladdin Books 86, 136, 155, 379
Aladdin MIX 130
Alaska Northwest Books 52, 360
Alaska's Heroes 52
Alcott, Louisa May 213, 224, 225
Alexander, Elizabeth 19
Alexander, Lloyd 82, 140
Alexander, Robert 10
Alexander, Sally Hobart 20
Alexander, Sue 177, 182, 183, 184, 380, 381
Alexie, Sherman 126, 208
All-American Quilts 122
Allie Finkle's Rules for Girls 134
Almost Heaven 337
Alphin, Elaine Marie 68, 69, 71, 195, 198, 200, 201, 202, 348, 356
Altman, Lynn 324
Amadi's Snowman 23
Amazing Journeys 139
American Born Chinese 126
American Cheerleader 32
American Cheerleader Junior 139
American Girl 32, 118, 120
American Library Assn. (ALA) 10, 125, 155, 260, 261, 298
American Society of Journalists and Authors 256, 260
The Amethyst Road 76, 78, 83

Amistad Books 373
Amulet Books 76, 78, 82
The Amulet of Samarkand 83
Ances, Becky 41
Anderson, M. T. 126, 170, 172, 208
Andrews, Benny 126
"Angels and Ages" 227
Animal Dads 67
Animals & nature 36, 66, 67, 131
Anna of Byzantium 203, 207
Anne Frank: The Diary of a Young Girl 222
Anne of Green Gables 216
Annette, Lynnea 306
Appearances, author 272, 273, 275, 276, 277
Appelt, Kathi 13, 17
AppleSeeds 41, 162, 237
Arch Books 325
Arihara, Shino 106
Aronson, Marc 375
Art and artwork 21, 31, 40, 121
Art Education 40
Arts & Activities 40
Asher, Jay 277, 278
Asher, Sandy 63, 158
Ask 138, 237
Assn. of Authors' Representatives 243, 245, 250, 251
Assn. of Booksellers for Children 260, 261
The Astonishing Life of Octavian Nothing 126
Atheneum Books 11, 13, 17, 21, 73, 82, 126, 127, 135, 224, 225, 291, 373, 377
Atria Books 10
At the Sign of the Star 338
Audiobooks 126, 133, 267, 280
Audubon 361
AuthorHouse 128, 129
Authors Guild 135, 236, 257, 260, 272, 298
Autobiography 221-229, 314
Avalon Books 129
Aver Magazine 133
Avi 216
Awards 113, 125, 126, 127, 128, 256, 259, 261, 401-437

Babbitt, Natalie 153
Baby Bear, Baby Bear What Do You See? 125
Babybug 35, 36, 59, 138, 237
Baby Couture 133
Baby Talk 139
Backlist 112, 113, 265, 268
Backstory 91, 171, 172, 309-319
Bad Men 363
Baker, Rosalie 117, 118, 119, 121

Balliett, Will 138
Balouch, Kristen 127
Bantam Delacorte Dell 222, 272
Barefield, Shannon 129
Barker, Cicely Mary 14
Barrett, Tracy 75, 76, 78, 83, 203, 207, 209
Barry, Sheila 119, 121
Bartimaeus trilogy 83
Bartoletti, Susan Campbell 349, 350, 351
Baseball Saved Us 105
Baseball Youth 32
"The Basement Ghost" 88
Bates, Amy 108
Bauer, Joan 13
Bauer, Marion Dane 154
Bauer Pub. 32
Beaks! 67
Beanbag Buddies and Other Stuffed Toys 122
Beast 73, 82
Beckett Media 132
Beery, Ariel 132
Beginnings 154, 169, 310, 318, 319, 374
Behold the Trees 380
Belanger, Jeff 91
Belling the Tiger 140
Bellows, Melinda 131
Benchmark Books 70
Benton, Lori 137
Benz, Derek 279, 280
Bergman, Alan and Marilyn 152
Berkowitz, Lisa 129
Between Golden Jaws 82
Be Well 43, 46, 47
Bick Pub. House 325
The Big Field 13
Big Mouth & Ugly Girl 147
Bilich, Karin 292, 295
Billy Hooten: Owlboy 86
Biography 20, 21, 52, 53, 55, 95, 110, 161, 184, 309, 310, 314, 348, 352, 353, 364
Birmingham, 1963 19
Bishop, Gerald 139
Blackbirch Press 101
The Black Cauldron 141
Black Potatoes 349, 351
Blackwood, Gary 68, 69, 70, 301, 302, 307
Blazanin, Jan 310
Bleddingvoode 314
Block, Francesca Lia 216
Blogs 7, 39, 252, 276, 277, 278, 296, 331, 343
Blood and Chocolate 341
Bloody Jack 193
Blooming Tree Press 273, 279
Bloomsbury 15, 134, 138

Blount, Roy Jr. 257
Blue 203, 204, 207, 210
The Blue Review 139
Blume, Judy 257
Board and concept books 63, 131
Body of Evidence series 86
Boedeker, Bill 14, 16
Bog Child 11
Book producers and packagers 96, 130, 137
Booksellers and bookstores 263–270, 272, 273, 274, 279
Book Sense 76, 275
The Book Thief 10, 126
Boring, Mel 163, 166
Boughton, Simon 129
Bourland, Annette 137
Bowen, Brenda 130, 137
A Box Full of Kittens 135
Boxing Day Books 131
Boyds Mills 17, 19, 188, 193
Boy Girl Boy 147, 148
Boy: Tales of Childhood 222
Boys' Life 32, 43, 45, 118, 232, 233, 234, 236, 238, 239, 305
Boys' Quest 120
The Boy Who Couldn't Die 92, 93
Brainstorming 86, 282, 306, 307, 321-330
Bray, Libba 74, 77, 82
Breakaway 223
Breier, Davida 263, 265, 266, 268, 269
Brewer, Paul 23
Bridge to Terabithia 201, 215
Brimner, Larry Dane 193
Brimstone Journals 144
Brio 139, 223
Britton, Tamara L. 99, 100, 102
Brooks, Geraldine 213
Brooks, Max 92
Brothers in Hope 109
Brown Bear, Brown Bear What Do You See? 125
Brown, Erin K. 328
Brown, Monica 106
Bruchac, Joseph 106
Bryant, Jamie Gleich 31
Bryson, Bill 339
Buddy Books 99
Buffalo Song 106
Bulla, Clyde Robert 140
The Bumblebee Queen 53
The Bundle Book 59
Buried 127
Burke, Judy 88
Burningham, John 61
Burroughs, Augusten 10
Bush, Laura and Jenna 135
Busy Book series 123
Butler, Dori Hillestad 107, 306, 308, 311, 318
But That's Another Story 152
By These Ten Bones 74, 76, 77, 80, 81, 82
By Venom's Sweet Sting 82

Cabot, Meg 134
Cahill, Bryon 38, 39
Calkins Creek 203
Calliope 41, 117, 237
Campbell, Bebe Moore 107
Campus Life 32, 33
Cam's Quest 290
Canadian magazines 42, 44, 47
Candlewick Press 86, 90, 92, 93, 126, 137, 144, 168, 222
Caney, Steven 122
Canoe & Kayak 32
Jonathan Cape 128
Capstone Press 98, 100, 102, 103
Captain Underpants series 296
Card, Orson Scott 308
Career development 65-72, 249, 250, 255-262, 271-280, 301
Career World 40
Carella, Katie 17, 19
Carey, Janet Lee 74, 77, 81, 82
Carle, Eric 125
Carlsen, Joy 29
Carlson, Dale 325, 327, 328
Carlson, Lori 21
Carolrhoda 68, 69, 195, 348
Carus Pub. 36, 37, 43, 46, 120, 237
Carver: A Life in Poems 19
Cash, Mary 138
Castillo, Ana 21
The Cat Ate My Gymsuit 224, 225
Catherine, Called Birdy 378
The Cat in the Hat 125
Celebrate Cricket 152
Celebrities, magazines 32, 35
Celia's Island Journal 222
Center for Children's Books 127
A Certain Slant of Light 92, 93
The Chalk Box Kid 140
Chambers, James 100, 104
The Chaos King 85, 92
Chapter books 15, 188
Chapters 147, 179, 182, 183
Characters 50–52, 59, 61, 74, 75, 78, 80, 81, 87, 89, 90, 108, 109,143–148, 153, 155, 159, 165, 167, 169, 170–172, 174, 177, 187–191, 195, 196, 198, 199, 201–211, 214, 216, 218–220, 223, 224, 226, 228, 309–319, 326, 328, 357, 374, 375
Charkin, Richard 138
Charlesbridge Pub. 13, 14, 15, 21, 50, 53, 67, 203
Charlotte's Web 17
Checkerboard Library 99
Chelsea Green 130
Chelsea House 348, 353
Chess Rumble 17
Chewy Louie 141
Chicken House 134
Chicken Soup for the Soul 239
Child 139
Child Development 34, 150
Childhood Education 40
Children's Better Health Inst. 237

Children's Book Council 135, 259, 260, 298
Children's Book Press 127-128
Children's Lit. Web Guide 298
China 117
Choices 40
Chorlian, Meg 116, 118, 121
Christian Focus Pub. 168
Christie, R. Gregory 109
The Christmas Adventure of Space Elf Sam 141
Chronicle Children's Group 13, 14, 21, 108, 113, 168
Chronicles of Chrestomanci series 83
Cicada 46, 237
Cirque du Freak series 93
Cisneros, Sandra 21
City Foxes 360
Clap Clap: Clapping Games 116, 121, 124
Clarion Books 13, 15, 20, 55, 76, 78, 83, 125, 143, 154, 165, 312, 315, 352, 377
Clark, Christine French 155, 237, 240
Class of 2k7 278–280
Classroom magazines 28, 37, 38, 39, 40–42, 95, 97, 131
Clear Light Books 275
Clementine 379
Clements, Andrew 127
Clichés 167–175, 195, 216
Click 237
Clifford the Big Red Dog 110
Climax 196, 197, 198
Clips and credits 244, 291
Clique series 8
Close Kin 82
Club Connection 139
Clubhouse, Clubhouse Jr. 137, 162
The Clue of the Linoleum Lederhosen 170
Coaches, writing 331-336
Cobblehill Books 140
Cobblestone 37, 41, 116, 118, 237
Cobblestone Group 37, 41, 43, 233, 236, 237, 241, 305
Cobb, Steve 138
Cobb, Theo 292, 295, 296
Cobb, Vicki 290, 292, 293, 296
Code Orange 219, 220
Collard, Sneed B. III 52, 54, 66, 67, 68, 69
Collegebound Teen 139
Colophon House 349
Come Away from the Water, Shirley 61
Come Look with Me: Asian Art 15
Coming of age 213-220, 224
Concept Books 107
Conferences 191, 246, 247, 250, 256, 261, 373-382, 383-400
Conflict 75, 144, 216, 304, 310, 315
Connolly, John 363

Constable, Tina 137
Contests and awards 401-437
Continents of the World 342
Contracts 65, 231-242, 244, 245, 249, 251, 257, 266, 273, 350, 351
Cookie 46
Cooney, Caroline B. 219
Coop. Children's Book Center 127
Cooper, Floyd 20
Cooper Square Pub. 106, 128
Cooper, Susan 78, 83
Copper Sun 126
Cordray, Chuck 45
Robin Corey Books 131
Cornish, D. M. 14
CosmoGIRL! 27, 45
Costales, Amy 111
Joanna Cotler Books 144, 216
Counterfeit Son 68
Coville, Bruce 155
Cowboy José 190
Cowell, Cressida 73, 82
Crafts 31, 115-124, 130
Crane, Cody 39
"Creating Buzz: Native Bees" 361
Creative nonfiction 49-56
Cricket 67, 151, 152, 237
Cricket Pub. 43, 131, 344
Crisler, Curtis L. 20
Critiques 244, 379, 380
Crossover books 10, 15
Crown Books 92, 137
Crow Toes Quarterly 42, 43, 44
Crystal, Billy 9
C. S. Lewis 349
CTB/McGraw-Hill 344
Cuffe-Percz, Mary 17
Cunane, Kelly 127
Cunningham, Barry 134
Cunningham, Linda 129
Cures for Heartbreak 215
Curmi, Serena 188
Current Events 40
Current Health 1 & 2 40, 139
Cushman, Karen 377

Da Capo Press 129, 138
Dahl, Roald 222
Daisyworld Press 130
Dalheim, Mary 139
D'Alto, Nick 116, 118
Daly, Joe Ann 140
Daly, Kristin 23
Dane County Kids 139
The Dangerous Book for Boys 133
A Dangerous Engine 127
Danziger, Paula 224, 225
Darby Creek 50, 290
Darragh, Aileen 22
Dash, Joan 127
David, Laurie 112
Davies, Sarah 137
Davis, Deborah 165
Davis, Terry 179, 184, 185, 186
Davy Crockett 356
Dawson, Kathy 76

Day, Larry 22, 127
Day of the Scarab 82
DC Comics 16, 129, 134
Dead Girl series 89
Dead Girl Walking 89
Dead Sea 92
Deane, Linda 133
Dean, Zoey 14
Debon, Nicolas 127
Decker, Timothy 17
Defending Irene 205
DeKeyser, Stacy 12
Delacorte Press 74, 82, 83, 86, 90, 134, 145, 148, 164, 179, 203, 205, 215, 219, 271, 341, 345, 380, 382
Demarest, Chris L. 188
Dendy, Leslie 163
Dessen, Sarah 13, 217
Details 18, 19, 23, 45, 51, 53, 55, 75, 80, 81, 111, 159, 161, 162, 163, 171, 338, 340, 352, 357
Developmental stages, children 34, 58, 59, 60, 61
DeVito, Carlo 138
Dial Books 136, 160, 214, 216, 218, 272, 275
Dialogue 52, 53, 54, 165, 167, 174, 185, 203-211
Dig 117, 237
Dilkes, David 342, 343
Disabilities 29, 133
Disney 137
Disney Adventures 139
Distribution, book 7, 263-270
Ditlow, Anthony, Helen, and Tim 137
DK Pub. 130, 136
Dlouhy, Caitlyn 11, 13, 17, 21
Does My Head Look Big in This? 107, 109
Dog and Bear: Two Friends, Three Stories 126-127
Dolan, Eamon 136
The Donkey Cart 140
Doorasamy, Sharon 95, 98, 100
Dorchester Pub. 92
Doughty, Rebecca 112
Dowd, Siobhan 11
The Down-to-Earth Guide to Global Warming 112
Dragon 139
Dragon Naturally Speaking 9, 284
Dragon's Keep 74, 75, 77, 81, 82
Draper, Sharon 126
Driggs, Lorin 100, 102, 103
Driscoll, Susan 128
A Drowned Maiden's Hair 168
Paul Dry Books 222
Dryden, Emma 377
DuBurke, Randy 17, 106
DUDE! Stories and Stuff for Boys 152
Duel: Burr and Hamilton's Deadly War of Words 22
Duey, Kathleen 126
Duffield, Katy 162
Dungy, Tony 135

Dunham, Jennie 246, 247, 249, 250, 251, 252
Dunkle, Clare B. 74, 76, 77, 80, 81, 82
The Dust Bowl and the Depression 350
Dutton Books 11, 126–128, 136, 137, 140, 309, 323, 329, 376
Dyer, Brooke 59
DynaMath 40

Eagan, Cindy 131
Earley, Tony 216
Early readers 15, 93, 94
Easterly, Sara 272
Easton, Emily 15, 22
Eble, Diane 332, 333, 335, 336
E-books 137, 266, 267
Eclipse 92
Edmunds, Page 138
Educational pub. 38, 39, 40, 41, 49, 95-104, 131, 238, 239
Educational Week 40
Edwardson, Debby 203, 204, 206, 208
Edwards, Sue Bradford 181, 182, 184, 185, 186
Eek and Meek 141
Ehrlich, Amy 137, 222
Eighth Mountain Press 150
Eleven 12
Elijah Helps the Widow 325
Elsewhere 93
Elya, Susan Middleton 190
Encyclopedia Horrifica 91
Enderle, Judith Ross 187, 188, 192, 193
Endings 154, 168, 169
English, Karen 15
Enslow Pub. 98, 100, 102, 104, 342, 347, 348, 349, 350, 352, 353
Enter the Earth 130
Eos 73
Epiphanies 195-202
Escaping Tornado Season 193
Evans, Dilys 21
Even Firefighters Hug Their Moms 323
Experts 55, 75, 225, 236, 340, 341, 365, 367-372
Exploding the Myths 375

Faces 41, 237
Facts on File 100, 102, 104, 128
Fagan, Deva 82
Fairy tales 11, 65, 170
Fallen Angels 374
The Fallen series 92
Family Circle 133
Family Energy 139
FamilyFun 120
The Family Groove 133
Fantasy 11, 73–81, 85, 89, 92, 93, 134, 155, 159, 166, 168, 169, 170–172, 199, 214, 345, 357
Farmer McPeepers and His Missing Milk Cows 162

Farnsworth, Bill 106
Farrar, Straus and Giroux 54, 93, 126, 127, 128, 161, 196, 222, 337, 338
Fartiste 23
Fashion, magazines 31, 32, 34
Fatal Charm 87
Faze 223
Fear Street series 93
Feed 208
Feiwel, Jean 135
Feldman, Jody 341
Felin, M. Sindy 126
Ferber, Brenda 128
Ferguson Pub. 104
Ferrell, Nancy Warren 52, 53
Fiesta Fiasco 374
Filter Press 364
Fink, Andy 132
David Finkling Books 11, 128
Fireflies 127
First-person accounts 201, 221, 223, 227, 234, 339
First Second 126
Fishbone, Greg R. 278
Fisher, Catherine 73
Fisher, Dorothy Canfield 216
Fisk, Karen 22, 23
Flanagan, John 14
Fleischman, Paul 144
Fleming, Thomas 234
Flipped 143
Florence, Debbi Michiko 117
Flotsam 125
Flux 12, 89, 326
The Fold 13, 107
Forbes, Esther 217
Ford, Beth 138
Fortune's Folly 82
47 73, 82
For You Are a Kenyan Child 127
Frances Foster Books 127
The 14 Fabulous Fibs of Gregory K 276
Fowler, Susi Gregg 306
Fox, Jennifer 17, 105, 106, 109, 113
Fox, Mem 151, 378
Fradin, Dennis Brindell 22
Fragnito, Michael 138
Franklin Watts 189
Frazee, Marla 378
Freaks: Alive, on the Inside! 341, 344
Freedman, Russell 55, 56, 127
Freeman, Laura 15
Fresh.Magazine 133
From the Desk of Septina Nash: The Penguins of Doom 279
Front Street 17, 18
Fuge, Charles 61
Full Cast Audio 133
Fun for Kidz 120, 305

Gaia Girls series 130
Gale, David 23
Gallagher, Liz 12
Games: A Tale of Two Bullies 316

Gates, Lisa 331–333, 335, 336
Gee, Joshua 91
George's Secret Key to the Universe 135
Get Born 133
Getting Air 290
Gettysburg Ghost Gang series 86, 87, 92
Ghost Girl 312
The Ghost Sitter 89
Ghoul 92
Giblin, James Cross 152
Douglas Gibson Books 226
Giff, Patricia Reilly 12
Gifted Education Press Quarterly 40
Gildiner, Catherine 222
Gillespie, Jenny 138
Gimme a Call 134
Giovanni, Nikki 9
Girl 132
A Girl Named Zippy 11
Girl of the Moment 11
Girls Can Do Anything 42
Girls' Life 223
Give a Goat 22, 23
The Giver 216
Glass Dragons 357
Glazer, Joshua 91, 92, 93, 94
Globe Pequot Press 137
Gods of Manhattan 11
Go! Exploring the World of Transportation 41–43
Going and Going 111
Golden, Christopher 86, 89
The Golden Dream of Carlo Chuchio 82, 141
The Golden Hour 77, 78, 83
Goldman, Michael 45, 46
The Golem's Eye 83
Golfer Girl 29, 30, 32, 43, 132
Golio, Gary 20
The Gollywhopper Games 341
Gone Wild: An Endangered Animal Alphabet 126
Goodstein, Anastasia 34
Goosebumps series 93, 134
Gopnik, Adam 227
Gordon, Cambria 112
Gordon, Jeffie Ross 187
Gordon, Roderick 134
Gordon, Stephanie Jacob 187, 188, 193
Gorman, Carol 311, 312, 316, 318
Gossip Girl series 8, 131
Gothic: Ten Original Dark Tales 92
Goyette, Cecile 216, 218, 220
Grand & Humble 145
The Grand Tour 83
Graphia 92, 93
Graphic novels 16, 17, 93, 106, 130, 131
Graphic Planet 131
Graphic Universe 129
Gratz, Alan 160, 161, 162, 163, 273, 275
Graves, Trina 132

Grayson, Ashley 87, 93
A Great and Terrible Beauty 74, 82
The Great Gilly Hopkins 215
The Great Pumpkin, Charlie Brown 129
Greenberg, Melanie Hope 235
Greenhaven Press 101, 348
Green, John 126, 375, 376
Greenwillow 61, 82, 83, 199, 341
Grey Griffins series 279, 280
Grey, Mini 128
Griffin, Adele 145, 190
Griffin, Amy 379
Griffin, Peni R. 89
Griffin, Regina 138
Griffiths, Rachel 378
Grimes, Nikki 126
Grosset & Dunlap 15
Groundwood Books 127
Grove, Vicki 178, 181–183, 185
Guinea Pig Scientists 163
Gutman, Dan 289, 290, 291, 292, 293

Hachette Book Group 16, 129, 136, 138
The Halloween Book of Facts and Fun 352
Hallowmere series 75, 79, 81, 82, 160, 164
Halls, Kelly Milner 50, 51, 55, 365
Hamilton, Virginia 140
Hand Print 19
Hank Zipzer #14 15
Hanson, Lisa 123
Hanukkah at Valley Forge 128
Harcourt 74, 76, 82, 83, 133, 137, 147, 157, 170, 190, 193, 378
Hard Love 375
Hard Shell Word Factory 224
Harlin, Greg 128
Harness, Cheryl 65, 66, 67, 68, 69
HarperCollins 11, 23, 59, 61, 69, 73, 85, 92, 126, 127, 130, 134, 135, 137, 138, 144, 145, 147, 157, 168, 193, 290, 304, 312, 316, 373
Harrington Park Press 130
Harrison, Lisi 134
Hartinger, Brent 145
Hartman, Bob 308
Hartnett, Sonya 126
Hattie Big Sky 205, 210, 271, 272, 273, 382
Hautala, Rick 86
Hawking, Steven 135
Haworth Press 130
Hayes, Kathleen 36, 62
Hearst 27, 35, 43, 45, 138
The Heart of the Beast 50
Hedquist, Aaron 273
Hees, Miriam 273
Help! A Story of Friendship 61
Henkes, Kevin 58
Henry David Thoreau 353
Herrera, Juan Felipe 111
Hesse, Karen 19
Hess, Nina 169, 171, 172

Hidden Talents 292
Hide-and-Seek Turkeys 188
Hieroglyphics Magazine 132
The Higher Power of Lucky 125, 373
The High King 141
Highlights for Children 36, 43, 67, 88, 115, 116, 118, 120, 122, 124, 150, 155, 162, 191, 192, 209, 237, 239, 240
Highlights High Five 35, 36, 43, 62
Hijuelos, Oscar 21
Hi-lo books 95, 96
Hillyer, Lexa 138
Hinton, S. E. 125
Historical fantasy 73-81
Historical fiction 54, 70, 73, 78, 79, 80, 143, 144, 146, 205, 207, 214, 217, 224, 271, 312, 313, 341, 344, 368, 377
History 19, 20, 21, 22, 37, 41, 55, 65, 66, 68, 73-81, 87, 91, 118, 122, 131, 189, 205, 207, 312, 313, 314, 341, 344, 345, 348, 349, 350, 352, 363, 364
Hitler Youth 349
Hoffman, Tiffany 115, 118, 119, 122, 124
Holiday House 126, 138, 196, 271, 374
Hollow Kingdom trilogy 74, 77, 80, 82
Holm, Jennifer 224, 225
Henry Holt 74, 82, 83, 125, 141, 163, 197, 209, 213, 214
Holtzbrinck 129, 134, 135, 138
Hongying, Yang 130
Hooton, Claude 30, 132
Hopscotch 32, 118, 120, 305
Horne, Richard 15
Horror 75, 85-94
Hostetter, Joyce Moyer 203, 204, 205, 207, 208, 209, 210
Hotel Kid 222
Houghton Mifflin 13, 52, 67, 129, 136, 222, 308, 314, 347, 349, 377, 380
Hour of the Cobra 83
Hour of the Outlaw 83
Houts, Amy 116, 119, 121, 124
Howard Kids 135
Howell, Theresa 106, 111, 114
How I Live Now 217–220
How It's Done 326
How to Train Your Dragon 73, 82
How-to writing 111, 116, 130, 221, 369
Hudson Pub. 131
Hudson, Wade and Cheryl 131
Hughes, Catherine 232, 233, 239
Humanics Learning 120
The Humming of Numbers 82
Humor 61, 93, 118, 155, 168, 172, 215, 218, 224
Hunter, Elizabeth 35, 36
Hurst, Carol Otis 140
Hurston, Zora Neale 100
Husni, Samir 25, 26

Hyman, Trina Schart 21
Hyperion 82, 83, 126, 127, 138, 379
I Capture the Castle 216
Ideas 87, 153, 189, 281, 282, 301-336
I Face the Wind 290
I Get So Hungry 107
Iggulden, Conn and Hal 133
Ignite Your Faith 33, 43, 234, 240-241
Imagery 159-166, 199
In the Coils of the Snake 82
"The Indian Camp" 214
Inheritance trilogy 166
Innerst, Stacy 190
In the Serpent's Coils 75, 82, 159
Instructor 40
"Intentional Living" 326
International Gymnast 32
International Reading Assn. 259, 260
Interviews 343, 358, 359, 361, 365, 370, 371, 372
Into the Land of the Unicorns 155
The Inuit 189
The Invention of Hugo Cabret 16, 110, 126, 127
iUniverse 128, 129

Jablonski, Carla 75, 79, 81, 82
Richard Jackson Books 125
Jacob Have I Loved 215
JAKES 32
Janssen, Heather 133
Jazz 126, 127
Jenkins, Jerry B. 173
Jennifer the Jerk is Missing 318
Jennings, Crystal H. 47
Jeremy Thatcher, Dragon Hatcher 157
The Jewel and the Key 78
Jim the Boy 216
Joan Lowery Nixon 353
Johnny Tremain 217
Johnston, Allyn 137, 378
Johnston, Tony 190
Jones, Carrie 12
Jones, Diana Wynne 83
Joncs, Lynn 365
Jones, Traci L. 126
Journey Stone Creations 168, 173
Jove Books 302
Joyce, William 9
Julia's Kitchen 128
Jump at the Sun 126
Jump the Cracks 12
Jump Start Press 96, 102
Junior Baseball 32
Junior Scholastic 40
Junior Shooters 132
Just for Daddy! and Just for Mommy! 135
Just for You to Know 69
Just in Case 128
Just Us Books 131

Kadohata, Cynthia 128, 224, 225
Kaleidoscope Kids 117
Kaline Klattermaster's Tree House 11
Kanninen, Barbara 88
Karp, Cindy 106
Karre, Andrew 89, 93
Keenan, Josephine Rascoe 153
Keene, Brian 92
The Keeper of the Grail 134
Keeping Score 13
Keller, Holly 61
Kempskie, Heather 123
Kensington Pub. 131
Ketchum, Liza 143, 144, 146
Khan, Ausma 27, 28, 132
KidHaven Press 101
Kids' America 122
Kids Can Press 119, 120, 121, 122, 138
Kids Play 130
Kids' Rooms, Etc. 139
Kid Zone 120
Kiki 29, 30, 31, 43, 132
Kim, Emily Sylvan 246, 247, 249, 250, 252
Kimmel, Eric 152
Kimmel, Haven 11
Kingfisher Books 129
The King of Attolia 82
King of Ithaka 75
King of Shadows 78, 83
Klause, Annette Curtis 145, 341, 344
Knopf 10, 78, 83, 126, 127, 143, 216, 222
Knots in My Yo-Yo String 222
Knowles, Jo 93
Know Your World 40
Kochan, Susan 107, 108, 114, 190
Koellhoffer, Tara 348, 351–353, 356
Koelling, Holly 10
Koertge, Ron 144, 147, 148
Kohn, Betsy 239, 240
Kolosov, Jacqueline 82
Koochin, TeLeni 42, 44
Korczak, Ayal 27, 132
Kozlowicz, Neil 292, 294, 295
Kraus, Marisa 130
Krauss, Ruth 59
Krebs, Gary 137
Kremer, John 271, 274
Krensky, Stephen 128
Krieger, Ellen 130, 136
Krienke, Martha 139
Krull, Kathleen 23
Kulikov, Boris 23

Ladybug 138, 237
Lamb, Wendy 12, 214–217, 337
Lamplighter series 14
Landau, Elaine 348, 349, 351, 352
Lane, Kimberly 15
Lane, Shannon Hurst 357, 358, 359
Langeland, Deirdre 138
Language Arts 40
Larbalestier, Justine 128
Lark Books 120

Larson, Kirby 205, 210, 271, 273, 382
The Last Snake Runner 78, 83
LàTeen 27, 43, 132
Latinos 21, 26, 27, 132
Law, Elizabeth 136
Lazar, Daniel 246, 247, 248, 250, 252, 253
Leading Student Ministry 139
Learning Books 131
Learning and Leading with Technology 40
Lee, Dom 105
Lee & Low 17, 105, 106, 108, 113
Lee-Tai, Amy 127
Left Behind series 173
The Legend of Zoey 164
LeGuin, Ursula K. 150, 151
L'Engle, Madeleine 135, 140, 196
Lerner Pub. 52, 129, 347, 348, 356
LeRoy, Yolanda 13
Lessons from a Dead Girl 93
Letvin, Alice 36
Levine, Arthur A. 127, 276, 378–381
Lewis, Jon 279, 280
Lewis, Kevin 57
Licensing 8, 9, 102
Lieberg, Carolyn 309, 311, 317
Lieurance, Suzanne 336
Lifelong Books 129
Life's Little Instruction Book 112
Lilly books 58
Lily Dale: Believing 15
Lily's Ghosts 85, 87, 92
Listening Library 137
Little, Brown 8, 10, 16, 73, 82, 92, 93, 126, 127, 131, 134, 136, 168, 177, 205, 216, 222
The Little Engine that Could 9
Little, Kimberly 78, 83
The Little Lutheran 35, 36, 43, 132
Little Scholastic 131
Little Simon Inspirations 135
Live Journal 276
Liwska, Renata 17
Lizzi, Marian 136
Llewellyn Worldwide 12, 87, 89, 93
Lock and Key 13
Lockhart, Doug 137
Logan Magazine 29, 43, 133
Loggia, Wendy 134
Lohse, Joyce B. 363
Looking Back 222
Looking for Alaska 376
Looking Glass Library 131
Lopez, Rafael 106, 111
Lord, Cynthia 224, 225
The Lord Is My Shepherd 18
Lord, Michelle 106
Walter Lorraine Books 222, 308
Love (and Other Uses for Duct Tape) 12
The Lovely Bones 93
Lowell House 92
Lowry, Lois 127, 216, 222

Lubar, David 292, 297
Lucent Books 101
Luna Rising 106, 128
Lupica, Mike 13
Lurie, Stephanie Owens 11
Lutes, Chris 33, 234, 240
Luxbacher, Irene 119
Lynch, Chris 190
Lyons, Lisa 138
Lyons Press 358

Maass, Donald 315
MacCready, Robin Merroe 127
Macken, JoAnn Early 98, 100, 103, 104
Mackenzie, Catherine 168, 170, 171, 172, 175
MacLean, Christine 323, 326, 327, 329
Macmillan Books 15, 129, 137, 138
Made in China 189
The Magazine 139
Magic, The Gathering 139
Magicians of Quality 83
Magic in Manhattan series 134
The Magic Kerchief 271
Magic or Madness 128
Magic Wagon 131
Magination Press 311
Make It About Me! 129-130
Making Comics 127
Mama Always Comes Home 59
Mañana, Iguana 374
Manlove, Melissa 108, 113, 168, 170, 171, 175
Manning, Suzanne 47
Manzano, Sonia 135
March 213, 218
Margaret Chase Smith 21
Marimba Books 131
Marino, Krista 90, 92, 380
Marion Wright Edelman 352
Marketing 113, 244, 248, 249, 264, 266, 269, 271, 272, 273, 274, 278, 280, 324
Markinko, Dorothy 140
Marlowe & Company 129
Marr, Melissa 11
Marshall Cavendish 70, 348, 380
Martin, Bill Jr. 125
The Marvelous Misadventures of Sebastian 141
Marx, Trish 106
Mary Margaret and the Perfect Pet Plan 329
MATH 40
Matthews, Meredith 139
Maude, Rachel 131
Max and Felix 193
The Mayflower and the Pilgrims' New World 21
Mayflower: A Story of Courage, Community, and War 22
McArthur, Debra 347, 349, 350, 351, 353, 356
McBratney, Sam 61
McCarthy, Pat 353

McCarthy, Peter 127
McClafferty, Carla 49, 51, 53, 54, 55, 161, 162
McCloud, Scott 127
McClure, Wendy 107, 109, 112, 114
McCormick, Patricia 127
McCutchan, Ron 131
McDonald, Joyce 148
Margaret K. McElderry Books 78, 83, 188, 245, 341, 377
McFerrin, Samantha 190
McGraw-Hill Education 136
McIntosh & Otis 140
McKissack, Patricia 301
McLimans, David 126
McMullen, Sean 357
McNeese, Tim 353
McPhail, David 21
McPheters & Company 25
McVeigh, Mark 136, 379, 380
Meadowbrook Press 120, 122, 123
Mebus, Scott 11
Meckler, Caroline 213, 214, 215
Melodrama 167-175
The Melting of Maggie Bean 130
Menaker, Daniel 137
Meredith Books 129
Meriwether Pub. 369
Metaphor 159, 160, 162, 165, 166, 167, 179
Metsch, Amy 137
Meyer, Daniel 359
Meyer, L. A. 193
Meyer, Stephenie 10, 92, 168
Michaelis, Antonia 82
Michael, Livi 190
Middle East Nations of the World 342
Middle-grade 11, 12, 14, 22, 31, 32, 34, 93, 94, 130, 155, 196, 214, 224
Middleworld 130
Millbrook Press 120
Millicent Min, Girl Genius 276
Millin, Christopher 44
Mirrorstone Books 82, 160, 169, 171
The Mislaid Magician 83
Mis Quince 27, 43
Miss Crandall's School for Young Ladies & Little Misses of Color 19
Mitchell, Barbara 95, 99, 100
Mitchell Lane 95, 100, 102
Mlynowski, Sarah 134
Mochizuki, Ken 105
MOM 43, 46, 47, 48
Monster 373
Monster Blood Tattoo 14
Moo-Cow Fan Club 41, 43
Moon Plane 127
Moonshower, Candie 164, 166
Moose Enterprise 169
Mooser, Stephen 380, 381
Moran, Lisa Singer 139
More Super Scary Stories for Sleep-Overs 92

444

Morgan, Cal 138
Morgan Reynolds 95, 100, 103
Moriarty, Laura 263, 264, 265, 266, 267, 268, 269
Morris, Bill 126
Morrow, Paula 131
Moses: When Harriet Tubman Led Her People to Freedom 126
Mosley, Walter 73, 82
Motherwords 43, 48
Mousseau, Richard 169, 170, 172, 174
Movie Girl 224
Moyers, Scott 136
Mrs. McMurphy's Pumpkin 304
Muhammad Ali 112
Multicultural 15, 19, 21, 23,105, 106, 107, 108, 109, 111, 122, 124, 131, 189
Multnomah Books 138
Murfin, Teresa 188
Murphy, Erin 246, 247, 249, 251, 252, 253
Muse 237
Muslim Girl 27, 28, 43, 132
My Brothers' Flying Machine 205
Myers, Christopher 126
Myers, Garry Cleveland 155
Myers, Walter Dean 126, 373, 374
My Friend 139
My Friend Rabbit 9
My Grandpa Had a Stroke 311
My Name is Celia 106
My Sister's Keeper 10
My Teacher Is an Alien 155
Mysteries 87, 91, 131
Mysteries of the Mummy Kids 50
Mysterious Ways 179
Mystery Bottle 127
Mystery Writers of America 127, 260, 261
My Weird School series 291

Na, An 13, 107
Napoli, Donna Jo 73, 82
Narrative 143, 150, 166, 184, 196, 214, 215, 314, 339
Nathan, Jan 141
National Book Network 264
National Council of Teachers of English 260
National Geographic Children's Books 66
National Geographic Explorer 131
National Geographic Kids 232, 241, 361
National Geographic Little Kids 35, 43, 131
National PAL CopsNKids Chronicles 139
National Writers Assn. 260
National Writers Union 236
Natural Jewish Parenting 139
Naughty Ma Xiaotao series 130
Negotiation 238, 239, 241, 242, 245, 250, 251, 266, 350, 351
Nelson, Judy 10

Nelson, Kadir 126
Nelson, Marilyn 9, 19
Nelvana, Ltd. 9
Neri, G. 17, 106
Networking 250, 258, 262, 369
New Age Dimensions 139
Newbery, Linda 128
New Lit Generation 267
Newman, Aline 361, 364
New Moon 30, 92
Nick Jr. Family 31, 34, 43, 139
Niehaus, Alisha 136
Nikki and Deja: Birthday Blues 15
Ninjas, Piranhas, and Galileo 177
Nitz, Kristin Wolden 205, 207, 208, 209, 210, 211
No Dogs Allowed! 141
Northland Pub. 106, 128
North Texas Teens 140
NorthWord Books 128
Not in Room 204 109
Not Like You 165
Novelists, Inc. 258, 260
Novelty books 130, 131, 134
Noyes, Deborah 92
Nurss, Sally 58, 60, 149

Oates, Joyce Carol 9, 147
Oceans of the World 342
O'Dell, Kathleen 218
O'Dell, Scott 140
Odyssey 237
"Ohoyo Osh Chisba: The Unknown Woman" 153
Old, Wendie C. 352, 353
Oliver, Lin 15, 373, 380
Olsen, Logan and Laurie 29, 133
Olson, Gillia 98, 99, 100, 101, 102, 103, 104
101 Things series 15
O'Neill, Alexis 193
One More Time, Mama 380
On Etruscan Time 78, 83, 209
One-Eye! Two-Eyes! Three-Eyes! 291
On Her Way: Stories and Poems About Growing Up Girl 152
On the Road 358
1,000 Years Ago on Planet Earth 66, 67
123 I Can Paint and *123 I Can Sculpt* 119
Open Horizons 274
The Opposite of Invisible 12
The Oracle Betrayed 82
Oracle Prophecies trilogy 73, 82
Orange Avenue 130
Orchard Books 279, 379
Outcast series 86
Out of the Ball Park 135
Out of the Dust 19
The Outsiders 125
Owen, J. D. 233, 236, 238, 239

Pacific View Press 189
Pack-o-Fun 120
Painting the Wild Frontier 20
Palmquist, Vicki 289, 292, 295,

297
Paolini, Christopher 166
Paper Towns 13
Paranormal Powers 70
Pardonable Lies 363
Parenting 46, 47, 48, 133
Parents for Parents 133
Parisi, Elizabeth 379, 380
Park, Linda Sue 13, 70, 152
Parrotfish 375
Parties & Potions 134
Partridge, Elizabeth 373
Paterson, Katherine 201, 215
Patrick, Philip 137
Patron, Susan 125, 373
Patterson, James 9
Pattison, Darcy 304, 306–308
Paul, Ann Whitford 374
Paulsen, Gary 234
Payment 231-242, 257
Peachtree Pub. 205, 311
Pearce, Q. L. 87, 90, 92, 94
Pearson Education 116, 136, 348
Pearson, Mary E. 196-198, 202
Peck, Richard 216
Pederson, Marissa 12
Peeled 13
PEN American Center 259
Penguin Group 9, 13, 14, 75, 120, 134, 136, 137, 190, 275, 277
Penny from Heaven 225
Pennypacker, Sara 379
Perfection Learning 95, 100, 103
The Perfect Shot 68, 195, 198, 200, 201
Pericoli, Matteo 127
Perigee Books 137
Permissions 241, 348, 350
Perseus Book Group 129
Personal experience 221-229
Peterson, Julie 59
Peterson, Ken 138
Philbrick, Nathaniel 21-22
Philomel 13, 14, 17, 18
Photographs, research 347-356
Picador 10, 363
Picoult, Jodi 10, 359
Picture books 8, 15, 17, 18, 19, 20, 21, 22, 57, 59, 66, 67, 110, 131, 205, 206, 213, 291, 378
Pilkey, Dav 292, 296
Pimm, Nancy Roe 50
Pincus, Gregory K. 276
Pingry, Patricia 117
Pitlock, Julie Carnagie 101, 104
Pitzer, Susanna 127
The Place at the Edge of the Earth 314
Place, research 203, 337-346
A Place Where Sunflowers Grow 127
Plant, Tamara 47, 48
Plot 52, 53, 93, 153, 154, 167–171, 175, 177, 187, 189, 190, 191, 214, 218, 223, 281, 304, 309, 315, 316, 317
Plourde, Lynn 21
Plushie Pals 132

Pocket Books 129, 363
Pockets 232, 363
Poetry 19, 20, 60, 76, 269
*Poetry for Young People:
 Langston Hughes* 126
Poison Ink 86
Polvino, Lynne 15, 20
Poploff, Michelle 272
Poppy imprint 8, 131
Neal Porter Books 127
Poseur series 131
Positive Teens 140
The Prairie Builders 52, 67
PreK 32, 34, 36, 57-64, 130, 131
PresenTense 132
Price Stern Sloan 87
Princess Nevermore books 290
Print-on-demand 266, 267
Profopin, Romana 138
Promotion 77, 113, 123, 250,
 264, 266, 272–280, 369
Proposals 121, 123, 291, 325
Prose, Francine 157
Ptolemy's Gate 83
Puffin 128, 222, 225, 292, 302
Puget Sound Parent 140
The Purple Balloon 110, 113
The Purple Crayon 298
Putnam 13, 14, 22, 77, 107, 108,
 114, 126, 134, 145, 178, 185

Q 47
The Queen of Attolia 82
The Queen with Bees in Her Hair
 65
Quince Girl 26, 43

Rabb, Margo 215
Rachel Carson 52
Rader, Laura 23
Raglin, Tim 190
Raising the Griffin 337, 340, 344
Raisin Wine 226
*Ralph Masiello's Ancient Egypt
 Drawing Book* 16
Random House 11, 12, 61, 86,
 109, 128, 129, 131, 137, 214,
 216, 225, 380
Rangel, Angie 44
Ranger Rick 139
*Ranger's Apprentice Book Five:
 The Sorceror in the North* 14
Ransom, Jeanie 71
Raoul Wallenberg 347
Raschka, Chris 110
Rayburn, Tricia 130
Ray, Delia 312, 313, 315
Raymond, Carl 136
Razorbill 14, 75, 82, 86, 92, 128,
 138, 277
Reaching Dustin 185
READ 38, 40
Reader's Digest Assn. 128
Reading Like a Writer 157
The Reading Teacher 40
Reading Today 40
Real Sports 140

Rebel Angels 74, 82
The Recess Queen 193
Rector, Rebecca Kraft 345
Red Fox imprint 61
The Red Queen's Daughter 82
Reference books 95, 96
Regan Books 138
Regan, Dian Curtis 290–293
Regenold, Michele 41, 42
Reich, Susanna 20
Reidy, Carolyn 136
Religious publishing 18, 33, 35,
 36, 38, 88, 132, 173
Remainders and returns 268
Resales and reprints 237, 239,
 241, 326
Research 52–55, 66, 69, 70, 72,
 73, 76, 80, 86, 87, 98, 116,
 173, 241, 263, 302, 312, 313,
 325, 326, 337-372
Résumés 69, 101, 103
Retellings 86, 170
Return to Fairyopolis 14
Revenge of the Shadow King 280
Rhiannon 178
Rhyme and rhythm 52, 57,
 60–62, 146, 150, 151
Rice, Bebe Faas 309, 314
Rico, Gabriele Lusser 325
Riggs, Shannon 109, 110
Rights 231, 235, 236, 243, 257,
 291, 326, 350
The Rise of the Black Wolf 279
Rising Moon 106, 113, 128, 162
Rivers, Randi 15, 50, 53, 56
The Road to Paris 126
Roaring Brook 9, 126, 129, 138
Robinson, Marileta 150, 151, 192
Roca, Francois 112
Rodriguez, Alex 135
Rohmann, Eric 9
Romanos, Jack 136
Room One: A Mystery or Two 127
A Room on Lorelei Street 197,
 198, 202
Rose, Naomi C. 275, 276
Rosen, Michael 128
Rosinsky, Natalie 237, 242
Rosoff, Meg 128, 217
Ross, Steve 137
Roth-Ey, David 138
Rowling, J. K. 7, 8, 134, 169, 294
Rowman & Littlefield 128
Royalties 238, 239, 351
Ruby, Laura 85, 87, 92
Rules 224, 225
Run Far, Run Fast 17
Running Press 129
Running with Scissors 10
Ryskamp, Bruce 137

Saint-Lot, Katia Novet 23
St. Martin's Press 216, 374
Samoun, Abigail 245, 246, 250,
 251
Samurai Shortstop 160, 163, 273,
 275
SandCastle Books 99

Sandell, Lisa 107, 109
Santa trilogy 23
Saving the Griffin 205, 207, 208,
 210
Say It with Music 131
Sayre, April Pulley 54
Scarecrow Press 375
Scary Stories for Stormy Nights 92
Scenes 50–53, 55, 89, 94, 164–166,
 177, 179, 184, 185, 201
Schlitz, Laura Amy 168
Schmidt, Gary D. 13
Schneider, Howie 141
Scholastic 16, 19, 38, 39, 40, 43,
 91, 107, 110, 112, 127, 131,
 134, 141, 155, 188, 193, 216,
 224, 225, 237, 276, 291, 347,
 349, 378, 379
Scholastic News 40
School and library market 77, 95-
 104, 113, 238, 261, 264, 267,
 272, 273, 275, 347, 348
Secular Homeschooling 133
SchoolArts 40
School Library Journal 277, 279
Schrock, Jan West 22
Schulz, Charles 129
Schwartz & Wade 109, 110
Science 36, 39, 55, 66, 67, 68,
 131, 225, 290
Science Activities 40
Science fiction 92, 345, 357
Science Fiction and Fantasy Writers
 of America 76, 251, 260, 261
Science Weekly 40
Science World 39, 40
Scope 40
Scott, Elaine 14
Screenplays 282, 285, 287
Second Sight 70, 302
Secret of the Three Treasures 196,
 197
*The Secret Rites of Social
 Butterflies* 11
Secrets of the Cirque Medrano 14
Secrets of the Unexplained series
 70, 303
SeedFolks 144
Seeger, Laura Vaccaro 127
Seer series 87
Seesaw Girl 70
Self-publishing 129, 263, 264,
 266, 291
Selznick, Brian 16, 21, 110, 126
Sendak, Maurice 9, 94
Sensel, Joni 82
Senses 45, 46, 51, 159, 160, 161,
 163, 166
Sentences 119, 179, 182, 207
Series 14, 15, 93, 170, 224
A Series of Unfortunate Events 168
Set in Stone 128
Setting 50–52, 55, 76, 77, 79–81,
 87, 111, 166, 171, 172, 187,
 191, 214, 223, 337, 341, 344,
 345, 374
Seuling, Barbara 63, 64, 131, 154
Dr. Seuss 125

Seventeen 27, 45, 138, 223
Seybold, Alice 93
The Shakespeare Stealer 302, 307
Shan, Darren 92, 93
Shannon, David 21
The Shape of Water 12
Sharing Our Homeland 106
She Got Up Off the Couch 11
Shellenberger, Susie 139
Shepard, Aaron 291, 292, 297
Shep: Our Most Loyal Dog
   52, 54, 68
She Touched the World 20
Shoket, Ann 138
Show and Tell 21
Shura, Mary Francis 155
Shutterfly 129
The Siblings Busy Book 123
Silent Echoes 75, 79, 82
The Silver Kiss 145, 341
Simner, Janni 196, 198, 202
Simon & Schuster 10, 23, 57, 73,
   86, 125, 127, 129, 130, 134,
   135, 136, 190, 290, 291, 318,
   375, 379, 380
Simonsen, Reka 74, 77, 79, 80, 81
The Simple Guide to Cats 322
Singing Hands 315
Singleton, Linda Joy 87, 89
Six78th 42, 43, 44
Skating 32
Skin Hunger 126
Skolnick, Elise McKeown 359
Skylar 17
The Slam 46
Slap 32
Slashdot 276
Sleator, William 92
Sleeper Code 86, 87
Sleeping Bear Press 52, 54, 69, 101
Sleeping Freshmen Never Lie 292
Sliding into Home 311
SM 43, 46, 47
Small, David 17
Small presses 141, 263–268, 273,
   349
Smile, Principessa! 188
Smith & Kraus 130
Smith, Bryan 129
Smith, Cynthia Leitich 85, 86, 91,
   92, 373
Smith, Dodie 216
Smith, Greg Leitich 177, 182,
   184, 186
Smith, Lane 21
Smith, Molly 96, 102
Lemony Snicket 168
Sniegoski, Tom 86, 87, 92, 94
"Soccer in Any Language" 209
Social Studies and the Young
   Learner 40
Society of Children's Book Writers
   and Illustrators 127, 189, 245,
   251, 256, 260, 373
Softball Youth 32
Software 281-287
Sold 127
The Soldier in the Cellar 92

Some Helpful Tips for a Better
   World and a Happier Life 112
Someone Like You 217, 218
Something Out of Nothing: Marie
   Curie and Radium 54, 161
Song for Cambodia 106
Sorcery and Cecilia or The En-
   chanted Chocolate Pot 83
Soto, Gary 21
So Totally Emily Ebers 276
The Sphere of Secrets 82
Spider 237
Spiegler, Louise 76, 78, 83
Spinelli, Jerry 130, 216, 222
Spirin, Gennady 18
Spollen, Anne 12
SportingKid 32
Sports 30, 32, 132, 224
Sports Illustrated 27
Sports Illustrated for Kids 32
Spradin, Michael P. 134
Spudvilas, Anne 18
Square Fish 135
Standing Against the Wind 126
Starscape 292
Staub, Wendy Corsi 15
Stebleton, Joelle 361
Steering the Craft 150
A Step from Heaven 107
Steptoe, Javaka 20
Sterling Pub. 91, 120, 126, 138
Stevenson, Dinah 377, 378
Stevermer, Caroline 74, 83
Stine, R. L. 134
Stirnkorb, Patricia 168, 170, 173,
   174
Stolz, Mary 140
Stormwitch 71
Story of a Girl 126
A Story of the Young Jimi Hendrix
   20
Storyworks 40
Strauss-Gabel, Julie 376
The Strongest Man in the World:
   Louis Cyr 127
Stroud, Jonathan 83
Stuart Goes to School 379
Stuart's Cape 379
Sturtevant, Katherine 338, 339
Suicide Bombers 348
Super Scary Stories for Sleep-
   Overs 92
SuperScience 40
Surrender 126
Surviving the Applewhites 216
Swallowing Stones 148
The Swan Maiden 82
The Sweet Far Thing 82
Sweet 16 139, 239, 240
Sykes, Shelley 86, 92
Szymanski, Lois 86, 87, 92, 93

T&N Children's Pub. 128
Talent 14
Talewinds Books 203
Tantalize 86
Teacher 140
Teachers College Press 348

Teaching Elementary Physical
   Education 140
Teaching Music 40
Teaching PreK-8 40
Technology & Learning 40
Technology 7, 17, 33, 34, 38, 89,
   101, 267, 272, 279, 281-287,
   331
Teen Light 140
Teen People 140
Temairik, Jaime 273
Ten Naughty Little Monkeys 61
Terrible Storm 140
Tessitore, Joe 137
TFH Pub. 322
That Bookwoman 17
Thaxter, Celia 222
Themes 37, 58, 85, 86, 109, 112,
   113, 116, 122, 159, 169, 170,
   183, 187-193, 223, 307
There's a Girl in My Hammerlock
   130
Theroux, Paul 339
The Thief 82
Thies, Sue 95, 100
Think & Discover 140
Thirteen Reasons Why 277, 278
This House is Ours 111
Thomson Gale 101, 103, 136
Thorsen-Snipes, Nanette 325
Thrasher 32
Three Leaping Frogs 140
The Three Pigs 125
Three Rivers Press 137
The Three Silly Girls Grubb 308
Three Young Pilgrims 66
Thrilling Tales series 172
Tibetan Tales for Little Buddhas 275
Tiger Beat 34
Tiger Moon 82
Tilbury House 22, 23
Time for Kids 100, 102, 103
Time Out New York Kid 139
Time Quintet 135
Tintin in the Congo 136
Tiny Tummies 140
Tips on Having a Gay (ex)
   Boyfriend 12
To Fly 352
Tofu and T. rex 177
Tokunbo, Dimitrea 23
Tolan, Stephanie F. 216
Tomlinson, Heather 82
Toney, Sandra 322, 323, 326, 329
Too Close to the Falls 222
Tor Books 357
Torchlight 140
To Tell Your Love 140
Touching Snow 126
Tough Boy Sonatas 20
Townsend, Beth 98, 100, 104
The Trailblazing Life of Daniel
   Boone and How Americans
   Took to the Road 66
Transitions 81, 177-186
Travaglini, Timothy 22, 77, 79, 80,
   134
Travel 225, 227, 338, 357

The Treasury of New England Folklore 146
Trent, Tiffany 75, 79, 80, 82, 159
Tria and the Great Star Rescue 345
Tricycle Press 245, 251
Trigger 71
Trouble 13
The True Confessions of Charlotte Doyle 216
A True and Faithful Narrative 338
The True Story of Stellina 127
The Truth About Truman School 107
Tuck Everlasting 153
Tuesday 125
Tundra Books 125
Tunnels 134
Turner, Megan Whalen 82
Turner, Philip 138
Turner, Tracey 15
Turn-Here Inc. 134
Turrisi, Kim 379
Turtle 61
Tuthill, Kate 341, 344
Tweit, Susan J. 360, 361
Twenty-First Century Books 348
Twilight 10, 92, 93, 168
Twist 32
Two Badd Babies 188
Two-Can 128
Tyndale House 138

The Underneath 13, 17
Understood Betsy 216
Unsinkable: The Molly Brown Story 364
An Unspeakable Crime 348
Upfront 40
USA Gymnastics 32
U*S*Kids 140
U·X·L 101

Vacuum Cleaners 69
Van Doren, Liz 137
Van Draanen, Wendelin 143
Van Metre, Susan 76, 77, 89, 93, 94
Vaught, Susan 68, 71, 72
The Very Hungry Caterpillar 9
Vetter, Deborah 46, 151, 153
Viewpoint 55, 144, 145, 146, 147, 150, 187, 191, 328
Viking Books 11, 13, 179, 217, 222
Vision Quest 179
Voekel, Pamela and John 130
Voice 52, 68, 143-148, 165, 190, 203, 214, 215, 331
Voices in First Person 21
The Voice that Challenged a Nation 55

Wade, Lee 109, 112
Wade, Mary Dodson 349, 351, 356
Wadsworth, Ginger 52, 54, 56
The Wager 82
Walker Books 15, 126, 127
Walker, Craig 141

The Wall and the Wing 92
Walton, Rick 304
Waniewski, Liz 214, 272
Frederick Warne Books 14
Warner Books 129
Waryncia, Lou 37, 41, 233, 234, 236, 241
WaterBrook Multnomah 138
Watrous, Scott 137
Watson, Jesse Joshua 17
Watts, Suzanne 61
The Wayfinder 199
Wayman, Anne 331, 333, 335, 336
Wayshak, Deborah Noyes 90, 93
Weatherford, Carole Boston 19, 126
Websites 7, 34, 35, 39, 45, 46, 236, 237, 241, 259, 272–274, 276, 289-300, 370
Weedflower 128, 224, 225, 226
Weekly Reader Corp. 38, 40, 43, 128, 139
Weetzie Bat 216
Weisner, David 21
Weiss, Jennifer 190
The Well-Centered Child 58, 149
Welles, Lee 130
Wernick, Marcia 76, 79
Western Writers of America 260
West with Hopeless 309, 317
Whale Snow 203, 206
Whales on Stilts 170
Whatever Happened to Uncle Albert? 380
What's Hers 140
When I Was Your Age 222
When Santa Lost His Ho! Ho! Ho! 23
Where the Great Hawk Flies 143, 144, 146
Where I Want to Be 145, 190
Where the Wild Things Are 94
The Whispering Road 190
A Whisper of War 87
Whitcomb, Laura 92, 93
Whiteman, Douglas 9, 14
White Mane Pub. 86, 92
Whitman, Stacy 159, 160, 163, 166
Albert Whitman 107, 113, 352
Who Is Haunting the White House? 91
Wicked Lovely 11
Wiechmann, Angela 122, 123
Wiesner, David 125, 152
Wild, Margaret 18
Wiley Children's Books 120, 136
Wilky, the White House Cockroach 141
Williams, Brian 134
Williams-Garcia, Rita 208
Williams, Julie 193
Williams, Maiya 77, 78, 83
Williams, Mary 109
Williamson Books 117, 120
Williams, Suzanne 61, 189, 192
Will Third Grade Ever End? 188
Wilson, Karma 59
The Windchild 65
Winding Oak 289

Wingertzahn, Jennifer 165
Winkler, Henry 15
Winspear, Jacqueline 363
Winter, Jonah 112
Witness the Boston Tea Party 348
Wittlinger, Ellen 375, 376
Wizards of the Coast 159, 160
Wohl, Lauren 138
Wojtyla, Karen 245
The Wolf Who Cried Boy 308
Wolves Chronicles 83
Wondertime 46
Wong, Karen 139
Wood, Bruce 141
Woodson, Jacqueline 108, 190
Woolvs in the Sitee 18
WORD 39
Wordsong 19, 20
Working Partners 137
Workman, Katie 138
Workman Pub. 120, 122, 138
World Pulse 140
World War Z: An Oral History of the Zombie War 92
The Worm Family 190
Wrede, Patricia 74, 83, 346
Wringer 216
A Wrinkle in Time 135, 140, 196
Writer's block 282, 327
Writers' groups 255-262, 273, 371
Writing 40
Writing for the Soul 173
Wyatt, Melissa 337, 338, 340, 345

Yang, Gene Luen 126
A Year Down Yonder 216
Yearling Books 86
Yee, Lisa 276
Yes We Can! 61
Yolen, Jane 68–70, 205, 208, 301
Yoon, Salina 134
You Can Do It 135
Young Adult Library Services Assn. 10, 126, 261
Young adults 8, 9, 10, 11, 12, 13, 14, 26, 27, 33–35, 38, 42, 46, 74, 89, 92–94, 107, 125, 130, 132, 134, 136, 143, 165, 190, 214, 216–218, 223, 224, 310, 337, 341, 368, 375, 376
Young, David 138
Youngest Templar trilogy 134
Young Urban Viewz 132
Ypulse 34
Yudkin, Marcia 324
Yu-Gi-Oh 140
Yummy: The Last Days of a Southside Shorty 17, 106

Zamoof! 42–44
Zarr, Sara 126
Zest Books 130
Zevin, Gabrielle 93
Zindel, Lizabeth and Paul 11
Zonderkidz 137
Zusak, Markus 10